# CONFEDERATE "TALES OF THE WAR" IN THE TRANS-MISSISSIPPI PART TWO

# Area Battle Map 1862

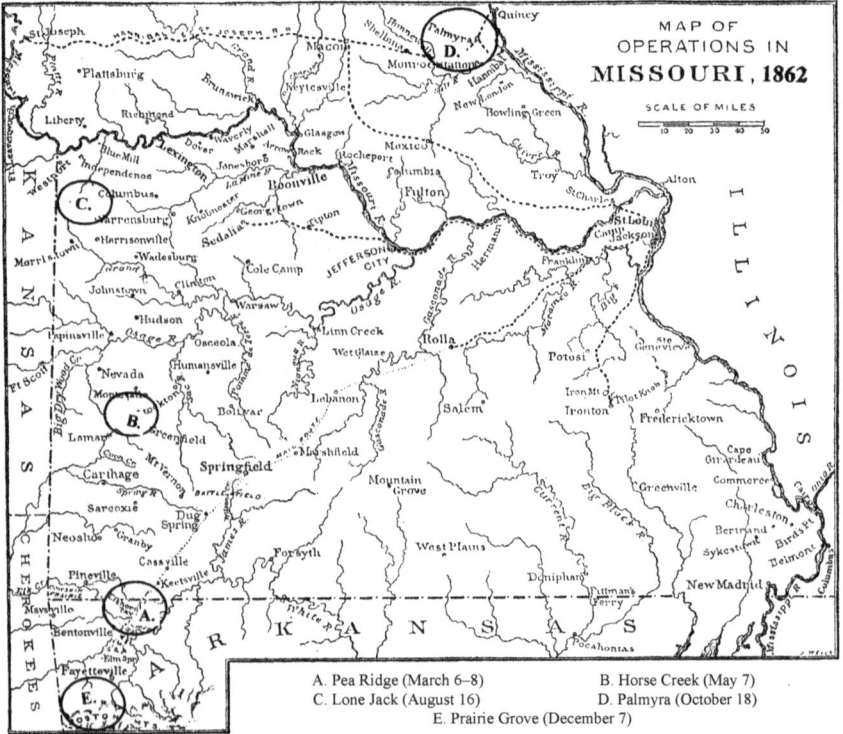

MAP OF
OPERATIONS IN
**MISSOURI, 1862**

SCALE OF MILES

A. Pea Ridge (March 6–8)     B. Horse Creek (May 7)
C. Lone Jack (August 16)     D. Palmyra (October 18)
E. Prairie Grove (December 7)

UNWRITTEN CHAPTERS OF
THE CIVIL WAR
WEST OF THE RIVER

VOLUME VII

# Confederate
# "Tales of the War"
# In the Trans-Mississippi
## Part Two: 1862

Author/Editor Michael E. Banasik

Camp Pope Publishing
2011

Library of Congress Control Number: 2011936483

ISBN: 978-1-929919-36-9

Camp Pope Publishing
P.O. Box 2232
Iowa City, Iowa 52244
www.camppope.com

## Series Dedication:

Dedicated to the forgotten soldiers of both North and South, who fought in the American Civil War west of the Mississippi River; their deeds of perseverance and valor shall not be lost through the ravages of time, but rather recorded for all to remember.

## Volume VII, Part Two Dedication:

To my wife Brenda. I will love you forever.

## Acknowledgement:

I would like to thank James McGhee of Jefferson City, Missouri, who encouraged me to do this book and who has been a constant supporter of my work.

# CONTENTS

# Photographs and Illustrations

# Maps

# Series Introduction

The Civil War in the Trans-Mississippi region provides a fascinating study of Nineteenth Century warfare under the most severe conditions. Soldiers serving in the region faced an almost complete lack of a railroad net, a decrepit road system, and terrain that varied from arid deserts to rugged mountains. Battles were few, but the constant strain of living under less than ideal conditions wore heavily upon the soldiers serving west of the Mississippi River. Often the stories told by the frontier soldiers were not of great engagements, but of long marches, poor living conditions, or of simple survival. And for each story told there were always two parts, one told by a man in gray and another by one who wore the blue.

# Introduction to Volume VII, Part Two

This latest volume of my series comprises an extensive group of reminiscences published by the St. Louis *Missouri Republican* between 1885 and 1887. These pieces were written by the participants in the Civil War and cover the entire conflict from the firing of the first guns until the surrender of the Confederate armies in 1865. The first story appeared on July 4, 1885, and the last one, that I have discovered, on July 2, 1887. In all 94 pieces were published. Typically, in each Saturday issue, the *Republican* printed assorted reminiscences by the lowliest private to the most exalted general, all veterans of the war, covering the Civil War from every aspect, both North and South and from every front of the action, including the high-seas. For this volume of the series only those pieces dealing with the Trans-Mississippi theater, and from the Southern point of view, will be presented. Because of the extensive nature of the material, Part Two of Volume VII will deal exclusively with the events of 1862, while future volumes will cover the period 1863–1865 and will follow in the coming years. The pieces from the Northern point of view will also be presented in later volumes of this series.

As to why these articles were published, the *Missouri Republican* wrote the following:

> The publication of the official orders and correspondence of the war of the rebellion made it comparatively easy for military writers to get at the exact facts of many disputed questions, and all the campaigns have been discussed by the record in recent years by competent officers of both the contending armies. Probably it is the publication of these numerous volumes, which, as much as anything else, has aroused a renewed interest in all manner of literature based on the incidents of the civil war. In response to what seems a public desire the *Republican* will hereafter publish in its Saturday edition a series of war papers, either original or selected from the

best current sketches in contemporary publications.

It is not desired to make this department especially a medium for criticism of military operations. The incidents of camp life and the experiences of the private soldier will find as ready access to these columns as the history of great campaigns. What ever war reminiscences will interest the thousands of old soldiers and the greater thousands of their children, will gladly be published in the full ballet that these chronicles of personal experiences from both sides, while reviving the memories, will at the same time aid in obliterating the animosities of the great struggle.[1]

The 1862 portion of these "Tales of the War" covers in great detail the Battle of Pea Ridge, Arkansas (March 6–8, 1862), as well as the engagements at Lone Jack, Missouri (August 16, 1862) and Prairie Grove, Arkansas (December 7, 1862). Also presented are various pieces concerning the "Palmyra Massacre" (October 18, 1862), soldiering in Arkansas with an Arkansas regiment, and some short "Bits and Pieces" that are associated with the Trans-Mississippi, but have no real date associated with them. The Appendices include the most comprehensive Confederate Order of Battle ever presented on the Battle of Pea Ridge as well as the first recorded publication of General Blunt's request for a truce at the Battle of Prairie Grove, that had been lost since 1862.

I hope you find these pieces as fascinating as I did in researching and preparing them for your reading pleasure.

Michael E. Banasik

Nameplate which appeared ahead of most of the "Tales of the War" in the *Republican.*

1. Editorial Comment, *The Missouri Republican* (St. Louis, Missouri), July 4, 1885.

Chapter 1

# Spring 1862:
## The Battle of Pea Ridge, Arkansas (March 6–8, 1862) and Incidents Surrounding the Battle

**Item:** From Lexington, Missouri, to Pea Ridge (September 1861–March 8, 1862); the Life and Death of Churchill Clark, by N. P. Minor.[1]
**Published:** May 8, 1886.

### Capt. Churchill Clark's Indian.

Bowling Green, Mo., April 30
Editor, *Republican*

    Capt. Churchill Clark,[2] the hero of only two battles, was the grandson of Gen. William Clark, who was the compeer of Gov. Meriwether Lewis with whom he explored the sources of the Missouri and Columbia Rivers, under the auspices of

---

1. N. P. Minor was born about 1823, and enlisted in what became Company B, Second Missouri Infantry (Confederate) on December 9, 1861. Following the Battle of Pea Ridge, Arkansas (March 6–8, 1862), he was left behind at the White River as a nurse and never returned to his unit. On February 28, 1863, his unit listed him as a deserter, from March 1862. National Archives, Record Group M322, (roll no. 109), Confederate Compiled Service Records, Second Missouri Infantry.

2. Samuel Churchill Clark, also known as "Churchy," was born on September 12, 1842, in St. Louis, briefly attended St. Louis University, before being admitted to West Point with the Class of 1863. His father was General Meriwether Lewis Clark, commander of the Ninth Division, Missouri State Guard (MSG). At the beginning of the Civil War, the young Clark resigned U.S. service and offered his services to Missouri. He commanded a two gun battery at the Siege of Lexington, Missouri, in September 1861, for which action he was praised. Later he served as a drillmaster and an instructor of tactics. In December 1861, his battery entered the Confederate service and fought at the Battle of Pea Ridge. While protecting the withdrawal of the rebel forces, Clark was struck by a cannonball and decapitated—he was nineteen years old. United States War Department, *The War of the Rebellion: A Compilation of the Official Records of the Union and Confederate Armies*, 70 vols. in 128 (Washington, D. C. 1880–1901) Series 1, vol. 3:186, 189; 8:306, 311; 53:450 (hereafter cited as *O.R.*; all citations of *O.R.* refer to Series 1 unless indicated otherwise); Joanne C. Eakin, *Confederate Records From the United Daughters of the Confederacy Files*, 8 vols. (Independence, MO, 1995–2001), 2:60; Richard C. Peterson, James E. McGhee, Kip A. Lindberg, and Keith I. Daleen, *Sterling Price's Lieutenants: A Guide to the Officers and Organization of the Missouri State Guard, 1861–1865* (Shawnee Mission, KS, 1995), 151, hereafter cited as Peterson; Wayne Schnetzer, *More Forgotten Men: The Missouri State Guard* (Independence, MO, 2003), 46; Phillip Thomas Tucker, *The South's Finest: The First Missouri Confederate Brigade from Pea Ridge to Vicksburg* (Shippensburg, PA, 1993), 7–8, hereafter cited as Tucker, *South's Finest*.

Mr. Jefferson,[3] early in this century, and died in St. Louis about 1840, having served his country faithfully as Indian agent for many years.

By his gentle bearing Gen. Clark had endeared himself to all who knew him and specially was held in high reputation by the Indians who then held sway over the vast wilderness lying on the headwaters of the Missouri and stretching to the base of the Rocky Mountains. Spring and fall they made semi-annual pilgrimages to their great father in St. Louis for counsel and supplies. They will not forget the "pale face" who passed through their country years before going westward and who returned months afterwards, bearing evidence of immense travel. This together with his unwearied kindness inspired them with profound respect and confidence. No Indian ever went to St. Louis without calling on Gen. Clark and he was sure to heap additional obligations upon them.

Samuel Churchill Clark

No doubt in council the aged warriors often spoke in eulogy of the brave, pale face who had made the long voyage through their country and returned, only to be kind to the "child of the forrest," and so his name came down the stream of time, the father teaching it to his children, and his children's children to the third and fourth generation. At any rate Gen. Clark became the idol among them, and

## An Indian Brave

among them, whose name I have forgotten, for some cause not now necessary

3. William Clark, an explorer from Kentucky and companion of Meriwether Lewis was born in Virginia in 1770. An officer in the United States Army, Clark was a major when appointed the territorial governor of the Louisiana Territory in 1813, which included Missouri. He served as governor until Missouri became a state in 1821 and died on September 1, 1838. David B. Guralnik, ed., *Second College Edition Webster's New World Dictionary of American Language* (New York, 1972), 262, hereafter cited as Guralnik; Francis B. Heitman, *Historical Register and Dictionary of the United States Army From Its Organization, September 29, 1789, to March 2, 1903*, 2 vols. (Washington, 1903; reprint ed. Gaithersburg, MD, 1988), 1:306, hereafter cited as Heitman; *History of Audrain County, Missouri, Written and Compiled from the Most Authentic Official and Private Sources Including a History of Its Townships, Towns and Villages* (St. Louis, 1884), 6–7, 27, 38, 145.

Meriwether Lewis was born in 1774, in Virginia, joined the military in 1795, and was a captain when he, with William Clark, was commissioned in 1803 by President Thomas Jefferson to explore the northwestern part of the United States. In 1807, Lewis was appointed the territorial governor of the Louisiana Territory. On October 11, 1809, Lewis committed suicide. Guralnik, 813; Heitman, 1:631; *History of Audrain County*, 6.

to be stated, became an outcast. He had lost his heritage in his tribe and became a wanderer on the face of the earth. Homeless and without friends, he left his native wilds reckless of the future. In grief he remembered the traditions of his tribe and concluded to throw himself upon the kindness of his "great father" and come to St. Louis. Just then the curtain had risen upon the bloody drama, Camp Jackson had fallen, blood had been shed in the streets of St. Louis.[4] The old war horse, Sterling Price, had made his brief but eloquent speech to the Missourians from the steps of the Planter's House,[5] the legislature at Jefferson had passed their Military Bill,[6] bought their powder and been dispersed by [Nathaniel] Lyon,[7] the

---

4. On May 6, 1861, Governor Claiborne F. Jackson called for the Missouri Militia to assemble through-out the state for "instruction in military tactics." In St. Louis, Camp Jackson was established on the outskirts of St. Louis in Lindell Grove, bordered by Grand Avenue on the west, Compton Avenue on the east and Lindell on the north. On May 10, U.S. Captain (later General) Nathaniel Lyon captured the camp without firing a shot. Lyon feared that the pro-secession Jackson was using the lawfully as-sembled Missouri Militia as a ploy to capture the St. Louis Arsenal, with its large store of weapons and ammunition. Following the capture of the Missouri Militia Brigade, the prisoners were marched off to the St. Louis Arsenal. En route, a mob attacked the Federal troops, resulting in the killing of 25 civilian men, women and children along with 3 unarmed prisoners from Camp Jackson. This then became known as the "St. Louis or Camp Jackson Massacre" and propelled Missouri into the Civil War. Hans Christian Adamson, *Rebellion in Missouri, 1861: Nathaniel Lyon and His Army of the West* (Rahway, NJ, 1961), 62–64, hereafter cited as Adamson; Michael E. Banasik, *Missouri Brothers in Gray: The Reminiscences and Letters of William J. Bull and John P. Bull* (Iowa City, IA, 1998), 9–10, 12; R. S. Bevier, *History of the First and Second Missouri Confederate Brigades 1861–1865. And From Wakarusa to Appomattox, A Military Anagraph* (St. Louis, 1879), 24–25, hereafter cited as Bevier; "Governor's Proclamation—General Orders No. 7," *The Missouri Republican* (St. Louis, MO), May 2, 1861; William C. Winter, *The Civil War in St. Louis: A Guided Tour* (St. Louis, 1994), 34–35, 46, hereafter cited as Winter.

5. Sterling Price was born in September 1809 in Virginia, and moved to Missouri in 1831. He served in the U.S. Congress, was governor of Missouri (1852), and became a brigadier general during the Mexican War. At the beginning of the Civil War he cast his lot with Missouri and subsequently the Confederacy. He died in St. Louis in 1867. For a complete biography see Banasik, *Missouri Brothers in Gray*, 148–150; Mark Mayo Boatner III, *The Civil War Dictionary* (New York, 1959), 669, hereafter cited as Boatner.

The Planter's House was a four and one-half story hotel, located on the west side of Fourth Street, between Pine and Chestnut streets. It began construction in 1837, and opened for business on April 3, 1841. Prior to the Civil War it was an important social center and meeting place, characterized as "the epitome of elegance and grandeur, a place of romance and gaiety, a center of lavish entertaining and extravagant spending." A fire in 1887 closed the hotel. It was later refurbished, a new hotel opened in 1922, and still later it was converted to an office building. Winter, 67–68.

6. The "Military Bill" was written by Thomas A. Harris, future commander of the Second Division, MSG. This bill, which organized the Missouri military force, was passed following the Camp Jackson Affair, and was signed by Governor Jackson on May 14, 1861. The provisions of the bill organized Missouri into nine Military Districts or Divisions and provided the guidelines for the establishment of the MSG, including the appointment of its officers. Griffin Frost, *Camp and Prison Journal* (Quincy, IL, 1867; reprint ed. Iowa City, IA, 1994), 2, hereafter cited as Frost; Peterson, 5, 22–23; State of Mis-souri, *An Act to Provide For the Organization, Government, and Support of the Military Forces State of Missouri Passed at the Called Session of the Twenty-first General Assembly* (Jefferson City, MO, 1861; reprint ed. Independence, MO, n.d.), 3–6, 77; Thomas L. Snead, *The Fight For Missouri From the Election of Lincoln to the Death of Lyon* (New York, 1866), 173, 184, hereafter cited as Snead.

7. General Nathaniel Lyon was born in Connecticut on July 14, 1818, attended West Point (number

Gasconade bridge had been burnt, "there was mounting in hot haste," the dogs of war were unleashed.[8]

The exiled Indian when he reached the future capital inquired for his "great father," and was amazed when told he was dead. His son was next inquired for. Maj. Meriwether L. Clark[9] was in Richmond, Va., at the call of the Confederate government and could not be reached. "Has he no son I can see?" inquired the lone Indian, and was told that Churchill Clark, then on the eve of resigning his cadetship at West Point, would reach St. Louis, in a few days, and sure enough the young artillerist, then in his 18th year, arrived an immediately tendered his sword to Gen. Jackson and was ordered to report to Gen. Price, then on his march north from the bloody field of Wilson's Creek. The Indian warrior sought the boy and told him in his high-wrought language of his tribe the story of his wrongs and self-exile and his determination

---

11 of 52), and served in the U.S. Army until his death at Wilson's Creek, Missouri, on August 10, 1861. His actions in Missouri, during 1861, propelled that state into the Civil War. Banasik, *Missouri In 1861: The Civil War Letters of Franc B. Wilkie Newspaper Correspondent* (Iowa City, IA, 2001), 353–355; Ezra J. Warner, *Generals in Blue: Lives of the Union Commanders* (Baton Rouge, LA, 1964), 286–287.

8. Following the signing of the Military Bill, Governor Jackson sent squads of men, under Colonel N. C. Claiborne, to protect the bridges over the Gasconade and Osage River, which led to Jefferson City. "In the excitement of the hour the detachment," under the command of Basil Duke of St. Louis, "which was sent to guard the Osage Bridge set it on fire and partially destroyed it," as a precaution against capture. The bridge over the Gasconade was left untouched, contrary to the author's comments. Robert E. Shalhope in his book on Sterling Price also stated that the Gasconade bridge was burnt, but provided no supporting documentation. However, the *Confederate Military History* makes the same claim. Clement A. Evans, gen. ed. *Confederate Military History*, 13 vols. (Atlanta, 1899; reprint ed. Secaucus, NJ, 1974), vol. 9: *Missouri*, by John C. Moore, 43, hereafter cited as Moore, *Missouri, Confederate Military History*; John McElroy, *The Struggle For Missouri* (Washington, DC, 1909), 90, hereafter cited as McElroy; James Peckham, *Gen. Nathaniel Lyon, and Missouri in 1861: A Monograph of the Great Rebellion* (New York, 1866), 167–168; Robert E. Shalhope, *Sterling Price Portrait of a Southerner* (Columbia, MO, 1971), 158, hereafter cited as Shalhope; Snead, 173.

9. Meriwether Lewis Clark was born on January 10, 1809, in St. Louis. His father was William Clark, of the Lewis and Clark Expedition. Meriwether Clark graduated from West Point in 1830, served in the Black Hawk War in 1832, and the Mexican War in 1846. At the beginning of the Civil War, Clark was living in St. Louis as an architect, engineer and Surveyor-General for Missouri. Shortly thereafter, Clark was appointed a brigadier general commanding the Ninth Military District, vice Daniel M. Frost, who was captured at Camp Jackson. On November 11, 1861, Clark was appointed a major in the Confederate Service, was transferred to the east side of the Mississippi River, and promoted to colonel on April 16, 1862. Clark competed his military service on the east side of the Mississippi River, being captured at Sayler's Creek, Virginia, on April 6, 1865. After the war, Clark moved to Kentucky, where he worked as an architect and taught mathematics at the Kentucky Military Institute. He died in Frankfurt, Kentucky, on October 28, 1881, and was buried in St. Louis. For a complete biography see Appendix B. *O.R.*, 8:792; Bruce S. Allardice, *More Generals in Gray* (Baton Rouge, LA, 1995), 61–62, hereafter cited as Allardice; Clement A. Evans and Robert S. Bridgers, gen. eds., *Confederate Military History Extended Edition*, 19 vols. (Atlanta, 1899; reprint ed., Wilmington, NC, 1987), vol. 12: *Missouri* by John C. Moore, 258–259, hereafter cited as Moore, *Missouri, Confederate Military History, Extended*; Donald R. Hale, *Branded as Rebels Volume 2* (Independence, MO, 2003), 58–59, hereafter cited as Hale.

# Never to Return

to his home. "Many snows have fallen, many summers have fled," said the exile, "since your grandfather rested in peace in the wigwam of my fathers in that wild land where the Muddy River is an infant. They were friends in right whereof we shall be friends. I will be to you what they were to him." The flush of pride mantled the cheek of the young officer at the voluntary tribute paid to his noble ancestor. The compact was made. Their paths through life lay together.

September, 1861, beheld a gallant army of Federal troops at Lexington, Mo., commanded by the heroic [James] Mulligan,[10] environed by an undisciplined army under Gen. Price. All that foresight, bravery and energy could do to prevent the fall of the beleaguered city and the capture of the Federal Army had been tried. Bastines [bastions], trenches, redoubts, pits, wires and all the appliances of the highest military skill had been brought into requisition, but all were in vain. Nothing could extricate them from the strong grip of Price. From Wednesday at 7 a.m. till Tuesday at 3 p.m., day and night, the fight raged furiously without intermission.[11] The brave men within met the charge from without with unflinching

---

10. Lexington was the county seat of Lafayette County and the site of a siege from September 13–20, 1861. Located about 300 miles from St. Louis on the Missouri River, Lexington's population at the beginning of the war was near 5,000 inhabitants, who participated primarily in the hemp growing industry. The city consisted of some manufacturing (hemp) with two colleges. The Masonic College, which embraced some fifteen acres, served as the Federal defensive point during the siege. *O.R.*, 3:171; McElroy, 206–207.

James Mulligan was born in Utica, New York in 1830. He commanded the Twenty-third Illinois Infantry Regiment, and by virtue of seniority assumed command of the Lexington garrison in September 1861. Captured at Lexington, Mulligan was exchanged in October 1861, for General Daniel M. Frost and served the rest of his Civil War years on the east side of the Mississippi River. On July 24, 1864, Mulligan was wounded at Kernstown, Virginia, and captured; he died shortly thereafter. *O.R.*, vol. 37, pt. 2:601; *O.R.*, Series 2, 1:554; McElroy, 206.

11. On September 12, 1861, General Price's army was within two miles of Lexington and halted for the night, having pushed back the enemy's outlying forces. Reinforced the next morning, Price closed in on Lexington, investing the city on all sides, with the exception of the river which was still open to the Federal command. September 14–17 saw little action, save sniping that was meant to cut off the water access to the Federals. During this time the rebel forces continued to increase to about 18,000 by the siege's end. The common soldier saw no reason for the delay, leading one to record—"Hell is full of better Generals…God give us success, we have no leaders." This delay, according to another soldier, was necessary because: "We had to mold our bullets and make our cartridges and when sufficient ammunition was prepared we were ready." Those in the artillery had similar problems, having to "manufacture ammunition" before an attack could begin. At 6 a.m., on the morning of the 18th, the attack began in earnest, with the State Guard attacking along the river bank from two points, successfully cutting the Federals' water supply and capturing the a steamboat that was laden with Federal supplies. Finally, after fifty-two hours of continuous combat, Mulligan surrendered the city, at 2 p.m. on September 20. The critical soldier, who previously despaired at his general's tactics now recorded—"Gen. Price's tactics proved to be the best. If we had charged them our losses would have been heavy." At Lexington the Federals surrendered 3,500 men, 5 pieces of artillery, 2 mortars, 3,000 stands of small arms, 750 horses, $100,000 worth of commissary supplies, and the Great Seal of Missouri. Price put the rebel losses at 25 killed and 72 wounded. *O.R.*, 3:185–188; Banasik, *Missouri In 1861*, 182 (n. 79); Joanne Chiles Eakin, *Diary of a Doctor Missouri State Guards, 1861* (Independence, MO,

courage, until weary and worn out with ceaseless fight and no possibility of aid, they reluctantly yielded, and the stars and stripes were lowered to the broad blue folds of the state flag. Churchill Clark, in charge of one gun,[12] "flashed his maiden sword" around the walls of this historical fort. I shall never forget his appearance; in fact, it seemed but yesterday when the young boy stood by his gun, his light and agile form, his jaunty artillery cap with its all-meaning colors,

## His Boyish Face,

upon which the callow down of youth had not yet come, all blackened and be-grimed with the powder; his intrepid manner as gun after gun was discharged impressed me with the profoundest respect for the youthful warrior.[13] The army had witnessed his feats and appreciated them, and in a few weeks he was placed in command of a battery sent from Richmond.[14] He had tutored and disciplined the Indian who became one of the best soldiers. Gen. Price and his army finally rested at Springfield, waiting in vain for help from the Confederate government. On the 13th of February, 1862, pressed by [Samuel R.] Curtis[15] on the east side

---

1999), 23–28 (hereafter cited as Eakin, *Diary*); J. W. (Watt) Gibson, *Recollections of a Pioneer* (St. Joseph, MO, n.d.; reprint ed., Independence, MO, 1999), 114–117; James E. McGhee, *Service With the Missouri State Guard: The Memoir of Brigadier General James Harding* (Springfield, MO, 2000), 45 (hereafter cited as McGhee, *Service with the Guard*); Jeffery Patrick, ed., "Remembering the Missouri Campaign of 1861: The Memoirs of Lieutenant William P. Barlow, Guibor's Battery, Missouri State Guard," *A Journal of the American Civil War* 5 (No. 4, 1997), 45 (hereafter cited as Patrick).

12. During the course of the siege of Lexington, General Mosby M. Parsons "loaned" two guns to Captain Clark, for use during the siege. These two guns would subsequently constitute two of the four guns that Clark would later command at the Battle of Pea Ridge, Arkansas. *O.R.*, 53:450.

13. During the Siege of Lexington, General James Rains challenged his battery commanders to strike down a Union flag which was flying on the southeast corner of the Federal entrenchments. Within a short time Churchill Clark's battery won the prize of a "gold medal" for leveling the flag. *Ibid.*, 3:189.

14. Not true. According to Peterson, Clark's Battery, also known as the "Boy Battery" or the Second Missouri Artillery, initially contained two 6-pound guns, which they received at Lexington while as-signed to Parsons's Eighth Division, MSG. Following the capture of Lexington, Clark was given another two 6-pound guns, making a total of four. In October 1861, the battery was transferred from Parsons's Division to William Slack's Fourth Division, MSG. During November 1861, two of the six pound guns were exchanged for two 12-pound howitzers, giving Clark's Battery two 6-pound guns and two 12-pound howitzers for the fight at Pea Ridge in March 1862. Following the Battle of Pea Ridge, Clark's Battery was transferred to the east side of the Mississippi River, where it completed its military service. Carolyn M. Bartels, *Trans-Mississippi Men at War Volume I Missouri C.S.A.* (Independence, MO, 1998), 140; Peterson, 151–152, 286; William L. Shea and Earl J. Hess, *Pea Ridge: Civil War Campaign in the West* (Chapel Hill, NC, 1992), 336, hereafter cited as Shea & Hess; Jo. A. Wilson, "Clark's Battery," *Missouri Republican* (St. Louis, MO), November 28, 1885 (hereafter cited as Wilson, "Clark's Battery").

15. Samuel R. Curtis was born on February 3, 1805, in Clinton County, New York. He attended West Point, graduated in 1831, and served one year at Fort Gibson, Indian Territory, before resigning. Curtis worked as an engineer in Ohio until the Mexican War when the governor made him colonel of the Second Ohio Infantry. After the war, he returned to Ohio and moved to Keokuk, Iowa. He practiced engineering and law, was elected mayor of Keokuk, and served three terms in the U.S. Congress. When the Civil War began, Curtis became colonel of the Second Iowa Infantry and was appointed a brigadier general on May 17, 1861. He commanded the Army of the Southwest, won the Battle of Pea

and [Franz] Sigel[16] threatening from the west, Gen. Price commenced a retreat, which for endurance and success, has no parallel in the history of armies. The fight commenced north of Springfield by the advance of Curtis' column, and the cavalry command of Col. [Elijah] Gates,[17] which was kept up with slight intermission for nearly a hundred miles. Gen. Price, in addition to his army train, covering an entrant train of nearly 2,000 wagons, without the loss of property.[18] In this

---

Ridge, and was promoted to major general for his efforts. In September 1862, Lincoln appointed him Department of Missouri commander, a post he held until May 1863. Curtis finished the war serving as commander of the Department of Kansas and then of the Northwest. For a complete biography and photograph see Michael E. Banasik, *Reluctant Cannoneer: The Diary of Robert T. McMahan of the Twenty–fifth Independent Ohio Light Artillery* (Iowa City, IA, 2000) 279–281; Warner, *Generals in Blue,* 107–108.

16. Franz Sigel was born on November 18, 1824, in the Grand Duchy of Baden (Germany), graduated from the military academy at Karlsrule in 1843, and fought on the losing side in the German Revolution of 1848. Immigrating to the United States in 1852, Sigel was living in St. Louis in 1861 when the Civil War began. During the early months of the war, Sigel proved to be a recruiting magnet for Federal troops in Missouri as the phrase "I fights mit Sigel" became a rallying cry for the German population. Sigel was made a brigadier general on August 7, 1861, and for gallantry at Pea Ridge he was promoted to major general. After Pea Ridge, Sigel was reassigned to the Eastern Theater of operations, where he completed his Civil War service. He died in 1902, in the state of New York. For a complete biography see Banasik, *Missouri In 1861,* 362–364.

17. Elijah Gates was born on December 17, 1827, in Lancaster, Kentucky, moved to Missouri in 1847, uprooted his family and moved to California in 1852 in the search for gold. Returning to Missouri, Gates settled near St. Joseph, on the western border, where he raised hemp. A Democrat in politics, and slave owner, Gates joined the MSG in May 1861, served for three months and subsequently organized a cavalry company in James T. Cearnal's Cavalry Regiment. In December 1861, Gates resigned from the MSG and organized the First Missouri Cavalry Regiment (Confederate), being elected colonel of the command. Gates fought at Wilson's Creek and Lexington in Missouri and at Pea Ridge in Arkansas before being transferred to the east side of the Missouri River in April 1862, where he completed his military service. Gates, known as a "cool and courageous man," was wounded five times, captured three times, and lost an arm at the Battle of Franklin, Tennessee, on November 30, 1864. Gates returned to St. Joseph following the war, where he was elected sheriff of Buchanan County, served four years, and in 1876, was elected Missouri State Treasurer. He died at his home in St. Joseph on March 4, 1915. Eakin, *Confederate Records,* 3:98–99; *History of Audrain County,* 39; Suzanne Staker Lehr, *As the Mockingbird Sang: Civil War Diary of Pvt. Robert Caldwell Dunlap, C.S.A.* (St. Joseph, MO, 2005), 36; Tucker, *South's Finest,* 5–6.

18. At dusk on February 12, Elijah Gates's First Missouri Cavalry attacked the advance pickets of Curtis's army to cover the rebel retreat from Springfield, which began shortly after midnight. By 10 a.m., on February 13, Federal troops had entered Springfield, followed by a vigorous pursuit, which did not abate until February 18. Of the fighting retreat General Price wrote: "Retreating and fighting all the way to the Cross Hollow, in this state [Arkansas], I am rejoiced to say my command, under the most exhausting fatigue all that time, with but little rest for either man or horse and no sleep, sustained themselves, and came through repulsing the enemy upon every occasion with great determination and gallantry." The final Federal attack occurred at Sugar Creek on February 17, with a loss 13 killed and 20 wounded, while the rebels lost 3 killed and 14 wounded. *O.R.,* 8:757; Michael E. Banasik, *Duty, Honor and Country: The Civil War Experiences of Captain William P. Black, Thirty-seventh Illinois Infantry* (Iowa City, IA, 2006 ), 73–75; Ephraim McD. Anderson, *Memoirs: Historical and Personal; Including the Campaigns of the First Missouri Confederate Brigade* (St. Louis, 1868; reprint ed. Dayton, OH, 2005), 140–141, hereafter cited as Anderson, *Memoirs*; Frost, 5.

retreat [William] Wade,[19] [Hiram] Bledsoe[20] and Clark did noble duty, but the end was nigh, the bright sun of a March day saw Clark joyously move his battery into battle at Elkhorn,[21] not grudgingly, but as if he loved the sound of the guns as they thundered in the narrow passes. It was a grand sight to see him move the boy battery, in the very paths of the blue-coats and open great lanes through their brave ranks and to behold him in the very gates of death and hear his orders given as cool as on a field day.

That Elkhorn or Cox farm on Pea Ridge, as you may please to call it, was

---

19. William Wade was born in Maryland in 1819, and later moved to St. Louis, where he was elected captain of the Washington Guards (Company B), Missouri Militia, on October 9, 1858. Later he was elected captain of the Emmet Guards (Company D), and was captured at Camp Jackson, on May 10, 1861, while serving as a common private. Paroled on May 12, Wade joined the MSG and was elected major of an artillery battalion on November 5, 1861. Wade entered the Confederate Service on December 28, 1861, as the captain of a battery of artillery. At the Battle of Pea Ridge, Wade now a Confederate major, was noted for his "distinguished conduct." In April 1862, Wade and his command were transferred to the east side of the Mississippi River where they completed their service. Wade was promoted to colonel in December 1862, but did not survive the war. On April 29, 1863, he was struck by a fragment of a shell and killed at Grand Gulf, Mississippi. "There was not a more popular or a more deserving officer," recorded one veteran, "and every soldier felt his death as a personal loss." Of Wade, Confederate General Dabney Maury recorded: "He was always cheerful and alert, and never grumbled...He was but little over five feet high. I do not think any man in the army, up to the last, was more respected than Wade." *O.R.*, 8:284–285; "The Grand Military Encampment," W. R. Babcock Collection, Missouri Volunteer Militia Scrapbook, page 17 of unnumbered pages, Missouri Historical Society (hereafter cited as Missouri Militia Scrapbook); D. H. Maury, "Recollections of the Elkhorn Campaign," *Southern Historical Society Papers*, 52 vols. (R. A. Brock, gen. ed.; Richmond, VA, 1876–1859; reprint ed. Wilmington, NC, 1990–1992), 2:192, hereafter cited as Maury; "Military Encampment," *Missouri Republican*, May 7, 1861; Moore, *Missouri, Confederate Military History*, 72, 117; Hale, 335; Peterson, 132.
20. Hiram Bledsoe was born on April 25, 1825, in Bourbon County, Kentucky, moved to Missouri, in 1839, and settled in Lafayette County, near Lexington. During the Mexican War he joined Company B, First Missouri Mounted Volunteers Regiment and participated in Doniphan's Southwest Expedition. At the beginning of the Civil War, Bledsoe organized a mounted command, but took on a battery of three guns in May 1861. He fought at Carthage (July 5, 1861), Wilson's Creek, and Dry Wood Creek (September 7, 1861), where he was wounded. Bledsoe returned to duty in the final days of the Siege of Lexington and subsequently commanded the battery at Pea Ridge, in March 1862. The battery, with Bledsoe in command, moved to the east side of the Mississippi River in April 1862, where they completed their military service. Returning to Lexington, Bledsoe married in 1869, and was elected presiding judge of Cass County in 1872; he served three terms. In 1878 he was elected County Collector and died at his home in Pleasant Hill, Missouri, on February 7, 1899. Bartels, *Trans-Mississippi Men*, 136–139, 160; Peterson, 287; W. L. Webb, *Battles and Biographies of Missourians or the Civil War Period of Our State* (Kansas City, MO, 1900), 316–321, hereafter cited as Webb.
21. The Battle of Pea Ridge, Arkansas (Elkhorn Tavern was the Confederate name) took place on March 6–8, 1862, in northwest Arkansas. According to a newspaper correspondent, General Curtis selected the Union name for the engagement even as the battle was raging. William Fayel recalled that one man wanted to call it "Ozark Mountains," but Curtis thought it too general. Another suggested Leetown. Fayel suggested Sugar Creek. "The general objected to this on account of the affair two weeks before." Curtis then questioned a local as to the name of the distant ridge. "'Pea Ridge!' said the Butternut. 'That's just it,' said the general." Specifics on the battle to follow in other notes. Wm. Fayel, "Curtis Withdrawal From Cross Hollows," *Missouri Republican*, December 19, 1885.

# A Bloody Fight,

and skulkers had no business there.[22] A lovely spring sun witnessed its beginning and its end. The Federal troops fell back stubbornly and bravely contesting every inch until Cox's barn, containing their commissary stores, was captured.[23] When their front lines were partially doubled back on their rear the infantry were busy and yet it was an artillery fight, as demonstrated by the damage done to the forrest trees, which were cut off or shattered to pieces. Clark's battery had performed prodigies of valor on various parts of the field until finally the enemy, rallying at a particular point, he ran his battery very near the advancing column apparently without sufficient infantry support. Gen. Price with an eagle eye saw his danger in a moment, rode up hurriedly to Clark, and seeing yet another column of Federals advancing upon him obliquely, pointing in that direction he said: "Give it to them there." As quick as thought his guns were sighted, but before their contents were discharged a round shot from an opposing battery

## Struck the Brave Boy

on the head carrying away at least half of it.[24]

---

22. The writer was referring to the combat that occurred on the Confederate left near Elkhorn Tavern. Between 6–7:00 a.m., on March 7, General Curtis heard that the rebels were pressing his rear. By 8:00 a.m. the head of Price's column had cut the Telegraph Road, north of Elkhorn Tavern and Curtis had called a conference of his commanders to discuss the situation. At about 9:00 a.m., Curtis dispatched Colonel Eugene A. Carr and the Fourth Division, to protect Elkhorn and his rear, while other units moved off to confront the rebels reported about Leetown. Reaching the Elkhorn area about 10:00 a.m., Carr attacked the advancing Missourians under General Price, who quickly deployed to flank Carr's small command. The remainder of the day would see attack and counterattack by the two foes, until late in the day, when the Federals would withdraw, their ammunition exhausted. The rebels called the Union retreat a "rout," while the various Federal commanders noted that their troops "fell back," "retired," or "retreated" from the rebels at Elkhorn Tavern. Carr's command numbered 2,463 men with 12 guns while Price fielded 6,818 men with 43 pieces of artillery. Note: See Appendix A for a further explanation of Price's strength at Pea Ridge. *O.R.*, 8:258–261, 264: Boatner, 627–628; Suzanne Staker Lehr, *Fishing on Deep River: Civil War Memoir of Pvt. Samuel Baldwin Dunlap, C.S.A.* (St. Joseph, MO, 2006), 70; Maury, 187–188; Franz Sigel, "The Pea Ridge Campaign," *Battles and Leaders of the Civil War*, 4 vols. (New York, 1887–1888), 1:321, hereafter cited as Sigel; Shea & Hess, 336–339; Phillip Thomas Tucker, *The Confederacy's Fighting Chaplain Father John B. Bannon* (Tuscaloosa, AL, 1992), 43, hereafter cited as Tucker, *Father Bannon*.
23. The barn was part of Elkhorn Tavern, which was owned by the J. C. Cox family, and contained a large supply of "flour and other commissary stores," including desiccated vegetables. The captured supplies also included "several sutler wagons," which contained such delicacies as "candies, tobacco, canned fruit, and other useful articles." The barn did not fall until the final charge of March 7, which sent the Unionists reeling across the Cox field to their final position for the night. The captured supplies turned out to be a welcome relief for the Missourians, who had not eaten anything for thirty-six hours. *O.R.*, 8:313; Elmo Ingenthron, *Borderland Rebellion: A History of the Civil War on the Missouri-Arkansas Border* (Branson, MO, 1980), 156, hereafter cited as Ingenthron; McGhee, *Service With the Guard*, 70–71; W. L. Truman, "Battle of Elkhorn—Correction," *Confederate Veteran Magazine* 12 (January 1904), 27–28, hereafter cited as Truman.
24. By all accounts, Captain Clark died in the waning moments of the battle, while covering the Confederate retreat on March 8. The round took off his head. *O.R.*, 8:310, 329; Maury, 189; McGhee,

Thus perished with the dew of youth upon him this gifted child of artillery. The Indian was one of the stricken in heart that saved the guns and the corpse of this beloved leader.[25] Three times during the eventful day did those devoted battery men move the mangled remains of Churchill Clark to save it from capture. In all the sad scene that preceded the fall of the Confederacy none excelled in sadness the sight of those devoted men as they followed their boy leader to his last resting-place upon the banks of the Arkansas River at Fort Smith and with tearful eyes and aching hearts fired the last artillery salute leaving the young soldier to sleep until the morning of the resurrection in his narrow home with no sounding requiem but the flow of the river to the ocean. The Indian lingered the longest at the grave of his last friend. His after-career is a mystery. Whether he perished or survived the war, or whether he followed or abandoned the Confederate cause after the death of Clark, or wandered back to the graves of his fathers, will perhaps remain a secret forever. Be that as it may, if I have faithfully put on the record the heroic qualities of the young Confederate officer, and at the same time did justice to the fidelity of the untutored Indian to his only friend, the object of this communication will have been accomplished.

N. P. Minor.

\* \* \* \* \* \*

---

Service With the Guard, 74.

25. There appears to be some disagreement as to the disposition of Clark's body, following the battle. Harding stated that "an ineffectual attempt was made to bring off the body," while Bevier noted that one of his lieutenants carried the body from the field. Settling the argument Shea & Hess state: "Survivors of the wrecked battery left Clark on the ground and dragged off their crippled weapons." Clark's body was later retrieved by Captain Wright Schaumberg of General Henry Little's staff, and returned to Van Buren, Arkansas, for burial on March 29. His funeral was attended by General Price, with a large number of officers and the men of his battery. Bevier, 110; McGhee, Service With the Guard, 74–75; Shea & Hess, 250; Tucker, Father Bannon, 55; Tucker, South's Finest, 42; Wilson, "Clark's Battery," Missouri Republican, November 28, 1885.

**Item:** A brief statement on the life of Captain S. Churchill Clark, ex-tracted from an article entitled "Clark's Battery." Except for a few paragraphs, herein presented, the article deals with Clark's Battery on the East side of the Mississippi River, by Jo. A. Wilson, member Clark's Missouri Battery.[26]

**Published:** November 28, 1885.

## Clark's Battery [Extract].

The following account of the service of this noted Confederate battery is fur-nished by Jo. A. Wilson, now a civil engineer at Lexington, Mo., and is made up from a diary he kept throughout his four years' service:

S. Churchill Clark, a cadet from West Point Class of 1861, son of Col. Meriwether Lewis Clark, late of the Confederate Army, formerly of the United States Army, joined Gen. Price's command just before the Battle of Lexington, Missouri, and commanded a part of Gen. Parsons's artillery during the battle. Among the ordnance captured at Lexington were two six-pounder field pieces, one brass, one iron. These Gen. Price turned over to Capt. Clark, with authority to raise a company of artillery for the "Missouri State Guard," which he did, and afterwards received two twelve-pounder howitzers, making a four-gun battery. In December, 1861, when the State Guard began to enlist in the Confederate service, Clark, holding a captain's commission in the Confederate Army, commenced recruiting a company for "three years or during the war," retaining the same guns.

The battery was at this time known as "Clark's Battery," or "Second Missouri Artillery," was attached to the First Missouri Brigade in Springfield, Mo., then in winter quarters, and soon became noted for proficiency in drill and military maneuvers.

On the retreat to Cross Hollows, Ark., Clark's Battery generally marched with the rear guard, being frequently engaged with the enemy—assisted Gate's regiment in giving the Federal's a severe check at Sugar Creek—took an active part in the engagement at Elkhorn, where

## Capt. Clark was Killed

while gallantly sustaining a heavy fire from the enemy's artillery and infantry.[27]

---

26. Joseph A. Wilson was born on the Sac & Fox Indian Reservation, Iowa, on January 30, 1840. At the beginning of the Civil War he lived in Lexington, Missouri. As a civilian he served as a guide and messenger for General Rains's Division at the Siege of Lexington. Afterwards, he attached himself to Company D, Second Infantry Regiment, Eighth Division, MSG, and moved with them to Springfield, Missouri. Wilson joined Clark's Missouri Battery in December 1861, and continued on in the service until the end of the war, surrendering in Alabama in April 1865. As an added duty, Wilson served as "Drill Master" in Clark's Battery. He died at Lexington on March 20, 1913. Eakin, *Confederate Records*, 8:78, 80; Peterson, 221, 224; Schnetzer, *More Forgotten Men*, 247.

27. On February 17, Curtis's advance engaged Price's command at Sugar Creek, Arkansas. Clark's Missouri Battery held the rebel center, when Federal cavalry charged across Sugar Creek, up a hill

This was about the close of the second day's fighting, while our main army was in retreat. The officers and men of the battery were favorably mentioned by Gen. [Henry] Little[28] in his report of the battle. Owing to the rapid advance of the enemy Clark's body was left on the field and buried with the dead of both armies. Capt. Wright Schaumberg of Van Dorn's staff was afterwards sent in with a flag, and brought the body to Van Buren where it was buried with military honors.[29] Capt. Clark was an officer of great promise, full of ardor and of a buoyant, cheerful disposition; nothing seemed to depress his spirits. Thoroughly posted in tactics

---

after some distant fleeing rebels. To the Federals surprise, they were met by Clark's artillery fire, followed by the popping of assorted small arms. The Unionists, led by Major James Hubbard of the First Missouri Cavalry U.S., had found a hornet's nest of Confederate troops. After an hour engagement, the Federals broke off the attack, having lost 13 killed and about 20 wounded. The rebels for their part recorded their losses as three killed and fourteen wounded. *O.R.*, 8:61, 752; Bevier, 315–316; Frank Moore, ed., *The Rebellion Record A Diary of American Events*, 12 vols. (New York, 1861–1868; reprint ed. New York, 1977; hereafter cited as *Rebellion Record*), 3: Diary–35; Shea & Hess, 39–43; W. H. Tunnard, *A Southern Record: The History of the Third Regiment Louisiana Infantry* (Baton Rouge, 1866), 123, hereafter cited as Tunnard.

28. Lewis Henry Little was born on March 19, 1817, in Baltimore, Maryland, and received a direct commission into the U.S. Infantry on July 1, 1839. He served in the Mexican War, was breveted a captain, and participated in Johnston's Mormon Expedition in 1858. At the beginning of the Civil War, Little was stationed at Jefferson Barracks in St. Louis, where he resigned his commission on May 7, 1861, and joined the MSG on May 18, as a colonel. Little was latter commissioned a major in the regular Confederate Army. On January 23, 1862, Little was given the command of the First Missouri Brigade, which he led with distinction at Pea Ridge. Little was transferred to the east side of the Mississippi River in April 1862, and was commissioned a Confederate brigadier general on April 16, 1862. Little did not survive the war. He was killed at the Battle of Iuka, Mississippi, on September 19, 1862. See Appendix B for a compete biography of Henry Little. *O.R.*, 8:285, 739; Albert E. Castel, "The Diary of General Henry Little, C.S.A." *Civil War Times Illustrated* 11 (October, 1972), 4; William C. Davis, "Lewis Henry Little," *The Confederate General*, 6 vols. (William C. Davis, gen. ed.; Harrisburg, PA, 1991), 6:78–79, hereafter cited as *Confederate General*, 34.

29. Wright C. Schaumberg, a resident of New Orleans, joined the Fifth Division, MSG, in 1861, as a lieutenant colonel and aide-de-camp. On December 9, 1861, Schaumberg was serving as a Confederate captain and adjutant and quartermaster for Henry Little's "Volunteer Corps," which became Little's First Missouri Brigade on January 23, 1862. At the Battle of Pea Ridge, Schaumberg was noted for his "distinguished conduct." Following the battle, Schaumberg spent a short time on the east side of the Mississippi River, eventually becoming General Van Dorn's adjutant general. Schaumberg returned to the Trans-Mississippi in 1863, as a major and Inspector General of the department. On June 13, 1864, he was promoted to lieutenant colonel. Schaumberg completed his military service in the Trans-Mississippi and returned to New Orleans following the war, where he became the personal secretary to Mayor Shakespeare of the city. He died sometime before 1900. *O.R.*, 8:285, 312, 739; vol. 22, pt. 2:1053; vol. 26, pt. 2: 1068; vol. 34, pt. 4:669; vol. 41, pt. 4:1072; 53:759–760; Bevier, 70, 77–78; Eakin, *Confederate Records*, 7:1; Peterson, 155; Frank Von Phul, "General Little's Burial," *Southern Historical Society Papers*, 29: 212–214.

Schaumberg arrived at Curtis's headquarters on the evening of March 10, with one hundred men (William Watson has the number at 30 men) to assist in burying the dead. He was still part of Little's staff, though temporarily attached to Van Dorn, as Van Dorn had no staff. The exchange of prisoners followed on the eleventh with the burying of the dead shortly thereafter. *O.R.*, 8:193, 285; Tucker, *Father Bannon*, 55; William Watson, *Life In the Confederate Army Being the Observations and Experiences of an Alien in the South During the American Civil War* (London, 1887; reprint ed Baton Rouge, LA, 1995), 313–317, hereafter cited as Watson.

and army regulations, he labored to bring his company up the highest standard of efficiency. Though small in stature, his figure was graceful and his physical powers well developed. In the management of the horse and the use of the saber he excelled. Beloved and respected by all, his death, at any early age of 20, cast a gloom over all who knew him....

\* \* \* \* \* \*

**Item:** Traces the events from the retreat from Springfield, Missouri, in late February 1862 to the Battle of Pea Ridge, March 6-8, 1862, by Colonel R. H. Musser, late Judge Advocate General, Third Division, MSG.[30]
**Published:** November 21 and 28, 1885.

## The Battle of Pea Ridge.

The following description of the Battle of Pea Ridge by Col. R. H. Musser contains some points that are new:

I was serving on the staff of the Third Division, Missouri State Guard,[31] as judge-advocate. I had been appointed to the position after the Battle of Boonville[32] by Gen. John B. Clark, Sr.[33] For what distinguished services I was promoted from

---

30. Richard H. Musser was born on February 6, 1829, in Claysville, Kentucky, moved to Missouri in 1849, and settled in Brunswick, Chariton County. Admitted to the Missouri Bar in 1854, he was elected a Court of Appeals Judge in 1855. Musser started the Brunswick *Gazette* newspaper and later bought the *Brunswicker*, which he combined with his previous newspaper to form the *Brunswicker and Gazette*. At the beginning of the Civil War, Musser was appointed Judge Advocate General of the Third Division, MSG on June 23, 1861. He was at the Battles of Wilson's Creek and Lexington, where he served as aide to the division commander. At Pea Ridge, Musser had a horse shot out from under him while rallying some troops. Following Price to Mississippi, Musser spent a short time east of the Mississippi River, returned to the Trans-Mississippi Department and raised a battalion of infantry in late November 1862. His new command was known as Musser's Battalion or the Eighth Missouri Infantry Battalion. On January 4, 1863, it united with Clark's and Mitchell's Missouri Infantries, and Ruffner's Missouri Battery to form John B. Clark's Missouri Infantry Brigade. On September 30, 1863, Musser's Battalion and Clark's Infantry were consolidated to form a new regiment. On December 15, 1863, per Special Order No. 177, Headquarters, Price's Division, the unit was designated the Ninth Missouri Infantry. Musser later participated in the Campaign for Little Rock (August 1–September 14, 1863), the Red River Campaign (March 10–May 22, 1864) and the Camden Expedition (March 23–May 3, 1864). Following the war he settled in St. Louis, practiced law in the city until 1877, when he returned to Brunswick, where he reestablished himself. Date of death unknown. *O.R.*, 8:320; vol. 22, pt. 2:851; vol. 34, pt. 1:603, 812; 53:423, 439, 824; Michael E. Banasik, *Serving With Honor: The Diary of Captain Eathan Allen Pinnell of the Eighth Missouri Infantry (Confederate)* (Iowa City, IA, 1999), 44–45, 93; *History of Howard and Chariton Counties, Missouri, Written and Compiled from the Most Authentic Official and Private Sources Including a History of Its Townships, Towns and Villages* (St. Louis, 1883), 761–764; National Archives, Record Group 109, Confederate Muster Rolls, Ninth Missouri Infantry; Peterson, 108; Schnetzer, *More Forgotten Men*, 171.
31. The Third Division, MSG was commanded by John B. Clark, Sr. It was organized from men from the Missouri counties of Adair, Boone, Chariton, Howard, Linn, Macon, Putnam, Randolph, Schuyler and Sullivan. State of Missouri, *An Act for Military Forces*, 4; Peterson, 107.
32. Boonville was located in Cooper County, Missouri, on the south side of the Missouri River. On June 17, 1861, Nathaniel Lyon engaged the MSG at Boonville and easily dispersed them after a only a few minutes. During the engagement, Lyon lost 2 killed, 9 wounded (2 mortally) and 1 missing out of 1,700 men engaged. Lyon reported capturing 60 rebels, 500 arms, and 2 brass cannon. The rebel forces engaged numbered between 300–500 men with the loss of between 3–5 killed, about 6–20 wounded and another 20 captured. *O.R.*, 3:11–14, 809; Christopher Phillips, *Damned Yankee: The Life of General Nathaniel Lyon* (Columbia, MO, 1990), 217–220; McGhee, *Service With the Guard*, 31–32 (n. 45); Moore, *Missouri, Confederate Military History*, 45; "The Battle of Boonville," *Rebellion Record*, 1: DOC 408–410; "A Secession Account," *Rebellion Record*, 1: DOC 410–411; Snead, 213–214.
33. John B. Clark, Sr. commanded the Third Division, MSG. He was born on April 17, 1802, in

a private to the rank of lieutenant-colonel it is not necessary here to mention. The old general had been sent to the Confederate Congress by the Neosho legislature[34] and his successor to the command, Gen. E. W. Price[35] had been captured on the Osage and was a prisoner of war. The command of the division devolved, therefore, on Col. John B. Clark, Jr.,[36] who was ranked only in seniority by Col.

Kentucky, moved to Missouri in 1818, and became a lawyer and a successful politician. At the beginning of the Civil War he was appointed a general in the MSG, was wounded at Wilson's Creek and subsequently became a Confederate Senator from Missouri. After the war, Clark fled to Mexico, but later returned to Missouri, where he resumed his practice of law. He died in October 1885, in Fayette, Missouri. For a complete biography see Banasik, *Serving With Honor*, 282–283; Allardice, 59–61; Peterson, 107.

34. In June 1861, the Missouri government fled Jefferson City, and, at the call of Governor Jackson was supposed to meet on October 21 at Neosho, in the southwestern part of the state. On October 23, the legislature met at Neosho and on October 28 (Eakin says October 29), they passed an Ordinance of Secession. The legislature adjourned on October 29, and reconvened on October 31, at Cassville to complete their business. Laughlin in her article has the legislature well short of a quorum necessary to pass the Ordinance with 39 House and 10 Senate members present out of the 67 and 17, respectively that were required. However, Union newspapers, at the time, reported as "reliable," that the legislature fell only four votes short of a quorum—though not specifying which branch or branches. With another take on the vote General Franz Sigel, a Federal officer, also reported the same numbers and date as did Laughlin. Lucia Rutherford Douglas, ed., *Douglas's Texas Battery, CSA* (Tyler, TX, 1966), 173; Eakin, *Diary of a Doctor*, 35–37; "From Missouri," *Chicago Daily Tribune* (Chicago, IL), October 31, 1861; "From St. Louis," *Chicago Tribune*, November 2, 1861; Frost, 2; Sceva Bright Laughlin, "Missouri Politics During the Civil War," *Missouri Historical Review* 23 (July 1929), 617–618; Lehr, *As the Mockingbird Sang*, 26; Sigel, 1:315; Tunnard, 95.

35. Edwin William Price, the eldest son of Sterling Price, was born on June 10, 1834, in Randolph County, Missouri. Price received a degree from the University of Missouri at Columbia, and was a farmer by profession. At the beginning of the Civil War, he was elected captain of the Central Missouri Guards of Chariton County. Price later joined the MSG and rose to the grade of brigadier general commanding the Third Division. He "gallantly" fought at the Missouri Battles of Carthage, Drywood Creek, Wilson's Creek and Lexington. In the latter part of 1861, Price was captured near Warsaw, on the Osage River. Sent to Alton Prison, in Alton, Illinois, Price was paroled on February 26, to Chariton County, and exchanged in October 1862. He returned to Missouri, took the Oath of Allegiance to the United States in October 1862, and was pardoned by President Lincoln in November. After the war Edwin lived out his remaining days raising wheat and running a tobacco factory in Chariton County. He died in St. Louis on January 7, 1908. *O.R.*, 3:31; *O.R.*, Series 2, 4:642–643, 742; Allardice, 187–188; Carolyn M. Bartels, *The Forgotten Men Missouri State Guard* (Shawnee Mission, KS, 1995) 296; Hale, 258–259; Peterson, 107, 116; Winter, 121.

36. John B. Clark, Jr. was born in Fayette, Missouri, on January 14, 1831, educated at the University of Missouri (Columbia) and received a law degree from Harvard in 1854. At the beginning of the Civil War, Clark was elected captain of Company C, First Infantry Regiment, Third Division, MSG in May 1861. He subsequently rose in rank, commanding his regiment and then the Third Division. While serving in the Guard, Clark fought at Wilson's Creek, Lexington, and Pea Ridge. Clark was appointed a colonel in the Confederate Army on June 28, 1862, and in November 1862 he commanded what would later become Ninth Missouri Infantry, which he led at the Battle of Prairie Grove, Arkansas (December 7, 1862). He subsequently commanded a brigade in the Trans-Mississippi, and was promoted to brigadier general on March 8, 1864, having fought in most major engagements west of the Mississippi River. After the war, Clark was elected to the U.S. Congress (1873–1883) from Missouri. He died on September 7, 1903. For a complete biography see Banasik, *Serving With Honor*, 380–381; Moore, *Missouri, Confederate Military History*, 206–208; National Archives, Record Group M861 (roll no. 36), Records of Confederate Movements and Activities, Ninth Missouri Infantry; Peterson,

Congreve Jackson,[37] then absent on recruiting service.

We had evacuated Springfield on the 13th day of February, 1862, fallen back to Crane Creek, thence to Keytesville, down the Wire Road through the Cross Hollows to Mudtown and thence over the range to Dripping Spring and Cove Creek. Gen. Ben McCulloch,[38] who might have supported and reinforced us so as to enable us to remain in Missouri, had sulked, like Achilles at the siege of Troy.

The retreat from Springfield had been the result of the want of harmony between Gen. Price and Gen. Ben McCulloch, the latter having reluctantly made a stand at Wilson's Creek in August, 1861, on the condition that Gen. Price would

## Waive the Right to Command,

to which his rank entitled him.[39] He then ran away from victory and failed to sup-

---

107, 113, 115; Special Orders No. 38 (November 10, 1862), Special Order Letter Book (June 1–Dec. 18, 1862), Hindman's command, 111–112, Peter W. Alexander Collection, Columbia University, New York, (hereafter cited as Special Order Book No. 1); Ezra J. Warner, *Generals in Gray: Lives of the Confederate Commanders* (Baton Rouge, LA, 1959), 52.

37. Congreve Jackson was born in Howard County, Missouri, near Glasgow, in the early part of the nineteenth century. He received little schooling during his life, but was called a "man of wisdom... and his judgement without error." A Democrat and a slave owner, Jackson served as a militia general, during the "Mormon difficulties," in 1838. Jackson, then served in the Second Seminole War as a captain, commanding Company D, First Missouri Volunteers under Colonel Richard Gentry. During the Mexican War, Jackson commanded a battalion and served as the executive officer (lieutenant colonel) in the First Missouri Mounted Volunteers. At the beginning of the Civil War he was elected colonel of the Second Infantry Regiment, Third Division, MSG, on August 11, 1861. He led his command at Lexington and Pea Ridge, where he was noted for "great bravery during the hottest part of the engagement." Due to age and "infirmities," which made him unfit for service, Jackson left the Guard in April 1862. Indications are that he organized an irregular force in the spring of 1863, and led it into southwest Missouri, in conjunction with Tom Livingtston. No further Civil War record is known on Jackson. In 1865, following the war, Jackson returned to his home in Howard County, where he died, unmarried, in about 1883. *O.R.*, 3:191; 8:319; vol. 22, pt. 2:109, 225; 53:438–439; Heitman, 2:56, 281; *History of Audrain County*, 55–56; Peterson, 15; Musser, "Two Missouri War Characters," *Missouri Republican*, November 14, 1885.

38. Born in Tennessee in 1811, Ben McCulloch fought at the Battle of San Jacinto, prospected for gold in California in 1849, and was a U.S. Marshall in Texas. He received the surrender of the Federal forces in San Antonio, Texas, in February 1861, and was commissioned a Confederate brigadier general on May 11, 1861. McCulloch commanded the District of the Indian Territory, which embraced the territory south of Kansas and west of Arkansas in the early part of the war. He was killed at the Battle of Pea Ridge on March 7, 1862. For a complete biography see Banasik, *Missouri In 1861*, 356–357; *O.R.*, 3:575; Warner, *Generals in Gray*, 200–202.

39. Price yielded command of the Missouri troops to General McCulloch on August 4, 1861, and following the Battle of Wilson's Creek resumed an independent command. Additionally, long before the Confederates gave up Springfield on February 13, 1862, Price and McCulloch had been in a fundamental disagreement over the conduct of the Missouri Campaign. According to Shea & Hess, "Price saw the war entirely in terms of liberating Missouri; McCulloch's primary concern was the defense of Confederate Arkansas and the Indian Territory in accordance with orders from Richmond." The Battle of Wilson's Creek and its aftermath highlighted those difference, resulting in the departure of McCulloch's command back to Arkansas. By the time that Price's Missouri army had entered winter quarters on December 23, 1861, at Springfield, messages had already been flowing to anyone in power who would listen, on the fate of the Missouri army and Price's desire to again return to the Missouri

port Gen. Price in his advance to the Missouri [River], even after he had captured Lexington.[40] As Price fell back from the Missouri for want of his support, McCulloch retreated into the deep valley in which is situated the Wire road, felling the trees across it for fear of an enemy, not at the time threatening him or within reach. He not only undertook to make the roads impassable, but destroyed the crops and forage in Missouri he ought to have consumed, and then went into winter quarters near Cross Hollows in Arkansas.[41] This movement of McCulloch not only left open to the enemy the well-supplied country of Southwest Missouri inhabited by a friendly people, but practically abandoned the lead mines at Granby,[42] the only source of supply for bullets short of Mexico. The retrograde movement of McCulloch had compelled Price to leave the Missouri River. Reluctant to leave his

---

River. Initially all the responses were non-supportive, but finally the tide turned and the Confederate Government promised support by early March 1862. In northwest Arkansas, Colonel Louis Hébert promised to march to Price's support if the Unionists advanced on his position at Springfield. By January 29, 1862, Hébert was ready to march but a tremendous snowstorm kept his troops in camp. As late as February 9, Price was still hopeful that the bluecoated army could be met and defeated, all depended on assistance from Arkansas. But time had run out. On February 16, Hébert marched from Fayetteville heading to Price's assistance. However, Price had already abandoned Springfield on February 13 and was moving rapidly south towards Arkansas. *O.R.*, 8:702, 712–715, 730, 741–742, 745, 747–748, 750, 753, 756; 53:720; Eakin, *Diary of a Doctor*, 46; Janet Hewett, ed. *Supplement to the Official Records of the Union and Confederate Armies,* 100 vols., in three parts, (Wilmington, NC, 1994–2001), pt. 3, 3:646–647 (cited hereafter as *O.R.S.*); Alvin M. Josephy, Jr., *The Civil War In the American West* (New York, 1992), 335; Shea & Hess, 19.

40. McCulloch moved his command back to Arkansas on August 25, 1861, citing the following:

I am in no condition to advance, or even meet the enemy here, having little ammunition or supplies of any kind. In fact, with the means of transportation now at my disposal I find it impossible to keep my force supplied, and will, in consequence, shorten my line, by falling back to the Arkansas line…and there proceed to drill and organize a force to meet the enemy when they take the field again in this quarter.

Latter, after fully reviewing the subject, McCulloch would add that he had no support from the troops under Colonel William J. Hardee in eastern Missouri and the strength of his command was much reduced due to the loss of the Arkansas State Troops. *O.R.*, 3:672, 747; Tunnard, 79.

41. In late September 1861, Price retreated from Lexington due to the advancing elements of John C. Frémont's army. Price crossed the Osage River on October 10, and continued southward on October 17. Meanwhile, Frémont pressed forward and occupied Springfield for the second time on October 26. While the Federals were still in Springfield, McCulloch, Price and Governor Jackson met at Keetsville, on November 6 to discuss the military situation in southwest Missouri. All parties agreed to await the advance of the enemy, while Generals Price and McCulloch would pick the location for the battle. On November 10, Frémont was reported to be advancing, prompting McCulloch to order McIntosh's command to devastate the countryside. "Everything that would or could aid" the enemy "was destroyed—corn fodder, oats, hay and wheat-stacks—while the roads were thoroughly and completely blockaded by felling timber across them. It showed how imminent the danger was considered." Banasik, *Duty, Honor and Country*, 32, 37; *Confederate Military History*, vol. 10: *Arkansas*, by John A. Harrell, 64, hereafter cited as Harrell, *Arkansas, Confederate Military History*; Lucia Rutherford Douglas, ed., *Douglas's Texas Battery, CSA*. Tyler, TX, 1966, 176, hereafter cited as Douglas; Lester Newton Fitzhugh, ed., *Cannon Smoke: The Letters of Captain John J. Good, Good-Douglas Texas Battery, CSA* (Hillsboro, TX, 1971), 113–114, 121, hereafter cited as Fitzhugh; Tunnard, 105.

42. The Granby lead mines were located in Newton County, in southwest Missouri.

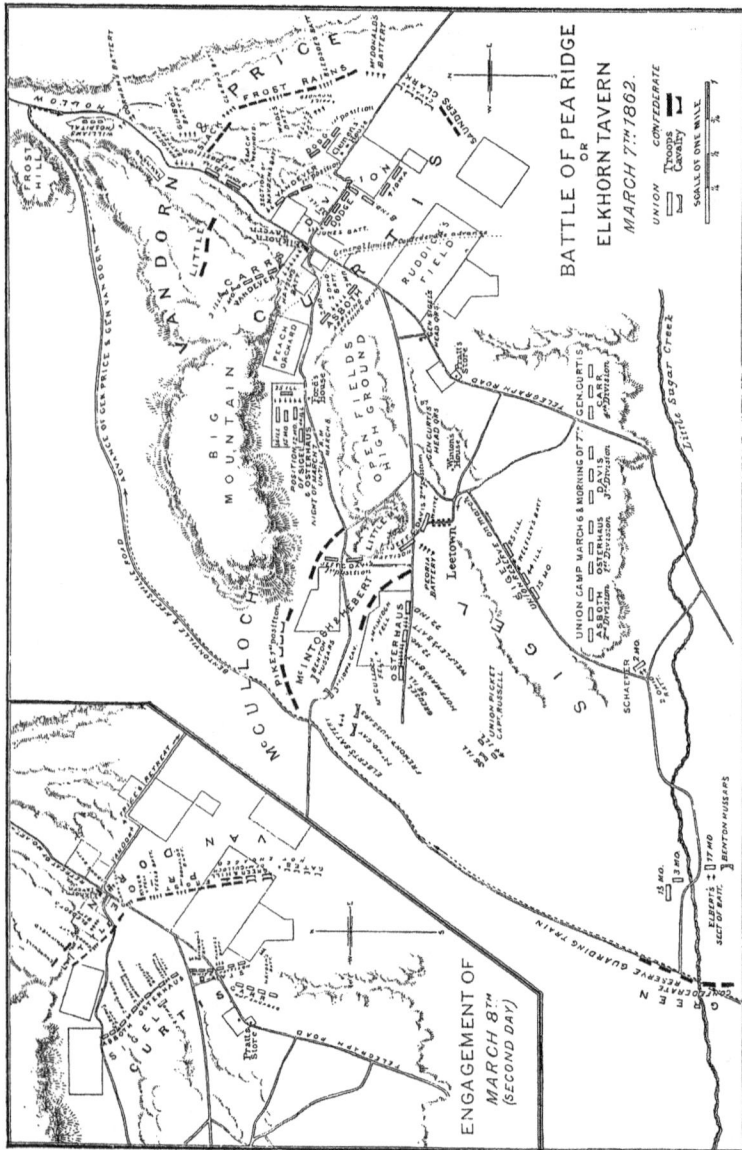

Battle of Pea Ridge, Arkansas (March 7–8, 1862)

own state he made a stand at Springfield,[43] and sent courier after courier to urge Gen. McCulloch to send him reinforcements. The Texas, Louisiana and Arkansas troops with the Indians would have enabled Gen. Price to hold Southwest Missouri and the country was more abundantly supplied with food and forage for them than Arkansas. They are the same army with which the Battle of Pea Ridge was fought at such disadvantage.[44] Gen. Price, duly informed of the enemy's movements, strength and purposes,

## Urged Every Consideration

and offered every inducement, proposing again to waive command and give McCulloch command. He continued to hope for this assistance at Springfield till the enemy in force pressing on his pickets and threatening his rear induced him to order a retreat. The same conditions and inducements were again offered to Gen. McCulloch by Gen. Price, who insisted on making a stand at Cross Hollows.[45]

---

43. To the surprise of the rebel command, the Federals abandoned Springfield, beginning on November 9, 1861, with the bulk of the army leaving by the tenth. McCulloch received news of the Federal evacuation of Springfield on November 15, and promptly advanced with his "available mounted troops"—about 1,500 troops—entering Springfield, for the second and final time, on November 19. The following day, McCulloch removed the remnants of his command from Missouri, sending them into winter quarters on November 29, in Arkansas, even while Price's command again moved northward towards the Missouri River. To facilitate the quartering of his command, McCulloch split his army with a brigade under Louis Hébert occupying positions from Bentonville to Fayetteville, Arkansas, including Cross Hollows. The other brigade, under James McIntosh, wintered near Fort Smith on the Arkansas River. Meanwhile, Price's command, without support from McCulloch, pulled back from Osceola, Missouri, on the Osage River, on December 19, and moved back to Springfield, where they entered winter quarters on December 23. *O.R.*, 3:742–743, 748; 8:730, 746; 53:763; William G. Bek, ed., "Civil War Diary of John T. Buegel, Union Soldier," *Missouri Historical Review* 40 (April 1946), 217; Wiley Britton, *The Civil War on the Border A Narrative of Military Operations in Missouri, Kansas, Arkansas, and the Indian Territory, 2 vols.* (New York, 1899), 162, 182, 197, hereafter cited as Britton, *Civil War on the Border, 1861–1862*; Douglas, 176; Eakin, *Diary of a Doctor*, 43, 46; E.p.m., Letter to the Editor, *Waukegon Weekly Gazette* (Waukegon, IL), November 30, 1861; Fitzhugh, 123; Frost, 3; Henry Ketzle, Typescript manuscript, "Military History of the 37th Reg. Ill. Vol. Infantry," Aledo Museum (Aledo, IL), 3; James E. McGhee, *Letter and Order Book Missouri State Guard 1861–1862* (Independence, MO, 2001), unnumbered page 50 (entry page 98); Tunnard, 109; Watson, 267–268.

44. See Appendix A for organization of the Confederate forces at the Battle of Pea Ridge.

45. On December 22, 1861, McCulloch wrote Confederate Secretary of War J. P. Benjamin a long letter detailing the relationship between himself and General Price. On the matter of where to best defeat the Federal army, McCulloch wrote:

> I wrote him [General Price], proposing to draw the enemy, if he did advance and follow us, into Arkansas, to what is called the Boston Mountain. If we could have effected this it would have doubled my force, by calling in my two regiments from Texas, then in the Indian Nation, and the Indian regiments also. This he objected to, saying his men would not consent to go out of the State of Missouri, at the same time expressing a desire to see me. I again met him, and told him if we fought the enemy where we were it would amount to nothing but a repulse of his infantry, as he would never bring his baggage wagons and artillery into so rough a country; whereas if he could be got down to the Boston Mountain, some 60 miles, we would get all his cannon, 120, and most of his army, with their arms. He said again his men

How far we should have fallen back cannot be told if we had not been joined in the latter days of February by Gen. Earl Van Dorn[46] who took command of the entire forces, ranking both Price and McCulloch.[47] Van Dorn was an able and dashing cavalry officer from the regular army and a West Point graduate. He took command and reorganized the forces the best he could in the short time and patched up a sort of harmony between the two generals. The order to move northward toward our own state was gratefully heard on dress parade on the evening of the 1st of March, and the Missouri infantry were on the second morning along the deep valley which

## Perforated the Ranges

of the Boston Mountains.[48] It was the 3rd when we reached the Cane Hill neighborhood, famous for its apples and fruits.[49]

---

would not leave the State; whereupon I agreed to fight them in our present position, though I believed it would result in little good to Missouri.
*O.R.*, 3:748.

46. Earl Van Dorn was born in 1820, in Mississippi, attended West Point where he graduated in 1842 (number 52 of 56). During the Mexican War Van Dorn received two brevets, after which he fought in the Seminole War. At the beginning of the Civil War, Van Dorn, now a major, joined the Confederate Army. He was appointed a brigadier general in April 1861, and a major general in September. Van Dorn fought and lost the Battle of Pea Ridge and then led his army to the east side of the Mississippi River. He was killed on May 8, 1863, by a disgruntled husband for violating "the sanctity of the home." When Van Dorn joined the army in Arkansas he was received with mixed emotions. One soldier in the Third Louisiana recorded that Van Dorn "was not fit to enter a ten acre field with McIntosh." This did not bode well for the soldier knowing that Van Dorn was being placed in command over McCulloch, whom the soldier liked and respected. However, this same soldier also noted that others thought that Van Dorn was a "bold and dashing officer," who "would do wonders and revolutionize matters." For a complete biography see Banasik, *Missouri Brothers in Gray*, 157, 160; Boatner, 867; Watson, 281.
47. General Earl Van Dorn arrived in Little Rock on January 29, and hurried on to Jacksonport where he arrived two days later. Lingering for a time, Van Dorn moved on to Price's headquarters on Cove Creek, where he arrived on March 2, 1862. Note: Many of the period writers have various dates for the arrival of Van Dorn at Price's headquarters. Maury has the date as March 1, Tunnard and Douglas stated March 2, while Harding has the date as March 3. Father John Bannon, the chaplain for Little's Missouri Brigade, recorded that Van Dorn arrived on March 2 at 4:00 p.m. Most authors of secondary material have the arrival date as March 3, with the exception of Shea & Hess, who have the arrival date as March 2. *O.R.*, 8:197; *O.R.S.*, pt. 3, vol. 1:641; Walter Lee Brown, "Pea Ridge: Gettysburg of the West," *The Arkansas Historical Quarterly* 15 (Spring, 1956), 8, hereafter cited as Brown; Douglas, 182; Douglas Hale, *The Third Texas Cavalry in the Civil War* (Norman, OK, 1993), 88, hereafter cited as Hale, *Third Texas Cavalry*; Harrell, *Arkansas, Confederate Military History*, 66–67; Lehr, *As the Mockingbird Sang*, 34; Josephy, *Civil War In the American West*, 338; Maury, 183; McGhee, *Service With the Guard*, 64; Shea & Hess, 56; Tucker, *Father Bannon*, 32; Tunnard, 129.
48. Shortly after arriving at Price's camp on March 2, Van Dorn issued orders for the army to march northward to engage Curtis's Federals. On March 4, the Missourians broke camp and headed north. *O.R.*, 8:283; L. G. Bennett and Wm. M. Haigh, *History of the Thirty-sixth Regiment Illinois Volunteers During the War of the Rebellion* (Aurora, IL, 1876; reprint ed., Marengo, IL, 1999), 128, hereafter cited as Bennett & Haigh; Lehr, *As the Mockingbird Sang*, 35; Maury, 183; McElroy, 313; McGhee, *Letter and Order Book*, unnumbered page 75 (entry page 148); Shea & Hess, 56; Tunnard, 129.
49. Northwest Arkansas was famous as a fruit growing region, particularly its "big red apples," with Fayetteville being the center of the trade. Harrell, *Arkansas, Confederate Military History*, 70.

It was between Cane Hill and Fayetteville we passed the house of Mr. Heagan, a blind gentleman of great intelligence and hospitality. Some of the Missouri soldiers went to his well and began drawing water. The water soon gave out, but on examination the supposed bottom of the well was found to be a barrel of whiskey. Confederate enterprise was equaled to the occasion. The barrel and four of its brothers were rescued from drowning. Mr Heagan was blind and could not see it, and it soon became apparent from the number of soldiers reeling under the burden of their canteens. Unfortunately for the cappers [captors] of the whiskey Gen. Martin Green[50] came along, discovered the cause of their joy and ordered the barrels decapitated. Much to their disgust and eternal regret it was done.

On the 4th we passed through Fayetteville and on the evening of the 5th we bivouacked at a dismantled overshot mill known as the Elm Springs.[51] It was here that we got our first definite information of the enemy. Maj. Lowther,[52] in com-

---

50. Martin Green, of Canton, Missouri, was born on June 3, 1815, in Virginia, married in the spring of 1836, and moved west. By the beginning of the Civil War, he was a successful farmer, businessman and politician, having been elected to the Missouri State House in 1854, and a county judge in 1856. Elected colonel of an irregular, pro-Confederate militia regiment, Green lost the Battle of Athens, Missouri (August 5, 1861) and later joined Sterling Price at the Siege of Lexington. On December 2, 1861, Green was elected a brigadier general of the Second Division, MSG, which he led at Pea Ridge. After the battle, Green was transferred with his command to the east side of the Mississippi River, where he completed his military service. Green was appointed a Confederate brigadier general on July 23, 1862, and killed by a Union sniper on June 26 at Vicksburg, Mississippi. See Banasik, *Missouri In 1861*, 347, for a complete biography. *O.R.*. 8:316–318; Warner, *Generals in Gray*, 116–117.

51. Elm Springs, Arkansas, was located about 10 miles north of Fayetteville on a road that ran parallel to the Telegraph or Wire Road, which eventually led to Springfield, Missouri. One participant in the campaign described it as "a small town, the buildings of which are mostly old & dilapidated, while another called the area a 'little paradise.'" It also served as a training post for the Confederate Army during the summer of 1862. From Elm Springs it was about 13 miles to Bentonville, Arkansas, and 27 miles to the Pea Ridge battlefield. Michael E. Banasik, *Embattled Arkansas: The Prairie Grove Campaign of 1862* (Wilmington, NC, 1996), 185–186; George B. Davis, et al, *Atlas to Accompany the Official Records of the Union and Confederate Armies* (Washington, DC, 1891–1895), plt. 10, no. 2, hereafter cited as Davis, *Civil War Atlas*; Frank Allen Dennis, ed., *Recollections of the 4th Missouri Cavalry, William S. Burns Captain Co. I, 4th Missouri Cavalry (Union)* (Dayton, OH, 1988), 27, hereafter cited as Dennis; Josephy, *Civil War In the American West*, 339; Lehr, *As the Mockingbird Sang*, 36.

52. This was probably Major Robert R. Lawther of the First Missouri Cavalry Regiment (Confederate). He was born in Kittanning, Pennsylvania, in about 1837. Prior to the war Lawther was a resident of Muscatine, Iowa, where he was a businessman and served as the treasurer of a local Presbyterian Church. Running afoul of the local police for "cheating his business partner," defrauding his church and the city, Lawther left Iowa. At the beginning of the war he was living in Jefferson City, Missouri, joined the MSG, and was latter elected major of the First Missouri Cavalry Regiment (Confederate) when the regiment was organized on December 30, 1861. Lawther departed the First Missouri on June 12, 1862, with the permission of President Jefferson Davis to organize the First Regiment, Missouri Partisan Rangers during the summer of 1862. His command was later incorporated into the Tenth Missouri Cavalry, with Lawther elected the colonel of the regiment on April 20, 1864. Lawther led his command until he resigned on February 27, 1865 (his service record has the date as January 10), with a surgeon's Certificate of Disability. During the war, he participated in the major battles or engagements in Arkansas at Pea Ridge, Pine Bluff (October 25, 1863), the Camden Expedition (March–May 1864) and Price's 1864 Missouri Raid. He was paroled at Galveston, Texas on June 20, 1865. *O.R.*, vol. 22,

mand of some scouts, captured a forage party of the enemy with a small escort on the Wire road, that is, the road in which the telegraph line from Springfield to Fayetteville and to a point south was built.[53] The road we were bivouacked on was the Bentonville road, parallel to the Wire road, and from ten to fifteen miles west.

## The Unsuspecting Foraging Party

were bagged, trains and all, together with their escort. From them Gen. Price gained information as to the enemy's position and a knowledge of the fact that Gen. Franz Sigel was in his front only a few miles and possibly had no knowledge of his proximity.[54] The march had been a hard one that day, and the weather quite

pt. 1:731–732; vol. 34, pt. 1:781; vol. 41, pt. 1:698; *O.R.S.,*, pt. 2, vol. 38:253; Bevier, 77; Joseph H. Crute, *Units of the Confederate States Army* (Midlothian, VA, 1987), 203, hereafter cited as Crute; Joanne C. Eakin and Donald R., *Branded As Rebels: A List of Bushwhackers, Guerrillas, Partisan Rangers, Confederates and Southern Sympathizers from Missouri During the War Years* (Independence, MO, 1993), 261, hereafter cited as Eakin & Hale; "The 'Invader'," *Muscatine Daily Journal* (Muscatine, IA), May 28, 1863; McGhee, *Missouri State Guard Letter Book,* unnumbered page 29 (entry pages 56–57); National Archives, Record Group M322, (roll no. 57), Confederate Compiled Service Records, Tenth Missouri Cavalry Regiment.

53. On the evening of March 5, the Confederate Army was encamped about Elm Springs, with Price's command in advance. Van Dorn's plan called for a quick advance that would take in Sigel's Federals in the Bentonville area, before they could react to the rebel move and concentrate their scattered command. To deceive the Federals, McIntosh's Confederate Cavalry Brigade was detached from the main body on March 5, and sent up the Telegraph Road, toward Mudtown, in an attempt to make the Federals believe that an attack was coming from that quarter. During the day, on March 5, Colonel B. W. Stone's Texas Cavalry captured 7 wagons with 38 prisoners. (Note: Stone in his official report places the number of captured wagons at 10 and prisoners at 40; however, two other participants in the campaign noted the number as 7 wagons and 36–38 prisoners, including one soldier who made a diary entry on the day of capture to that effect.) Early on the morning of March 6, the advance continued, on the road to Bentonville, with Gates's First Missouri Cavalry (Confederate) leading the way. Gates's unit, by all accounts, did not capture any wagons or prisoners on March 5, though Federal reports indicate that their picket was fired upon just north of Elm Springs on that date. *O.R.,* 8:209, 307; Richard Lowe, ed, *A Texas Cavalry Officer's Civil War: The Diary and Letters of James C. Bates* (Baton Rouge, 1999), 75–77, hereafter cited as Lowe; Tunnard, 130.

54. General Curtis, the Federal commander, received news of the rebel presence at Fayetteville at 2:00 p.m. on March 5, from Private William Miller, Third Iowa Cavalry, who was acting as a spy at the time. While heading to the rebel army, Miller was detained by some Texas cavalry, interviewed and released. Having determined the rebels' intentions, Miller hurried back to Federal lines and reported his information to Curtis. Miller reported that the rebels were marching north toward Bentonville and would be at Elm Springs by the evening. Curtis believed the report and immediately called in his scattered command, including Sigel's two divisions which were in the vicinity of Bentonville. Private George B. Raymond, Company D, Thirty-sixth Illinois Infantry, an orderly for General Curtis, was given the mission to deliver orders to Sigel to withdraw. Raymond, accompanied by a guide, wound his way to Sigel's camp, losing his companion in the process, shot dead by a rebel patrol. Raymond finally reached Sigel's headquarters sometime after nightfall on March 5. William S. Burns, a member of the Fourth Missouri Cavalry, stated that Sigel received the dispatch at 10:00 p.m., the same time that Sigel received reports from his advance near Elm Springs that the Confederates were approaching. With Curtis's orders in hand and reports from his scouts, Sigel immediately ordered his forward outpost near Osage Mills, just north of Elm Springs, to withdraw immediately to Bentonville, while the rest of his command was ordered to evacuate the Bentonville area at 2:00 a.m. on March 6. *O.R.,* 8:197, 208–209, 592; Edwin C. Bearss, "The Battle of Pea Ridge," *Arkansas Historical Quarterly* 20

cold. It was too late to press forward and the soldiers were tired and very hungry. The supper was cooked and heartily eaten, and we lay down for rest, expecting an early reveille. It came at 4 o'clock in the morning, and after bolting a hasty cooked breakfast we moved out. Early in the day we ascertained that our cavalry had struck Sigel, who was at a mill somewhere north and west of us, and were pressing him. He had gotten information of our neighborhood and force, and was active and early as usual.[55] He got into Little Bentonville Prairie a little too soon for us, but our infantry entered the park of the beautiful meadow in time to see his rear guard, skirmishing with our advance, escape into the canyon of Sugar Creek. Thus, like a good soldier, he deployed, masked his field pieces and held us at bay till he

## Made Good His Escape.

I never saw so handsome a retreat, nor a corps extricated so skillfully in the presence of a superior force. No man even saw all of the battle but from our standpoint and information Sigel's escape was the question of the diligence that enabled him to enter Bentonville Prairie ahead of us and escape into Sugar Creek Valley. The chances of war, however, turn more upon diligence and endurance than upon genius. It is the staying qualities that make the soldier. From Julius Caesar to Grant the pluck that never gave up the fight and could often retrieve disasters has always been worth the price of armies. Sigel deployed every few hundred yards and masked his pieces. We advanced cautiously with skirmishers in front and flanking parties on the heights on either side till halted by a ricochet round shot and shell or volley of canister. Availing himself of our prudent halt Sigel would unlimber and gallop forward till the approaching shadows of nightfall rendered it necessary to cease the pursuit and enable him, by following the course of the creek, to

## Make His Junction

with Curtis's command at Elkhorn Tavern.[56] Sigel's retreat was not without casu-

---

(Spring, 1961), 77–78; Bennett & Haigh, 129; Dennis, 28; H. D'B. C., "History of the Third Iowa Cavalry," *The Daily Gate City* (Keokuk, IA), November 14, 1863; Sigel, 1:319.

55. On the morning of March 6, the First Missouri Cavalry (Confederate) led the rebel advance toward Bentonville, not the Third Texas Cavalry as stated by Shea & Hess in their book on Pea Ridge. In his official report on the battle, General Price clearly stated that "Colonel Gates's regiment of cavalry led the advance of the whole army." A close review of source cited by Shea & Hess has the Third Texas Cavalry leading the advance, however, the source is unclear as to what advance the Third Texas was leading—I believe it to be McIntosh's Cavalry Brigade, which was on the road to Bentonville via Osage Mills, which was to the west of the main body. McIntosh's command was essentially screening the rebel army to the west, while Gates's Missourians were leading the advance on the most direct route to Bentonville. *O.R.*, 8:297, 307; Josephy, *Civil War In the American West*, 339; Shea & Hess, 65, 73.

56. Sigel's command began moving out of the Bentonville area at 2:00 a.m. and by 8:00 a.m. the trains had passed through Bentonville, en route for Curtis's main body at Little Sugar Creek. Sigel tarried

alties, and he did not extricate himself without loss. I saw a poor soldier wounded and very cold, without his boots. A Confederate being in need of such articles, had anticipated his death and pulled them off him while alive. He was placed in charge of the surgeon and taken care of. I hoped he lives to remember his bootless condition, and pardon the over hasty enemy who gave him so much suffering that day.[57]

Gen. Curtis, as afterwards we learned, expected us to advance on the Wire Road and had made dispositions on the south of his camp to impede our march. I suppose his theory of our advance from that side was based upon the fact of Lowther's capture of his foragers and wagons. We, however, being well informed of the country turned north after the long skirmish with Sigel and moved around on a road which intersected the Wire Road just north of Pea Ridge. We bivouacked in the woods very hungry and quite cold, and were early in the morning on the march, reaching the Wire Road north of Curtis's rear just before daylight.[58] The road passes

---

at Bentonville waiting for his picket guard from Osage Mills to pass through town, when at 10:10 a.m. he was informed that the enemy was approaching his position. Sigel, with 600 men (Bennett & Haigh place the number at 800), hastily evacuated Bentonville closely pursued by rebel cavalry which were enveloping the town from three sides. With great skill, Sigel retreated from the near trap, setting ambushes to lure in the pursuing rebel cavalry, firing and then retreating. By this method did Sigel successfully retreat from Bentonville. In all, according to Sigel, he fended off three attacks from 10:30 a.m. until reinforcements met him at 3:30 p.m., and he safely rejoined Curtis's main body. *O.R.*, 8:210, 283; Bennett & Haigh, 136; Sigel, 1:319–320.

57. The Federals lost 16 killed, 30 wounded and 26 prisoners, according to one Federal source, while Curtis reported only losing "some 25 killed and wounded." The prisoners all came from Company B, Thirty-sixth Illinois Infantry, except for 2. Rebel losses on March 6, occurred mainly in the Third Texas Cavalry, with one source reporting losing 10 killed and 20 wounded; however, in his official report on the Elkhorn engagement, Colonel Greer reported the loss of the regiment as 2 killed and 12 wounded. Other Confederate losses are not known. *O.R.*, 8:198, 299; *O.R.S.*, pt. 2, vol. 10:607; Haigh & Bennett, 138; Victor M. Rose, *Ross' Texas Brigade Being a Narrative of Events Connected With Its Service In the Late War Between the States* (Louisville, KY, 1881), 57, hereafter cited as Rose; A. W. Sparks, *The War Between the States, As I Saw It. Reminiscent, Historical and Personal* (Tyler, TX, 1901), 173, hereafter cited as Sparks.

58. Once Curtis became aware of Van Dorn's approach he concentrated his command at Little Sugar Creek. As the writer noted, Curtis felled timber to block the approach to the Union position, including covering the roads that flanked his position to both the right and left. Meanwhile, Van Dorn called a conference of his primary commanders at 6:00 p.m. and determined to move around Curtis's right flank, via the eight mile "Bentonville Detour" and gain the Wire Road in the rear of Curtis; this in turn allowed Van Dorn to avoid a direct assault on the Federal entrenchments at Little Sugar Creek. At 8:00 p.m. on March 6, Price led out his command to Curtis's rear, but found the going extremely difficult as the road had been previously obstructed. Working through the night, Price's command finally cleared the obstructions at 6:00 a.m. and continued its march. The first elements of Price's column reached the Wire Road at about 8:00 a.m., well after what Van Dorn had envisioned. In his official report, Van Dorn stated that the Wire Road was reached at 10:00 a.m.; however Henry Little, who commanded Price's advanced brigade recorded that he reached the road at 8:00 a.m. In other reports, and from the writer's comments, it was clear that Van Dorn probably reached Price's advanced elements at 10:00 a.m. *O.R.*, 8:197–198; 283, 305, 307; Alvin M. Josephy, J., *War On the Frontier* (Alexandria, VA, 1986), 141; Lehr, *As the Mockingbird Sang*, 36; Maury, 187.

# Through A Deep Canyon

or creek valley, into high and precipitous cliffs on either side. Flanking parties moved along the table-lands and hills on either side, and the infantry and artillery of the Missouri troops, under Gen. Price, moved along the valley on the Telegraph Road. The Texas, Arkansas and Louisiana troops, with the Indians, under Gen. Albert Pike,[59] were moved by a different route to the rear of Curtis's position, so that when about 9 o'clock in the morning, we were near the Elkhorn Tavern. There was an elevated and almost impassable hill between the two wings of our army. This was known as Big Mountain, and extended longitudinally from the point where the Missourians debouched into the canyon on the Wire road, some four miles north, and overlooked Curtis' camp. This ridge was taken possession of by Gen. [Daniel M.] Frost,[60] who was in command of the artillery, rather by instinct than by reason of any orders from the commanding general.[61] The right and left

---

59. Albert Pike was born in Boston, Massachusetts, on December 29, 1809. Educated at Harvard, he went west in 1831, and taught school in western Arkansas near Fort Smith. Pike raised a company of Arkansas volunteers for the Mexican War, after which he returned to Arkansas, practiced law, and became the attorney for the Creek Indians. At the beginning of the Civil War, Pike was adamantly against secession, but joined the Confederacy to protect his property interests in Arkansas. His principle contribution to the Confederate war effort was convincing the five civilized tribes of the Indian Territory to sign a treaty with the Confederacy. Pike was made brigadier general on August 15, 1861, fought at Pea Ridge, and resigned his commission on July 12, 1862, following a bitter disagreement with General Thomas C. Hindman over the extent of Pike's command. Following the war, Pike moved to Washington, DC, where he wrote "legal treaties" and expounded "the morals and dogma of the Masonic order." He died in Washington on April 2, 1891. Banasik, *Embattled Arkansas,* 102–103; Harrell, *Arkansas, Confederate Military History,* 408–410; Heitman, 2:64; Warner, *Generals in Gray,* 240–241.

60. Daniel M. Frost was born on August 9, 1823, in New York, graduated from West Point (number 4 of 25) in 1844, served in the Mexican War, being breveted a first lieutenant "for gallantry and meritorious conduct in the Battle of Cerro Gordo, Mexico." On May 31, 1853, Frost resigned from the army and moved to St. Louis, Missouri. At the beginning of the Civil War, he ran a "planing mill" in St. Louis, and was a general in the Missouri State Militia. Captured at Camp Jackson on May 10, 1861, Frost was exchanged in November 1861. As a general in the MSG, Frost was at the Battle of Pea Ridge in March 1862, and was promoted to a Confederate brigadier general in October 1862, effective March 3. At the Battle of Prairie Grove Frost commanded a Confederate division, and a brigade at Little Rock in September 1863, after which he submitted his resignation and escorted his wife to Canada via Mexico. Unfortunately, Frost's resignation was never accepted and he was listed as a deserter, the only Confederate general officer so listed at the end of the war. Frost later returned to St. Louis and became a farmer. He died on October 29, 1900, and was buried in St. Louis. For additional information on Frost see *Missouri Brothers in Gray.* Banasik, *Missouri Brothers in Gray,* 138; Boatner, 318; Heitman, 1:438; Warner, *Generals in Gray,* 94–95.

61. Frost commanded a mixed unit at the Battle of Pea Ridge consisting of the Seventh and Ninth Divisions, MSG and the Third Confederate Brigade under Colton Greene. Of the three units, the Ninth was primarily made up of two artillery batteries, containing seven pieces of artillery. As to Frost making the decision to occupy the heights, not true. According to General Price, when he saw that a Federal battery was being placed to cover the main road, he ordered his command to deploy. He sent Little's and Slack's commands to the right of the road and directed General Frost to occupy the heights, which gave his artillery a "very commanding position" from which to "check the enemy's advance." This occurred at about 10:00 a.m. *O.R.,* 8:305, 323, 325–326.

wing of our army, although they had turned the enemy's rear, were in sight of each other, or rather in sight of the enemy from Pea Ridge, but

# Seven Miles Apart

by the long detour which was alone practicable for assisting and reinforcing each other. The commander-in-chief could not go from one wing to the other or superintend the whole battle.

This disposition was unknown to Gen. Price till after his own line of battle had been determined on and we were about to go into battle. Gen. Van Dorn, who had been with McCulloch's wing of the army at that time, rode up.[62] Gen. Price said to him: "Ah, general, I am glad to see you for I have just made a disposition of my forces." He then explained to him his plans and pointed out the line of battle, stating to him if he did not like it he could change the orders as the men were just about being put into these positions. After asking a few questions as to the order and arrangement of the several commands, Gen. Van Dorn said he did not think the order of battle could be improved.

Gen. Price then said: "How long will it be before Gen. McCulloch will be up?" Gen. Van Dorn replied that Gen. McCulloch

# Would Not Come

there at all, that he had sent him to attack the enemy on the other side of the mountain.

Gen. Price remarked, seeming greatly surprised: "Gen. Van Dorn, I am exceedingly sorry to hear it, sir! I am *exceedingly* sorry to hear it, sir."

Gen. Van Dorn asked in a very quiet, soft manner: "Why, general?"

Gen. Price said: "Because, sir, it is eight miles around that mountain and two miles across it and there is no mule in the Confederacy that can climb over it. Should the enemy concentrate against me, before he could get to my assistance, I fear they would prove too much for me; and should the enemy concentrate against him, there would be nothing left of him, sir, before I could go to his assistance. I was in hopes that you would bring his men and put them into this fight, side by side, with mine. If you had done so, there is such a spirit of emulation existing between them that they would have done such fighting as you never saw, Gen. Van Dorn!"

Gen. Van Dorn, with characteristic magnanimity, said: "General, I believe you are right. He begged so hard that I yielded very reluctantly to his solicitation to go there, but I will send a courier at once to him to come here."[63]

---

62. Secondary accounts have Van Dorn with Price's column and not McCulloch's column as the writer has indicated. Edwin Bearss, "The First Day At Pea Ridge, March 7, 1862," *Arkansas Historical Quarterly* 17 (Spring 1958), 133; Brown, 11; Frank Cunningham, *General Stand Watie's Confederate Indians* (San Antonio, TX, 1959), 59; Hale, *Third Texas Cavalry*, 94; Shea & Hess, 86.

63. This portrayal by Musser does not coincide with Shea & Hess's account on Pea Ridge or Duncan's

He sent a courier, but before McCulloch's wing was reached he was engaged with the enemy and could not withdraw his forces, and he fell very early in the action.[64]

[Part II of the Article]

From the canyon following the Wire Road and east of Big Mountain the valley widens somewhat into a wooded plain. It is on the elevated part of the valley, and as the valley of Sugar Creek goes into it, there is situated the Elkhorn Tavern. Around the tavern, and old fashioned hostelry, where the stage-coach and weary travelers were wont, before the railroad was known, to find comfort and rest, men cultivated fields with deadened timber still standing in them. We advanced and took position under this plateau in the timber. The enemy seemed not to be looking for us on the flank, for our cavalry captured some of his forage wagons and caissons of the Dubuque Battery, which we kept until the surrender at Shreveport.[65]

Col. Bob McCullough's [McCulloch] cavalry[66] protected our front and left

---

*Reluctant General.* Shea & Hess have Van Dorn deliberately assessing the situation at about 8:00 a.m. on the morning of March 7, with Van Dorn dividing his army to more quickly concentrate the army at Elkhorn Tavern. Duncan has Van Dorn sending a courier, directing McCulloch to attack Curtis from the west. However, D. H. Maury, Van Dorn's Chief of Staff, recorded that "McCulloch sent a request that instead of closing up and joining in our attack, he should strike the enemy from where he was. Van Dorn assented." Alvin N. Josephy supports Maury's account stating that McCulloch "requested permission to leave the Bentonville road and attack Curtis." Musser's account of Van Dorn's and Price's meeting, concerning McCulloch's movements, seems to support what Maury recorded and Josephy later recounted. Further, it was evident from Musser's account, that Van Dorn did not join Price until about 10:00 a.m., as Van Dorn stated in his official account of the battle, just as Price was preparing to attack the Union rear. Van Dorn was not "at the head of Price's division," as Shea & Hess have stated. Robert Lipscomb Duncan, *Reluctant General: The Life and Times of Albert Pike* (New York, 1961), 211–212, hereafter cited as Duncan; Josephy, *Civil War In the American West*, 341; Maury, 187; Shea & Hess, 86–87; Tucker, *Father Bannon*, 43.

64. Between 1:30–2:00 p.m., while performing a reconnaissance, McCulloch was struck and killed instantly from a volley fired by Company B, Thirty–sixth Illinois Infantry. The men of Company B raced forward, with Peter Pelican securing McCulloch's gold watch, when a volley from nearby Arkansas troops sent the Illinois troops back to their cover. The incident occurred about an hour and a half after McCulloch became engaged. *O.R.S.*, pt. 3, 2:173; Bearss, "First Day At Pea Ridge," 150; Bennett & Haigh, 148; Brown, 14; Duncan, 213–214; Shea & Hess, 96, 110.

65. Three forage wagons were captured early in the morning by Gates's First Missouri Cavalry (Confederate), while the caisson was taken in the middle of the afternoon. The caisson was captured by either Gates's command or Colonel Benjamin A. Rives's Third Missouri Infantry (Confederate). The Dubuque Battery or Third Iowa Battery was commanded by Captain Mortimer M. Hayden. The battery was organized in Dubuque, Iowa, in September 1861, and spent most of its service in the Trans-Mississippi region. In addition to the Battle of Pea Ridge, the battery also fought at Helena (July 4, 1864) and took part in the Little Rock Expedition of 1863. The battery did not arrive at the battlefield until about 12:30 p.m. on March 7. *O.R.*, 8:268, 272, 307–308; S. H. M. Byers, *Iowa In War Times* (Des Moines, IA, 1888), 601–603, hereafter cited as Byers; Shea & Hess, 170, 178.

66. Robert A. McCulloch, Sr. was born in Albermarle County, Virginia in 1825, and moved to Missouri with his parents, settling in Howard County. Shortly thereafter, the family moved to Cooper

flank, while our artillery, under Emmett McDonald [MacDonald][67] and Capt. [Henry] Guibor[68] opened fire upon the enemy's lines. There was another artillery officer, not a Missourian, who commanded some guns that day. He was an expert artillerist, but so far failed in the field that he never more was [an] officer of a Missouri command.[69] Our division commanded by Col. J. B. Clark, Jr., supported the battery commanded by Capt. Emmett MacDonald.[70] These pieces were of iron,

County, where they made their permanent residence. In 1849, McCulloch joined in the California gold rush with his brother and later returned to Missouri. At the beginning of the Civil War, McCulloch lived in Boonville, and organized one of the first MSG units in the state on May 12, 1861. His Cole & Cooper Counties Cavalry Company became part of the First Cavalry Regiment, Sixth Division, MSG. He led the command at the Battle of Second Boonville and was elected lieutenant colonel of his command on June 27, 1861. He also fought at Carthage and Wilson's Creek and in October 1861 was elected colonel of his command. Known as "'White headed Bob,"' McCulloch commanded a battalion, of four companies, at Pea Ridge (See Appendix A for details on McCulloch's Battalion), after which he transferred to the Confederate Service, commanding the Second Missouri Cavalry Regiment (Confederate). He served the remaining years of the Civil War under General N. B. Forrest, being wounded at Old Town Creek, Mississippi on July 15, 1864. Following the war McCulloch returned to Missouri and was elected County Collector of Howard County in 1878, and served as the Missouri State Register of Lands and Secretary of Treasure during John S. Marmaduke's tenure as Governor. McCulloch died at his home in Boonville in 1911, at the age of 86. *O.R.S.*, pt. 2, vol. 38:142, 146, 150–151, 153, 160–161; Bartels, *Trans-Mississippi Men*, 19–21; Eakin, *Confederate Records*, 5:105–106; McGhee, *Service With the Guard*, 19; Peterson, 174–175; Schnetzer, *More Forgotten Men*, 154; Snead, 185–186.

67. A St. Louisian, Emmett MacDonald, commanded a squadron of cavalry at Camp Jackson. At Lexington, he led a battery of artillery. He died on January 11, 1863, as a colonel, leading a brigade of cavalry at the Battle of Hartville, Missouri. For biography and photo see *Missouri Brothers in Gray*. Banasik, *Missouri Brothers in Gray*, 143–144.

68. Henry Guibor was born in 1823 in France and moved to St. Louis as a child. A carpenter by trade, Guibor fought in the Mexican War, returned to St. Louis where he became a deputy marshal. A member of the St. Louis Volunteer Militia, Guibor commanded an artillery company at Camp Jackson in May 1861, which was captured. After his parole, he joined Sterling Price's army, where he commanded a six gun battery. He participated in the Missouri battles of Carthage, Wilson's Creek, Lexington, and Pea Ridge, Arkansas. Captured at Wilson's Creek, Guibor escaped shortly before the battle had ended and went on to finish his service in the Guard. After Pea Ridge, Guibor completed his military service on the east side of the Mississippi River, serving in the Army of Tennessee. He was wounded during the Vicksburg and the Atlanta Campaigns and was present at the surrender of Joe Johnston's Confederate Army in North Carolina. After the war he returned to St. Louis and became superintendent of the "House of Refuge." Guibor died from cancer on October 17, 1899. *O.R.*, 3:32, 101, 186; vol. 17, 1:24, 32, 38, 39; Series 2, 1:556; Banasik, *Missouri In 1861*, 381; Mudd, "What I Saw At Wilson's Creek," *Missouri Historical Review* 7 (January 1913), 101; Snead, 217; Shea & Hess, 162–164; Winter, 137–138.

69. Of the Missouri battery commanders at Pea Ridge, only one failed to have a stellar career in the military service—Ephriam V. Kelly. A merchant from St. Joseph, Missouri, at the beginning of the war, the twenty–two year–old Kelly was born in Kentucky and resigned from the MSG just prior to the Battle of Pea Ridge; however Price did not accept the resignation until after the battle. Kelly then departed the army and was captured on April 15, 1862, while heading home. Bartels, *Forgotten Men*, 195.

70. Also known as the "Saint Louis Battery" or the "Third Battery, Missouri Artillery (Confederate), the battery began recruitment on October 6, 1861. Originally intended as a horse artillery company, the command received three 6-pound smoothbore guns on November 1, 1861, and was assigned to duty in James McBride's Seventh Division, MSG. Emmett MacDonald was elected the first captain

and while cumbersome in the field were very efficient when once in position.[71] I ought here to state, the while [we] bivouacked the night before we were joined by Col. Congreve Jackson and a considerable body of recruits. The rank of Col. Jackson entitled him to the command, but being on the eve of battle he generously waived in the favor of the young John B. Clark in compliment to his personal valor and deference to the young man's ambition.[72] We shelled the enemy in our front and pressed him until we ascertained his line of defenses, which were on the edge of the deadened timber.

## A Hastily Prepared Stockade

of rails in the edge of the red oak bushes, which carry their leaves until spring, showed his wonted skill in improvised field work. We saw what we had to do.[73] Gen. Price made his dispositions rapidly. He was a man whose instincts were particularly military and on the field possessed all his faculties intensified by the danger and the ambition for victory. We were posted on the extreme left of the line and our flank covered by the cavalry, the artillery being unlimbered and in hand to be disposed of as occasion required. Little's brigade of Confederate infantry[74] was on the extreme right, as I now recollect, with [James] Rains's,[75] [Mosby M.]

---

of the battery and served with the command until he resigned on September 10, 1862. The unit fought at Pea Ridge, after which it received another 6-pound gun, captured from the Dubuque, Iowa Battery, as a "token of the services rendered that day." After Pea Ridge, the company moved to the east side of the Mississippi River, where they completed their military service. *O.R.S.*, pt. 2, vol. 38: 343–345.

71. On February 26, 1862, General Price gave MacDonald command of a five gun battery. At Pea Ridge the battery contained only three guns— one 6-lb iron smoothbore and two 12-lb howitzers, according to Shea & Hess. However this was unlikely given Musser's comment that the guns were iron. The standard 12-pound howitzer was made of brass and the iron model was not produced by the Confederacy until 1862. It was highly unlikely that Richmond would have sent the iron model to Arkansas, or that the gun was even available, until it was fully tested under field conditions in the east. MacDonald's Battery, like Gorham's Battery, may have had problems with manning all the guns. Gorham's Battery which contained six guns had only enough men to man four of the guns, while the other two guns were left with the trains. *O.R.*, 8:323; Banasik, *Missouri Brothers in Gray*, 25; Crute, 209–210; McGhee, *Letter and Order Book*, unnumbered pages 72–73 (entry page 143); Peterson, 293; Warren Ripley, *Artillery and Ammunition of the Civil War* (New York, 1970), 46.

72. During the battle Congreve Jackson commanded the Second Infantry Regiment of Clark's division and was cited for his "great bravery" during the engagement. *O.R.*, 8:319.

73. This stockade was made of rail fence by Grenville Dodge's Brigade and was located on Clemon's farm near the Huntsville road. Wm. Fayel, "Curtis's Withdrawal from Cross Hollows," *Missouri Republican*, December 19, 1885; Shea & Hess, 190.

74. Little's Brigade consisted of three regiments with two batteries of artillery. Of the three regiments one was cavalry, commanded by Elijah Gates, while the other two were infantry, commanded respectively by John Q. Burbridge and B. A. Rives. The artillery was commanded by Captains Churchill Clark and William Wade. For more details on Little's Brigade see Appendix A. *O.R.*, 8:307.

75. James Spencer Rains was born on October 2, 1817 (William Cravens, a biographer of Rains, has his birth date as October 12, 1807), in Tennessee, later moved to southwest Missouri, settling near Sarcoxie. He served in the militia in pre-Civil War days, and was a state senator (1854–1861) when the war began in April 1861. Appointed a brigadier general in the MSG, Rains served throughout the war. After the war Rains settled in Texas, where he died on May 19, 1880. See Michael E. Banasik, *Confederate "Tales of the War" In the Trans-Mississippi Part One: 1861* (Iowa City, IA, 2010), 190–191, for

Parsons's,[76] [James] McBride's[77] and [William Y.] Slack's divisions[78] in the center in the order named, from left to right, with [Colton] Greene's[79] and [Alexander] Steen's[80] divisions, reduced in number by recruiting for Confederate service in

a complete biography. Allardice, 190–192; Letter (February 16, 1914), William M. Cravens to Walter B. Douglas, Staff Correspondence (folder no. 1), Missouri State Guard, Missouri Historical Society.

76. Parsons's Sixth Division, MSG was led by Major D. H. Lindsay at the Battle of Pea Ridge—Mosby M. Parsons, a resident of Jefferson City, Missouri, was born in Virginia in 1822, moved to Missouri at age thirteen, and served in the Mexican War. At the beginning of the Civil War, Parsons was appointed a brigadier general, on May 17, 1861, commanding the Sixth Division, MSG. Parsons led his command in all the 1861 battles of his division, but was not present at the Battle of Pea Ridge, being at the time in Richmond, Virginia. Parsons succeeded Price as commander of the MSG on April 8, 1862, and on November 5, 1862, he was commissioned a brigadier general in the Confederate Army. Parsons spent his Civil War years, except for three months, in the Trans-Mississippi Department. At war's end he went to Mexico, where he was killed on August 17, 1865. See Banasik, *Missouri Brothers in Gray*, 146–148, for biography and photo; Banasik, *Missouri In 1861*, 380–381; Peterson, 34; Snead, 313.

77. At Pea Ridge, McBride's Division was under Daniel M. Frost, though the troops were commanded by Major James Shaler. James Higgins McBride was born in Kentucky in 1814, moved to Paris, Missouri, and later relocated to Springfield. A lawyer by profession, McBride was appointed a Circuit Judge in 1860, and lived in Houston, Missouri, at the beginning of the Civil War. Governor Jackson appointed McBride a brigadier general, commanding the Seventh Division, MSG on May 18, 1861, in which position he served until resigning on February 23, 1862. In the summer of 1862, General Thomas C. Hindman breveted McBride a general in the Confederate Service, subject to the approval of the Richmond government. Not receiving his commission, McBride resigned in September 1862, and returned to the MSG. McBride contracted pneumonia in March 1864 and died at his home in Yell County, Arkansas. He was buried at Bluffton. See Banasik, *Serving With Honor*, 388–389 for a complete biography. *O.R.*, 8:323–325; Moore, *Missouri, Confederate Military History*, 80.

78. William Yarnel Slack commanded two units at Pea Ridge—the Second Brigade of Missouri Volunteers and his own Fourth Division, MSG. Slack was born on August 1, 1816, in Kentucky, and moved to Missouri at the age of three. His family settled near Columbia, where the young Slack was educated. A lawyer by profession, Slack moved to Chillicothe and joined in the Mexican War, commanding a company under Sterling Price. At the beginning of the Civil War, Slack was appointed a brigadier general, commanding the Fourth Division, MSG. He was severely wounded at Wilson's Creek and did not command his division during the Siege of Lexington. Slack was wounded again, near Elkhorn Tavern on March 7; Slack was moved to another location some seven miles from the battlefield, where his condition deteriorated rapidly. He died on March 21, 1862. Of General Slack, one Confederate veteran recorded, "he was a man of much more than ordinary ability, cool and clear-headed, and a more gallant soldier never lived." *O.R.*, 8:285; McGhee, *Service With Guard*, 67; Peterson, 136; Warner, *Generals in Gray*, 278.

79. Colton Greene commanded the Third Brigade, Missouri Volunteers and was a resident of St. Louis at the beginning of the war. See Appendix B for a biography of this officer. *O.R.*, 8:325–326; Allardice, 104–105.

80. Steen's Fifth Division, MSG was commanded Colonel James P. Sanders at the Battle of Pea Ridge. Colonel Alexander Early Steen was born in 1828, in St. Louis. His father, Enoch Steen, was a colonel in the U.S. Army and remained loyal to the Union at the outbreak of the Civil War. The younger Steen served during the Mexican War, receiving a brevet for "gallant and meritorious conduct in the battles of Contreras and Churubusco." Steen was mustered out of the army in 1848, but reentered the service in 1852, only to resign on May 10, 1861, upon the capture of Camp Jackson. Joining the MSG, Steen rose to the rank of brigadier general, commanding the Fifth Division, MSG. He fought at Wilson's Creek and was present at the Siege of Lexington, Missouri, though ill at the time. At Pea Ridge, Steen was absent from his command, being in Richmond, attempting to secure a generalship in the Confederate Army. On November 10, 1862, Steen was appointed a Confederate colonel and given command of the Tenth Missouri Infantry. Steen was killed at Prairie Grove on December 7. *O.R.*, 8:321; 53:444;

position among them. Gen. Frost was nominally in command of the artillery but could get but one battery in hand—Guibor's, if I remember right.[81]

It was past noon when these dispositions were made[82] and we could hear the conflict on the right wing beyond Big Mountain, which was hot and heavy.[83] Gen. Price, who was in the rear of Col. Clark's division, directed me to carry orders to Clark to move forward and charge the enemy in his stockade. Gen. Price had with at this time two of his staff, one was his son, a young lad just from school, possibly twenty years of age,[84] and Capt. Gage, a Louisianan, who had volunteered as an aide-de-camp. The orders were delivered to Col. Clark to charge and by him promptly obeyed.[85] He directed me to take command of the right of the division;

---

Allardice, 215–216; Banasik, *Missouri Brothers in Gray*, 155; Heitman, 1:919.

81. In recalling General Frost's role in the battle one veteran wrote: "Frost was assigned the command of General McBride's division, but declined so small a command, and watched the battle from a convenient height." Frost had two batteries in the battle—Guibor's and MacDonald's. *O.R.*, 8:323; Moore, *Missouri, Confederate Military History*, 79–80.

82. Between 8:00 a.m. and 10:00 a.m. Price made his initial dispositions as he developed the Union position. Little's First Missouri Brigade filed off to the right of the road followed by Slack's Brigade. Clark's command came next, filed to the left, followed by Frost's troops, which also filed to the left of the main road. The rebel artillery occupied the left center supported by Clark's Division on their left and Frost's troops on the right. Even as these initial dispositions were taking place an artillery duel commenced between the First Iowa Battery and Price's rebel guns. Between 10:00 a.m. and noon Price's troops continued to move into position. Colton Greene's Missouri Brigade moved behind the rebel batteries, supporting them from the rear. James P. Sanders came next with the Fifth Division, MSG, and took a post to the left of Clark's Division. Rains's Division came last and took a position in support of the rebels guns and to their right rear. For a reserve Price held back Lindsay's Sixth Division.
Note: In Edwin Bearss portrayal of the battle, he has Saunder's command arriving on the scene before Clark's Division. However, this does not seem to coincide with either the order of march in Price's command or Clark's report on the deployment of the troops. *O.R.*, 8:284, 307, 319, 321, 325; 53:790–791; Bearss, "First Day at Pea Ridge," 145; Lehr, *Fishing on Deep Water*, 70; Moore, *Missouri, Confederate Military History*, 79; Shea & Hess, 159–163.

83. The battle on March 7 was divided into two distinct areas; the one "beyond Big Mountain" was taking place in the vicinity of Leetown, about two miles to the west. The Confederates in that quarter were commanded by General Ben McCulloch. The firing began there just before noon. Bevier puts the time at 11:00 a.m. Bevier, 102; Hale, *Third Texas Cavalry*, 96; Shea & Hess, 96.

84. Musser was referring to Celsus Price, who was born in March 1841, in Chariton County, Missouri. When the war began, Celsus was attending school at the University of Virginia. He later joined his father's staff and served with him throughout the war. During the Battle of Pea Ridge, Colonel Clark recalled the incident in his official report to General Price. Clark wrote: "Your orders were conveyed to me during the day by Celsus Price, of the Third Division, one of your volunteer aides. He was always cool and collected, so that I never mistook the order, and allow me to say that in the earnest face of the son I could see the heroism of the father." After the war Celsus lived for a time in Texas and Mexico and finally settled in St. Louis. With his father and brother Edwin, Celsius open a tobacco commission. He died on September 5, 1909, was cremated and his ashes spread behind the Price Monument at Bellefontaine Cemetery. *O.R.*, 8:320; Hale, 358; Shalhope, 36.

85. As the day slipped away Price's command continued to flank the Union forces to the rebel left, until, as described by Musser, all was ready for what would amount to the final assault of the day. By this time, between 3:00–4:30 p.m., the Federal line had been bent back into a "V" shape, with the Confederates overlapping both of the Union flanks. This assault would finally break the Union line and shatter the its right at Elkhorn Tavern, but it would come too late for the rebels as night was fast

Lieut.-Col. Joseph Vaughan[86] to lead in the left, and we doubled-quicked on the enemy through the deadened timber. In about forty yards of the stockade

## We Received a Volley

which was deadly and point blank. It unhorsed Clark and myself and killed and wounded many men and officers. Had we been sufficiently victorious to have passed forward we could have carried the stockade by storm, but the men yielded to their instincts to return fire without orders, and our staggered column hesitated; some of the men took cover and others lay down in the field. The enemy continued to pour in his vollies, and we were in a critical situation. Clark on foot, and Joe Vaughan rallied the men and we held them to their work. But our fire was comparatively ineffective against the troops behind stockades.[87] At that juncture Gen. Price, who had been wounded in the fleshy part of the lower arm, had sent orders to the cavalry to advance.[88] Bob McCullough lost not a second, and he came in on the enemy's flank just in time to force the enemy to yield the stockade to us and retire. There was an officer commanding a battalion of cavalry, who refused to obey the order to charge. Maj. Caleb Perkins,[89] his next in command, summarily charged him with

---

approaching. Shea & Hess, 183–190.

86. Joseph P. Vaughan or Vaughn, a resident of Benicia City, California, was elected a major of the Second Infantry Regiment, Third Division, MSG on August 20, 1861, and a lieutenant colonel on December 12, 1861. As a member of the Guard he fought at Dry Wood, Lexington and Elkhorn. Vaughn later joined the Confederate service and was elected major of the Sixth Missouri Infantry. He was killed at Corinth, Mississippi, on October 3, 1862, while leading a charge. *O.R.*, vol. 17, pt. 1:390; *O.R.S.*, pt. 2, vol. 50:533; Peterson, 118; Schnetzer, *More Forgotten Men*, 234.

87. At 3:00 p.m. (Shea & Hess place the time at 4:30 p.m.), General Price ordered his left wing, including Clark's Missouri Division to advance. Clark's command with the rest of the left wing was momentarily halted for about 30 minutes, while both sides kept up a furious pace of fire. To the far right of the Confederate lines, Little was ordered to advance, but only after he heard the firing commence on the left. Within a short time Price's entire line became engaged and finally drove the enemy from the vicinity of Elkhorn Tavern. According to Price the enemy were "completely routed." *O.R.*, 8:305, 308, 319–320; Moore, *Missouri, Confederate Military History*, 80; Josephy, *Civil War In the American West*, 345; Shea & Hess, 185; Tucker, *Father Bannon*, 45.

88. Price had been wounded between 2:00 and 3:00 p.m., but remained on the battlefield, having his wound wrapped in a handkerchief. McGhee, *Service With the Guard*, 68; Shea & Hess, 180.

89. Caleb Perkins was born in 1830, and lived in Rennick, Missouri, at the beginning of the Civil War. He joined H. T. Fort's Randolph County Company, MSG, and later became captain of the unit. On September 24, 1861, upon organization of the Fifth Infantry Regiment, Third Division, MSG, Perkins was elected major of the unit. Perkins later left the unit and operated for a time as a guerrilla, serving with Bill Anderson, while recruiting for the Confederacy. During Price's 1864 Missouri Raid, Perkins joined the Confederate Army and went south back to Arkansas with his recruits. Following the raid Perkins was elected colonel of an infantry regiment in the fall of 1864, but never saw any action. Perkins died in 1901 and was buried in Chariton County. *O.R.*, vol. 40, pt. 1:415–418; Banasik, *Serving With Honor*, 202 (n. 4); Michael E. Banasik, *Cavaliers of the Brush: Quantrill and His Men* (Iowa City, IA, 2003), 81 (n. 240); Bartels, *Trans-Mississippi Men*, 33; William Niel Block, *Shades of Gray Confederate Soldiers and Veterans of Randolph County, Missouri* (Shawnee Mission, KS, 1996), 56; Crute, 209; Eakin & Hale, 344; National Archives, Record Group M322 (roll no. 175), Confederate Compiled Service Records, Perkin's Infantry Battalion; Peterson, 126, 128.

cowardice and led the squadron into the fight.[90] Perkins now lives in Rennick, in Randolph county. We were victorious in our combined attack on our left wing, due to the prompt gallantry of Bob McCullough. I had no time to notice how Parsons's, Rains's, Little's and other corps behaved on our right. I found them, however, doing their work well when I was unhorsed and had leisure to look. Had we failed or given way on the left they hardly would have been able to sustain the battle. Gen. Slack had been killed earlier in the day, or rather fatally wounded.[91] The casualties in our division were not heavy as to fatal wounds,[92] but there were many among these, Capt. [James C.] Wallace[93] of Chariton County, hors au combat for several months; Lieut.-Col. William S. Hyde[94] of Chariton County, was also wounded and fatally.

---

90. At the time of the battle, the Fourth and the Fifth Infantry Regiments, Third Division, MSG, were combined into one command under Colonel John Poindexter, with Lieutenant Colonel X. J. Pindall and Major Perkins as field officers (The *Official Records* have Pindall as L. A. Pindall, but that was not correct, per references below. Additionally L. A. Pindall was in the Second Division not the Third.). In the *Official Records,* Colonel Clark makes no mention of the incident detailed by Musser. Be that as it may, the officer in charge at that time, of the Fourth/Fifth Infantry, after Poindexter's wounding would have been Xenophen J. Pindall or Pindle. A resident of Macon County, Missouri, Pindall was elected third lieutenant of Company A, First Cavalry Regiment, Third Division, MSG on June 16, 1861. Pindall was promoted to major of a mounted infantry battalion in August 1861, and became the lieutenant colonel of the Fourth Infantry Regiment, Third, Division, MSG, on September 26, 1861. According to official casualty reports, for the Battle of Pea Ridge, contrary to what Musser wrote, the report stated that Pindall did "his duty bravely as an officer." Pindall latter joined the regular army and was paroled out of the service in 1865. He was the brother of L. A. Pindall. (For a biography see Harrell, 549). *O.R.*, 8:319, 888; Bartels, *Forgotten Men*, 290; Bartels, *Trans-Mississippi Men*, 31, 189, 294; Eakin, *Confederate Records*, 6:106; *Confederate Military History, Extended*, vol. 16: *Arkansas* by John A. Harrell, 549; W. M. Moore Letter, May 10, 1915, Skaggs Collection, Arkansas History Commission; Peterson, 111, 123, 131.

91. Shea & Hess have Slack being wounded around 1:00 p.m. in an encounter with Vandever's command, while Colonel Thomas Rosser, who took command of Slack's brigade after Slack was wounded, stated that the event occurred in "the early part of the engagement." Edwin Bearss supports Shea & Hess, placing the time sometime after the noon hour, following the arrival of Vandever's command. *O.R.*, 8:312; Bearss, "First Day At Pea Ridge," 139; Shea & Hess, 175.

92. According to Clark's official report the Third Division, MSG, lost 14 dead and 103 wounded in the charge out of 500 men. However, in an addenda to his report he listed his losses as 11 killed, 101 wounded and 35 missing—the missing probably occurred on the retreat. *O.R.*, 8:319–320.

93. James C. Wallace was born in 1840, and enlisted in the Missouri State Militia on April 17, 1861. On August 17, 1861, he was elected a lieutenant in Company B, Third Infantry Regiment, Third Division, MSG, the position he was serving in when wounded at Pea Ridge. After he recovered, Wallace joined the Confederate Army on October 3, 1862, and was elected captain of Company E, Eight Missouri Infantry Battalion (Confederate). Wallace's unit later became Company I, Ninth Missouri Infantry and surrendered at Shreveport, Louisiana, in May 1865. Wallace returned home and died at Keytesville, Missouri, on March 15, 1916. *O.R.S.*, pt. 2, vol. 38:586, 591; Bartels, *Trans-Mississippi Men*, 299; Eakin, *Confederate Records*, 8:11; Peterson, 121.

94. William S. Hyde was born on November 13, 1827, in Spotsylvania, County, Virginia. He moved to Missouri and at the beginning of the Civil War lived in Brunswick, Chariton County, Missouri, serving as the editor of the *Brunswicker*, a local newspaper. He enlisted in Company I, First Infantry Regiment, Third Division, MSG and was later elected first lieutenant of his company. Hyde fought at Carthage, Wilson's Creek and Lexington. On September 20, 1861, he was elected lieutenant colonel of the Third Infantry Regiment of his Guard Division. Severely wounded at Pea Ridge, Hyde died on March 22 at Elkhorn Tavern. Bartels, *Trans-Mississippi Men*, 29; Eakin & Hale, 225; Peterson, 117, 120.

Just as we were satisfactorily resting from our labors the news from the right wing spread among the troops that Ben McCulloch had been killed and his command having devolved on Gen. McIntosh, who was likewise killed—that Gen. Herbert [Hébert] of the Third Louisiana, next in command, had been severely wounded[95] and the command devolved upon Gen. Albert Pike commanding the Indians; that Pike had been unable to keep his Indians in hand and had withdrawn from the field.[96] The news of disaster had come to dispel the joy of victory, but we went into bivouac with the declining sun, on the enemy's ground, with some prisoners and captured artillery as trophies, full of hope that the morrow's daybreak would awaken us to renewed battle.[97]

## Second Day.

The Missouri troops bivouacked upon the field and many were regaled with captured suttler stores of the enemy and other luxuries. There was much suffering during the night among the wounded of both armies, for it was very chilly and the wounded suffered from both cold and thirst. They were relived as fast as the surgeons and infirmary corps could reach them. For myself, being unhorsed and having lost part of my blankets I fell back upon the hospital, some two miles down the canyon, when I saw Dr. [John J.] Grinstead,[98] an able and sympathetic

---

95. McCulloch was killed between 1:30–2:00 p.m. and McIntosh was slain about half an hour later; both men were killed by elements of the Thirty-sixth Illinois Infantry. About 3:00 p.m. initial reports reached Van Dorn that stated that McCulloch, McIntosh and Hébert had been killed. Hébert was not killed or wounded, but was captured by members of Cavalry Company B, Thirty-sixth Illinois Infantry between 4:00–4:30 p.m. As such, within a two hour period the Thirty-sixth Illinois had destroyed the leadership of the Confederate army about Leetown and essentially won the battle for the Federal arms, though another day of battle remained. *O.R.*, 8:284; *O.R.S.*, pt. 3, 2:173; Bennett & Haigh, 148, 151; Shea & Hess, 113–115.

96. Following the deaths of McCulloch and McIntosh, no one informed Pike of the situation, and from 1:30 p.m. until 3:00 p.m., according to Pike, he "received no orders whatever nor any message of any type." At 3:00 p.m., upon investigation, Pike was informed by Major J. W. Whitfield that the other two general officers were dead. Pike took charge of a few scattered regiments and did little more than maintain a defensive position, while he sought guidance from Van Dorn. Meanwhile Colonel Elkanah Greer, commander of the Third Texas Cavalry, took command of another group of regiments and directed their actions for the remainder of the day. Pike and Greer eventually led their troops to join Van Dorn, which they did before daylight on March 8. During the night march to join Van Dorn, continued confusion led several of the rebel regiments from the right flank to move away from Van Dorn and join the trains. Overall, McCulloch's wing of the army was shattered and would do little on March 8. *O.R.*, 8:289–290, 283–294; Shea & Hess, 142–146.

97. During the first day, Van Dorn reported capturing 200 prisoners and 7 cannon. *O.R.*, 8:284.

98. John J. (or I.) Grinstead (or Grinsted) was a resident of Keyteville, Chariton County, Missouri, when the war began. He was appointed the regimental surgeon, First Infantry Regiment, Third Division, MSG on June 23, 1861, and transferred to the Third Infantry Regiment on November 5, 1861. Grinstead was promoted to lieutenant colonel and division surgeon general on December 3, 1861. He later left the Guard and joined the First Missouri Infantry Battalion (Confederate) under Waldo P. Johnson. At Pea Ridge, Colonel Clark commended Grinstead "for his kindness and attention" to the wounded. The Confederate hospital, a "log house," was situated on the Wire Road at a place known as "Sugar Hollow." *O.R.*, 8:320; Bearss, "First Day At Pea Ridge," 144; Bartels, *Trans-Mississippi Men,*

surgeon from my own county, attending to the wounded, of whom there were many of our own neighbors. We made a rail pen in the neighborhood of the hospital and with Col. Joe Finks[99] and Col. [Gustavus A.] Elgins[100] passed the night in comfort a soldier earns by fatigue and danger. There never was a more charming night's sleep. We were awakened by the sound of field artillery and we repaired to the front.[101] I saw my poor horse George lying dead on the way and realized with regret that I was a cavalier with only a saddle and a bridle. I remembered his behavior in battle and the peculiar groan he emitted when the bullet cut the halter rein and penetrated his chest just in front of my knee, and how he gradually filled up with blood and died.

There was a heavy skirmish going on when we reached the front. All night Gen. Pike's command had been making the detour from the position of the right wing, and we felt confident, occupying, as we did, the enemy's ground, we could with reinforcements

## Drive Him Out

from his position, even if he retreated over the ground formerly threatened by our right. But Gen. Van Dorn, who had not learned to appreciate the value of the volunteer soldier, as illustrated afterwards in both the American armies, North and South, determined to retreat and leave the field we had won to the enemy.[102] [Ben-

25, 29; Harrell, *Arkansas, Confederate Military History*, 381; McGhee, *Service With the Guard*, 67; Peterson, 108, 114, 120.

99. Joseph H. Finks was born on August 7, 1838, in Green County, Virginia. In July 1861, he enlisted as a private in the Third Division, MSG in Fayette, Missouri. At the Battle of Wilson's Creek he was a captain and served as a volunteer aid under General John B. Clark, Sr. Finks was also at the Siege of Lexington, as an aide to Governor Claiborne F. Jackson. On November 4, 1861, Finks was promoted to lieutenant colonel in the Guard. Finks later joined the Confederate Army and was paroled out of the service in June 1865, as a major and quartermaster. He died on April 24, 1915, in Howard County, Missouri. *O.R.*, 53:423, 439; Eakin, *Confederate Records*, 3:46; Peterson, 109.

100. Gustavus A. Elgin (or Elgins), was a resident of Fayette, Howard County, Missouri, and at the beginning of the war he organized the Howard County Volunteers Company and was elected captain of the unit. On July 3, 1861, Elgin was promoted to lieutenant colonel and assigned to duty as the division quartermaster, Third Division, MSG. Following the Battle of Wilson's Creek, Elgin supervised the burial of Nathaniel Lyon, when his body was abandoned by Federal troops in Springfield. As a Guard member Elgin also fought at Boonville, Carthage, Dry Wood and Lexington. Elgin left the MSG after Pea Ridge, initially serving as a private and later as a Quartermaster under John B. Clark, Jr., first in Clark's Missouri Regiment, in November 1862, and then in Clark's Missouri Brigade. He was paroled out of the army at Shreveport, Louisiana in 1865. *O.R.*, vol. 41, pt. 2:1095; *O.R.S.*, pt. 2, vol. 50:650–651; McGhee, *Service With the Guard*, 80; Richard H. Musser, "The War in Missouri," *Southern Bivouac*, 6 vols. (Reprint ed. Wilmington, NC, 1993), 4:679; National Archives, Record Group 109, Confederate Muster Rolls, Ninth Missouri Infantry; Peterson, 108, 112; Schnetzer, *More Forgotten Men*, 73.

101. The cannon firing began about 7:00 a.m. on March 8 and continued for three hours before the final assault began. *O.R.*, 8:214, 284, 309; Bevier, 104; Josephy, *Civil War in the American West*, 346; Lehr, *As the Mockingbird Sang*, 36–37; McGhee, *Service With the Guard*, 73.

102. During the night Van Dorn reassessed his situation and found that his command was short of ammunition and many of his troops had not eaten since March 6. His quartermaster was sent to bring in

jamin] Rives's regiment[103] and some reliable infantry had been thrown forward to cover a movement which looked to us like a retreat, but, we were assured, was only a strategic change of front.[104] This movement involved the loss of that gallant officer Capt. Churchill Clark, commanding a battery of artillery—a young officer of great skill and judgement, who was universally regretted. He was a descendent of the first governor of Missouri. There is no pleasure in recounting the details of disaster. Suffice it to say we retreated in excellent order, as much to the surprise of the enemy as ourselves. We had lost very few prisoners and no standards. We had several pieces of artillery and caissons more than we went in with, which was saved by the soldierly instincts of the battery commanders, and ultimately reported safely to headquarters at Van Buren.[105]

the trains but failed to find them at Camp Stephens, about eight miles from Van Dorn's position. By mid-morning, with his artillery out of ammunition and finding the enemy concentrated in his front, Van Dorn gave the order to withdraw. Price, for his part, withdrew reluctantly, still feeling that the battle could be won. About 10:30 a.m., the Federals sensing the rebel movement to the rear began their final push to drive the Confederates off the battlefield. By noon, according to General Curtis, the "firing ceased. The enemy had suddenly vanished." The battle was over, with little effort on the part of the Unionists to pursue their victory. *O.R.*, 8:202, 215, 284, 306; Bearss, "First Day at Pea Ridge," 132; Hale, *Third Texas Cavalry*, 93; Josephy, *War On the Frontier*, 141; Lehr, *As the Mockingbird Sang*, 37; Shea & Hess, 243.

103. Benjamin A. Rives commanded the Third Missouri Infantry Regiment (Confederate), which was organized on January 16, 1862, at Springfield, Missouri. The regiment was part of Little's Brigade of Missouri Volunteers. After the Battle of Pea Ridge, the regiment moved to the east side of the Mississippi River, where it completed its military service. Rives was born in 1822, in Buckingham County, Virginia, attended the University of Virginia and obtained a medical degree from the University of New York City in 1844. Settling in Virginia, Rives married in 1846, and moved to Ray County, Missouri in 1850, where he and his wife Eliza had six children. Prior to the war, Rives was a doctor, banker, farmer and a member of the Missouri General Assembly (1858–1860). On April 27, 1861, he was appointed captain of what became Company A, First Cavalry Regiment, Fourth Division, MSG. He fought at Carthage, and Wilson's Creek, after which he was promoted to colonel of his regiment on August 11, 1861. At Lexington, in September 1861, Rives commanded his Guard division. Rives left the Guard in January 1862, being elected colonel of what became the Third Missouri Infantry (Confederate), on January 16, 1862. He led his regiment at the Battle of Pea Ridge, where he received a mortal wound on March 8 and died two days later. *O.R.S.*, pt. 2, vol. 38:444, 448; Bevier, 77; Crute, 198; McGhee, *Service With the Guard*, 53–54; Peterson, 136–138; "Sketch of Colonel B. A. Rives of Ray County, Missouri," Col. B. F. Rives Papers, Missouri Historical Society.

104. As the Confederate forces fell back from Elkhorn Tavern, they split into two groups; most of the artillery, three companies of Rives's Regiment, 1st Arkansas Mounted Rifles and the 17th Arkansas Infantry headed north up the Wire Road; the second group comprising the main body of Van Dorn's army took the road to Huntsville. Others in the rebel command also thought like Musser did and believed that they were not retreating. James Harding recorded: "Many of our men in fact thinking the movement was merely a change of position preparatory to a renewed attack." Walter P. Lane wrote of his Texans: "not one of those composing my command supposed for a moment that a retreat was contemplated, nor were they undeceived until the order came from General Van Dorn." A private soldier in Lane's command believed that the "beaten enemy was not entitled to the possession of the field of battle" feeling that the rebels had been "defrauded of their well-earned dues" of victory. Another from the Ninth Texas Cavalry simply wrote: "Our Army was not whipped but the fighting ceased for want of ammunition." *O.R.*, 8:300; Lowe, 84; McGhee, *Service With the Guard*, 74; Shea & Hess, 249; Sparks, 178.

105. Many in the rebel command believed that the artillery train was lost and captured following the

Our orderly retreat was impeded by the immediate extent of fallen timber found in the road. This forest had been felled by Gen. Ben McCulloch a few months before, while Price was between him and the enemy.

Our wearied and breakfastless march was enlivened by few incidents. The situation was hardly realized till we found it so bad, no amount of execution could do it justice and the very excellence of its badness made it rather charming than disgusting.

We reached Van Winkle's mill[106] in the charming valley of one of the White Rivers, a place to us ever famous. For at the mill we found a field of turnips and a drove of shoats. The pig impaled on a bayonet yielded his flesh to the hungary Missourian and we broke our nearly two day's fast in a menu that would have charmed a Parisian *chef de cuisine*.

Squealing pig spitted on bayonet and ramrod. Raw turnips.

\* \* \* \* \* \*

---

battle. However, after a circuitous route the artillery showed up at Van Buren, Arkansas. During their retreat from Pea Ridge, Van Dorn reported the loss of one piece of artillery which he abandoned after it became disabled. Van Dorn also stated that he brought off four pieces of artillery and burned another three that could not be removed from the field of battle. Curtis for his part reported capturing 500 prisoners over the course of several days following the battle as well as five pieces of artillery. Many of Curtis's prisoners were probably Missourians, who had been discharged, prior to the battle, and were captured on their way home—they were in the wrong place at the wrong time and counted as captures from the battle, even though they were not. Also included in the captures were 40 prisoners captured before the battle and a number of "citizens" as recalled by one captured prisoner who escaped—W. D. Kittle of the First Arkansas Mounted Rifles noted the Federals "took 490 prisoners of our men—officers, citizens, privates and all."

As to artillery losses, part of the confusion can be explained by Confederate batteries abandoning their old iron guns in favor of brass pieces which they had captured. According to Hunt Wilson (see next article), Gorham's command left their four old iron guns on the field in favor of captured guns. Hiram Bledsoe would also noted that his command abandoned one gun following the battle but gives no reason why. *O.R.*, 8:194, 271, 284–285, 322; vol. 32, pt. 3:694; *O.R.S.*, pt. 2, vol. 2:594; pt. 2, vol. 2:159–160; pt. 3, vol. 2:191; Dispatch (March 19, 1862), *The Washington Telegraph* (Washington, AR), March 26, 1862; Douglas, 189; Lehr, *As the Mockingbird Sang*, 34, 37; Lehr, *Fishing on Deep Water*, 75; McGhee, *Service With the Guard*, 76–77; Rose, 63; Shea & Hess, 252, 264, 271; Hunt Wilson, "Battle of Pea Ridge," *Missouri Republican*, July 11, 1885.

106. Van Winkle's Mill was located about eight miles (Tunnard has it as six miles, Anderson seven, Brown ten and Lehr twelve) from the battlefield, on War Eagle Creek on the road to Huntsville. The mill was owned by Peter Van Winkle, a Dutchman, who was born in New York City on February 25, 1814. In 1839, Van Winkle moved to Greenland, Arkansas, a short distance from Fayetteville. Van Winkle subsequently acquired 17,000 acres of timberland in northwest Benton County, where he open a sawmill. During the winter of 1861–1862, the mill provided material for McCulloch to build his winter quarters in northwest Arkansas. Anderson, *Memoirs*, 178; Brown, 15; Lehr, *As the Mockingbird Sang*, 38; Ernest Scott, "Peter Van Winkle," *Arkansas Historical Quarterly* 21 (Summer, 1962), 170–172; Tunnard, 145.

**Item:** The Battle of Pea Ridge as recalled by a Confederate artillery-man, by Hunt P. Wilson, Guibor's Missouri Battery.
**Published:** July 4 and 11, 1885

# The Battle of Elkhorn

Hunt P. Wilson[107] whose likeness accompanies this sketch is probably best known in St. Louis and neighboring cities as one of the best trap shots in this part of the country. During the war he used a different kind of shell from those he handles now, being a member of Guibor's Battery,[108] which went from St. Louis to join the Confederate Army. Some of his personal experiences he has neatly told in several papers read before the Southern Historical and Benevolent Society. One of these papers, describing the Battle of Elkhorn, or Pea Ridge, is in part given here. The battle took place March 6, 7 and 8, 1862. Mr. Wilson first briefly describes the retreat of Gen. Price's little army from Springfield to Cove Creek, near the Boston Mountains, and the junction with Van Dorn, McCullough [McCulloch] and McIntosh. Thus strengthened, the Confederates turned and raced Sigel's wing of Curtis's army into and through Bentonville, Ark., without however, bringing him to serious battle until the field of Pea Ridge was reached. Curtis's position

---

107. Hunt P. Wilson, a painter by trade and resident of St. Louis was born about 1842. He joined the MSG in April 1862, because of the "excitement and circumstances over which he had no control"; besides which he was "out of employment." On June 15, 1862, Wilson entered the Confederate service in Guibor's Missouri Artillery at Priceville, Mississippi, where he served as a sergeant and chief musician (armed) of the battery. Captured at Vicksburg, Wilson was sent to Gratiot Street Prison in St. Louis on July 16, where he offered to take the Oath of Allegiance. In his petition to take the Oath, to General James Totten, Wilson stated, that previous to his capture he had "no opportunity to escape" from the rebel service and further desired to "become once more a citizen of the United States." Totten refused the petition, not believing that Wilson was sincere, and sent him to Camp Morton, Indiana, for exchange on November 20, 1863. Wilson was held in Indiana, until March 19, 1864, when he was forwarded to Fort Delaware, where he was discharged on June 1, 1864, after taking the Oath of Allegiance. According to Wilson's statement to Federal authorities, he did not list participation in the Battle of Elkhorn, even though his article clearly shows that he did participate in the battle. At the time of Elkhorn, Wilson probably was not a member of the MSG and was simply acting as a private citizen. National Archives, Record Group M322 (roll no. 81), Confederate Compiled Service Records, First Missouri Battery Light Artillery; Schnetzer, *More Forgotten Men*, 247.
108. Guibor's Battery, also known as the "First Missouri Artillery (Confederate)," had its beginnings in pre-Civil War St. Louis. Organized as a St. Louis Missouri Militia unit, the battery was captured at Camp Jackson on May 10, 1861. The paroled men made their way to Price's camp, and Henry Guibor was given the task of organizing a battery in M. M. Parsons's Sixth Division, MSG. Initially equipped with three 6-pound smoothbores, the battery added a fourth 6-pounder by the Battle of Wilson's Creek. While serving in the Guard, Guibor's Battery fought at the Missouri battles of Carthage, Wilson's Creek and Lexington. The battery disbanded in October 1861, and the men journeyed to Memphis, Tennessee, where they were organized into a new battery and joined General Daniel M. Frost en route to join Price at Springfield, Missouri. The new, "provisional" MSG command consisted of four 6-pound smoothbores and two 12-pound howitzers, with Guibor as the commander. Following the Battle of Pea Ridge, on March 25, 1862, the battery was reorganized as a Confederate battery and moved to the east side of the Mississippi River, where it completed its military service. *O.R.S.*, pt. 2, vol. 38:340–341; pt. 3, vol. 1:618–619; Banasik, *Missouri Brothers in Gray*, 19; Patrick, 28–31, 50.

was on strong ground, which the Federal troops had occupied long enough to fully learn its advantages. As the Confederates divided their forces and attacked on both flanks, two battles were fought in some respects entirely independent of each other. Mr. Wilson says:

Gen. McCulloch attacked in two columns, on right and left flank, sending Pike and his Indians over the ridge while he turned in at the Foster place and marched down the skirt of the mountain. It is perfectly clear now that he should have kept his men together and gone on the ridge himself which would have brought him in Sigel's rear, dividing the Federal army into two isolated commands.

Old Chief Stand Watie[109] swept down from this position with his Indians, stampeding the Federal cavalry and capturing a four gun battery, which they immediately burned up, and celebrated the event by a war dance.[110] In the midst of their excitation a Federal rifled battery, which had been moved on to Little Mountain, opened on them, and they scattered to the four winds. This was the last of them as a body, though some of them remained and skirmished all through the day.[111]

Gen. McCulloch and McIntosh were both killed nearly at the same time and but a short distance apart while forming their men on the south or left flank of the Federal position. Gen. Herbert [Hébert] was also taken prisoner. The Texans pressed [Alexander S.] Asboth's right, and he withdrew his cavalry through the

---

109. Stand Watie was born on December 12, 1806, in what became modern-day Georgia. He was educated at a mission school, served as a deputy sheriff, clerked in the Cherokee Supreme Court and edited a newspaper. As a member of the "Treaty Party," Watie helped negotiate a treaty which sold the Cherokee lands east of the Mississippi River. Relocated to the Indian Territory (modern-day Oklahoma) in 1837, Watie assumed the leadership of his party in 1839, following the assassination of three of its prominent members. Prior to the Civil War, Watie served on the Cherokee Council and was speaker of the Council from 1855–1861. With the beginning of the Civil War, the Five Civilized Tribes joined the Confederacy in October 1861, and Watie became the colonel of the First Cherokee Mounted Rifles. In addition to the Battle of Pea Ridge, Watie also fought at Wilson's Creek in Missouri and Honey Springs (July 1863) and Cabin Creek (September 1864), in the Indian Territory, to name but a few of his engagements. He was promoted to general officer on May 10, 1864, and was the last Confederate general to surrender on June 23, 1865. Following the war, Watie returned home, in what is now Delaware County, Oklahoma, where he died on September 9, 1871. For a complete biography see Banasik, *Reluctant Cannoneer*, 292–294.

110. Watie's command, by most accounts, did not capture the three-gun Federal battery. Shea & Hess credit McIntosh's cavalry for capturing the Federal guns, while Pike's Indians hit Companies A and B, Third Iowa Cavalry, who were guarding the left flank of the Union guns. Later in the day, after the battle on the Confederate right was lost, Colonel E. Greer, not Watie or Pike as the writer states, ordered the carriages of the captured Federal guns burned,. *O.R.*, 8:293; Bearss, "First Day At Pea Ridge," 152; Shea & Hess, 99–101.

111. After the capture of the three Federal guns, Pike's Indians swarmed about the prize, celebrating their good fortune. For twenty minutes Pike waited for new orders, while his command languished about the captured battery. Meanwhile, Colonel Stand Watie informed Pike that a new Federal battery was sighted and preparing to fire. Pike attempted to gain control of his command but failed as two rounds from the new threat sent the Indians scattering into the nearby woods. For all intents and purposes Pike's command was finished for the day as his men remained in the woods and refused to advance. Putting a positive face on the dilemma Pike recorded that the Federal "battery was thus, with its supporting force, by the presence of the Indians, rendered useless to the enemy during the action." *O.R.*, 8:288.

gap and around the base of Little Mountain, from whence he struck McCulloch's men on the south, then swung around and struck the other column, thus beating them in detail.[112] Gen. [Frank A.] Rector[113] withdrew his men to the twelve-cornered school-house and so discontinued the fight. These events consumed nearly all day. McCulloch's men were in the fields, on level ground, while the Federals were on the hills or rising ground, well covered by artillery. The Texans and Arkansans were without generals, poorly armed, and on bad ground, and could not cope with the superior appliances of the enemy. Yet they made a good fight.

## Gen. Price's Battle.

In the meantime, the brave old hero, Gen. Price, with his Missourians, had turned Curtis's right flank and formed line of battle, directly in his rear, facing southward, and was having everything his own way. His command consisted of the following brigades, (so called though they were mere skeletons): Little's, Slack's,

---

112. The Hungarian born Alexander S. Asboth was educated in Europe, and immigrated to the United States in 1851. At the beginning of the Civil War, he was Frémont's Chief-of-Staff, and on September 3, 1861, Frémont appointed Asboth a brigadier general and assigned him to command his Fourth Division. Asboth was reappointed brigadier on March 21, 1862, for his actions at the Battle of Pea Ridge. In mid-1862, Asboth moved to the east side of the Mississippi River, where he completed his Civil War service. He died in 1868, in Argentina, from the effects of an operation on an old Civil War wound. Boatner, *Civil War Dictionary*, 27–28.

With the death of McCulloch and McIntosh, and the disorganization of Pike's command, the only viable Confederate force still on the Leetown front was Hébert's Brigade, which contained only four regiments at the time—the Third Louisiana, Fourth, Fourteenth, and Fifteenth Arkansas Infantries. About 2:00 p.m. Hébert led his command southward from Little Mountain and collided with Julis White's brigade of Federals from Davis's Third Division. For one hour the two commands slugged it out in the heavy brush. Hébert then ordered his brigade forward and in the process captured two pieces of artillery, but a portion of his command became so disorganized to be labeled no better than an "armed mob" by Shea & Hess. Davis reinforced the area with Thomas Pattison's First Brigade on Hébert's left, while Peter Osterhaus's Second Brigade formed on the rebel right. Pressed on three sides, and with no support or reinforcements, Hébert's Brigade fell back. The battle on the Confederate right flank was at an end. Asboth was not present at the engagement. Bearss, "First Day At Pea Ridge," 150–152; Shea & Hess, 120, 125, 128, 133–134, 139–142.

113. Frank A. Rector, a resident of Fort Smith, was the adjutant general of the First Division, Arkansas Volunteers at the beginning of the Civil War. In October 1861, he was elected the commander of the Seventeenth Arkansas Infantry, which he led at Pea Ridge. Following the battle he moved to the east side of the Mississippi River, was furloughed in June 1862 (William L. Cabell has Rector resigning because of his health), and returned to Arkansas. General Thomas C. Hindman, in need of troops, appointed Rector to command what became the Thirty-fifth Arkansas infantry on July 11, 1862. Rector's appointment "did not give satisfaction to the Arkansas men" nor to the Missourians who were placed in his regiment. On August 11, Rector resigned and was appointed a major and quartermaster of the Northwest District of Arkansas by Charles A. Carroll. He served throughout the war, remaining a major and quartermaster. *O.R.*, vol. 22, pt. 2:1099; *O.R.S.*, pt. 1, vol. 1:155; pt. 2, vol. 2:588, 776; William L. Cabell, "Reminiscences From the Trans-Mississippi," *Confederate Veteran* 12 (April 1904), 173, hereafter cited as Cabell; General Orders (July 11 and August 11, 1862), by Charles A. Carroll, in General Orders (1862–1864), Various Generals, Peter W. Alexander Collection, Columbia University, New York; National Archives, Record Group M317, Confederate Compiled Service Records (roll no. 219), Thirty–fifth Arkansas Infantry; John P. Quensenberry Diary, State Historical Society of Missouri, July 14, 1862.

Rains's, Jno. B. Clark's, Steen's, Green's and Frost's. The Missouri army, by an all-night march, had passed completely around the Federal right flank, marching to the north and east of Big Mountain, then forming line of battle facing south on the Keitsville and Fayetteville or "Wire" Road directly in Gen. Curtis's rear. The country this side of the hill is broken, with high ridge and deep hollows, though which the Wire Road runs. The column entered by what is called the Cross Timber Hollow. Some of the ridges are 150 feet high. In the valley of this defile is located what is known as the tan-yard, three-fourths of a mile from Elkhorn Tavern. From the tan-yard there is a gradual ascent, and alongside the road runs a deep hollow, reaching up to the spring near the tavern. At the head of this and crossing it is a "bench" along the base of the mountain. Along this bench was the United States cavalry under Gen. [Eugene A.] Carr.[114] Along the road leading down from the tavern were the Iowa troops, with artillery, and on their right, leading to the east, on the Van Winkle Road, on which are a few clearings, Gen. Curtis prolonged his line of battle. Another hollow leads from the tan-yard to the southeast, and at the head of this hollow rested the Federal right. This ground was all well wooded.[115]

The first indication of the opening ball, or series of military balls, was the display of a yellow flag on a stick fastened to the gable end of a house near by. Then fourteen soldiers belonging to Asboth's division marched down the hill and surrendered. They had got lost. Then some forage wagons, well laden, drove out of a hollow and were taken in. Then an aide galloped up and said,

## "Van Dorn Wants A Battery."

This suited Capt. Guibor who wanted to try the metal of his new guns and men, and waiving his hat he ordered the battery forward at a trot. The aide pointed out the way, the battery turned into the left, up a steep hill, and came into position under a hot fire of grape, canister and shell; for directly in front, on the opposite ridge, on the Wire Road, 250 yards distant, was a famous Iowa battery of four

---

114. Eugene A. Carr was born on March 20, 1830, in Erie County, New York, and graduated from West Point in 1850 (number 19 of 44). At the beginning of the Civil War, he commanded Company I, First U.S. Cavalry, which he led with gallantry at the Battle of Wilson's Creek. Carr was commissioned the colonel of the Third Illinois Cavalry on August 16, 1861. He led the Fourth Division at the Battle of Pea Ridge, where he was wounded three times and received the Congressional Medal of Honor for his service. Effective March 7, 1862, Carr became a general officer and on March 11, 1865, he was breveted a major general. Carr died on December 2, 1910, and was buried at West Point. *O.R.*, 3:56, 89; Boatner, *Civil War Dictionary*, 127–128; Warner, *Generals in Blue*, 70–71.

115. When the Federal command initially deployed for battle, only General Carr's Fourth Division was present; Vandever's Brigade held the left while Dodge's command was positioned on the right. The Third Illinois Cavalry held the far right of Carr's line on the Van Winkle-Huntsville Road. The hollow leading from the tanyard was known as the "Tanyard Hollow" and it pointed due south to the west of Elkhorn Tavern. The "Williams Hollow" ran southeast, parallel to the Van Winkle-Huntsville Road, and would provided an avenue for Price's rebels to turn the Union right flank later in the day. Shea & Hess, 177–178.

guns, supported by Iowa troops with two more of their guns 150 yard further up the road.[116]

While forming in battery two horses were shot down, and the writer's caisson was noted absent. The captain ordered him down the hill to bring it up; going down he found the team had balked and would not pull. A Federal forage wagon stood near, and he proceeded to press the mules. The Federal driver, a tall son of Illinois named "Abe," objected to losing his mules; he said they were wild and hard to handle by strangers, and asked permission to stay with them. The mules were hitched to the caisson, Abe cracked his bullsnake whip, and pulled into position in rear of the guns, Abe sitting composedly in the saddle viewing the fight. After awhile the captain noticed him and ordered him down the hill to a place of safety, but he refused to go without mules. The captain having no time to argue went back to his duties, and Abe drove his team all though the fight, eight or nine hours under heavy fire, most of the time at 250 to 400 yards from the enemy's line of battle.

The other batteries with the infantry came up the same road, took position farther to the left and opened on the enemy's right wing, as there was a Federal battery in the field on the Van Winkle Road.[117] Some State Guard cavalry under Bob McCullough and Congreve Jackson formed on the extreme left. Then on their right came Bledsoe's,[118] Clark's and McDonald's [MacDonald's] batteries, Rains's infantry,[119] Wade's battery,[120] a regiment of infantry and then Guibor's bat-

---

116. Guibor's command took a position on "Broad Ridge," to the northeast of Elkhorn Tavern, and engaged the Third Iowa Artillery, which was positioned just to the north of Elkhorn Tavern. Shea & Hess, 162, 177.

117. The Battery on the Van Winkle Road, or the road to Huntsville, was the First Iowa Battery. Shea & Hess, 177.

118. Bledsoe's Battery consisted of four guns; according to Shea & Hess three 12-pound Napoleons and "Old Sacramento," which was not correct. The initial battery consisted of one brass 6-pound smoothbore and "Old Sacramento." The battery added one 6-pound, Model 1841, iron gun, from the Liberty Arsenal and added another Model 1841 gun following the Battle of Wilson's Creek. Ibid., 339; Bartels, *Trans-Mississippi Men*, 136; Peterson, *Price's Lieutenants*, 287.

119. Rains's infantry consisted of four regiments from his Eighth Division, MSG—Sixth Infantry Regiment, Tenth, Eleventh and Thirteenth Cavalry Regiments (all Dismounted). *O.R.*, 8:327–328; Bevier, 96; Peterson, 212, 227, 231, 239–242, 273–282.

120. Wade's Missouri Battery (Confederate) was organized on December 28, 1861, at Springfield and assigned to Little's Brigade. The unit contained six guns, which according to Shea & Hess, consisted of four 12-pound howitzers and two 6-pound smoothbores. However this seems to go against normal Confederate practice at the time, where a six-gun Confederate battery normally contained two 12-pound howitzers and four 6-pound smoothbore guns. Further, when Wade's guns arrived in Springfield in late November 1861, they were part of a twelve gun shipment that consisted of eight 6-pound smoothbore and four 12-pound howitzers; Little's Brigade received six of the guns. It seems unlikely that Price would have placed all the howitzers in one battery. According to J. A. Wilson, a member of Clark's Battery, also part of Little's Brigade, Clark's command received two twelve-pound howitzers between November and December 1861, giving the command four guns, which they used at the Battle of Pea Ridge; this corresponds with the arrival of the four 12-pound guns at Springfield. The remaining two 12-pound howitzers were then given to Wade's Battery; and with the two extra six-pound guns from Clark's Battery and two additional 6-pound guns from the just arrived guns would give Wade's

tery; this filled out the ridge. Little's Confederate brigade was on the right, across the tan-yard hollow. This constituted

## The First Position.

As on top of the hill was open woods and underbrush, some confusion ensued in getting things in shape. Gen. Van Dorn rode up, and, pointing over, told Capt. Guibor he wanted that battery silenced. "Very well, sir; I will do the best I can," was the reply, and "commence firing" was ordered. At this time the other side was pouring in a well directed fire, knocking off limbs of trees and tearing up the ground in fine style. Our battery opened a rapid fire. The writer, noticing some people on top of the mountain, three-fourths of a mile distant, turned his piece in that direction, and was boring a shell at four seconds to get their range, when the captain asked him what he was about. On being told, the captain said they were Confederates, and ordered the gun pointed to the front again, and also ordered that the piece and the next one decreased more. Up to this time the other guns were aiming at the smoke, probably doing little damage, and it is reasonable to suspect the other side were doing the same, as their shots went over us. The next piece was commanded by Johnny Bull,[121] with Ben Von Phul[122] as gunner. The writer

---

Battery its six guns. Following the Battle of Pea Ridge, Wade's Battery moved to the east side of the Mississippi River where they completed their military service. Anderson, *Memoirs,* 99; Bevier, 77; Jack Coggins, *Arms and Equipment of the Civil War* (Wilmington, NC, 1987), 63, hereafter cited as Coggins; Crute, 210; J. Gorgas, *The Ordnance Manual for The Use of The Officers of The Confederate States Army* (Charleston, SC, 1863; reprint ed. Dayton, 1976), 346; Shea & Hess, 336; Wilson, "Clark's Battery," *Missouri Republican,* November 28, 1885.

121. John P. Bull was born in Vicksburg, Mississippi, on December 4, 1840, moved to St. Louis at the age of eight, and was educated at St. Charles College in St. Charles, Missouri. In 1857, he was a founding member of the Second National Guard Company of St. Louis. As a private he was captured at Camp Jackson on May 10, 1861, and exchanged on December 2. With his brother William, John joined Guibor's MSG Battery on December 15, 1861. He fought at Pea Ridge, transferred briefly to the east side of the Mississippi River, and returned as a member of Gorham's MSG Battery. In September 1862, Gorham's Battery was transferred to the Confederate service. John Bull left the artillery on December 2, 1862, and fought at Prairie Grove as a lieutenant and aide to Colonel Emmett MacDonald. On May 1, 1863, John was promoted to major in the Fifth Arkansas Cavalry Regiment. He fought at Helena (July 4, 1863) and commanded the Fifth Arkansas during the 1863 Campaign for Little Rock and at Pine Bluff, Arkansas on October 25, 1863. In March 1864 John Bull was married and received his promotion to lieutenant colonel the same evening. He participated in the Camden Expedition and Price's 1864 Missouri Raid. After the war he returned to St. Louis, and with his wife Zanobia he had four children. He later died in his home town. *O.R.,* vol. 22, pt. 1:156, 540, 737; vol. 34, pt. 1:792, 794; Banasik, *Missouri Brothers in Grey,* ix, 19, 27–28, 36, 45, 112, 118; Eakin, *Confederate Records,* 1:183; Schnetzer, *More Forgotten Men,* 34.

122. Benjamin Von Phul, a St. Louis resident, was captured at Camp Jackson on May 10, 1861, and joined Guibor's MSG in September 1861. According to Peterson, Von Phul was appointed adjutant and first lieutenant in William Wade's MSG Artillery Battalion on November 20, 1861, but the battalion disbanded in December. At Pea Ridge, Von Phul served as a gunner in Guibor's MSG Battery. In September 1862, Sterling Price recommended Von Phul for a position in the Ordnance Department and during the 1863 Campaign for Little Rock, Von Phul commanded a 6-gun battery. Banasik, *Missouri Brothers in Gray,* 25, 107, 129; Eakin, *Confederate Records,* 7:173; National Archives, Record

acted as gunner of his own piece. The two pieces were depressed and at their next discharge a loud explosion was heard and a column of black smoke arose, in the Iowa battery. We had struck a limber chest. Two more shots and a louder explosion, followed by a longer and denser column of smoke. A caisson was blown up. The fire of our four guns was now concentrated, as we had a good mark to shoot at and the battery in front ceased to answer. It was fairly knocked out and by a battery of the same caliber and number of guns. The St. Louis boys did it and did it fair and in less than an hour.[123]

Gen. Price and staff passed by and the old general was wounded in the arm shortly after passing. Gen. Frost came up in the rear, dismounted, came to the gun, loaded and fired it. Gen. Van Dorn passed away from the rear of the guns.

Gates's regiment of cavalry then came up the hollow in front of the guns and went half way up the slope, dismounted, every fourth man holding the horses, then formed and moved up to the brow of the hill. At the same time Little's Confederate brigade, which had by this time got into line opened on the Iowa troops in their rear, with Gates in their front, which was answered by the brave boys from Iowa. The rattle of musketry was terrific. A great number of balls came over by the battery, but got high. The poor horses of Gates's regiment received a large number of stray shots and the horse-holders lying down, the horses all came galloping down the hill in riderless yet regular order as if guided by unseen hands. A few horse holders could be seen slipping down the hill. A demoralized cannoneer exclaimed, "My God they have all been killed." Soon a loud cheering was heard and a guard came down with some prisoners. Little's brigade had swung around and cut off a part of the Federals line and the others, unable to stand the hot fire escaped up to the tavern.

"Limber to the rear—places, pass your caissons—by piece from the right, front into column—trot—march," rung out, and down this hill went the battery, then around past the tan-yard, and up to the position of the Iowa battery, where they halted to give the infantry time to reform. Here was a scene of wreck and disaster. The remains of a part of a Federal battery were scattered around and the effect of the explosion could be plainly seen. Dead horses and dead and wounded infantry told of the storm of iron which had beaten them down. One gunner in particular presented a horrible sight. He was an Austrian judging from his flaxen almost white hair, one side of his face was scorched black, the other side a deep red, while his light blue glassy eyes started from the sockets. No wound could be seen. He had been killed by concussion. An officer had his body dragged to the side and covered with leaves. There were many wounded lying around, and the boys attended to them as best they could. A captain was lying at the foot of a tree with a cap over his face. The writer went to him and took his pistol, a fine one, then, raising the cap, saw a handsome face, that the gaze of a pair of mournful hazel eyes and heard a "Please do not kill me." "No, my friend, you are safe. We are not savages."

---

Group M322, Compiled Service Records, Von Phul's Battery; Peterson, 132; Schnetzer, *More Forgotten Men*, 235.
123. Guibor's command had hit the limber chest of the First Iowa Battery. Shea & Hess, 162–164.

Dr. Tom Staples[124] came along, and seeing an ambulance near, called it over; seated inside was a partly intoxicated Confederate surgeon, who declined to get out. Staples, a man of herculean proportions, seized the Esculapian [or aesculapian] by the collar, literally lifted the man out, and threw him across the road; he got up shook his fist, and, threatening vengeance, slunk off down the hill. The Federal captain was given a drink of brandy, placed in the ambulance with several of his wounded comrades, and sent to the hospital. Two minnie balls struck the ambulance while these Federals were being placed in it.

## Second Position.

As Gorham's battery[125] had gone up with Little's line our pieces were placed in position on the same line and to the left. Gorham's battery was the old battery that Guibor and Barlow commanded at Carthage,[126] Wilson's Creek, Dry Wood[127]

---

124. Thomas E. Staples was born in Henry County, Virginia, on December 7, 1823, and later migrated to Missouri. During the Mexican War, Staples served in the Company D, First Missouri Regiment, Mounted Volunteers, as a member of Doniphan's Expedition. A resident of Georgetown, Saline County, Missouri in 1860, Staples commanded a company of Missouri Militia during the Southwest Expedition in the Winter of 1860–1861. At the beginning of the Civil War Staples organized an independent cavalry company for the Sixth Division, MSG, which he led at Wilson's Creek, where he was wounded. On September 14, he was elected major of the Second Cavalry Regiment, of his division. By the Battle of Pea Ridge, Staples was an assistant surgeon within his Guard division. Staples later joined the Confederate army, Wood's Cavalry Battalion, and was captured during Price's 1864 Missouri Raid, sent to St. Louis, where he was released on bond. On June 7, 1865, Staples was paroled out of the army at Shreveport, Louisiana, and returned to Missouri. He died in Nelson, Missouri, in October 1899. *O.R.*, Series 2, 1:361; Bartels, *Forgotten Men*, 340–341; Eakin, *Confederate Records*, 7:74; Peterson, 177.

125. Gorham's battery was organized at Lexington, Missouri, on September 19, 1861. The battery obtained their guns—four 6-pound smoothbores—from Guibor's Battery, which disbanded in October 1861. The guns came from the Liberty Arsenal, while the battery was part of the Sixth Division, MSG. James C. Gorham, commander of the battery, was from Marshall, Missouri (Saline County), and remained with the battery until General Thomas C. Hindman replaced him with Alexander B. "Buck" Tilden on November 10, 1862. Banasik, *Missouri Brothers in Grey*, 43; Patrick, 49–50, 59; Peterson, 192.

126. The Battle of Carthage took place on July 5, 1861. It was actually a running fight of about ten miles that began at the Spring River and proceeded northward into and through Carthage. Nightfall terminated the action. The rebel force numbered about 4,000 effectives while the Federals fielded about 1,100 men. The Unionists lost 18 killed, 53 wounded, and 5 missing; Confederates lost about 12 killed, 64 wounded and 1 missing. David C. Hinze and Karen Farnham, *The Battle of Carthage: Border War in Southwest Missouri, July 5, 1861* (Campbell, CA, 1997), 202, 205, 278; Ward L. Schrantz, *Jasper County, Missouri in the Civil War* (Carthage, MO, 1923; reprint ed. Carthage, MO, 1992), 23, 31–33.

127. A portion of Price's army under General James Rains left Springfield on August 22, 1861, and moved to Stockton, Cedar County, Missouri. By August 25, the remainder of Price's command had concentrated at Rains's location. Four days later Price's rebels moved off in the direction of Fort Scott, Kansas, in an attempt to take the fort before moving on to the Missouri River. On September 1, a 786-man MSG force under General Alexander Early Steen captured 80 mules two miles from Ft. Scott and moved back to the Confederate main body. In response, the fort's commander, Jim Lane, sent a 500-man force and one mountain howitzer from the Third, Fifth and Sixth Kansas Cavalries in pursuit. About 4 p.m. on September 2, the two forces collided near Dry Wood Creek. Following a sharp

and Lexington. The caissons were placed down the hill to shelter them from the enemy's fire, which came hotly from up the road from sixteen guns, two six-gun batteries and four mountain howitzers, formed in a line from the side of the hill at the tavern and across the Wire Road to the Van Winkle Road, their left supported by cavalry placed along a bench of the mountain, under command of Col. Carr.[128] Their guns were served rapidly. A long line of Confederate soldiers stretched along a ravine over to the right, but they were not firing as horsemen could be seen through the trees, and it was not certain who they were. On the captain making inquiry, Lieut. Moulton of the battery volunteered and rode down and up the other side of the hollow, where he found out who they were, for about a hundred Feds began to pop at him with their Sharps carbines. Moulton came flying back, yelling, "It's them, it's them, it's them!" The guns and the battery opened fire and the Federals soon withdrew, after suffering severely in men and horses. The lines were not 200 yards apart at the nearest point.

## A Hot Spot.

The writer's gun was moved about fifty yards to the left, to command a blind road, where they soon had a small battle on their own hook. There was no infantry on the left on that side of the ridge, as they had their hands full with the Federal lines on the Van Winkle Road and had not yet moved up. Consequently, as the gun was being placed, skirmishers began to make it warm, but a few rounds of canister drove them off. Then a full battery, about 500 yards in front, opened a salvo, which had the aim been lower, must have destroyed the detachment. To say that the writer felt no apprehension of danger to himself would be ridiculous affection. A soldier going into battle is always ready to let his comrades be shot in his own sted and seldom awards to his own life to the cause. So the writer generously killed off (in his mind) half of the men in the battery, and stood up to the work, not from any motives of bravery, but from sheer compulsion—because he had it to do. The fire from the Federal battery was so strong and so sudden that some of the cannoneers ran away down the hill. There remained but four men—Bat Leahey, No. 1, with his clothes torn almost off him; Tom Kelly, bare head and bleeding at

engagement of about an hour the outnumbered Federals withdrew back to Ft. Scott. Price reported losing 2 killed with 23 wounded, while Federal losses numbered 5 killed and 12 wounded. Following the engagement, Price turned away from Ft. Scott, being informed that the fort had been deserted, and moved toward Lexington on the Missouri River. *O.R.*, 53: 435–436; Britton, *Civil War on the Border, 1861–1862*, 127–128; Eakin, *Diary of a Doctor*, 16–17; T. F. Robley, *History of Bourbon County, Kansas to the Close of 1863* (Fort Scott, KS, 1894), 169–170.

128. By 3:00 p.m., when the battle on the rebel left was reaching a climax, the Federal lines consisted of fifteen pieces of artillery. The First Iowa Artillery (4 guns), Third Iowa Artillery (4 guns) and the First Indiana Battery (3 guns) occupied the center near Elkhorn Tavern. To the right, on the Van Winkle–Huntsville Road, General Carr placed a two-gun section of the First Iowa Artillery and on the far left, two 12-pound mountain howitzers of Bowen's Missouri Cavalry Battalion. The troopers on the far right of the Union line belonged to the Third Illinois Cavalry. In all the Federal line consisted of fifteen guns, with about 2,500 men. Byers, 121; Shea & Hess, 178–180, 182.

the nose; Sam Marks,[129] knocked flat and rolling on the ground, with his mouth full of dirt; and Wilson, with the flap of his coat shot away, his hat knocked off and a singing sensation in his ears. The balance of the detachment were gone, and three of them, who shall be nameless, turned up missing; one never stopped until he reached St. Louis. The gunner or corporal of the piece was found lying down behind a log a few paces to the rear. Refusing to get up and do his duty, the writer laid hold of his collar, but he laid so close that the collar was torn off in trying to drag him up; failing to fetch him, a few heavy kicks in the ribs were given, and he was left there; he soon got up and scurried down the hill, and was seen no more during the fight. The four men now worked the gun; Marks at the trail handspike and lanyard, Kelly inserting the shot, Leahey running and sponging, the writer serving vent and aiming. Soon the limber chest was exhausted of ammunition, and the young man who replenished from the caisson could get no further up the hill than to a big tree that stood some fifty yards in the rear, where he deposited quite a pile of shell and canister. The Federal skirmishers came prowling back on the left front, and every few seconds a minnie ball would come singing past, or thud against the gun. One of the limber drivers called "Ktuch," who had been a newsboy in St. Louis, not over 16 years old (his real name was Johnny Fee) came up to the gun with two rounds of canister and a shell; he had heard the calls for ammunition and seeing the timidity of the others left his team and responded to the call. The charge of powder was taken from one canister, the two rammed home and the gun slewed [sloughed] around and pointed to sprinkle the skirmishers. As the writer was sighting, a skirmisher stepped from behind a small tree, not sixty yards away; standing in the position of a rifleman target-shooting he took a long, deliberate aim at the head of the devoted gunner, whose sensations were horrible at this moment, as he could almost feel the bullet boring a hole between his eyes; a puff of smoke came from the rifle and a sharp metallic ring told that the aim was too low; the ball struck the face of the muzzle of the gun, leaving a large dent; one

129. Bartholomew or Barthold "Bat" Leahey, a member of Guibor's First Missouri Battery, was a resident of Pettus County, Missouri, at the beginning of the Civil War. Though Leahey was a member of the MSG, no date of entry could be found. Leahey entered Confederate Service on April 5, 1862, was promoted to corporal on December 1, 1862, and was captured at Vicksburg, Mississippi, on July 4, 1863. Sent to Gratiot and Myrtle Street Prisons, in St. Louis on July 15, 1863, Leahey was forwarded to Camp Morton Prison in Indianapolis, Indiana, on August 1, 1863. Leahey was never exchanged, taking the Oath of Allegiance to the United States on January 2, 1865, after which he was released.
Though a member of the MSG, Samuel U. Marks had no record of his entry date into the Guard. On April 5, 1862, Marks entered Confederate service as a corporal in Guibor's Battery. He was captured at Vicksburg on July 4, 1863, later exchanged, and completed his service with Guibor's Battery on the east side of the Mississippi River. Marks was paroled out of the army on May 1, 1865, in North Carolina.
No record is found in Guibor's Battery on a Tom Kelly. Boatner, 118; Joanne C. Eakin, *Missouri Prisoners of War From Gratiot Prison & Myrtle Street Prison, St. Louis, Mo. and Alton Prison, Alton Illinois Including Citizens, Confederates, Bushwhackers and Guerrillas* (Independence, MO, 1995), "Leahey, Barthold" entry; National Archives, Record Group M322 (roll no. 81), Confederate Compiled Service Records, First Missouri Battery Light Artillery.

inch higher and these papers would never bored a respectable audience. Marks pulled the lanyard and the skirmisher rallied on the great reserve.

Lieut. William Corkey[130] now came up with a supply of ammunition. A shell was then bored at two seconds and sent over to the opposing battery, followed by several more and some canister showered into the bushes to keep the sharpshooters at a healthy distance. A friction primer failed, and lodging in the vent the gun was spiked. The writer ran to the other pieces for a gunner's pincers, but could find none, and reported to Lieut. William Corkery who solved the problem in a rough and ready manner by pulling out the stump of the primer with his teeth.

The action on this part of the line now became very hot. The Confederate infantry and artillery fire being generally up hill was low and deadly, while the enemy, aiming down hill naturally fired high and did little execution. A magnificent black Federal horse came galloping down the road, with head up and distended nostrils. The writer caught and tied him to a tree-top which had been conveniently shot off nearby; blood was seen on the saddle, which showed the rider had suffered. Poor brute, he had run the gauntlet unscathed to die an instant later by a shell from his former owners. A pair of beautiful pistols were taken from the holsters and in the haversack was found a nice lunch of real wheat bread and butter and ham, wrapped in a white napkin, and a flask of brandy. How high those fellows lived. These articles had just been removed when a shell struck the noble animal full in the chest and exploding left the poor creature a quivering pile of flesh. The captain got part of the lunch, but the brandy was too precious for unwounded men to drink.

The firing in front began to lull and Slack's brigade with Reeve's [Rives's] and [John Q.] Burbridge's regiments[131] came up on a left wheel with Rains on their

---

130. William Corkey or Corkery was born in Ireland and lived in Missouri at the beginning of the Civil War. He joined the MSG on August 1, 1861, being elected a second lieutenant of artillery. On March 25, 1862, Corkey was appointed a first lieutenant in Guibor's Battery. Captured at Vicksburg on July 4, 1863, and exchanged, Corkey lost his position in the battery when it was consolidated on October 3, 1863. Corkey remained on the east side of the Mississippi River for the remainder of the war while still retaining his rank. He was paroled out of the service in Mobile, Alabama, in 1865, as a first lieutenant, still assigned to Guibor's Battery, but not serving in the command. *O.R.*, vol. 24, pt. 1:668; vol. 24, pt. 2:111; *O.R.S.*, pt. 2, vol. 38:340–341; National Archives, Record Group M322 (roll no. 81), Confederate Compiled Service Records, First Missouri Battery Light Artillery; Schnetzer, *More Forgotten Men*, 54.

131. John Q. Burbridge commanded the Second Missouri Infantry (Confederate), which was organized on January 16, 1862. Following the Battle of Pea Ridge the regiment moved to the east side of the Mississippi River where it completed its military service. Burbridge was born about 1830, educated at St. Louis University and was a banker in Louisiana, Missouri, at the beginning of the Civil War. Prior to the war, Burbridge led the local Pike County Militia, serving also as the "drill master" of the unit. During the course of the war, Burbridge led troops in the MSG and commanded regular Confederate troops, serving mostly in the Trans-Mississippi. One old veteran described Burbridge as "a man of less than medium height, very erect and graceful…[and] made a notable appearance on the" battlefield. After the war he moved to Alabama. He died on November 14, 1892. For Burbridge's complete military service record see Banasik, *Serving With Honor*, 378–380; Eakin, *Confederate Records*, 2:1866; Letter (October 31, 1914), Ben Burbridge to Stella Dunn, Staff Correspondence (folder no. 1),

left, crossed the hollow and the whole line charged up with a wild cheer.[132] Capt. Guibor who well understood how to fight artillery in the brush took all the canister he could lay hands on, and with two guns went up in the charge with the infantry. Gen. Rains' brigade on the left led by Col. Walter Scott O'Kane[133] and Maj. [Charles C.] Rainwater,[134] made a brilliant dash, and routed out a battery which

---

Missouri State Guard, Missouri Historical Society; Joseph A. Mudd, "What I Saw At Wilson's Creek," 91; Tucker, *South's Finest*, 1.

132. In describing the final rebel push of the day, Wilson first related the events on the right of the Confederate line, which took up the assault as the battle rolled from the Confederate left to the right. As March 7 was fading Price made his final grand assault to drive the Federals from their position about Elkhorn Tavern. Slack's Brigade, commanded by Thomas H. Rosser, was located on the far right of the rebel line, next to John Q. Burbridge's Missouri Regiment, and overlapping the Federals left. At the "double–quick" and for "a distance of 300 yards," Slack's command charged, dispersing the enemy "in every direction." A portion of Slack's command followed up the retreating bluecoats, but were stopped dead in their tracks in Ruddick's field. This, according to Shea & Hess marked "the high-water mark of the Confederate war effort in the Trans-Mississippi." *O.R.*, 8:313; Shea & Hess, 193–197.

133. Walter S. O'Kane was born in Virginia about 1835, and a resident of Independence, Missouri, at the beginning of the Civil War. He was sent to Warsaw, Missouri, by Governor Jackson, to organize the local militia and on May 6, 1861, was elected captain of the Warsaw Grays. On July 4, O'Kane was elected lieutenant colonel of the 4th Infantry Regiment, 8th Division, MSG and served with them until December 31, 1861. O'Kane became an aid-de-camp for General Rains on January 1, 1862, was captured in June 1862, while recruiting in northern Arkansas and was exchanged in September 1862. O'Kane completed his military service on General Marmaduke's staff, having been passed over for regimental command of the Eighth Missouri Infantry by General M. M. Parsons. While in the Guard, O'Kane fought at Cole Camp and Wilson's Creek in Missouri and Pea Ridge, Arkansas. He later participated in the Battle of Prairie Grove, Arkansas and assorted cavalry raids under General Marmaduke. *O.R.*, 8:328; 13:45; vol. 22, pt. 1:77, 736; Bartels, *Forgotten Men*, 278; Bartels, *Trans-Mississippi Men*, 237; Letter (December 26, 1862), Hindman to Anderson, Copy Letter Book, Hindman's Command (June 11–December 30, 1862), 187–188 (hereafter cited as Copy Letter Book No. 2); Kathleen White Miles, *Bitter Ground: The Civil War in Missouri's Golden Valley Benton, Henry, and St. Clair Counties* (Warsaw, MO, 1971), 34, 40, 214, hereafter cited as Miles; Peterson, 211, 232, 234.

134. Charles Cicero Rainwater was born at Knoxville, Ray County, Missouri, on April 6, 1838, graduated from Central College at Fayetteville, Missouri, in 1858, and married in September of the same year. In October 1858, Rainwater, with his new bride, settled about one mile from Cole Camp, Missouri, where he entered the mercantile business. In April 1861, he entered the Missouri Militia and was elected a lieutenant in the Warsaw Grays in June 1861. He fought at Cole Camp on June 17, 1861 "and took part in every engagement of importance west of the Mississippi until 1864." During the war, Rainwater served in assorted staff positions including Assistant Division Commissary of Subsistence and Aid-de-Camp in the Eighth Division, MSG under General James Rains; within the regular Confederate army, Rainwater served on John S. Marmaduke's staff as Acting Division Commissary of Subsistence, Aid-de-Camp and Chief of Ordnance & Artillery. Rainwater was wounded in the head at Bayou Meto, Arkansas on August 26, 1863, and in the hip at Lake Chicot, Arkansas on June 6, 1864 [Note: Winter has incorrectly identified the wounds as occurring at Vicksburg and during the Atlanta Campaign]. On December 2, 1864, Rainwater was retired from the service with a Medical Certificate of Retirement. However, he joined the staff of General Joe Shelby in February 1865, and served "in a crippled condition" until the end of the war. Following the war, Rainwater returned to St. Louis in August 1865, where he again entered into the mercantile business. He served as the President of the Police Commission (1870–1874) and from 1889 as the President of the Merchant's Bridge Association. He died on November 10, 1902. *O.R.*, vol. 22, pt. 1:198, 528; vol. 34, pt. 1:946–947, 971; Eakin, *Confederate Records*, 6:142; Eakin & Hale, 363; Hale, 266; Miles, 52, 228; Peterson, 209–212; Medical Certificate (December 2, 1864), Rainwater and Fowler Family Papers, Western Historical

had been playing on them for an hour or more from its position in an old field. Col. O'Kane turned their right flank and drove them out in disorder. This charge brought good fruits, for eight guns, four of them dismounted, were captured along the line.[135] The Federal troops being dislodged from the woods, began forming in the fields, and planted some new batteries back on the knobs in the rear, which opened fire, and now the battle grew furious. Gorham's battery could not hold its position and fell back to its old place. Guibor planted his two pieces directly in front of the tavern and opened at close quarters with grape and canister on the Federal line in which great confusion was evident, as officers could be seen trying to rally and reform their men. Gen. Curtis, who was a veteran of Mexico and a good officer, was in person hurrying forward the troops from Sugar Creek, and it was well he did, for in a few moments more his troops engaged would have been demoralized.[136]

## Rock Champion's Charge.

It is necessary to give some description of the different lines of battle and happenings thereon for a particular understanding of the desperate charge of Capt. J. R. (Rock) Champion.[137] As this exploit has seldom been equalled in war in

Manuscript Collection, State Historical Society of Missouri; Moore, *Missouri, Confederate Military History, Extended*, 391–392; Mrs. C. C. Rainwater, "Reminiscences From 1861 to 1865," in *Reminiscences of the Women of Missouri During the Sixties* (Jefferson City, MO, 1911), 17–18, 26, hereafter cited as *Missouri During the Sixties*; Winter, 114.

135. In assaulting the Union center, to the left of Slack's Brigade, Little's Brigade led the way; Burbridge's Regiment was on the right, next to Slack, while Rives's and Gates's commands were on the left of Burbridge. Sandwiched between Rives's and Burbridge's commands came Lindsay's Sixth Division, MSG, and Colton Greene's Third Brigade, Missouri Volunteers. To the left of Rives and Gates, Rains's Eighth Division, MSG, took their post and operated with Price's assault on the Union right. The situation was confusing, and, according to Shea & Hess, "Little gave up trying to form the 1st Missouri Brigade and its myriad supporting units into an organized line. He simply ordered everyone to charge." In the charge, three pieces of artillery, belonging to the Third Iowa Artillery, were captured, not eight as Wilson recorded; one was captured by Rosser's Battalion, Slack's Brigade, while the other two were taken, according to Colonel Henry Little, by Rives's and Gates's Regiments. *O.R.*, 8:308, 312, 322, 325, 327; Shea & Hess, 188–189.

136. After the Confederates broke the Union center and left, the rebels looted the Union camp and the tavern, thus momentarily breaking the momentum of their charge. Meanwhile, Guibor's Battery moved up and placed their guns in front of the tavern and began firing on the newly forming Union line. Finally, after about thirty minutes, the various rebel commanders reestablished control over their troops and renewed their attack. Into the thicket, south of the tavern, went the Confederate right and center. Curtis for his part hurried up troops to support Carr's hard pressed Unionists. Portions of the Second Missouri and Twenty-fifth Illinois Infantries and eight guns from the Second and Fourth Ohio Batteries established his final line on the southern side of Ruddick's field, even as Carr's command came rushing back across the field. Shea & Hess, 191–195, 204.

137. A Missouri Minuteman, John Rockham "Rock" Champion organized St. Louis Volunteer Militia companies in early 1861. Champion was absent from his unit when it was captured at Camp Jackson on May 10, 1861. He later fought at Wilson's Creek, Lexington, and Pea Ridge, leading a company in the Sixth Division, MSG. On March 25, 1862, he joined the Confederate Service and was later elected captain of Company K, Second Missouri Cavalry. He was a daring and reckless cavalryman and died, shot in the head, on August 30, 1862, while leading a charge into Bolivar, Tennessee. *O.R.*, vol. 17,

any country it is worthy of detailed description. The entire Confederate line was charging up to the Elkhorn Tavern. Col. Carr, the Federal cavalry commander, had withdrawn his command from the bench of the mountain on the Confederate right. The Illinois battery, at first planted in the horse lot west of the tavern, had limbered to the rear and taken a new position in the field.[138] The Federal mountain howitzer battery[139] had also moved away. The Eighth Iowa Battery, which had poured such a hot fire down the road upon Guibor and Gorham, had by this time lost the use of two of its guns, dismounted by the fire of Guibor's Battery, but continued to fight its two remaining guns until the Confederate regiment of Col. "Clint" Burbage[140] was upon them, when, their horses being killed, that regiment took them in, and at nightfall brought them down the road. To the left, on the Van Winkle Road, the batteries of Emmett MacDonald, Bledsoe and Wade had been engaged in a severe artillery duel, in which the Federal batteries held their own until the Confederate infantry got within range, when they were forced back, leaving two guns captured by Rains's men, led by the gallant O'Kane. The cavalry on the extreme left under Gen. John B. Clark and Col. Robert McCullough,[141] had turned the Federal right wing, and the latter's entire line was falling back to meet reinforcements hurrying to their assistance from Sugar Creek, on their left rear. The Federals placed eighteen or twenty guns to command the tavern.[142] Guibor moved up with the Confederate line, or a little in advance, and formed in battery in the narrow road in front of the tavern, losing several horses in the movement, and now commenced a hot fight. The rapid fire of twenty pieces of Federal artillery, and not "one thin red line," but three or four heavy blue ones, commenced wavering and balking in his front, while the two guns were replying with grape and canister. Now came the crisis. A regiment of United States infantry[143] moved

---

pt. 1:120; *O.R.S.*, pt. 2, vol. 38:145, 165–166; Anderson, *Memoirs*, 215; Peterson, 183; Snead, 110.

138. Wilson was referring to the First Iowa Artillery. There were no Illinois batteries on this portion of the battlefield during the first day. *O.R.*, 8:265–266; Shea & Hess, 178.

139. This was a two-gun section of 12-pound mountain howitzers from William D. Bowen's Missouri Cavalry Battalion. *O.R.*, 8:270.

140. Wilson was referring to John Q. Burbridge's Missouri Regiment. The Battery was the Third Iowa Artillery. A review of various sources, including the *Official Records* and *Supplement to the Official Records*, reveals that only one gun in the Third Iowa Artillery was disabled during the battle, while another three pieces of the Third Iowa were captured. *O.R.*, 8:268–269; *O.R.S.*, pt. 2, vol. 15:542; pt. 2, vol. 19:440, 458; pt. 2 vol. 50:374–375, 387; Byers, 601; Shea & Hess, 189–191.

141. The cavalry on the Confederate left consisted of Cearnal's First Cavalry Regiment, Fifth Division, MSG and Robert McCulloch's Cavalry Battalion. Shea & Hess have mistakenly placed Gates's Missouri Cavalry Regiment and Shelby's Missouri Company on the far left of the Confederate line, but according to Henry Little's account of the battle, Gates's command was part of the charge that overwhelmed the Union center at Elkhorn Tavern. *O.R.*, 8:308, 317, 329; Shea & Hess, 198.

142. The final Federal line, in Ruddick's field, consisted of thirteen guns from four batteries "that had escaped capture or that had departed earlier to replenish their ammunition." Additionally, as the sun was fading, another eight guns from the Second and Fourth Ohio Artilleries arrived and helped stem the final rebel assault. *O.R.*, 8:200–201; Shea & Hess, 195–196, 204.

143. The incident that Wilson describes occurred late in the day on March 7, after the rebels had taken Elkhorn Tavern. The Union regiments in that area were the Ninth Iowa and Thirty-fifth Illinois Infan-

out of the timber on the left front of the guns, about 100 yards distant, with a small field intervening with the fences around it levelled to the ground. On Guibor's right was the tavern, on left a blacksmith's shop and in the lot some corn cribs. Behind these buildings Champion had placed his company of cavalry to protect their horses from the thickly flying bullets. Rock's quick eye saw the bayonets as they were pushing through the brush, and riding up, yelled in his rough-and-ready style, "Guibor, they're flank'n you!" "I know it but I can't spare a gun to turn on them," was the reply, pulling a handful of hair from his head in desperation, as there was no supporting infantry on his left. "By d—— I'll save you," said Rock. "How?" "I'll charge them!" This meant to attack a full regiment of infantry, advancing in line, 700 or 800 strong, with twenty-two men. Was anything more daring and apparently rash ever undertaken in battle? But Champion possessed the instinct of a born cavalry leader, and besides, his friend, his "fighting partner" was doomed to capture unless instant help was given. His quick brain reasoned; "It's a full regiment, consequently a new one; my men have been there before, and will go to h—— with me; they can't see us, and we can jump right onto them and they'll think we've got a thousand men." (These are Rock's own words, in relating the affair a short time after the battle.) Galloping back a few paces to his little band, his clear ringing voice could be heard by friend and enemy: "Battalion, forward, trot; march; gallop, march; charge," and with a wild yell, in they went, their gallant chief in the lead closely followed by "Saber Jack" Murphy,[144] an old regular dragoon, Fitzsimmons, Coggins, O'Flaherty, Pomeroy and the others.[145] The last named were old British dragoons; three of them had ridden with the heavy squadrons at Balaclava,[146] and all well knew what was in front of them.

---

tries. There was no mention of the incident in the Union accounts of the battle and Shea & Hess do not address the issue, though they do state that the Thirty-fifth Illinois was confronting Guibor's command at that time. The only descriptions of the charge were found in rebel accounts of the battle. *O.R.*, 8:324; Banasik, *Missouri Brothers In Gray*, 26; Shea & Hess, 190, 193.

144. There were two John Murphys that ended up in the Second Missouri Cavalry (Confederate) with Rock Champion—One was born in Kentucky, which could not be "Saber Jack," and the other deserted on September 24, 1862 at Baldwin, Mississippi. The second John Murphy also seems unlikely to be Saber Jack. National Archives, Record Group M322 (roll no. 17), Confederate Compiled Service Records, Second Missouri Cavalry.

145. Of the four mentioned names no record can be found on Fitzsimmons, O'Flaherty or Pomeroy, of their service. Patrick Coggins was born in Ireland, a laborer by trade, and a resident of Syracuse, Morgan County, Missouri at the beginning of the Civil War. He joined the MSG on June 3, 1861, and later transferred to Guibor's Battery. He fought at the Battles of Boonville, Carthage, Oak Hills and Lexington before joining Champion's Company. On March 25, 1862, at Van Buren, Arkansas, Coggins entered the Confederate service in what became Company K, Second Missouri Cavalry (Confederate). Coggins was wounded three times during the war, survived, and was paroled out of the service on May 17, 1865 at Columbus, Mississippi. National Archives, Record Group M322 (roll no. 17), Confederate Compiled Service Records, Second Missouri Cavalry.

146. The Battle of Balaclava occurred on October 25, 1854, during the Crimean War between the Russians and a combined British and French force. The Russian command attacked Balaclava in an attempt to break the allies' siege of Sebastopol. The Russian attack was foiled, but ensuing orders sent the "Light Brigade" on their famous charge. In the end the battle was a draw. The heavy unit at the battle was the Fourth Dragoons. Norman Stone and J. P. Kenyon, *The Wordsworth Dictionary of Brit-*

To falter now meant death, to charge in could bring no worse, and within thirty seconds they were right in the midst of the surprised Federal infantry, shouting, slashing, and shooting. Corporal Casey charged on foot, Guibor's two guns were at the same time turned left oblique and deluged the Federal left with canister. The result was precisely what Champion had foreseen and proved his reckless charge was directed by good judgement. The attack was a clear surprise, the result a stampede. The infantry fired an aimless scattered volley, then expecting a legion of horseman to fall on them, fled in confusion. Champion did not follow. Knowing when to stop as well as when to commence, he secured their flag, and quickly returned to the battery which he had saved, with a loss of only three of his gallant rough riders—two killed outright, whose names are forgotten, and Pomeroy, mortally wounded, died that night in the tavern.[147]

If this exploit was equalled by either side during our four years of hard fighting, or if it has ever been excelled in any war, the writer does not find it recorded. The simple facts seem like fiction, but they can be vouched for by several eye witnesses, now members of your society.

(Gallant, warm-hearted, faithful Rock Champion! When he finally went down leading this same devoted company in a charge near Bolivar, Tenn., bitter tears filled the eyes of many a hardened veteran, and the general expression was, "too brave to live long." How he was loved was shown by the conduct three of his men, who dismounted under a heavy fire to bring off his dead body. One was killed dead; the second wounded; but the third—brave old Coggins—balanced the lifeless body across his saddle and got safely off with it.)[148]

At this time a frightful accident occurred in the battery. In turning the pieces to the left to second Rock's charge, they were brought into the echelon formation. As the rear gun was discharged, Harry Gillespie, a brave Wheeling (W. Va.) boy, who was No. 1 on the front gun, thinking it was his own gun which had been discharged, jumped in and inserted his sponge-staff in the muzzle just as No. 4 pulled the lanyard. He was blown from the gun, horribly mangled.[149]

The movements were opportunely seconded by Gen. Slack's command, which had just got into line on the Van Winkle Road, some distance to the left of the guns. They fired a heavy volley into the woods at the critical moment, and this

---

*ish History* (Hertfordshire, England, 1994), 27–28.

147. According to General Frost's account of the incident, Champion did not capture the colors of the Federal regiment, but he did inflict six to eight casualties on the bluecoats, with the loss of two men wounded. *O.R.*, 8:324.

148. Coggins was wounded in the hand on the same day that Champion was killed, probably in the same charge. Officially the wound occurred at Middlesburg, Tennessee, on August 30, 1862, which was part of the "Operations on the Mississippi Central Railroad." The actual incident occurred at Bolivar, Tennessee. *O.R.*, vol. 17, pt. 1:43, 51, 120; *O.R.S.*, pt. 2, vol. 38:145, 165–166; National Archives, Record Group M322 (roll no. 17), Confederate Compiled Service Records, Second Missouri Cavalry.

149. According to William Bull, of Guibor's Battery, the injured man was "Louie Gilespie" not Harry. Bull recorded that Gilespie lost part of his skull and one of his arms to the blast. Gilespie was carried to the hospital, where he was left alive, as the battery left the area on March 8. Latter, in the article, Wilson will call Harry Gillespie "Larry Gillispie." Banasik, *Missouri Brothers in Gray*, 26.

lucky combination of attacks was more than those brave boys in blue could stand. They broke and fled in confusion, many throwing away their arms.

Gen. Slack was killed in this advance.[150]

The Federal commander, Gen. Curtis, while trying in person to check this retrogression of his lines, narrowly escaped injury, his orderly being killed and several of his attendants wounded.[151] The firing continued about half an hour, when Gen. Curtis reformed his line far out in the open. This was sensible, for it had been demonstrated that, while long range Springfield rifles could not cope with double-barrelled shotguns, loaded with buck-shot at close quarters in the underbrush, the latter had no show whatever over 400 or 500 yards in open fields.

Gen. Price had less than 1,700 bayonets in his entire command, but wished to charge with them; but Gen. Van Dorn refused, saying he did not wish such brave men killed.

Little's brigade was now posted on the mountain to the right. Bledsoe's battery was placed in the horse-lot previously occupied by the Illinois battery and Clark's battery was formed in the small field to the left of Guibor's southeast from the tavern. Guibor's guns were advanced a short distance up the road. On the left, on the Van Winkle Road, MacDonald's and Wade's batteries occupied the old field they had been shelling during the day. Gen. Price's men now held the identical line on which the Federals were formed in the morning.

The sun went down behind Little Mountain, red and angry, and the smoke of battle hung in palls over the low places and gathered amidst the dark brown trees at the base of the mountains. Save the cries and groans of the wounded, lying where they fell, the blue and grey mingled together, there was silence over the field. No exulting cheer, no answering shout of defiance, but the grim warriors of each side sank down to rest on the chill ground, and night spread her dark mantle over the fearful scene.

## Elkhorn Tavern

was a neat hostelry that afforded rest and shelter to the Wire Road travellers. It was two stories high, with a double porch in front, containing four rooms, with a long back area way or dinning room. A small building was used as a kitchen; underneath was a large cellar. The house had a good rock foundation, and in the center of the comb of the roof stood a large pair of elk horns, placed there by old Uncle Joe Robinson, who, away back in the forties, had shot the elk not far from

---

150. Not true. Slack was mortally wounded between noon and 1:00 p.m. *O.R.*, 8:312; Bearss, "First Day At Pea Ridge," 139; Shea & Hess, 175.

151. As night was setting in, a member of Company D, Bowen's Missouri Cavalry U.S. (Curtis's escort) was killed—decapitated; while one of Curtis's orderlies and General Asboth were both wounded. *O.R.*, 8:201; John D. Crabtree, "Recollections of the Pea Ridge Campaign, and the Army of the Southwest, in 1862," *Military Essays and Recollections. Papers Read Before the Commandery of the State of Illinois, Military Order of the Loyal Legion of the United States* (Chicago, 1899; 70 vols., reprint ed. Wilmington, NC, 1992), 12:214, 220 (hereafter cited as *MOLLUS*).

that spot. The tavern was snugged in on a point in the southeast corner of Big Mountain as the hill was called, and on a summit of a gradual rise from the hollow, where was located the tan-yard. Back of the tavern rises the bluff, and south is a plain of undulating fields, stretching some miles toward Sugar Creek, and alternating with prairies and timber, southwest to Bentonville. This is called "Pea Ridge," and the two hills, Big and Little mountain are merely large knobs on this ridge. It is walled in on the south by "Nubbin Ridge," towering over which, on a clear day, can be seen peeks of Boston Mountains, fifty miles distant.

The "Wire" or Springfield and Fayetteville Road runs north and south, directly in front of the tavern, and Bentonville and Van Winkle Road comes from the southwest, around the southern base of Big Mountain, crosses the wire road in front of the tavern and runs due east.

The prominent features of the tavern were two large rock chimneys, one on each end, in the capacious fireplaces of which the old brass-mounted andiron[152] and huge backlog added to the travellers comfort. The size of these chimneys is shown by one of them having, at a latter period, served as a hiding place for Capt. Peal (now living at Avoca), who being surprised by Federal cavalry, ascended the chimney, the rough stones afforded him a foot hold, and remained there twenty-four hours, when, finding his unwelcomed company intended staying longer, he slipped down, donned a blue coat, and walking, through his sleeping enemies, escaped. The tavern was burned down a few months before the close of the war.[153]

After the firing ceased the writer entered the tavern. Here was a scene he hoped he would never witness again. As the tavern was in the center of the Federal lines in the morning, they had converted it into a hospital. Its five rooms contained sixty wounded men, two-thirds of them Federals, and as fast as one answered to his last roll-call his body was removed and his place filled by another sufferer. Four surgeons—three Federals and one Confederate—were busy, and kindness and sympathy replaced the fierce passion and hate of battle.

Poor Larry Gillespie was lying on a blanket in fearful agony. Both arms were shot away, both legs broken, and a ragged wound across the face had destroyed his sight. He bore his suffering bravely, and was cursing a wounded Federal who, shot in the femora, with thigh-bone broken, was screaming so loudly his own surgeon had him removed to the hospital in the tan-yard hollow, and while being carried there his cries could be heard all over the field. Larry was alternately cursing and comparing this poor fellow's fate with his own. Pomeroy was also lying there, with his entrails protruding from a large wound in the abdomen. Both died before morning.[154]

---

152. Andiron: "Either of a pair of metal supports with ornamented front uprights, used to hold the wood in a fireplace." Guralnik, 51.
153. Elkhorn Tavern did not survive the war, being burnt in late 1862. It was rebuilt in 1885, burnt again, and rebuilt for the current National Battlefield Park. Shea & Hess, 327, 329.
154. According to William Bull, Gillespie was still alive when the command departed the area on March 8. Banasik, *Missouri Brothers in Gray*, 26.

The wounded of both sides were still lying thickly around, in the woods down by the road and down by the spring. Broken down wagons and dismounted cannon, dead horses and small arms thickly strewn the around, with the numerous killed of both sides, told of a terrible conflict.

During all this high carnival of death, Mrs. Cox, owner of the tavern, her son Joe, and his wife and sister-in-law were lying terrified in the cellar, though Joe most of the time had his head stuck up through the cellar door or out of the window, viewing the battle. Hundreds of bullets and grape and canister had struck the house on all sides, but only one cannon ball. This entered near a second-story window, striking one of the large studdings, and glancing down through the floor, spent its force in the hearth of the south fireplace. Mr. Cox still has the shell in his possession. It was evidently from Guibor's battery, as they were in line with the house.

During the night Capt. Guibor, who had a good idea of the general position, ordered the writer's pieces to a knoll to the right rear, where it commanded the tan-yard hollow, looking south, to prevent any flanking movement by the base of the mountain.

This gun, the tavern and south end of the hill were directly in line and range of the rifled Federal battery, as afterward appeared. About 10 o'clock Col. Chas. Blser [Biser][155] brought up part of the ordnance train, but owning to the retreat of McCulloch's men many wagons failed to arrive and there was a scant supply of ammunition for both infantry and artillery.[156] Our guns got fifteen rounds only. Some forage was found, horses fed and their harness loosened up to give them some rest. A small fire was started, screened by blankets to prevent interference

---

155. Charles T. Biser or Byser not Blser (this was probably a misprint in the newspaper) was born about 1838, a resident of St. Louis (Biser's service record has him a resident of Frederick County, Missouri), a civil engineer by profession, and a member of the "Old National Guard" of the St. Louis Militia prior to the Civil War. At the beginning of the war, Biser served under MSG Quartermaster General James Harding—position unknown. During the Battle of Pea Ridge, Biser served as a civilian aid to Colonel Little. He later joined the Confederate Army as a lieutenant in Company A, Lawther's First Missouri Partisan Regiment and was noted for bravery against Union forces in early August 1862. Captured in Osage County on September 1, 1862, while on recruiting service, Biser was sent to Gratiot Street Prison, in St. Louis. He was transferred to Alton Prison on January 7, 1863, and to Camp Chase, Ohio on January 30. Exchanged on March 28, 1863, at City Point, Virginia, Biser returned briefly to the Trans-Mississippi in April, 1863, and on December 8 was ordered to Richmond, Virginia for duty with the Quartermaster Department. Biser was reassigned to the post of Oxford, Mississippi, as its commander, on August 2, 1864, a position he held in late 1864. Final disposition unknown. *O.R.,* Index, 79, 1120, 1138; *O.R.,* 8:312; 13:200; vol. 39, pt. 2:748, 811, 889; Eakin, *Missouri Prisoners of War,* "Biser, Charles T." entry; McGhee, *Service With the Guard,* 39; "Old National Guard," Missouri Militia Papers; National Archives, Record Group M322 (roll no. 71), Confederate Compiled Service Records, Lawther's Partisan Regiment.

156. According to Van Dorn, D. H. Maury and Shea & Hess, Price's command received no ammunition during the night of March 7–8. Maury wrote: "The ammunition of the troops in action was exhausted, and to our dismay, when the reserve train of ammunition was sought for, it could not be found. The prudent and intelligent officer in charge of it had sent if off beyond Bentonville, about fifteen miles, and the enemy lay between." *O.R.,* 8:284; Maury, 188; Shea & Hess, 214.

by some meddling officer more than from the eyes of the enemy, and the boys prepared supper from the plentiful supply of sutler's stores which Champion's men had captured and divided with them. A large tin dish-pan served as a coffee-pot, and with ham, hardtack and cigars, matters assumed a more comfortable subject. "Abe," the prisoner, superintended making the coffee.

The boys had captured a mail-bag and amused themselves reading the letters, which were often peculiar. Some were from sons to parents, others to sweethearts and wives, and many contained money.

The Federal Prisoner.

After lunch "Abe" was sent with the caisson to the battery and lay down to sleep. Toward morning the captain heard a noise among the horses and a strange voice quieting them. He went over and asking whose there and what's the row, was answered, "Everything is all right now and its only me." "Well, who's me?" "I, sir, am the Federal prisoner." The captain was amused. Here was a Confederate battery on a battlefield, guarded solely by a Federal prisoner, all the men sound asleep. Abe could have walked up the road 400 or 500 yards and joined his own people.

Towards morning the sound of axes and rumble of wheels could be heard opposite our right. Gen. Curtis was preparing to cut his way out. Sigel realized from the pressure of McCulloch's men, had brought up his troops and the rifle battery (Welfley's)[157] which had done such service on Little Mountain, was placed on a commanding knoll in the field, behind their infantry. During the night two caissons and the captain of an Ohio battery drove into our lines and were captured.[158]

In the morning Little's brigade, on the right of the tavern and across the south end of Big Mountain, opened the ball by an advance down to the peach orchard, where the Federal left wing met them and a heavy fight ensued. The top of the mountain was swept by the rifled battery, which was well hauled, but the Confederates, sheltered by the brow of the hill and concealed by the thick brush, suffered little. The rifled battery's[159] line of fire was partly across the base of the mountain,

---

157. Welfley's Independent Battery of Light Missouri Artillery was organized on September 30, 1861 (Dyer says September 25) in St. Louis. The battery contained six guns: two 12-pound guns and four 12-pound howitzers and was commanded by Martin Welfley. Pea Ridge was the command's only major engagement, before it was reorganized in December 1862, and became Battery B, First Missouri Light Artillery Regiment. At the Battle of Pea Ridge one of the 12-pound howitzers was absent from the command. *O.R.*, 8:236; *O.R.S.*, pt. 2 vol. 36:157; F. H. Dyer, *A Compendium of the War of the Rebellion* (Des Moines, 1908; reprint ed. Dayton, OH, 1978), 1313, 1320, hereafter cited as Dyer.
158. Partially true. During the night, Corporal Conrad Ebner with three privates and one caisson from the Fourth Ohio Artillery, was sent to fill the chests with ammunition. Unfortunately they got lost during the night, drove up the main road into the rebel camp, which gladly took in the errant Federals and their precious ammunition for 6-pound rifled guns. *O.R.*, 8:238; *O.R.S*, pt. 2, vol. 50:387; Shea & Hess, 215.
159. On the morning of March 8, Sigel advanced his command into position on the Union left, covering the movement with the five smoothbore guns from Welfley's Battery and two 6-pound rifled guns from Hoffman's Fourth Ohio Artillery, commanded by Lieutenant Max Frank. *O.R.*, 8:214, 237–238; *O.R.S.*, pt. 2, vol. 50:387.

over the tavern and down the hollow where the single gun was posted. The boys at the gun, sound asleep, were rudely awaken by the shrill scream of a shell and a loud explosion in their midst. A rifled shell had passed over our infantry on the hill and struck the log behind which we were sleeping, burst, scattered dirt and splinter around promiscuously. A fragment struck the dish-pan, knocking sugar, coffee, ham and crackers into a cocked hat. The first impression was that the limber was blown up. Directly another shell came the same way, and yet another, all striking close to the gun. The limber was moved to the right and down the hill, out of the line, but not out of danger. The gun had to remain where it was ordered, and every minute or two a shell came down the hollow, some low, some high, cutting limbs from the trees. Another shell struck the log, and something had to be done, as to stay there and be knocked out in the cold blood was out of the question. The order was to open fire when it was necessary, and this now seemed to be the very quintessence of necessity. A shell and a fuse gouge was brought from the limber, and, watch in hand, the writer waited for the next shot. He knew that sound travelled 1,100 feet per second, and that the initial velocity of those shells ought to be about 1,400 feet, and tried to note the interval between the arrival of the sound of discharge and the shell. A shell was bored at four seconds, rammed home, and old Betty sent her compliments over to the boys on the other side. The result was three savage shots in return, passing close overhead. Several shells were sent, cut at four seconds, with no apparent effect. The greater "remaining" velocity of a missile from a rifled gun had not been allowed for and our shell burst short. About this time a dapper-looking officer galloped up and yelled out, "You're throwing shells among our own men; and what the h—— is going on here, anyway?" He was told to hold on a little and he would find out what was going on, and soon he was eminently satisfied, for another ringtail squealer came along, struck the ground, exploded and threw a bushel or two of dirt over the seeker for information, causing his horse to rear, and he lost his hat. Another shell bursting overhead completed the demoralization, and our friend spurred away, leaving his hat, which old Dennis O'Brien[160] instantly put on, saying, "Begob, he have a fine hat anyway."

The gent evidently came up to put on a little style, as we could see our shells passed a good sixty feet over and to the left of our men on the hill. A shell was now bore at past five seconds, and a double charge of powder used to send it on its mis-

---

160. Dennis O'Brien was a member of the pre-war Washington Guards, St. Louis, Militia. He joined the rebel cause on December 13, 1861, at Memphis, Tennessee, probably Guibor's Battery. This coincides with the arrival of steamer *Iatan* with 63 exchanged prisoners, who were captured at Camp Jackson on May 10, 1861. The *Iatan* transported the prisoners from St. Louis to Columbus, Kentucky, where they were transferred to a Confederate steamer. After a short stay at Columbus the men moved on to Memphis where they formed Guibor's Battery. O'Brien was later listed as a member of the First Missouri Field Battery (Confederate)—Westly Robert's command. He was paroled out of the service on June 1, 1865, at Alexandria, Louisiana, still a member of First Missouri Field Battery. Banasik, *Missouri Brothers in Gray*, 16, 19; "Washington Guards," Missouri Militia Scrapbook, page 17 of unnumbered pages; National Archives, Record Group M322 (roll no. 83), Confederate Compiled Service Records, First Missouri Field Battery.

sion. Relief came at last. From that time the enemy's fire was wild, and beyond an occasional low shot, all was well. Old Betty continued to answer back at intervals with sullen defiance. How she had escaped being dismounted, Providence alone could tell. Nineteen shells had struck within forty feet each side, many of them not over five feet high. Many struck in front and bounded over, bursting as they went by, and one rolled under the gun and stopped, when all hands made a dive for cover. The peaky black chunk of iron and lead commanded great respect for a few minutes, when, seeing it wouldn't "go off," it was placed in the limber as a memento. It was a James rifle shell.

During the night Gen. Curtis held a council of war, and it was decided to concentrate on the Wire Road and the tavern, and in case of failure to move out by their left flank over the mountain by a road then being cut over by its southwest end.[161] Little's brigade held its southeast end. At daylight the Federal infantry was formed three ranks deep across the fields, with batteries on the knolls in the rear, and Gen. Carr's cavalry in the woods, near Pratt's store, the Federal left wing resting on the space formed by the two spurs of the hill.[162] The Thirty-second Illinois was thrown upon the western spur. Gen. Little's Confederates charged down to the peach orchard, dislodging the Federal there, who re-formed 400 yards to the rear, and Little drew his men to the rear of the tavern, out of ammunition.[163] Capt. Hiram Bledsoe's battery had expended its last cartridge, Bledsoe having fired away his spare trace-chains and blacksmith tools, and Old Sacramento ceased to bellow. Guibor's pieces, on the left of the tavern, maintained a stubborn fire. Churchill Clark, the boy captain (19 years old) had been killed while sitting on his horse bravely directing his gunners where to fire, and his battery was ordered off the field.

161. Not true. During the night Curtis issued orders to his four divisions to redeploy for the morning battle, with General Sigel given command of the Union left, where the road for a retreat was supposedly cut. Of Curtis's main commanders it appears that only a despondent General Asboth was for cutting their way out through the enemy and "save by this if not the whole at least the greater part of our surrounded army." Curtis ignored Asboth's repeated requests, feeling confident that the morning would bring victory. About 2:00 a.m. on March 8, Sigel's command arrived in the vicinity of Pratt's store, supposedly moving to the Union left via his old camp at Sugar Creek, where he intended to get food for his men. Curtis halted the movement and had Sigel send for the food. Shea & Hess have Curtis meeting with Sigel during the night; however, General Sigel stated in his recollections of the battle that he never met with Curtis during the night nor was there any council of war. Instead, Sigel sent Captain Amussen to report his command present to Curtis, who gave no orders to Sigel for the coming battle. Sigel's command remained stationary through the night and finally completed their march to the Union left beginning at 6:30 a.m. on March 8. *O.R.*, 8:201; Sigel, 1:327; Shea & Hess, 217–22.
162. The Union right was held by Carr's Fourth Division; Davis's Third Division was placed in the right center and Sigel's two divisions held the left; Osterhaus's First Division was on the far left and Asboth's Second Division was positioned in the left center. Union cavalry was deployed on the two flanks; the Third Illinois and Third Iowa Cavalries were on Carr's right while the remaining Union cavalry covered Sigel's flank. Shea & Hess, 229.
163. The Thirty-second Illinois Infantry was not present at the Battle of Pea Ridge. Wilson probably meant the Twenty-fifth Illinois Infantry, which Sigel advanced to cover his artillery which was deploying to the west of the Telegraph Road. As the battle advanced on the eighth, the Twenty-fifth Illinois with the Twelfth Missouri Infantry moved into the wooded area occupied by Little's Brigade, where the two commands became engaged. *O.R.*, 8:215, 220, 222–223, 229.

Clark's section was replaced by a section of Emmett MacDonald's guns, whose battery had been in action all the day before on the left, and was admirably handled by that gallant and daring officer.

When the troops were falling back, MacDonald's color-bearer was shot, and Capt. Emmett, missing his colors, rode back in the face of a sharp artillery and musketry fire and found them leaning against a tree, where the bearer had left them. He waved the flag defiantly and galloped back to his company unhurt.

Clark's men and horses were badly shot up. Soon Gorham's battery, leaving behind them their old iron guns came along, bringing the brass pieces previously captured from the enemy,[164] and then Wade's battery moved down the road, all passing northward to the rear. Emmett MacDonald's and part of Bledsoe's batteries, with some infantry moved to the east on the Van Winkle Road.[165] Guibor's caissons and one gun now came down, under Lieut. Corkory, who was ordered to move his section to the tan-yard hollow; but as our gun was concealed from his view by the brush, and seeing some brass pieces farther down, he concluded we had proceeded him, under Lieut. Harrington. But that officer had taken the canteens and gone to the spring for water, some three hours before, and we did not see him again until reaching Van Buren, when he resigned and went home. Our swing-team driver went to look for him when that spent shell rolled under the gun and also forgot to return.

---

164. Not true. The only mention of Gorham's Battery, in the *Official Records,* taking on captured guns comes from Major D. H. Lindsay, commander of the Sixth Division, MSG. On March 8, according to Lindsay, Gorham "returned to the battle ground in the face of the enemy, and under the heavy fire of their guns, and brought off a 12-pounder howitzer that had been captured from the enemy." Lindsay makes no mention of Gorham leaving behind any of his guns or the complete exchange of Gorham's four 6-pounder iron guns. Overall, the complete exchange of Gorham's guns for the captured ones, did not happen as the same iron guns were present in the command on March 17, 1862. In addition to the one gun that Gorham's command dragged off the battlefield, John T. Hughes's Battalion brought off another two pieces, which places further doubt into Wilson's claim that Gorham's Battery was completely exchanged. However, this might explain why Curtis would later claim the capture of five pieces of Confederate artillery, while losing none of his own. A newspaper correspondent with Curtis's command sheds further light on the captured guns, recording that the Twelfth Missouri Infantry captured three guns in a charge, while another was "taken in the timber near by, and still another spiked piece" was found on the extreme right of the battlefield. Overall, it appears that the Confederates simply abandoned four old iron guns, from assorted batteries, while the fifth piece was lost, according to Van Dorn, on the retreat after it became disabled and was thrown into a ravine. *O.R.,* 8:195, 285, 315, 322, 788; "New-York 'Herald' Narrative," *Rebellion Record,* 4:258.

165. The bulk of the Confederate Army, that fought at Elkhorn on March 8, retreated on the Van Winkle–Huntsville Road. Heading north were the First Arkansas Mounted Rifles, the Seventeenth Arkansas Infantry and three companies of Burbridge's Second Missouri Infantry. Additionally, the bulk of the rebel artillery—nine batteries—headed north, including Clark's, Bledsoe's, Gorham's, Guibor's, Tull's, Wade's, Gaine's, Hart's and Good's commands. Contrary to what Shea & Hess recorded, Wilson has Bledose's battery moving East, down the Van Winkle–Huntsville Road. *O.R.S.,* pt. vol. 2:594; Shea & Hess, 240–242, 249, 252.

## An Eccentric Retreat.

Although our gun was screened from the sight of those passing down the road, we could see all that was passing, and when a battery went by at a gallop we thought some flank attack had been ordered. Lieut. Al Glanville of Bledsoe's battery, wounded in the leg by a spent grape-shot, rode up to see what we were doing and, telling us the artillery was ordered off the field, suggested the propriety of getting out of there, which advice was adopted instanter. As we moved out we saw scattered infantry falling back through the woods and down the road. Seated by the roadside was Kirk Anderson,[166] who waved his hat and told the writer to "git." Poor Kirk, unable to get up, was soon after passed by a regiment of Federal cavalry, and afterwards bitterly complained that they didn't even notice him.

When our gun reached the turn of the hollow, a confused mass of horsemen, wagons, and batteries could be seen a half mile in front and, moving a few hundred yards farther, on looking back, a column of United States cavalry was seen emerging from the hollow and forming in line. Capture now seemed certain. The gun detachment now consisted of four cannoneers and two drivers. The gun was unlimbered, prolongs fixed, and a shell fired at the pursuing cavalry. It seemed to explode in their front, and threw them into confusion; after a short drive another shell was fired. Some infantry came from our hill, followed by some cavalry. An excited officer, carrying a flag, halted, struck the staff on the ground, called on all to rally and die by it, then spurred away. A few men made a weak attempt to form by the flag, but the glittering steel of the dark blue cavalry looked too formidable and they passed on.[167]

The only remaining shell in the limber was now cut, the gun loaded, and the last representatives of Guibor's St. Louis battery and the last shot of the battle of Elkhorn was sent screaming and hissing back to the following horsemen.

It afterwards transpired that the Federal cavalry commander seeing this gun open fire, and the flag, and the numerous stragglers in the brush on either side, feared an ambuscade, and reversed his head of column. This gave those in front a little time to straighten out, an operation already accelerated by the firing. The flag was thrown on the limber, a cannoneer placed in the empty saddle and on a brisk gallop soon over took the battery.

---

166. Kirk Anderson joined what became Company A, Third Missouri Infantry Regiment (Confederate) on December 26, 1861. He served most of his time detached from his company, performing the duty as a clerk. In April 1863, he was transferred to the Windsor's Guard, a cavalry unit in General Price's Escort. There was no further record found of Anderson after his transfer. McGhee, *Service With the Guard*, 34; National Archives, Record Group M322 (roll no. 113), Confederate Compiled Service Record, Third Missouri Infantry.

167. According to W. L. Truman, of Wade's Missouri Battery, the excited officer was General Albert Pike. The flag that was abandoned, according to Shea & Hess, belonged to the Seventeenth Arkansas Infantry, and was saved by Rives's Missouri Regiment. However, Truman stated that Frank Dye, of Wade's Battery secured the abandoned flag. Eventually the flag was returned to the Seventeenth, though "it required the emphatic terms of two special orders from Gen. Van Dorn" to get the flag back from the Missourians. Cabell, 173; McGhee, *Service With the Guard*, 77; Shea & Hess, 254–255; Truman, 28.

Capt. Guibor was making a vain attempt to halt the scattered infantry to form a rear guard, and asked the captain of another battery which had ammunition, for two guns, which request was refused.

The brave Rock Champion, who with his company had voluntarily continued with Guibor, had his men deployed halting stragglers.

Gen. Albert Pike with about 150 men was along and Guibor asked him to take command, but he declined the honor and turned off to the left.[168]

All of Gen. Price's artillery, except Bledsoe's and MacDonald's batteries, was now marching due north towards Missouri, while Van Dorn with those batteries and the infantry had drawn off east by the Van Winkle Road, and Curtis was between.[169]

Gen. Martin Green, who had been left at Sugar Creek with 3,000 men to guard the trains,[170] fell back by the Bentonville road.

Col. John S. Mellon[171] had 140 wagons, now empty from their stores, having been served out. He turned his column back, and at Sugar Creek found a large quantity of stores hastily abandoned by two other commissaries. He loaded them up and carried them safely to Van Buren without the loss of a single wagon.

Capt. Guibor had received orders on the field from Van Dorn to march north on the Keitsville road and take the first left-hand road for the Indian Nation. This order, after careful consideration, he disobeyed and took a right-hand road through

168. Even while the Confederate retreat was in progress, General Pike received no information as to the status of the battle and that which he did receive only told of the Union advance. Pike followed along with the retreating troops, and, according to his report, he tried several times to cover the retreat with artillery or some of the scattered troops who were present—all to no avail. Believing that the retreating army would head down the Bentonville detour, back towards Camp Stephens, Pike left the main road and headed cross country in an attempt to get to the head of the retreating column. When Pike got to the top of a hill, he looked about, and to his dismay, saw that the retreating column was heading north toward Springfield, being pursued by Federal cavalry. Pike gave up the chase and headed down the Bentonville detour and did not catch the head of the retreating column in that quarter until he reached Elm Springs on March 9. Proceeding back toward the Indian Territory, Pike linked up with his brigade at Cincinnati on the border of the Indian Territory. *O.R.*, 8:291–292; Duncan, 220–223; W. Craig Gaines, *The Confederate Cherokees: John Drew's Regiment of Mounted Rifles* (Baton Rouge, 1989), 87, hereafter cited as Gaines; Shea & Hess, 254–255.

169. According to Shea & Hess, four rebel batteries were heading east down the Van Winkle–Huntsville Road—Jackson's, Kelly's, MacDonald's and Landis's. However, Landis's Battery was not present at the battle (See Appendix A, Jackson's Artillery for a comment on Landis's Battery), and, according to Wilson, Bledsoe's Battery was heading east, not north, as stated by Shea & Hess (252).

170. Green's command consisted of 2,000 men; 650 from his Second Division, MSG and another 1,350 men (probably stragglers) from all the other MSG Divisions. See Appendix A for more details. Bevier, 96; McGhee, *Service With the Guard*, 65.

171. John S. Mellon (or Melon or Melan) was a resident of St. Louis at the beginning of the Civil War. On September 21, 1861, Mellon was appointed the Division Commissary of Subsistence for the Second Division, MSG. Mellon later joined the Confederate Service, serving on the east side of the Mississippi, where he attained the rank of major and Chief Commissary of Subsistence, First District, State of Mississippi. Labeled as "one of the most efficient officers of his department," by General James R. Chamlers, Mellon held the post of Grenada, until it fell in early 1865. *O.R.*, vol. 24, pt. 3:1009; vol. 31, pt. 3:643; vol. 32, pt. 2:523; vol. 45, pt. 1: 869; Eakin, *Confederate Records*, 5:173; Peterson, 81.

Roaring River gorge, marching around to the eastward, then southward, with all the others following, the rear guard covered by Rock Champion and rejoined Gen. Price several days later; the general, knowing Guibor's orders, had given up all hopes of his artillery escaping, and all would have certainly been taken had not the latter disobeyed orders and used his own judgement.[172]

\* \* \* \* \* \*

172. Van Dorn's army began staggering into camp, near Van Buren, Arkansas on March 11, with Van Dorn arriving on March 13. Many in the army believed the artillery to have been destroyed or captured, but such was not the case; the artillery arrived about noon on March 15. By March 18, Van Dorn reported that the "entire army" that he had marched against the enemy was now in camp. However, at least one unit, the Fifth Division, MSG, did not arrive in Van Buren until March 19. In all it took eleven days for the Army of the West to complete their retreat from the Battle of Pea Ridge. *O.R.*, 8:789–790; Martha L. Crabb, *All Afire to Fight: The Untold Tale of the Civil War's Ninth Texas Cavalry* (New York, 2000), 80, hereafter cited as Crabb; Ingenthron, 159; Lehr, *As the Mockingbird Sang*, 25; Lehr, *Fishing on Deep River*, 74; Shea & Hess, 266; Sparks, 181–182.

**Item:** An incident from the Battle of Pea Ridge concerning General James Harding, by "Old Soldier."
**Published:** August 1, 1885.

## Llewellyn Held His Mule.

The recent appearance in the *Republican* of a paper read before the Southern Historical and Benevolent Association by Gen. James Harding[173] reminds me of an "Army lyric" written by that gentleman just after the Battle of Elkhorn. General Harding was Quartermaster-general of the Missouri State Guard, having a clerk in his department, a most estimable young gentleman, whom we shall call "Llewellyn."[174] During the heat of the battle, having occasion to consult Gen. Price, Harding on his large roan horse, accompanied by his clerk on his mule, rode towards the front where Gen. Price was engaged. Leaving his horse in charge of his clerk on his mule in a valley supposed to be safe, and repaired to the general on foot. It so happened, however, that the secluded spot selected for the safety of the animals was soon hotly peppered with shot and shell, but the clerk manfully stood his ground, holding the mule and the general's charger until the general's return.

After the battle while a number of officers were sitting around a camp fire, telling their stories of the battle, Llewellyn quaintly remarked the hottest places in which he ever got, was that while he was holding that mule of his in the secluded spot where Harding left him. This remark caused much merriment, and suggested

173. James Harding was born in Boston, Massachusetts, on February 13, 1830, educated in Boston and Springfield and moved briefly to St. Louis, Missouri in 1843, where he lived with a married sister. Returning to the East, Harding attended a secondary school for a short time, before signing on as a common seaman on a voyage to California in 1849. After two years in the West, Harding returned to the east coast, where in 1851 he worked on a survey crew. Moving westward with railroad work, Harding worked on the Missouri Pacific Railroad. Harding settled in Jefferson City, Missouri, where he married in 1855. Prior to the Civil War Harding was appointed the Chief Clerk for the Missouri State Auditor and in November 1860, joined the local militia company, the "Governor's Guard." By the end of 1860 Harding was a colonel in the Missouri Militia and Inspector General of the Fifth Military District. In February 1861, Governor C. F. Jackson appointed Harding a brigadier general and Quartermaster General for the State of Missouri. Harding left the Guard in April 1862, and joined the regular Confederate army as a major and Quartermaster of Sterling Price's Division. A short time thereafter, Harding was appointed a captain of artillery and completed his military service on the east side of the Mississippi River. Paroled out of the service in May 1865, Harding spent six years in Florida, before returning to Missouri in 1871, where he again worked for the railroad. Elected as the State Railroad Commissioner, Harding served for twelve years (1876–1888), after which he was made Secretary of the Commission. He died on April 4, 1902 on Jefferson City. Hale, 131; McGhee, *Service With the Guard*, vii–x; G. A. Parsons, Typescript Report (January 18, 1861), Missouri Militia Papers.

174. Lewis D. Allen, Jr., a grocer by trade and a member of the "Old National Guard" of the St. Louis Militia, was captured at Camp Jackson on May 10, 1861. Exchanged, Allen later joined the First Rifle Regiment, Sixth Division, MSG and later Guibor's Missouri Battery, where he served until the end of the war. From July 1863, to July 1864, he was listed as a clerk in the Adjutant General's Office, District of the Gulf, in Mobile, Alabama, serving under General Maury. "List of Members of the Old National Guard," Missouri Militia Papers, Missouri Historical Society; McGhee, *Service With the Guard*, 65, 68, 81; National Archives, Record Group M322 (roll No. 86), Confederate Compiled Service Records, Bledsoe's Missouri Artillery.

to Harding a parody he wrote upon the theme long known in the army as the story of "Llewellyn Held His Mule," fragments of which I now remember and give below, hoping that some old soldier may call to mind and supply the rest of the verses.

It was in March, first month of spring,
 An army brave and strong.
At Elkhorn made the welkin ring
 With shouts both loud and long
And while the battle raged so hot,
 And fighting was the rain.
In what was thought a sheltered spot,
 Llewellyn held his mule.
He did not hold a mule alone,
 For that was duty light.
He also held a noble roan
 Whose master shared the fight.

\* \* \* \* \* \* \*

**Item:** Scalping at Pea Ridge, by E. C. Boudinot.[175]
**Published:** January 2, 1886.

## Ross's Men Did the Scalping.

Fort Smith, Ark., Dec. 29, 1885
Editor, *Republican*

Among the "Tales of the War," published weekly in the *Republican,* appears in last Saturday's issue an interesting account of the last day's battle of Pea Ridge written by my old valued friend, Wm. Fayel.[176] In referring to the alleged scalping of Union soldiers on the battlefield by Indian troops of the Confederate Army, Mr. Fayel says: "No evidence of scalping were met with, it turning out that the men scalped were already buried." In reflection to this scalping business, some years after the war the late Col. W. P. Adair[177] of the Cherokee Nation assured me at the Planters' House that Stand Watie's men actually scalped a number of soldiers at Pea Ridge. "Better for them," added the humane Adair, "because when a man is stunned, scalping him starts the blood to running, and he recovers, gets up and runs away."

Knowing Mr. Fayel as I do, I am bound to believe Col. Wm. P. Adair made

---

175. Elias Cornelius Boudinot was born in 1835, in the Cherokee Nation, near modern-day Rome, Georgia. Raised in Vermont, Boudinot was living in Arkansas at the beginning of the Civil War, where he was the senior editor for the Little Rock *True Democrat.* Aligning himself with his uncle, Stand Watie, Boudinot joined Waite's Cherokee Regiment, being appointed a major. Boudinot fought at the Battle of Pea Ridge, and left the regiment in the middle of 1862, for a seat in the Confederate Congress as a representative of the Cherokee Nation. Following the war Boudinot represented the Cherokee Nation in several treaty negotiations and spent the remaining days in Washington. Boudinot died in 1890. See Appendix B for a complete biography. *O.R.S.,* pt. 2, vol. 73: 521; Washbourne Anderson, *Life of General Stand Watie* (Pryor, OK, 1915; reprint ed, Harrah, OK, 1995), 54; "The Confederate Congress: First Congress—Second Secession," *Southern Historical Society Papers,* 47: 69, 87, 89; Edward Everett Dale and Gaston Litton, *Cherokee Cavaliers: Forty Years of Cherokee History As Told in the Correspondence of the Ridge-Watie-Boudinot Family* (Norman, OK, 1939), xviii, 4, 84, 110–111, 230, hereafter cited as Dale & Litton; Margaret Ross, *Arkansas Gazette: The Early Years 1819–1866* (Little Rock, AR, 1969), 343, hereafter cited as Ross; Charles C. Jones, "Sons of Confederate Veterans," *Southern Historical Society Papers,* 18:93; Marcus L. Wright, "Colonel Elias C. Boudinot," *Southern Bivouac,* 2:433–435, 438, 440, hereafter cited as Wright.

176. William Fayel was a newspaper correspondent for the *Daily Missouri Democrat.* He wrote a series of articles concerning Curtis's campaign in southwest Missouri and northwest Arkansas which appeared in the *Missouri Republican,* in 1885–1886, and were part of the "Tales of War." These articles will be covered in detail in a future presentation of this series. William Fayel, "From Rolla to Springfield," *Missouri Republican,* December 5, 1885.

177. William Penn Adair of the Southern Cherokee Nation was a close friend of Stand Watie, and, a member of the Treaty Party. At the beginning of the Civil War he joined Watie's First Cherokee Mounted Regiment as the unit's assistant quartermaster. On February 3, 1863, he became the colonel of the Second Cherokee Mounted Rifles and remained so until the end of the war. In June 1865, with the war ending, Adair was appointed a member of the peace treaty delegation that negotiated the end of the war for the Indian Nations. He was a close personal friend of E. C. Boudinot and described by a biographer as "a handsome man of genial disposition…and able statesman." *O.R.S.,* pt. 2, vol. 73:521, 567, 571; Anderson, *Life of Stand Watie,* 54; Dale & Gaston Litton, 108, 117, 230.

the statement above quoted; but never was uttered a more infamous slander of the brave and generous Stand Watie and his men.

If my recollection serves me, Col. Adair

# Was A Prisoner

of war at some Northern prison when the Battle of Pea Ridge was fought,[178] and consequently could not have known the truth of his statement; however that may be, the defense he made of the barbarous act is sufficient evidence that he didn't know what he was talking about. No man in his senses would have given utterances of such ghastly twaddle. There were two regiments of Cherokees[179] at the Battle of Pea Ridge, one commanded by Stand Watie, while the other was raised by the late John Ross;[180] William P. Ross,[181] who is still living, was lieutenant-colonel of this regiment.[182] Ross's regiment deserted to the Federal Army soon after the

---

178. Not true. At the time of the battle, Adair was serving as Watie's assistant quartermaster. There was no indication in the *Official Records* that Adair was ever captured or for that matter, that he was ever at the Battle of Pea Ridge. However, given the close relationship that the Watie-Adair families had, it was quite likely that Adair was present at the battle. *O.R.*, passim; Dale & Litton, 117–118.

179. The First Regiment, Cherokee Mounted Rifles was commanded by Stand Watie and organized on July 12, 1861. It was mustered into the Confederate service after the Cherokee Nation joined the Confederacy in October 1861. John Drew commanded the other Cherokee regiment also known as the First Regiment, Cherokee Mounted Rifles or "Drew's Cherokee Mounted Rifles." Drew's Regiment was organized in June 1861, but not mustered into the Confederate service until November 5, 1861. *O.R.S.*, pt. 2, vol. 73:513, 521; Crute, 124, 126–127; Gaines, 15.

180. John Ross was the Principle Chief of the Cherokee Nation. He was born at Lookout Mountain, Tennessee, on October 3, 1790, and was one-eighth Cherokee. He fought at the Battle of Horseshoe Bend, Alabama, during the Creek Indian War, 1813–1814, as an adjutant to Andrew Jackson. In 1817, Ross was elected to the Cherokee National Council and two years later became the President of the Council. From 1819 to 1839, he fought against the relocation of his tribe to Indian Territory (Oklahoma), but failed. After the tribe relocated to the Indian Territory in 1839, Ross was chosen chief of the nation. Despite the relocation of the Cherokees to the West, Ross remained a strong Union supporter with dreams of possible statehood for the Territory. When the Civil War began Ross preferred neutrality to joining the Confederacy, but following the rebel victory at Wilson's Creek, Ross agreed to a treaty with the South. Ross was captured during a Union expedition to the Indian Territory in July 1862, and sent North, never to return. He died in Washington, DC in 1866, while trying to heal the wounds of the late war. Stewart Sifakis, *Who Was Who in the Union: A Comprehensive, Illustrated Biographical Reference to More Than 1,500 of the Principal Union Participants in the Civil War* (New York, 1988), 343; Larry C. Rampp and Donald L. Rampp, *The Civil War in the Indian Territory*, (Austin, TX, 1975), 173–174, hereafter cited as Rampp.

181. William Potter Ross, the nephew of the Principal Chief of the Cherokees, John Ross, was born in 1820. Graduating from Princeton (no. 1 of 44) in 1842, William Ross returned home where he served as a clerk in the Cherokee Senate in 1843. Prior to the war, Ross lived in Fort Gibson and edited the *Cherokee Advocate* (1844–1848). Ross was elected the lieutenant colonel of Drew's Regiment in November 1861, and was captured on July 15, 1862 at Park Hill, Indian Territory. Ross did not reenter the war, even though many of his men joined the Union, but remained neutral for the remaining days of the conflict. Following the war he was elected Principal Chief of the Cherokee Nation on October 19, 1866, to serve out the term of his uncle who had just died. Ross was again elected Principal Chief in 1873, and died on July 28, 1891 at the age of seventy-one. *O.R.*, 13:161–162; Gaines, 17, 121–122.

182. At the Battle of Pea Ridge, Colonel John Drew was present and commanded the regiment with Ross as his lieutenant colonel. *O.R.*, 8: 246, 289.

battle, *en-masse*, its lieutenant-colonel joining in the stampede.[183] I have no doubt that some of Ross's men did scalp some Union soldiers on that field.[184] A rigid investigation instituted by Stand Watie and myself proved beyond question that the scalping was done by Ross's regiment, and that no member of Stand Watie's command was guilty of the disgusting barbarity. In September, 1865, at the great council of the United States commissioners and fifteen or twenty Indian tribes, convened at Fort Smith, Ark.,[185] I held sworn documentary testimony not only that

## The Scalping Was Done

by Ross's regiment, but absolute proof of the very men who were guilty of the act; these men who tore the reeking scalps from dead and wounded soldiers were short-ly after mustered into the Union Army and exercised their skill in scalping rebel soldiers without exciting any loud cries of disapprobation from the Northern press.

---

183. Drew's regiment disbanded, surrendered, deserted, or was captured as the case may be, between July 4–15, 1862. On July 4, four hundred men of Drew's Regiment arrived at Round Grove, Indian Territory, where they surrendered to Federal authorities. Similarly, another 200 were "captured" with William P. Ross on July 15 at Park Hill, which effectively destroyed the command. Thomas C. Hind-man, the Confederate commander of the area at the time, simply labeled Drew's men as deserters. *O.R.*, 13:40, 161–162; Banasik, *Reluctant Cannoneer*, 46.

184. A total of eight Union soldiers from the Third Iowa Cavalry were scalped at the Battle of Pea Ridge. Of the eight, seven are known; from Company A—Carroll Foster and Elisha Hann; from Com-pany B—David Carroll and Casper French; James F. Mercer and Spencer Minor of Company D; and R. H. Williard of Company C. There was some confusion as to who actually performed the deed. Shea & Hess have Cherokees doing the deed, but don't state which command. Cunningham stated that Drew's Regiment "did the small amount of scalping in the battle." Monaghan tells a story of a Choctaw woman, who recalled "that her people mailed scalps back to friends and relatives in Mis-sissippi"—The only members of the Choctaw's present at the battle were the white troops of O. G. Welch's Squadron, who came from the First Choctaw & Chickasaw Regiment. Finally, Gaines sup-ports Monaghan's account stating "that several participants on the Union side…said that Texans not Indians, had mutilated the Union dead." *O.R.*, 8:206–207; *O.R.S.*, pt. 2, vol. 73:542–543, 549–550; Cunningham, 60; Gaines, 90; Jay Monaghan, *Civil War on the Western Border 1854–1865* (New York, 1955), 250, hereafter cited as Monaghan; "The Scalping At Pea Ridge," *Missouri Republican*, January 9, 1886; Shea & Hess, 102.

185. On September 8, 1865, a Grand Council, consisting of all the Indian tribes that supported the Confederacy, including Creek, Choctaw, Chickasaw, Seminole, Delaware, Wichita, Comanche, Great Osage, Senaca, Shawnee, Quapaw and Cherokee, met at Fort Smith to discuss the conditions upon which the Indian tribes would again enter the Union. The tribes, for their part, believed the meeting was to simply make peace with the United States, and were not prepared for any extensive negotiations on their relationship with the Federal government. After thirteen days of talks the council adjourned, with a treaty that simply ended the war between the Federal government and the various Indian tribes. The issues concerning an extensive Peace Treaty with the Federal government were tabled until the following spring when a lengthy Peace Conference was held in Washington, DC, which established a new relationship with the government. The primary provisions of the new agreement, which was signed on July 17, 1866, required the slave holding Indians to free their slaves and adopt them into their tribes with full rights to the Indian lands; Indian lands had to be forfeited to Northern friendly tribes from Kansas; and they were required to grant railroad access through their lands. Annie Heloise Abel, *The American Indian Under Reconstruction* (Cleveland, OH, 1925), 188–189; Edwin C. Bearss and Arrell M. Gibson, *Fort Smith Little Gibraltar on the Arkansas* (Norman, OK, 1969), 305–306, 308; Dale & Litton, 232–233.

Gen. [William S.] Homey [Harney],[186] Judge [Dennis N.] Cooly [Cooley][187] of Iowa, Gen. [Ely Samuel] Parker[188] of Grant's staff, Elijah Sells, now of Salt Lake, Utah, and other whose names I do not now recall[189] were commissioners on the part of the United States an this memorable council. They will each and every one bear me witness that in a speech made at that council I denounced the perpetrators of the scalping as cowards and a disgrace to the Cherokee people, and in the most positive, direct and conspicuous manner advanced to one of Ross's men sitting there in the uniform of a Union solider, charged him with being the chief of the scalping party, and dared him to deny it, shaking in his face the documentary

---

186. William S. Harney was born in Tennessee, joined the Regular Army in 1818, fought Seminoles in Florida, served in the Mexican War and combated Indians on the frontier. On June 14, 1858, he received a promotion to brigadier general in the regular army. Harney assumed command of the Department of the West, in St. Louis, on November 17, 1860. By the Civil War, Harney was one of only four general officers in the U.S. Army and expected to support the South, but he never did. St. Louis Unionists did not trust Harney and successfully had him removed from command following the Camp Jackson Affair. See Banasik, *Confederate "Tales of the War" in the Trans-Mississippi, Part One* for a complete biography. Boatner, 376; Dyer, 254; Heitman, 1:502; McElroy, 30–31; Warner, *Generals in Blue*, 208–209.

187. Dennis N. Cooley was born in New Hampshire in 1825, and moved to Iowa in 1854. President Lincoln appointed Cooley, a faithful Republican, Commissioner to South Carolina in 1864, to settle titles to cotton and land possession. With the end of the Civil War, President Johnson appointed Cooley Commissioner of Indian Affairs in 1865, primarily to provide relief for the destitute Indians in the Indian Territory. In August 1865, Cooley was assigned to the Peace Commission, at Fort Smith, serving as the body's president, and considered by the Indians to be a "most deplorable" choice. He resigned as Indian Commissioner in September 1866, following the Peace Conference in Washington, DC. Abel, *American Indian Under Reconstruction*, 174–175, 180; Dale & Litton, 239.

188. Ely Samuel Parker was born on 1828, on an Iroquois reservation near Indian Falls, New York. A full-blooded Seneca, Parker studied law in 1845, but was refused admission to the bar, after which he became a civil engineer in 1851. He worked on various waterway projects from 1851–1857, and while working in Galena, Illinois, befriended U.S. Grant in 1857. At the beginning of the Civil War, Parker attempted to join the Union cause but was rebuffed on several occasions. On May 25, 1863, with the support of President Lincoln, Parker was commissioned a captain and Assistant Adjutant General in the Seventeenth Corps under Grant. He was promoted to lieutenant colonel on August 30, 1864, and assigned as Grant's military secretary, a position he held until the end of the war. He was promoted to brigadier general on April 9, 1865, for "meritorious service during the war." After the war, Parker continued on with his service under Grant, resigning from the army on April 26, 1869. After Grant's election as President, Parker was appointed the Commissioner of Indian Affairs, the first American Indian to hold the post. Leaving Grant's administration, under a cloud of corruption, in 1871, Parker worked for a time on Wall Street and later on the New York Board of Police Commissioners. He died on August 30, 1895, in Fairfield, Connecticut. Boatner, 619; Frank R. Levstik, "Parker, Ely Samuel," *Encyclopedia of the American Civil War A Political, Social, and Military History* (David S. Heidler and Jeanne T. Heidler, gen. eds.; New York, 2000), 1456–1457; Heitman, 1: 769.

189. Elijah Sells was appointed superintendent of the Indian Southern Dependency in May 1865. He had previously been the "Third Auditor of the Treasury" under Secretary Simon Chase. Additionally, the only other major commissioner not mentioned by Boudinot was Thomas Wistar, a Quaker from Pennsylvania, who was appointed on August 12, 1865. Furthermore the various commissioners had numerous secretaries to assist them in the negotiations, including Charles E. Mix (assistant to Cooley), George L. Cook, W. R. Irwin, John B. Garrett and J. L. Harvey (assistant to Wistar). Abel, *American Indian Under Reconstruction*, 93, 176–177; Bearss & Gibson, *Fort Smith*, 305; Dale & Litton, 229.

proofs of his guilt. Let history tell the truth in this matter, and "Stand Watie and his men" will have nothing to be ashamed of.

E. C. Boudinot

\* \* \* \* \* \*

**Item:** Scalping at Pea Ridge by an officer who carried messages, concerning the incident, between General Curtis and General Pike, by P. S. Hocker, Lieutenant, Thirty-fourth Texas Cavalry (Alexander's Regiment).[190]

**Published:** January 16, 1886.

## The Scalping at Pea Ridge.

Centralia, Mo., Jan. 9, 1886

Editor, *Republican*

Being a reader of your paper and somewhat interested in your weekly publications relative to the late war, I have watched with interest the communications in reference to the scalping at Pea Ridge. In your issue of the 9th inst. I notice a copy of a communication written by Gen. Albert Pike to Gen. Curtis, March 15, 1862.[191] In reference to the same I was a lieutenant in Col. [Almerine M.] Alexander's regiment of Texas volunteers,[192] then under the command of Gen. Albert Pike, was appointed by Gen. Pike to carry the identical communication referred to and deliver the same to Gen. Curtis, who was then encamped on what was known as the Wire Road leading from Cassville, Mo., to Fayetteville, Ark. The headquarters of Gen. Curtis was then at the north end of the gorge which extends just south of Keyesville to Elk Horn tavern. Sergt. Philip Paris of Collins County, Texas, accompanied me under a flag of truce. We were three days in making the trip from Gen. Pike's headquarters[193] to that of Gen. Curtis, reaching the latter about

---

190. Phillip S. Hocker was originally a member of Company E, Twenty-second Texas Cavalry, but was transferred to the Thirty-fourth Texas Cavalry in mid-1862. *O.R.S.*, pt. 2, vol. 68: 130.

191. Hocker was referring to a special order issued by General Pike on March 15, 1862, that was partially printed in the January 9, 1886 issue of the *Missouri Republican*. See Appendix C for a complete copy of the general order. *O.R.S.*, pt. 3, vol. 2: 187–188; "The Scalping At Pea Ridge," *Missouri Republican*, January 9, 1886.

192. Almerine M. Alexander was born about 1819, in Kentucky, moved to Texas in 1849, and settled in Sherman. A wealthy merchant, Alexander was married with three children. In February 1862 Alexander began organizing his regiment, which was completed and mustered as a one year regiment on April 17, 1862, with Alexander elected colonel of the command. The regiment was variously known as Alexander's Texas Cavalry, the Second Texas Partisan Regiment or the Thirty-fourth Texas Cavalry Regiment; it was raised from the north Texas counties of Collins, Erath, Fannin, Grayson, Lamar, Palo Pinto, Red River, and Tarrant. The regiment was reorganized on June 27, 1862, by General Pike, "for the war," with Alexander still in command. During the year which he lead the Thirty-fourth, Alexander also served from time to time as a brigade commander. He led the regiment at the Battle of Newtonia, Missouri (September 30, 1862) and the Battle of Prairie Grove. Alexander resigned from the army on May 30, 1863 (Weddle has Alexander resigning on May 2), because of poor health. After Alexander's departure, the regiment continued on in the Trans-Mississippi Department and surrendered at Shreveport, Louisiana on June 2, 1865. *O.R.S.*, pt. 2, vol. 68: 289; Banasik, *Embattled Arkansas*, 497, 515; Crute, 341; National Archives, Record Group 109, Confederate Muster Rolls, Thirty-fourth Texas Cavalry; Harold B. Simpson, *Texas in the War 1861–1865* (Hillsboro, TX, 1965), 28, 121; Robert S. Weddle, *Plow-Horse Cavalry: The Caney Creek Boys of the Thirty-fourth Texas* (Austin, TX, 1974), 31–32, 89–90.

193. At the time Pike's headquarters were located at Dwight's Mission, which was forty-two miles

9 o'clock p.m. the third day, when we reached the Union encampment nine miles south of Gen. Curtis. Gen. [Jefferson Columbus] Davis[194] furnished us an escort the remainder of the way. Gen. Curtis treated us kindly and extended to us every accommodation and comfort at his command. He regretted exceedingly the scalping, and was much gratified to receive our message from Gen. Pike. From my

# Knowledge of the Facts

surrounding the scalping of white men by Indian allies under Gen. Pike, there is no doubt but the same was done, not, however, with the approval of Gen. Pike. I speak advisably when I say that no man regretted the savage practice more than Gen. Pike. Although it has been twenty-four years, I readily recall to mind his expressions of regret that he was unable to control a portion of his Indian soldiers.[195] It was impossible to control some of the wilder portion of the Indian allies on the Southern side for two reasons: 1. Their manner of warfare had always been the scalping knife and no quarter. 2. In this case it was well known in the Confederate Army that the Indians on the Union side and especially that portion commonly known during the war as Pin Indians, would, and did scalp Confederate soldiers.[196]

The scalping, however, was confined principally to Confederate Indians, but in a few instances some of our white soldiers were scalped, the greatest dread we had in the engagement the fear of being wounded and falling into the hands

---

southwest of Tahlequah, Indian Territory. *O.R.S.*, pt. 3, vol. 3: 187–188; Annie Heloise Abel, *The Slave Holding Indians: An Omitted Chapter in the Diplomatic History of the Southern Confederacy* (Cleveland, OH, 1915), 39.

194. Jefferson Columbus Davis was born on March 2, 1828, in Indiana and served in the Mexican War at age eighteen, for which he received a commission in the Regular Army. He was appointed colonel of the Twenty-second Indiana at the beginning of the Civil War and made an acting brigadier general on September 21, 1861. At the Battle of Pea Ridge, he led a division and then transferred to the east side of the Mississippi River. Davis was promoted to general officer, to date from December 18, 1861, and received a brevet to major general just before the war's end. During the war, he shot and killed his superior officer, William Nelson, which observers called murder, for which he was never held accountable. Davis completed his war service and became colonel of the Twenty-third U.S. Infantry after the war. He died on November 30, 1879. *O.R.*, 3:502; Warner, *Generals in Blue*, 115–116.

195. Immediately following the battle, Pike was savaged in the Union press. One piece claimed that Pike liquored up his Indian troops to commit the scalpings, another condemned him to "eternal infamy," while his home town of Boston wrote that Pike was "The meanest, the most rascally, the most malevolent of the rebels, who are at war with the United States Government." The attacks would never end, and, according to Robert Duncan, his biographer, "Albert Pike would be defending himself for the rest of his life against charges stemming from his three days at Pea Ridge." Duncan, 225, 228–229.

196. The practice of scalping was not limited to Native Americans or those who fought for the Confederacy. During the course of William Quantrill's 1863 Lawrence, Kansas Raid, three of Quantrill's men were scalped, by a Delaware Indian, which ultimately led to a flurry of scalping in Missouri by members of Quantrill's band. Union officials themselves did little to discourage the practice, particularly following the Lawrence Raid. On September 14, 1863, Colonel Charles Jennison, of Kansas Jayhawker fame, encouraged a multi-tribe group of Indians that "they should have his consent to scalp" guerrillas "from head to heels" whenever they were caught. But the question of who was a guerrilla seemed to be left up to the perpetrator to decide. Banasik, *Cavaliers of the Brush*, 33 (n. 82); "From Kansas," *Chicago Tribune*, September 18, 1863.

of the Pins, whose leading propensity seemed to be to separate from the white Union soldiers in order to satiate their thirst and secure a trophy of an enemy's scalp. The above knowledge engendered a spirit of retaliation, especially with the Confederate Indians. Col. [Cyrus] Bussey[197] says, "that some of those scalped were evidently first wounded in the battle and afterwards

## Murdered and Scalped

by a relentless foe." I doubt not that such was the case and readily call to mind a more horrible occurrence during the campaign of 1863. It was after the evacuation of Fort Gibson[198] by the Confederates.[199] The Confederates under Gen. [Douglas H.] Cooper[200] made a raid on a supply train en route from Fort Scott,[201] Kas.,

197. Cyrus Bussey was born on October 5, 1833, in Hubbard, Ohio. In 1837 his family relocated to southern Indiana and in 1855 Cyrus Bussey moved to Davis County, Iowa. As a Democrat, he was elected to the State Senate in 1858, and remained in that position until the war began. Bussey was appointed colonel of the Third Iowa Cavalry in August 1861. He commanded a cavalry brigade at Pea Ridge and accompanied them to Helena, Arkansas, in the summer of 1862. During the Vicksburg Campaign, Bussey commanded a division. He was appointed a brigadier general January 5, 1864, and breveted a major general March 13, 1865. After the war Bussey opened a business in St. Louis and then New Orleans. He died on March 2, 1915. *O.R.*, vol. 22, pt. 2: 694; A. A. Stuart, *Iowa Colonels and Regiments Being a History of Iowa Regiments in the War of the Rebellion; And Containing a Description of the Battles in Which they Have Fought* (Des Moines, IA, 1865), 583–585, hereafter cited as Stuart; *The Union Army A History of Military Affairs in the Loyal States 1861–1865—Records of the Regiments in the Union Army—Cyclopedia of Battles—Memoirs of Commanders and Soldiers*, 8 vols. (Madison, WI, 1908; reprint ed Wilmington, NC, 1998), 8:45; Warner, *Generals in Blue*, 58–59.
198. Fort Gibson was established as a military post in 1830, just prior to the relocation of the eastern Indians to the Indian Territory. It was located on the east side of the Grand River, about a mile from the river on a bluff, and about three miles from where the Grand met the Arkansas River. The post contained quarters sufficient to hold two companies of troops, along with two stone buildings for quartermaster and commissary stores. Wiley Britton, *The Union Indian Brigade in the Civil War* (Kansas City, MO, 1922), 209–210; Wiley Britton, *Memoirs of the Rebellion on the Border 1863* (Chicago, 1882; reprint ed., Florissant, MO, 1986), 207–209.
199. Union forces of the Indian Brigade, under Colonel William Phillips, occupied Fort Gibson on April 13, 1863. Britton, *Civil War on the Border, 1861–1862,* 37; Britton, *Union Indian Brigade*, 209.
200. Douglas Hancock Cooper was born on November 1, 1815, in Mississippi. He attended the University of Virginia from 1832–1834, returning to Amite County, Mississippi, to engage in farming. During the Mexican War, Cooper served in the First Mississippi Rifles without distinction. In 1853 President Franklin Pierce appointed him U.S. Agent to the Choctaw Nation in the Indian Territory. Cooper joined the Confederacy in 1861, and assisted General Albert Pike in negotiating a treaty with the Five Civilized Tribes in the Indian Territory. During the war, Cooper remained in the west, organized the First Choctaw and Chickasaw Mounted Rifles, and participated in fifteen engagements including Pea Ridge, Newtonia, Missouri, and Honey Springs, Indian Territory. He was promoted to brigadier general on May 2, 1863. Cooper assumed command of the Indian Territory on February 21, 1865. After the war Cooper remained in the Indian Territory, where he died in 1867. Boatner, 174; *Confederate Military History: Mississippi*, vol. 12: by Charles E. Hooker, 247–249; Rampp, 151–153.
201. Fort Scott was named after General Winfield Scott. The post was established on May 30, 1842, on the Marmaton River at the confluence with the Osage River, eight miles from Missouri. Initially established to protect the military road between Fort Leavenworth and Fort Gibson, Indian Territory, Fort Scott was virtually abandoned by the mid 1850's. With the beginning of the Civil War the fort was reopened and played a vital role throughout the war as a depot and guardian of the border between

to Fort Gibson, about five miles north of the latter place and just at the edge of the timber.[202] The train had made better time than our scouts had calculated on and was just entering the timber when attacked. The Union soldiers were in ambush and the Confederate soldiers were soon forced to abandon the coveted prize. They, however, captured two or three sutler's wagons in the rear which were soon retaken by the Union forces. When the wagons were captured they were turned west. With one of them there was a small boy, who told us that he thought his father was killed or wounded when the train was attacked. There were several prisoners besides the boy. When a few hundred yards west of the battlefield several Confederate Indians rushed up to where we were and before anyone suspected violence from them one of them drew a large hunting knife and literally disembowelled the little boy. His further atrocities and that of his three or four comrades, were only stayed by the instantaneous covering of the gang with a dozen or more revolvers or muskets. I never knew what became of the boy, as the Union soldiers came on us, and we left the wagons and prisoners.[203] I mention this simply to show the savage spirit which pervaded some of our Confederate Indian allies. There were some of the same kind on the Union side. There are many thrilling incidents yet unwritten which transpired in the Indian Department, whose field of operation embraced a strip of South Kansas, Southwest Missouri and Western Arkansas, besides bordering on the unfriendly Indians of the West. Through this section marauding bands and renegades found an open avenue to Texas and Mexico.

P. S. Hocker.

* * * * * * *

---

Missouri and the Indian Territory. Robert W. Frazer, *Forts of the West: Military Forts and Presidios and Posts Commonly Called Forts West of the Mississippi River to 1898* (Norman, OK, 1963), 57–58.

202. This raid occurred on May 25, 1863. Most sources have incorrectly identified the date as May 28; an engagement against a train did take place on May 28, but not the one where the sutler wagon was taken as described by the author of this piece. The engagement on the twenty-fifth took place about five miles from Ft. Gibson and occurred just before dawn. According to Union sources, the rebels lost 26 men, while the Federals lost 7 dead and 25 wounded. The only wagon lost was one sutler wagon. Assorted rebel accounts put their losses at 5 wounded in the Fifth Regiment Partisan Rangers (Texas) and 1 missing in the First Cherokee Mounted Rifles; other units losses are not known. Confederate sources also put Federal losses at 24 killed and 12 taken prisoner. *O.R.*, vol. 22, pt. 1: 341; Britton, *Memoirs of the Rebellion*, 266–269; Britton, *Union Indian Brigade*, 240; Dyer, 986; Witt Edwards, *"The Prairie was on Fire": Eyewitness Accounts of the Civil War in the Indian Territory* (Oklahoma City, OK, 2001), 50–52.

203. According to another Confederate, who participated in the attack, the Indians stripped the men naked, murdered one of the suttlers and the "gobbled" over the body. Edwards, *Prairie was on Fire*, 50.

**Item:** Comments on Snead's book *The Fight For Missouri*, the relation-ship between Generals Sterling Price and Earl Van Dorn at the Battles of Pea Ridge, Arkansas (March 6-8, 1862) and Corinth, Mississippi (October 3-4, 1862) and the death of General Henry Little at Iuka, Mississippi (September 19, 1862), by Colonel Celsus Price.
**Published:** June 5, 1886.

[Editor's Note: For the sake of continuity, this piece is presented in its entirety, including the parts from Mississippi, as they deal with the relationship between Generals Price and Van Dorn.]

## Gens. Price and Van Dorn.

(Paper read before the Southern Historical Society of St. Louis by Col. Celsus Price, June 3, 1886.)

On the first appearance of *The Fight For Missouri*, by Col. Thomas L. Snead,[204] I announced my intention to review it at length in a paper to be read before you at an early date. Much to my regret circumstances have prevented me from doing so, and from thus discharging what I regarded as my sacred duty both to living and dead Missourians who figure in its pages. Happily the book needs no endorsement from me to secure your favor, as its success is now assured by the favorable verdict of the highest critical authorities of both North and South, and the work has taken its place in our literature as an exceptionally fair and accurate history of events of which it treats.

As has been well said, the true history of our late Civil War, for obvious reasons, has not and cannot yet be written. But I venture to predict when it is written, the historian, when treating that portion of it relating to the fight for Missouri, will accept and adopt Snead's book as the highest and most undoubted authority upon the subject.

Col. Snead's relations to the principal actors in the drama enacted here in Missouri, and the important and active part he took in it, afforded him the best possible facilities for learning the facts; and he has so impartially related them that no survivor of the contest, on either side of it, has

## Challenged His Accuracy

or fairness.

---

204. Thomas Lowndes Snead was born on January 10, 1828, in Henrico County, Virginia. Educated at Richmond College, Snead received a law degree from the University of Virginia in 1850, and moved to St. Louis the same year. In 1860, Snead bought the *St. Louis Bulletin*, a decided "states rights" newspaper. At the beginning of the Civil War, he was an aide to Governor Jackson, then Sterling Price's Adjutant and finally became a Missouri Congressman, in 1864, for the Second Secession of the Confederate Congress. While in the military service, Snead took part in the Missouri engagements of Wilson's Creek and Lexington. After the war, he moved to New York City, where he worked for the *New York Daily News* and authored several pieces on the war including *The Fight For Missouri* (1866). He died on October 17, 1890, in New York and was returned to St. Louis for burial. Eakin, *Confederate Records*, 59; Moore, *Missouri, Confederate Military History, Extended*, 407 Peterson, 28; Winter, 128.

The work is eminently distinguishable in tone as well as in accuracy from the many similar books, which assuming the dignity of history, have been written for partisan purposes, or inspired by personal ambition or vanity.

Under the circumstance at this late day any extended review of the book would be superfluous and would seem obtrusive, and I will therefore confine myself to such suggestions as naturally occur to me from a perusal of it.

The author states in his preface that he wrote the book "because it was his duty to do so," the result of his labors more than justifies his assumptions of the task, and imposes upon him; we think, an additional and still greater duty.

*The Fight For Missouri* is but the initial chapter of the story of Missouri's active and important share in the war, and we who survive it have the right to claim that he alone possesses the materials and abilities to write it should complete the story.

The full and authentic narrative of the campaigns of the Confederate soldiers of Missouri is essential to the vindication of the truth of history and of the memories of the many of her gallant sons whose characters, motives and services have been misrepresented or forgotten.

In this connection I take occasion to state that Col. Snead was not only the trusted and confidential friend of Gen. Price throughout the war, but was also chosen by him to be his literary executor, and that in 1866, by Gen. Price's direction, I delivered to Col. Snead all the official papers and journals which had been accumulated by the general during the campaigns. When the true story of these campaigns shall be told, which can only be done by the aid of these documents, many errors, misrepresentations and wilful perversions of facts

# Will Be Exposed.

In this connection allow me to refer here to some of the facts to which I allude, which are within my personal knowledge and recollection. The personal relations between Gens. Price and Van Dorn have been, and still are, and very generally misunderstood to the prejudice of Gen. Van Dorn. I am happy to be able to state, from personal knowledge, that not only there existed no jealousy between them, but that each entertained for the other, the most cordial respect and esteem. Just after the Battle of Elkhorn, at an interview between Gens. Van Dorn and Price, the former expressly stated that if Gen. Price's plan had been carried out the Confederates would have won the battle, adding these words: "Gen. Price, I want you to know that this position is not of my seeking. I never commanded large bodies of men before; the President expects too much of me. Sir, you ought to be in command of this army, and I intend to say as much to the President."[205]

---

205. Celsus Price was referring to the original plan to concentrate all the troops at one point and not divide the army. In Colonel R. H. Musser's account on the battle, he provides a conversation that took place between Generals Price and Van Dorn on the disposition of the troops at the beginning of the battle. Van Dorn relates that McCulloch convinced him to split the command, but after conversing with Price agreed to recall McCulloch's Division to concentrate with Price's Missourians—unfortu-

The sincerity of Gen. Van Dorn in the expression is evident by the following extract from his letter to President Davis, dated Pricevale, Miss, June 9, 1862, in which he says:

I wish here to suggest to you, general, that the love of the people of Missouri, is so strong for Gen. Price, and his prestige as a commander there so great, that wisdom would seem to dictate that he be put at the head of affairs in the West. I see

## The Alluring Bait

to my ambition—the fall of St. Louis the recrimination of a rich segment of our beloved South from the grip of the enemy, and the glory that might be mine, but I shut all this out from me, because I think it is the best interests of the country to do so. I drop whatever glory there may be in it on the brow of Gen. Price, than whom there is no one more worthy to wear it, and than by whom I would rather see it worn. (*War of the Rebellion, Official Records*, Series I, 13:832.)

Gen. Price's appreciation of Gen. Van Dorn's magnanimity and merits as a soldier were often fully and freely expressed by him and no set or word of his ever evinced any want of respect or regard for him.

Again, it has been said and believed that Gen. Price objected to the assaulting of the inner works at Corinth[206] on the night of the first day's battle there, and dissuaded Van Dorn from doing so contrary to his instincts.

I know from personal knowledge obtained at the time and on the spot when I say that this is the exact reverse of the case. In corroboration of this I refer to an unpublished letter of Gen. John Tyler, Jr.[207] written to the honorable Wm. L.

---

nately it was already too late as McCulloch was already engaged and died shortly thereafter. D. H. Maury, Van Dorn's Adjutant General, would later record of the loss at Pea Ridge: "Had Van Dorn adhered to his original plan and fallen on the enemy's rear with all the forces of Price and McCulloch, the disasters of the day would have been averted. We may fairly conclude that it was lost through the want of discipline and cohesion in our army." Maury, 189; Musser, "Battle of Pea Ridge," *Missouri Republican*, November 21, 1885.

206. The Battle of Corinth, Mississippi, was fought on October 3–4, 1862, between the forces of Earl Van Dorn and William Rosecrans. Both sides were fairly equally matched with about 23,000 men. The first day belonged to the Confederate forces, while the second ended the battle in favor of the Union. Both sides lost about 2,500 killed and wounded, while the rebels lost an additional 1,763 men captured during the battle and the retreat that followed. Boatner, 176–177.

207. John Tyler, Jr., a Virginian by birth, was the son of the tenth President of the United States. At the beginning of the Civil War he worked in the War Department under L. P. Walker. When Walker resigned his post to accept a generalship, Tyler remained on his staff as his adjutant general until Walker left the military service in March 1862. Tyler joined Sterling Price's staff sometime in 1862, and was present at the Battle of Corinth in October 1862. Tyler accompanied Price back to the Trans-Mississippi in 1863, being appointed a volunteer aid-de-camp on April 1, 1863. He was present at the Battle of Helena, Arkansas on July 4, 1863. Tyler later returned to Virginia where he completed his war

Yancey,[208] Confederate senator, dated Holly Springs, Miss., October 15, 1862, a copy of which, made by the author at the time, I now have in my possession,[209] in which he makes the following statement:

> The day was now far spent and the excitement of the contest subsiding. Scores of men sank down exhausted by the heat and nearly famished for water. Gen. Price rode among them sympathizing with their suffering. Wherever he went cheers followed him; the wounded threw up their caps, and even the dying waved to him their hands.
> He dispatched his entire bodyguard

## With Canteens For Water

> and sent off courier after courier to hasten up surgeons, ambulances and restoratives. But notwithstanding the heat and fatigues of the day, and the exhausting effects and distractions of the battle, he saw his troops were inspired with enthusiasm and the prestige of victory, whereas, on the other hand, he felt assured the enemy were in confusion, and that, without reinforcements, which was reasonable to suppose had not yet arrived, they could not long maintain themselves against the vigor and fury of an assault; and he was frequently heard to exclaim, "Now is the time to push into Corinth! Now is the time to assure the victory!"

Gen. Tyler was actively engaged in the battle as voluntary aid-de-camp to Gen. Price and wrote this letter after it, while the facts were all fresh in his memory.

Again, it was also stated in a historical essay when we were encamped at

---

service as an adjutant general in the War Department. *O.R.*, 1:689; 4:476; vol. 17, pt. 2:674; vol. 22, pt. 1: 417; vol. 22, pt. 2: 811; vol. 46, pt. 3:1340; John Tyler, Jr. collection (C477), Western Historical Manuscript Collection, State Historical Society of Missouri, Columbia, MO.

208. William Lowndes Yancey was born at "The Aviary" plantation near Warren City in Hancock County, Georgia, on August 10, 1814. Educated in the North, Yancey returned to the South and settled in Greenville, South Carolina, by 1834, where he edited the *Greenville Mountaineer*. Yancey married in 1835, moved to Alabama in 1836, where he was elected to the Alabama Legislature in 1841, and the Senate in 1843. In 1844, Yancey was elected to the U.S. Congress, served two terms, but resigned in 1846, being "disgusted with compromises." Over the next several years Yancey became a strong advocate of Southern rights and was largely responsible for fomenting the Secession Crisis of 1860. His advocacy of the Alabama Platform, which Yancey wrote in 1848, at the Democratic Convention in Charleston, South Carolina, resulted in the split of the party and the eventual election of Abraham Lincoln. With the formation of the Confederacy, Jefferson Davis appointed Yancey to lead the diplomatic mission to France and England. Resigning his post as a diplomat, Yancey returned to Alabama, where he was elected to the Confederate Senate on March 27, 1862. Yancey did not survive the war, dying at his home in Montgomery, Alabama on July 27, 1863, of kidney disease. Patricia L. Faust, ed., *Historical Times Illustrated Encyclopedia of the Civil War* (New York, 1986), 845; Eric H. Walther, "Yancey, William Lowndes," *Encyclopedia of the Civil War*, 2157–2158.

209. The original copy of this extensive report on the Battle of Corinth can be found in the State Historical Society of Missouri. Tyler Collection, Letter to William L. Yancy (October 14, 1862), Western Historical Manuscript Collection, State Historical Society of Missouri.

Chewalla on the first night of the retreat from Corinth, Gen. Price urged Gen. Van Dorn to return to the attack on the following morning, when the facts are that Gen. Van Dorn issued an order that night directing Price to take the Rienzi Road at daylight with a view of renewing the attack on Corinth. Upon receipt of this order Gen. Price was greatly surprised, and taking three of his staff with him, including the writer, rode at once to Van Dorn's headquarters to

## Remonstrate Against It.

When we reached headquarters we found Gen. Van Dorn had gone to bed in his ambulance. Gen. Price awakened him, and referring to the order stated that as he (Price) commanded the larger portion of the army, and that part, too, which had done all the fighting that day, he felt that he had a right to be heard in the matter, said that he regarded it as madness to make the attempt, and thought it doubtful whether we would be able to extricate the army as it was, that he would much rather pull up stakes and cross the Hatchie River that night for he expected that we would be met by the enemy in force at the bridge the next morning.

Gen. Van Dorn yielded to Gen. Price's wishes and countermanded the order. The sequel proved that Gen. Price was correct in this anticipation, for we did meet the enemy in force at that point the next morning, and were compelled to fall back and cross the river below.

In support of my statements I quote the following from Gen. Tyler's letter to Senator Yancey; referred to above:

The artillery and ammunition wagons were first removed from the field. These were followed by a portion of [Mansfield] Lovell's command[210] that had bored but little of the fatigues and none of the perils of the day. And lastly followed by [Albert] Rust,[211] proceeded the war-worn, smoke-

---

210. Mansfield Lovell was born in 1822, graduated from West Point in 1842 (number 9 of 56), served in the Mexican War and resigned from the army in 1849. At the beginning of the Civil War he was an iron manufacturer in New York City and joined the Southern cause as a major general on October 7, 1861. Placed in command of New Orleans, Lovell was compelled to abandon the city in April 1862. He later lead a division at the Battle of Corinth. He was relieved of command in December 1862, for his loss of New Orleans and had no further leadership positions in the Confederate army. After the war he returned to New York City, where he was a civil engineer and surveyor. He died in 1884. Boatner, 494; Stewart Sifakis, *Who Was Who in the Confederacy: A Comprehensive, Illustrated Biographical Reference to More Than 1,000 of the Principal Confederacy Participants in the Civil War* (New York, 1988), 177.

211. Albert Rust was born in Virginia in 1818, moved to Arkansas in 1837, settling in Union County. At the beginning of the Civil War, Rust organized and took command of the Third Arkansas Infantry on July 5, 1861. He was promoted to brigadier general on March 6, 1862, and assigned to duty in the Army of the West under Earl Van Dorn. On May 27, 1862, Rust was sent to Arkansas, where he served under Thomas C. Hindman, for a short time, before returning to Van Dorn. Rust led a brigade at the Battle of Corinth, performed poorly and was again returned to the Trans-Mississippi on April 15, 1863. Rust never again played a major role in the Civil War and was eventually removed from duty. Following the war, he returned to farming, joined the Republican Party and was elected to the U.S.

begrimed and battle-scarred battalions of Gen. Price, he himself lingering with the rearmost files. After recrossing Cave Creek and again reaching the vicinity of Chewalla the column was halted and bivouacked for the night. Why it stopped here was to everyone an enigma. If retreating, and there seemed nothing else to do, we surely should have crossed the Tuscumbia River only four miles off, where our trains still reposed, if indeed, we did not continue

## Over the Hatchie,

requiring a march of only four miles more, while the bridges were yet in our possession. If food and water were absolutely necessary to the men, why not have gone where food and water were abundant, was the question on every lip. If rest was essentially demanded, the feeling in every heart was that they would repose better under the conviction that the army was secure.

But the commanding general said he did not mean to retreat, and, at a late hour his orders revealed the mystery as to our encampment. We were required to move by daybreak upon the Rienzi road preparatory to another attack upon Corinth. Gen. Price received the orders with amazement, and justly deemed them as coming from a mind rendered desperate by misfortune. He had previously, when directed to encamp, yielded with reluctant grace yet in the true spirit of the soldier to the wisdom of his superior. But he now considered it his imperative duty to interfere in behalf of the salvation of the army. To escape at all he felt that the gauntlet must be run, but the design of Gen. Van Dorn if persisted in assured destruction. To attack Corinth again with our broken forces was madness, and through his advice the purpose was abandoned and our bruised, sore and wearied men were permitted to sleep on.

In *The Fight For Missouri* occur the names of some whose subsequent services in the war contributed largely to the glory of the state, and the cause to which they devoted themselves, and whose lives and deeds are well worthy to be told in story and sung in song. There were Little, Green, McBride, Slack, Parsons, Champion, McDonald [MacDonald] and others.

Of these some sleep

## In Forgotten Graves

on distant battlefields, and their surviving comrades call for justice to their memo-

---

Congress in 1869. He died on April 4, 1870. See Appendix B for a complete biography. *O.R.*, 13: 829;

Boatner, 714; Faust, *Historical Times Encyclopedia of the Civil War*, 649; Sifakis, *Who Was Who in the Confederacy*, 249; Warner, *Generals in Gray*, 266–267.

ries. In reading *The Fight For Missouri* the allusion to the appointment of Henry Little upon the staff of Gen. Price recalls vividly to the memory the heroism, service and death of one of the noblest of them all.

Gen. Little served with distinction through all the campaigns of Gen. Price and up to the day of his death on the memorable battlefield of Iuka[212] when in command of his division.

Gen. Price had just given him an order to flank the enemy, and drive him across the road upon [Dabney H.] Maury's[213] masked batteries, and as Little reined up his horse to start in execution of the order he was struck and killed by a bullet passing through his brain over his left eye.

I was present near him at the time, and springing from my horse caught him before he fell, and he died in my arms. I had his body placed upon a blanket and carried into Iuka, where he was buried at about 12 o'clock at night, just before we started on our retreat, Col. Snead, I believe, superintending his burial. I state these facts with particularity because

## Many Different Accounts

of the circumstances attending his death have been related.

Dr. Luke Blackburn,[214] since Governor of Kentucky, Col. R. T. Morrison[215]

---

212. The Battle of Iuka, Mississippi, was fought on September 19, 1862. Sterling Price's command attacked William Rosecrans's Federals, suffering 1,516 casualties. The Federals lost 782 men. Of the Confederate losses, the death of General Little was probably the greatest casualty that the rebels suffered; he was shot in the head toward the close of the battle. Anderson, *Memoirs*, 222; Boatner, 428–429.

213. Dabney Herndon Maury was born on May 21, 1822, in Fredericksburg, Virginia, graduated from the University of Virginia in 1842, and later from West Point in 1846 (number 37 of 59). A veteran of the Mexican War, Maury was dismissed from the service on June 25, 1861, for "treasonable designs." Appointed a colonel, Maury served as General Van Dorn's Chief of Staff at the Battle of Pea Ridge, and was promoted to general officer on March 18, 1862, for his performance at the battle. Maury commanded divisions at Corinth and Iuka, Mississippi, and was promoted to major general on November 4, 1862. Maury completed his Civil War service commanding Mobile, Alabama. After the war, Maury returned to Richmond, Virginia, where he established the Southern Historical Society, and served as its chairman for twenty years. He died on January 11, 1900, at the home of his son in Peoria, Illinois. Boatner, 519–520; Faust, *Historical Times Encyclopedia of the Civil War*, 166, 386–387; Warner, *Generals in Gray*, 215–216.

214. Dr. Luke Pryor Blackburn was born on June 16, 1816, in Woodford County, Kentucky, and served as a rebel agent in Canada during the war. After the war Blackburn was tried in a Canadian court for shipping Yellow Fever infected clothing, which he obtained in Bermuda, to New Bern, North Carolina. The official charge was "conspiracy to commit murder." Yellow Fever subsequently broke out at the regimental hospital of the Ninth Vermont Infantry. Blackburn was acquitted of all charges in October 1865, as the count found no evidence that the trunks of clothing had never been in Canada. Returning to Kentucky in 1872, Blackburn was later elected governor (1879–1883). He died on September 14, 1887, and was buried in Frankfurt, Kentucky. John E. Kleber, *The Kentucky Encyclopedia* (Lexington, KY, 1992), 84; Sifakis, *Who Was Who in the Confederacy*, 25. Note: Yellow Fever is a mosquito borne disease which cannot be transmitted by "infected clothing."

215. Richard T. Morrison was appointed a lieutenant colonel in the MSG and Aid-de-Camp to General Price on May 18, 1861. He later joined the Confederate service, remaining as an aid to General Price

of St. Louis, and also, I believe, Gen. John Tyler, now of Washington City, were present at his death and know the facts to be as stated.

Time will not permit me to refer to many other named and unnamed heros, whose services and death reflected glory on the Confederate arms; the best tribute I can now pay to their memories is expressed in the words of our patriotic priest a poet when he says:

> Ah, fearless on many [illegible] for us
> They stood in their [illegible] fray for us.
> And held the foe [illegible] bay for us
> > And tears should fall
> > Forever o're all
> Who fell while wearing the gray for us.
> But their memories e're shall remain for us,
> And their names, bright names, without stain for us,
> The glory they won shall not wane for us:
> > In legend now lay
> > Our heros in gray
> Shall forever live over again for us.

* * * * * * *

---

with an initial rank of lieutenant. By Price's 1864 Missouri Raid, Morrison had risen to the rank of major, still on Price's staff. *O.R.*, vol. 22, pt. 1:416; vol. 22, pt. 2:811; vol. 34, pt. 1: 783; vol. 41, pt. 2: 1090; 53: 686.

**Item:** Price's retreat from Springfield in February 1862, Battle of Pea
Ridge (March 6-8, 1862) and movement to Memphis, by "R.," a member
of the Second Missouri (Confederate) Cavalry Regiment.
**Published:** October 9, 1886.

## Second Missouri Cavalry.

Springfield, Mo., Oct. 6
Editor, Republican

In giving my imperfect sketches of the war, I will have to confine myself to the
part played by McCullough's Second Missouri Cavalry, the nucleus of which was
sworn in for the war, at Springfield, Mo., in the winter of 1862.[216] We took an active part, in connection with Col. Gate's First Regiment and Gen. Rains's "Blackberry Cavalry," as rear guard in Gen. Price's famous retreat from Springfield to
Cove Creek in Arkansas, having neither sleep nor food during the time, winding
up with a pretty sharp skirmish at Sugar Creek, having in the meantime several
slight brushes with Gen. Curtis's advance, as at Crane Creek, Cassville, etc.[217]
These skirmishes had more of an amusement than danger in them as on more than
one occasion I remember that just as we had our corn-pone about ready to eat, a
few shots over on the next ridge would cause a hasty mount and forward march.

After we had rested and organized in Boston Mountains, and had given Gen.
Curtis ample time to choose his battleground, we returned to Pea Ridge, or, as we
called it, Elkhorn, via Bentonville, and tried

## To Surround the Enemy,

Gen. Price in command of the Missourians, McCulloch the Texans, McIntosh
the Arkansans, Gen. Pike the Indians and Gen. Van Dorn over all. Everybody
knows the result—a serious disaster to the rebels. Yet if all of Gen. Van Dorn's
army had been handled as Gen. Rains's Blackberry Cavalry were the first day of
that battle the second day would not have been fought, as the result would have
been very different. After the battle there was a long retreat over the mountains
to Van Buren, thence over the pine hills and Arkansas swamps to Des Arc, Ark.[218]

---

216. Robert A. McCulloch's Company, which became Company A, Second Missouri Cavalry Regiment, was organized on January 1, 1862, at Springfield, Missouri. At Pea Ridge the company was
commanded by First Lieutenant George W. Oglesby, while McCulloch commanded the battalion. The
remaining units of the Second Missouri were not organized until after the Battle of Pea Ridge, with
the regiment forming on July 2, 1862, at Priceville, Mississippi. See Appendix A for further details on
McCulloch's command at Pea Ridge. *O.R.S.*, pt. 2, vol. 50: 141.

217. Toward the evening of February 14, elements of the First Missouri Cavalry (Union) with William
Bowen's Missouri Cavalry Battalion, came upon the rebel camp at Crane Creek. After throwing ten
shells, from four mountain howitzers, at the Confederates, the Federals withdrew, taking thirty prisoners with them. There is no record of any skirmish at Cassville in the *Official Records*. The skirmish at
Sugar Creek occurred on February 17, 1862. See note no. 27 for details. *O.R.*, 8:2, 269.

218. Van Dorn's army departed Van Buren, Arkansas, on March 23, 1862, with the lead element of the
army under Henry Little arriving at Des Arc, Arkansas, on April 7. Little's Brigade quickly boarded

Then all the mounted troops had their horses taken away from them except the Second Missouri, they being the only cavalry enlisted for the war. At Des Arc we took steamers for Memphis. Our command with their horses were stowed away in and on the *Vicksburg*,[219] a Mississippi river steamer. Altogether we had 1,200 men aboard with just about states' room for the officers. However, a berth on top was very pleasant until the last night, when very soon after dark a violent rain with thunder and lightening and that almost amounted to a hurricane came on us.

The Wind Was So Violent

that the captain of the boat came round and advised us to keep a sharp lookout for the chimneys, pilot house and other possible dangers. However, we landed at Memphis about 11 p.m., rains still pouring. We were then transferred to a cattle boat alongside, where we slept till morning in manure half a foot deep. Early next morning we mounted and formed on the bluff in front of Memphis, and were just beginning to admire the beauties of the city when our horses began stamping, switching and biting. Buffalo gnats! so the natives told us, at the same time advising tar, feathers, etc., at our first chance. We were camped there about a week, losing at least two-thirds of our horses from this cause. Here we organized a full regiment by consolidating with a number of companies from southeast Missouri. Officered by such men as Sol. G. Kitchens,[220] William Cozens,[221] etc., we took

---

transports and arrived at Memphis, Tennessee, on April 11, never to return to the Trans-Mississippi until the war had ended. The remaining elements of Van Dorn's army followed over the next several days, with the last command arriving in Memphis on April 25. Banasik, *Embattled Arkansas*, 9–10.

219. The Confederate *steamer Vicksburg* (also known as *City of Vicksburg*) was a side-wheeled ship of 635 tons built in 1857 at New Albany, Indiana. She carried one gun, caliber unknown. Based out of New Orleans, the ship was used as a cargo ship throughout the Mississippi Valley region, including on the Arkansas, White and Black Rivers. Reported by Union officials as the "'largest and strongest steamer'" on the Mississippi, the *Vicksburg* was finally cornered by Federal ships on February 3, 1863, while lying at the wharf at Vicksburg, Mississippi. Rammed by the *Queen of the West*, which also fired hot shot into her, the *Vicksburg* refused to give in to the Union attack. The fires were put out, machinery stripped out of the vessel and sent to Mobile for use in another ship; the *Vicksburg* remained afloat as a wharf boat at her namesake city. On the night of March 29, the *Vicksburg* broke loose of her mooring and floated down to the Union fleet, which captured her. At 4:00 a.m. on March 31, Confederates sneaked board the vessel and burned her under the very eyes of its captors. Naval History Division, Navy Department *Civil War Naval Chronology* (Washington, DC, 1971), III–21, VI–319; United States War Department, *The War of the Rebellion: Official Records of the Union and Confederate Navies* (31 vols., Washington, DC, 1894–1922), 20:35–36, 735, 764–765 (hereafter cited as *O.R.N.; all citations* refer to Series 1 unless indicated otherwise).

220. Salomon G. Kitchen was from Bloomfield, Missouri. He served as a captain of Company C (Stoddard Rangers), Second Cavalry Regiment, First Division, MSG from June 15, 1861, until August 1 when he was elected major of his regiment. On September 17, Kitchen was promoted to lieutenant colonel and left the Guard upon expiration of term of service in December 1861. During 1862, Kitchen organized a cavalry battalion, which later became the Seventh Missouri Cavalry Regiment. Kitchen fought in forty-two engagements during the war and surrendered his command at Wittsburg, Arkansas in 1865. He died in St. Louis in 1891, at the of age 72. *O.R.*, vol. 22, pt. 2:921; Bartels, *Forgotten Men*, 206; Eakin, *Confederate Records*, 5:28; Peterson, 50, 52.

221. William H. Couzens (*Official Records* spelling) or Cozzens or Cousins or Cozens or Cozzine was born about 1817 in Missouri. He served in the Mexican War, and at the beginning of the Civil War was a lumber merchant in St. Genevieve. Couzens was elected captain of a cavalry company in the First

up our line of march east; reached Corinth in ample time to join the retreat south from that point after doing a few days' outpost duty. One incident of this retreat I remember quite well. We were sent to Boonville, a station south of Corinth, where about 1,800 sick and convalescent had been forwarded. I presume we were sent there

# As A Guard;

also to keep any raiding parties from destroying railroad and other property.[222] We reached Boonville in the night and very soon after were ordered to a bridge still south of Boonville, reaching it about daylight. We had hardly reached the bridge when we were ordered back to Boonville on the double quick. We made the five-mile run in wonderful time, but a little too late, for Col. [Edward] Hatch[223] of the Second Iowa, with (as I have always understood) Lieut-Colonel Phil Sheridan, had already been there, burnt the depot, destroyed other property and taken away all the rebels that could travel.[224]

My belief has always been that our hasty trip to the bridge was a wild goose chase and taken under orders from Cols. Hatch and Sheridan.

Another incident connected with this move was a report generally credited in

---

Division, MSG on August 16, 1861, and major of his command on October 5, 1861. He served in the Guard until December 27, 1861. Couzens subsequently joined the Confederate Army, being elected captain of a cavalry company on March 6, 1862, which became Company E, Second Missouri Cavalry Regiment (Confederate). On January 1, 1863, Couzens received a temporary promotion to major of the regiment, which was made permanent on August 14, a position he held until the end of the war. He was paroled out of the army on May 15, 1865, in Mississippi. *O.R.*, Index, 209; vol. 30, pt. 4:496; *O.R.S.*, pt. 2, vol. 38:144, 148; Bartels, *Forgotten Men*, 73; Bartels, *Trans-Mississippi Men*, 18, 59; Crute, 196; National Archives, Record Group M322 (roll no. 17), Confederate Compiled Service Records, Second Missouri Cavalry; Peterson, 54–55; Schnetzer, *More Forgotten Men*, 55.

222. The Confederate command had received word of an impending raid on Boonville, Mississippi, on May 27 and had dispatched a 400-man force, including the Second Missouri Cavalry (Confederate), to defend the place. During the night of May 29–30, Colonel Jehu A. Orr, commanding the Thirty-first Mississippi Infantry, ordered McCulloch's command to the Tuscumbia River bridge to protect it. On the morning of May 30, the Federal command under Colonel Washington L. Elliot took Boonville with its supply-ladened depot and train. Phil Sheridan was present on the raid, commanding the Second Michigan Cavalry. *O.R.*, Index, 729; *O.R.*, vol. 10, pt. 1, 862, 864–867.

223. Edward Hatch was born in Maine in 1832, and moved to Muscatine, Iowa, by the late 1850's, where he dealt in the lumber trade. On August 12, 1861, he joined the Second Iowa Cavalry, being made captain. Promoted to major on September 5, 1861, and lieutenant colonel on December 11, Hatch led the regiment at Corinth during the siege in April and May 1862. He was promoted to colonel on June 13, 1862, and general officer on December 15, 1864. After the war Hatch remained in the service, as colonel of the Ninth U.S. Cavalry, until his death on April 11, 1889. Boatner, 384; Heitman, 1:510; Stuart, 571.

224. The Federals reported destroying one train with 26 cars, 10,000 arms, 1000 sidearms, 100,000 rounds of ammunition, 3 cannon, 4 mortars and assorted infantry accouterments for 10,000 men. Additionally, they captured 2,000 sick and 500 convalescent soldiers, who were paroled. *O.R.*, vol. 10, pt. 1:862, 864–865.

our lines that Gen. John Pope[225] reported to the War Department, 18,000 rebels captured on this retreat,[226] thereby being at once promoted to the command of the Army of the Potomac for his remarkable exploit. Capturing sick men and multiplying by ten would be no difficult matter for a schoolboy.

R.

* * * * * *

---

225. John Pope was born on March 16, 1822, in Louisville, Kentucky. He attended the U.S. Military Academy, where he graduated in 1842 (number 17 of 56). During the Mexican War Pope was breveted a captain for gallantry. At the beginning of the Civil War, Pope was a captain of engineers and was promoted to brigadier general on June 14, 1861, to rank from May 17. Assigned to various positions in Missouri, including the command of a division under General Frémont, Pope would later leave the area to command the Army of the Potomac at the Battle of Second Bull Run or Manassas. For a complete biography see Banasik, *Duty, Honor and Country*, 449–450; Boatner, 658–659; Warner, *General in Blue*, 376–377.

226. On June 1, 1862, General H. W. Halleck, reported that he had a dispatch from General Pope which said he had captured 10,000 prisoners. This in turn was published in the Union newspapers and created quite a stir. Pope for his part would write General Halleck in 1865, in an attempt to set the record straight, that he sent no such dispatch. During the time of the incident, according to his biographer Peter Cozzens, Pope remained silent on the matter, "claiming that a higher sense of duty," compelled him to keep the matter private. *O.R.*, vol. 10, pt. 1:669; vol. 10, pt. 2: 635; Peter Cozzens, *General John Pope A Life for the Nation* (Chicago, 2000), 70.

Chapter 2

# Spring and Summer 1862:
## Horse Creek and Lone Jack In Missouri and Campaigning In Arkansas

**Item:** An engagement at Horse Creek, Missouri (May 7, 1862) between Colonel William F. Cloud (Actually a detachment of Company I,[1] Second Ohio Cavalry) and then Captain S. D. Jackman, by O. M. Snuffer.[2]
**Published:** March 13, 1886.

### Capt. Jackman's Escape.

At Home, Near Roscoe, Mo., Feb. 25
Editor, *Republican*

In the latter part of May, 1862, Col. (then Capt.) Jackman[3] (now United States marshal in Texas) collected about forty men, most of whom were his personal acquaintances, and started from Bates County to go south. At that time all southwest Missouri was swarming with Federal militia and Kansas men under Col. [William F.] Cloud,[4] who was operating between Fort Scott and Springfield.

---

1. There are no accounts of this skirmish in either the *Official Records* or *Supplement to the Official Records*, save a mention that the skirmish occurred on May 7, 1862. *O.R.*, 13:4.

2. Owen M. Snuffer was born about 1835 in Missouri and lived in St. Clair County at the beginning of the Civil War. He joined S. D. Jackman's regiment on July 19, 1862, and was elected second lieutenant of what became Company B, Sixteenth Missouri Infantry (Confederate). He resigned from the service on April 6, 1863 (Eakin & Hale have the date as April 20, 1863). *O.R.S.*, pt. 2, vol. 38:638; Eakin & Hale, 404; National Archives, Record Group M322 (roll no. 170), Confederate Compiled Service Records, Sixteenth Missouri Infantry.

3. Sidney D. Jackman was born in Kentucky, moved to Howard County, Missouri, in 1830, and settled in, Bates County, Missouri in 1855. At the beginning of the Civil War, Jackman raised a company in Bates County and was elected captain of the unit, which became part of the Ninth Cavalry Regiment, Eighth Division, MSG. Operating "behind enemy lines," Jackman raised two regiments during the war; the first was organized in the fall of 1862, and the second was raised in late spring of 1864. During the war, Jackman was basically a guerrilla leader, participating in only two major engagements: Lone Jack (August 16, 1862) and Westport (October 22–23, 1864). He moved to Texas following the war, where he died on June 2, 1886. See Appendix B for a complete biography. Allardice, 133–135; Crute, 201, 208; Mrs. Mary Jackman Mullins, "Sketch of Col. Sidney D. Jackman," *Missouri During the Sixties*, 93–96; Richard L. Norton, *Behind Enemy Lines: The Memoirs and Writings of Brigadier General Sidney Drake Jackman* (Springfield, MO, 1997), v, 3–9, 19, hereafter cited as Norton.

4. William F. Cloud was born and educated in Ohio, served in the Mexican War and lived in Emporia, Kansas, at the beginning of the Civil War. He organized Company H, Second Kansas Infantry and was made the unit's major on June 11, 1861. On April 3, 1862, Cloud became the colonel of the Tenth Kansas Infantry and on June 1 he was given command of the Second Kansas Cavalry. During the course of the war Cloud oftentimes served as a brigade commander, commanding brigades during the

These troops patrolled the whole country and Southern men who wanted to go south, as a rule, traveled by night and concealed themselves in the deep thickets by day. With the stars for his guide, Capt. Jackman crossed the Osage River at nightfall and marched south , arriving about sunrise at the head timber of Horse Creek, near the north edge of Vernon County.[5] The creek timber at this point was from 80 to 100 yards wide, there being a high bank or bluff on the east side, with rolling prairie land stretching on both sides of the timber towards the southeast. Capt. Jackman and his command selected a suitable covert, dismounted and tied their horses to saplings, expecting to stay in the brush till dark and then make another march for Cowskin Prairie in the northwest corner of Arkansas. Their position was on the east side of the creek. Near the steep bluff was an old stock trail. The men had all lain down on their blankets near their horses, and each one with his weapon at hand. Some of the men had fallen asleep. It was about noon when their doze was interrupted. It seems that Col. Cloud, with more than 100 men,[6] had got on their trail some miles to the north and had followed them down to the timber. Then by reconnoitering the creek he had succeeded in finding the exact spot where they were camped. By placing part of his force on the west side and a few to cover the creek valley north and south, with himself at the head of the main body strung along the top of the bluff, he had Jackman surrounded. With this beautiful disposition he called out from the heights: "Come out of there you d—— rebels, or we will kill every one of you!"

Thoroughly surprised Jackman and his men sprang to their feet, snatching up guns, pistols and blankets in all haste. Then there was lively mounting and quickly every soldier was in the saddle and in line, with eyes turned toward the gallant captain. With a bugle call for his men to follow he turned his dapple gray towards the bluff and they go up like a thunderbolt, attacking the head of Cloud's column so unexpectedly that it gives them a panic war chill. The colonel thought that there was only a dozen of them and they belonged to what were called the Mayfield boys. In the fight on the bluff Jackman and Col. Cloud met in hand-to-hand saber contest. The colonel rushed to the encounter. The captain warded off his stroke and gave him a wound in the hand. The colonel, however, returned to

---

1862 Indian Expedition and the Prairie Grove Campaign. In early 1865, Cloud was made the major general and commander of the Kansas Militia. After the war, Cloud resigned from his Kansas Militia post, moved to Carthage, Missouri, and entered into private business. See Appendix B for a complete biography. *O.R.*, 3: 56, 70; W. S. Burke, *Official Military History of Kansas Regiments During the War for the Suppression of the Great Rebellion* (Leavenworth, KS, 1870), 31–32, hereafter cited as Burke; Samuel J. Crawford, *Kansas in the Sixties* (Chicago, 1911), 207, 246, hereafter cited as Crawford; Alice L. Fry, *Kansas and Kansans in the Civil War: First Through Thirteenth Volunteer Regiments* (Kansas City, KS, 1996), 22, 53, hereafter cited as Fry; Webb, 351–353.

5. Not true. The engagement at Horse Creek occurred in the northeast corner of Barton County, twelve miles northeast of Lamar and about 35 miles southeast of Fort Scott. Banasik, *Reluctant Cannoneer,* 32–33; Davis, *Civil War Atlas,* plt. 161.

6. According to a member of the Second Ohio Cavalry, the force that Jackman encountered was a "large squad" from Company I. Jackman placed the Federals at forty men. Banasik, *Reluctant Cannoneer,* 32; Norton, 46.

the charge with so great purpose that Capt. Jackman was thrown out of balance in the encounter, his saddle girth broke and he fell to the ground, dropping his saber. He, however, quickly drew a Colt's dragoon revolver and fired, wounding the colonel in the side and convincing him it was time to quit. Meanwhile, during this duel between the chiefs, Jackman's men had driven the Federals to the brush. Several were wounded on each side. Jackman's horse fell into the hands of the enemy, as did also one mounted trooper. Two of the enemy with their horses fell into Jackman's hand. Jackman drew off without attempting to dislodge the Federals, who followed him and were repulsed in a spirited charge. In following them up one of Jackman's men, young [John O.] Summers[7] of Henry County, was killed, he having pushed the pursuit too rashly. Jackman soon arrived at Cowskin Prairie, and an exchange of prisoners arranged, Jackman getting his horse and trooper back for two Federal prisoners.[8] Col. Cloud was disabled for some months by his wounds.[9]

O. M. Snuffer

* * * * * *

---

7. Of John O. Summers, Jackman recorded—"He was of a good family, a brave man, and a gentleman. He was the first man I had killed during the war." Norton, 46.

8. According to Jackman, his command was at rest when the Federals stumbled upon him and demanded his surrender. When the Confederates failed to surrender, the Ohio boys beat a hasty retreat, with Jackman's troops hot on their trail. All the Federal losses came from Company I, Second Ohio Cavalry. Private William C. Mansfield was killed and Sergeant Francis C. Smith with privates Lyman P. Judson (blacksmith), and Milton M. Watkins captured. The Federals had one man wounded, John F. Mohn. Further, the Unionists reported capturing Jackman's "gray horse" and killing one rebel. James C. Howe, *Official Roster of the Soldiers of the State of Ohio in the War of the Rebellion, 1861–1866* (Akron, OH, 1893), vol. 11: 94–98; Norton, 44–46, 48–49.

9. Cloud was not at the engagement nor was he ever wounded during the course of the war. Webb, 352.

**Item:** The early happenings in the Twenty-seventh Arkansas Infantry, including its first scout and the assignment of James R. Shaler to command the regiment, by Silas C. Turnbo, Company A, Twenty-seventh Arkansas Infantry.[10]

**Published:** January 9, 1886.

# First Lessons in War.[11]

Pro Tem, Taney Co., Mo.

Editor, *Republican*

In June, 1862, our regiment, Twenty-seventh Arkansas,[12] was undergoing its organization at Yellville, Marion County [Arkansas]. In response to a military order a considerable number of citizens of military age had assembled from miles around to be "sweared in" for three years or the war. We were at first allowed to retain our horses, and passed as a cavalry command. Our arms were chiefly old squirrel-rifles and shot-guns. A few of the men had seen service under the earlier calls for troops, while the remainder were "raw hands." Any defects in arms and discipline the boys made manful efforts to supply in fun and frolic, and I believe we had as jolly a set as ever enlisted. Our rendezvous before completing our organization was at Camp Livingston, on the White River, opposite the little town of Mount Olive, in Izzard County [Arkansas]. Some other troops were camped near us, and probably altogether we numbered near 1,500 men, all under command of Gen. McBride. Our own regiment at the time was commanded by a heavy-set Dutchman named Clifford, who was supposed to rank as a major. The Federal Army under Curtis had by this time evacuated Forsyth, Taney County, Mo., and marched down through northeastern Arkansas to Batesville below us on the White River.[13] On the afternoon of June 28 scouts brought reliable information that a

---

10. Silas Turnbo was born in 1844 in the Ozarks of Arkansas, and at the beginning of the Civil War lived on a farm near the Arkansas-Missouri border on the "left bank" of the White River, in Marion County, Arkansas. On June 19, he entered military service at Yellville, Arkansas, and served the entire war in the Twenty-seventh Arkansas. Following the war Turnbo returned home, where he married and raised five children. About 1914, he moved with his wife, to Broken Bow, Oklahoma. He died in 1914, two years after his wife. S. C. Turnbo, "History of the Twenty-seventh Arkansas Confederate Infantry With Many Interesting Accounts of the Countries Through Which it Passed During the Civil War and Accurate Accounts of the Battles in which it Engaged," S. C. Turnbo Collection, University of Arkansas (Little Rock), intro, 7, 59–60, hereafter cited as Turnbo.

11. This is an abbreviated version of a similar piece that appeared in an undated typescript manuscript that Turnbo wrote following the war. Ibid., 65–77.

12. The Twenty-seventh Arkansas Infantry, also known as Shaler's Regiment, for its commander James R. Shaler, was originally a cavalry command, being dismounted on July 29, 1862. It was composed of men primarily from northern Arkansas and organized on July 31, 1862. The regiment fought in only one major battle during the war, Jenkins Ferry, Arkansas, on April 30, 1864. *O.R.*, vol. 34, pt 1:804–805; National Archives, Record Group M317 (roll no. 193), Confederate Compiled Service Records, Twenty-seventh Arkansas Infantry; Turnbo, 81–82, 98, 306.

13. Curtis's army entered Forsyth on April 10 and halted for a period of nine days, because of the rainy weather. On April 19, Curtis continued his march eastward, reaching Vera Cruz, thirty-seven miles to

body of Federals were passing down from Missouri to join Curtis at Batesville with a supply train. Orders were at once issued for a march to intercept them.[14] With much noise and confusion the horses were hastily saddled, and off we went "in a long string," fording the river, passing the village of Mount Olive and following the Wild Haw road toward

# Where the Enemy

were reported to be. The weather was dry and warm and the dust was almost unbearable. Near night we halted and camped by a stream which afforded water for the horses. Next morning, after the usual confusion in getting started, we pushed on, reaching Wild Haw[15] at noon, and halting to refresh ourselves at a splendid spring, continued on to Antioch church, where we arrived late in the afternoon. Some of our scouts had captured a Federal courier with dispatches and a lot of late newspapers. He had halted to take a swim in Mill Creek, and the scouts caught him at a disadvantage. The capture gave some information about the enemy and the report quickly spread that they were about four miles north of us and some 4,000 strong. We halted at the church and there seemed to be a kind of council of war held by some of the officers. How it terminated was never divulged, but anyhow we staid [stayed] there the whole night. Scouts and pickets were put out on all roads with instructions to keep on alert. The writer, with others under Lieut. [John C.] Ray [Rea],[16] after drawing a ration of one piece of bread for each man, was sent east half a mile to a cross-road. We were vigilant, but discovered nothing. At daylight we were ordered to rejoin the regiment, which was reported to be moving against the enemy. We were hungry and lank, and while mounting, asked permission from the officer to go hunt something to eat. This was promptly refused, his orders from the general being peremptory. However, I was determined to have something to chaw, and so told him, adding that I would join

the east on April 24. Curtis continued east and finally came to rest at Batesville, Arkansas on May 2, well before Turnbo's regiment was organized. Banasik, *Embattled Arkansas*, 5–6, 12.

14. On June 24, 1862, General McBride received orders at his Yellville headquarters from General Thomas C. Hindman, Commander of the Trans-Mississippi District, to "Gather all the people from the country about you. Follow and fall upon the rear of the enemy." McBride was to focus his attack on the Smithville, Arkansas area. The Twenty-seventh Arkansas and William O. Coleman's Missouri Cavalry Regiment were part of McBride's command at the time. McBride proceeded to Mt. Olive with Coleman's command, gathered up the Twenty-seventh Arkansas and on June 30 proceeded to Smithville via Wild Haw. McBride never completed his task, being turned away by a force that he described as being 1–2,000 Federal cavalry. William O. Coleman letter (November 20, 1914), W. L. Skaggs Collection (file no. 96), Arkansas Historical Commission, Little Rock, Arkansas; Telegrams (June 24 and 29, and July 4, 1862), Hindman to McBride, Copy Book of Telegrams (June 2–October 9, 1862), Peter W. Alexander Collection, Columbia University, here after cited as Copy Book of Telegrams.

15. Wild Haw was about sixteen miles northeast of Mt. Olive in Izzard County. Davis, *Civil War Atlas*, plt. 153.

16. John C. Rea (not Ray) was a lieutenant of Company A, Twenty-seventh Arkansas Infantry. He would become captain of the unit when Captain F. T. Wood resigned on March 3, 1863. *O.R.S.*, pt. 2, vol. 2:711; Turnbo, 67.

the troops as soon as I found the required rations. I was satisfied that there was plenty of provisions in the church, that had

## Been Brought There

by generous citizens and for the church. I struck out. Not a trooper was to be seen there, but in the church I found several pones of corn bread and some bacon and onions. I crammed my saddle-riders full and remounting with all I could hold in each hand, was on my way eating and rejoicing. I relate this and other incidents to show that we were still very young in the art of war. Following the trail of the troops for some distance north I came up where their horses were hitched. A few yards further in advance the men were in line of battle, all lying down. The position was near the road by which the enemy was expected to approach. I soon took my place in the line and seeing the grim expectancy of the men I felt just as though I was going to have a chill. The captain had something not very complimentary to say about my disobedience of orders and my rejoicing over the lunch evaporated rapidly. I soon discovered I was not the only one threatened with a chill. In a little while a reconnoitering party of the enemy came close up before discovering us. Some of the officers halted them and requested them to surrender, but they wheeled about and sped away. Some of our men gave chase but soon returned. We now expected an attack and made fresh preparations to receive it. The Federal officers, however, were just as cautious as our own, both evidently being determined not to be drawn into any traps. The suspense grew trying, and at length our officer moved us farther back. We were kept lying down again like our safety depended upon it. The boys would become restless and kept jumping up to have a look. Then the major would command" "Lie down!" and the men

## Would Drop.

In a minute another head would pop up, and the major would sing out: "Lie down, I say. When we are in camp I am no better than any of you, but when we are in line of battle you must obey my orders."

This was war indeed.

Still the boys would indulge their curiosity in spite of his military maximums. So it went until nearly noon, when Gen. McBride formed a reconnoitering party. It was composed of officers principally and the general led it. They went out to find what the Feds were up to. A similar party for a like purpose it seems had been sent out by the enemy at the same time. The two bodies met unexpectedly on the road, and then came the lively times among those dashing cavaliers. A few ineffective shots were exchanged, but the Federals soon got the best end of the horn and our men dashed back to our lines, being pursued so hotly that they scattered. Gen. McBride was cut off from the rest and chased over hill and across hollows in most exciting style. He finally escaped, but said he had to make a circuit of four miles to get back to his lines. The only loss was the general's hat, which fell off in the chase. Shortly after this the whole force received orders to mount and take the back track. We halted on Mill Creek for an hour. While remounting to continue the march a gun in the hands of Lafayette Ellison of Forsyth, Mo., accidentally went off, the discharge killing one of his best friends.[17] The body was left where it fell. I learned after the war that some citizens had found the remains a day or two afterwards and gave them as decent burial as their decomposed state would admit. This fatal accident cast a gloom over the whole command. We continued the retreat, arriving back at Camp Livingston late at night. This ended our regiment's first war experience. A few days afterwards Col. J. H. Shaler[18] of St. Louis arrived and superseded Clifford in command. Shaler was one of your strict disciplinarians and didn't suit the style of North Arkansas soldiers. He was seriously objected to and came near to causing trouble. Being only appointed over them and not elected, the men regarded him as simply a tyrant. I will write you of our later lessons in the art of war.

Silas C. Turnbo
Twenty-seventh Arkansas Regiment

* * * * * * *

---

17. Lafayette Ellison was the son of Jimmie Ellison and a member of Benjamin Crabtree's Company, Twenty-seventh Arkansas Infantry. For his part, it appears that Crabtree did not remain too long in the Twenty-seventh, probably resigning when the unit was dismounted. By November 1862 he was commanding a Missouri cavalry company, in Pocahontas in northeast Arkansas. *O.R.S,*, pt. 2, vol. 38:176; Turnbo, 76.

18. James R. Shaler, a resident of St. Louis and a member of the Volunteer Militia was captured at Camp Jackson and exchanged in October 1861. He fought at Pea Ridge, where he earned the praise of General Daniel M. Frost. When Thomas C. Hindman rebuilt the Trans-Mississippi Army, in the summer of 1862, he appointed Shaler colonel of the Twenty-seventh Arkansas Infantry Regiment. Shaler took command of his regiment on July 10, making a poor impression on his troops; many considered him a "tyrant" and openly questioned why Hindman appointed a Missourian to command an Arkansas regiment. In the latter part of 1863, Shaler was voted out as colonel of the Twenty-seventh Arkansas. Sterling Price subsequently appointed him major and inspector general of his command. *O.R.*, vol. 41, pt. 1:719; Series 2, vol. 1:117, 554; pt. 2, vol. 2:712; Turnbo, 81–82, 98, 306.

**Item:** Early happenings in an Arkansas Regiment in mid-July 1862, by Silas C. Turnbo, Company A, Twenty-seventh Arkansas Infantry.
**Published:** January 16, 1886.

## A Deserter Shot.[19]

Pro Tem, Mo., Jan. 14
Editor, *Republican*

On the 17th of June [July], 1862, our regiment, the Twenty-seventh Arkansas, left Camp Livingston, near Mt. Olive, Ark., with the rest of the cavalry, the whole being under Gen. McBride.[20] There was much dissatisfaction with the appointment of [Robert R.] Shaler as colonel of the regiment. At times mutiny was threatened, but the influences of Maj. [John W.] Methven[21] of Yellville and some company officers, with a few privates, was sufficient to prevent this. Shaler was a strict disciplinarian, and the men thought him unreasonably harsh. They were willing to drill and submit to camp discipline, but the excessive duty required on guard, and infantry drill, coupled with the hardships caused by the weather, wore the men out rapidly. The strongest and most vigorous broke down under the long strain. Some died, and others were disabled, and many left the ranks, some to join other commands and some, doubtless, going over to the Federals. We had 1,250 effectives when we organized, and in December the ranks were so depleted by death, disease and desertion that we had to be consolidated with another regiment.[22] When we left Camp Livingston on the 17th of July we

---

19. This is an abbreviated version of a similar piece that appeared in an undated typescript manuscript that Turnbo wrote following the war. Turnbo, 86–94.
20. McBride's Brigade consisted of three mounted regiments: Shaler's Arkansas, with William O. Coleman's and John Schnable's Missouri Regiments. Ibid., 86, 97–98.
21. John W. Methven or Methwin, a resident of Yellville, Arkansas and County Clerk of Marion County, was the first lieutenant in Company A, Twenty-seventh Arkansas Infantry. James R. Shaler appointed Methwen major of the regiment when the command was organized on July 31, 1862. The *Supplement to the Official Records* indicated that Methwen declined the promotion; however, later events would seem to show that he was the major of the regiment. He was captured, as a major, on October 17, during a night attack on a Union train near Mountain Home, Arkansas. He was sent to St. Louis where he died at Jefferson Barracks on December 8, 1863 (Turnbo has Methwen dying in Rolla, Missouri). According to Turnbo, Methwen "was a much respected citizen before war times and the soldiers held him in great esteem." Ibid., 95, 122–123; *O.R.*, 13:318; *O.R.S.*, pt. 2, vol. 2:711; Eakin, *Confederate Records*, 5:178.
22. The regiment was organized two days after they were dismounted on July 31, 1862. On December 15, 1862, Charles W. Adams's Arkansas Infantry Regiment reported 511 deserters, 325 absent/sick, 20 AWOL, 45 present sick and 170 present for duty. On December 17, Adams's Regiment was disbanded and the men sent to the Twenty-seventh Arkansas Infantry and Crawford's Cavalry Battalion. The Twenty-seventh received the following men, with the officers being sent to recover the deserters of the regiment—

| | | |
|---|---|---|
| Company A—20 men | Company B—35 men | Company C—19 men |
| Company D—36 men | Company E—18 men | Company F—none |
| Company G—15 men | Company H—18 men | Company I—25 men |

moved down to the mouth of the Sycamore and up that stream a few miles where we camped. Forage was very scarce and some of the boys, finding that Col. Shaler had plenty for headquarters use, raided it and divided it around. Thence we went to Camp Hindman[23] in the Buffalo Mountains near Burroughsville. Here a terrible tragedy was enacted in the name of martial law. A stripling of a boy named [Tom] Arnold[24] belonging to Co. H was condemned to be shot for desertion. The charge I suppose was correct, but it was well known that the boy was badly affected in his mind—considered a half idiot in fact. He had been raised as the pet of his family and was little more than a puny, sickly child. However, it was said an example was necessary and the sentence was executed in the hollow below the opening, and, according to orders, it was done in the presence of the command. The unhappy lad was marched to a tree by a detail of soldiers, who were compelled to guard him while another detail was compelled to shoot him. Tied to a tree and blindfolded he met death calmly, but many thought he did not appreciate his situation at all. This cruel execution will be remembered by all who were present, and whoever is responsible for it will probably have to answer at the judgment day.[25] It excited general indignation among the troops. Many of the men had purposely absented themselves contrary to orders, and some of those present turned their heads away and wept. We remained at Camp Hindman until the 23rd of July, when we took up the line of march to follow Gen. Curtis, who had retired from Batesville towards the Mississippi. On reaching White River

---

Company K—none

Total = 186

Note: The total received is in conflict with what Adams's Regiment says it sent and what the Twenty-seventh Arkansas received. In this case I've used the numbers supplied by the Twenty-seventh Arkansas. National Archives, Record Group 109, Confederate Muster Rolls, Adams's Arkansas Infantry; National Archives, Record Group M317 (roll No. 193), Confederate Compiled Service Records, Twenty-seventh Arkansas Infantry Regiment.

23. The camp was named after the District Commander Thomas C. Hindman.

24. Tom Arnold was a "conscripted" member of Company H, Twenty-seventh Arkansas Infantry. The company was organized on June 13, 1862. Arnold, recently married, "lived near Ben Brooks mill on Piney Bayou" in Izzard County, Arkansas. He was considered by those of his neighborhood to be an "imbecile." When he was executed, Turnbo noted that it was the third time that he had left the army without permission. *O.R.S.*, pt. 2, vol. 2:715, 721; Turnbo, 89–90.

25. In his expanded version of the ordeal, Turnbo noted that a party of twelve privates with an officer carried out the execution. Six of the muskets were loaded while another six were not. Turnbo, 92.

we went into regular camp fourteen miles above Batesville, called Camp Bragg. Here the regiment was dismounted and served during the rest of the war as infantry.[26]

Silas C. Turnbo.

\* \* \* \* \* \* \*

---

26. The Twenty-seventh was dismounted on July 29, 1862. *O.R.S.*, pt. 2, vol. 2:712–716.

**Item:** The Battle of Lone Jack, by D. C. Hunter.[27]
**Published:** September 12, 1885.

## The Right Wing Heard From.

Nevada, Mo., Sept. 8

Editor, *Republican*

Sometime since my attention was called to an article in the *Republican* written by Maj. [Emory S.] Foster,[28] in which the major drew a great many things from his imagination. I was requested to answer it at the time, but declined to do so, as I thought some other would improve the opportunity.

Next came "No. 2," from one Sidney D. Jackman, with a wood cut of his "phiz" and "general" prefixed to his name.[29] This is a peculiar piece of writing. For brag and bombast it has not its equal in ancient or modern history. I do not think any man since Adam was driven from his Eden pretended to write the history of any event and used as many "I's" as did our distinguished "general" in the very remarkable article.[30] When I was a boy there was a fight among Missouri Democrats, in which the Benton and the anti-Benton factions opposed each other bitterly. In speaking of the arrogance of Thomas H. Benton,[31] it was the custom of

---

27. Dewit Clinton Hunter was born in Illinois about 1829 and was a leading citizen of Nevada, Missouri, in 1861. A lawyer by profession, Hunter surveyed and built the first house in Nevada. At the beginning of the Civil War, Hunter was the circuit and country clerk for his home county. He was elected colonel of the Seventh Cavalry, Eighth Division, MSG on July 10, 1861, and resigned on December 10. While serving in the Guard, Hunter fought in only one battle, Wilson's Creek. He reentered the service, and as a Confederate major was sent into Missouri on July 11, 1862, to recruit a regiment of infantry. He organized a cavalry battalion on August 31, 1862, which formed the nucleus of his infantry regiment, which was organized on September 15. Hunter led his command at Prairie Grove on December 7, 1862, after which he resigned on February 4, 1863. Hunter again raised a cavalry regiment in the spring of 1864 and led the regiment at Marks' Mills, Arkansas (April 25, 1864) and during Price's 1864 Missouri Raid. Following the war Hunter returned to Nevada where he again practiced law. *O.R.S.*, pt. 2, vol. 38:273–274, 609; Bartels, *Forgotten Men*, 178; Crute, 208; Hale, 152–153; National Archives, Record Group 109, Confederate Muster Rolls, Eleventh Missouri Infantry; Snead, *Fight For Missouri*, 269; Special Orders 28 (July 11, 1862), Special Order Book No. 1.

28. Major Emory Foster was a major in the Seventh Missouri State Militia Cavalry and commanded the Federal force at the Battle of Lone Jack. Foster's Union account of the Battle of Lone Jack appeared in the *Republican* on August 1, 1885, and will be fully addressed in a forthcoming book in this series. For a biography of this officer see Appendix B.

29. Jackman's piece was printed on August 29, 1885, in the *Missouri Republican*, and was previously published in Norton's *Behind Enemy Lines*. For reference purposes it appears in Appendix F.

30. Hunter is clearly alluding to the lack of authenticity of Jackman's rank as "general." Kirby Smith assigned Jackman to duty as a brigadier general on May 16, 1865, but he was never confirmed in the rank, as by that time the Confederate government had long since fled Richmond, Virginia. Additionally, only President Jefferson Davis had the authority to appoint general officers, and many of Smith's late war promotions were repudiated by Davis. Allardice, 134; Boatner, 770.

31. Thomas Hart Benton was born in 1782 in North Carolina and studied law at the University of North Carolina. In 1782 he moved to Tennessee, where he was elected state senator. Benton moved to St. Louis in 1815, where he became the editor of the *Missouri Enquirer*. Elected as one of Missouri's first senators (1820–1850), Benton championed western causes like free navigation of the Mississippi

the anti-Benton partisans to denominate that distinguished worthy "Old I Did," and this would seem a fitting name for the heroic Jackman. Therefore, I will be pardoned for referring to him as "I Did."

The magnifying glasses worn by "I Did" make the "I!" very large, while the "Yous" are correspondingly diminutive. Yet many things that he relates are as near to the truth as a mind like "I Did's" can write. It is hardly necessary, then, to add that many of his statements are highly tinctured with "concentrated." Like the novel writer, he must have his hero and in his case the hero must be Jackman! In order to accomplish this, however, there were several other names

## To get out of the way.

And the first of these was Col. [Jeremiah V.] Cockrell.[32] This man was wanting in nerve—showed the white feather—started to run back, but "I Did" and "I Said" and, finally, we went on; and had it not been for "I Did," Col. Cockrell would have turned tail and run back to Frog Bayou. But "I Did" saved him, and we went ahead with flying colors.[33]

Dewitt Clinton Hunter

---

River and a national road to New Mexico. A tacit supporter of slavery, Benton was defeated for office in 1851, but won a U.S. House of Representatives seat in 1852. He died of cancer on April 10, 1858. James Neal Primm, *Lion of the Valley St. Louis, Missouri* (Boulder, CO), 1981, 113–114, 116–117, 120; James M. Volo and Dorothy Denneen Volo, *Encyclopedia of the Antebellum South* (Westport, CT, 2000), 30–31.

32. Jeremiah Vard Cockrell was born in 1832 and worked as a Methodist preacher in Warren County, Missouri, prior to the war. On June 13, 1861, he was elected a lieutenant in Company E, Second Cavalry Regiment, Eighth Division, MSG. During the summer of 1862, Cockrell recruited a regiment of cavalry, which was subsequently dismounted, causing Cockrell to lose command of the unit to Colonel S. D. Jackman. Cockrell never played a prominent role in the Civil War after losing his regiment. Following the war he resided in Texas and was elected to the U.S. Congress. Norton, 63–64, 70, 123–125; Peterson, 250, 284.

33. Missouri recruiters assembled in western Arkansas in the summer of 1862, preparatory to their return to Missouri. General Rains selected J. V. Cockrell to lead one of the expeditions into Missouri to procure recruits for the Confederate cause. Prior to this move, Cockrell established his camp on Frog Bayou near Van Buren. On July 27, Jo Shelby arrived in camp, joined his command with Cockrell's and proceeded into Missouri on August 1. Cockrell's force made contact with some Federal troops on August 8, near Newtonia, which produced little results. According to Jackman, the incident mentioned in the article occurred the following day, just as Cockrell and the other Missouri recruiters were moving into their areas of recruitment. Cockrell, supposedly "remarked that the responsibility was so great, that he was afraid to risk the command in Missouri." John N. Edwards, a Jo Shelby biographer, noted

After boosting Col. Cockrell in this style as long as necessary, "I Did" pets him up again, just as some men fondled a dog after having kicked him out of the path.[34] As to how Col. Cockrell would appreciate the treatment is not for me to say.

At Lone Jack the first strike "I Did" makes is at Col. Up. Hays,[35] who, I believe, is dead. Hays must not have even one feather in his hat, so "I Did" boots him clear out. Hays out of the way, branded as a coward, we will now proceed with the battle.[36] The lines were formed much as stated by "I Did"—Hunter on the right, Jackman in the center and [John C.] Tracy[37] on the left. Thus formed, we marched

---

that the incident involved a direct assault on the Newtonia defenses and made no mention of Cockrell's reluctance to proceed. However, in his latter years, Jo Shelby would support Jackman's statements regarding Cockrell's hesitation to proceed deeper into Missouri, though with a decidedly different bent than Jackman. Shelby wrote, that Cockrell "did not at the time, desire to hazard the lives of his devoted followers" and further was "a brave and good man and was as loyal to the South as any man who ever fought for her." *O.R*, 13:978–979; Joanne C. Eakin, *Battle of Lone Jack August 16, 1862* (Independence, MO, 2001), 78, hereafter cited as Eakin, *Lone Jack*; John Newman Edwards, *Shelby and His Men or the War in the West* (Cincinnati, OH, 1867; reprint ed. Waverly, MO, 1993), 69–70; Norton, 76, 78.

34. In his article on Lone Jack, Jackman would later write—"Col. Cockrell sustained the high opinion I had of him as a cool and brave man." Norton, 103.

35. Upton Hays was born in Callaway County, Missouri, on March 29, 1832, was a wealthy planter in Jackson County, and operated a freight line to Utah and Santa Fe at the beginning of the war. He was elected captain of Company E, First Cavalry Regiment, Eighth Division, MSG, and in December 1861, was elected lieutenant colonel of the regiment. Hays commanded a regiment of Confederate cavalry in the summer of 1862, and was killed on September 13, 1862, near Newtonia, at Page Crossing, while leading a charge upon some Federal pickets. See Banasik, *Cavaliers of the Brush*, 178–179, for a complete biography. *O.R.S.*, pt. 2, vol. 34:742; pt. 2, vol. 38:260; see "Col. David Shanks" entry, Eakin, *Confederate Records*, 7:14; John S. Krister, "Captured Guns At Lone Jack, Mo.," *Confederate Veteran* 24 (April 1916), 184; National Archives, Record Group 109, Confederate Muster Rolls, Twelfth Missouri Cavalry Regiment; Peterson, 244; Webb, 322–325.

Note: The *Supplement to the Official Records* states that Hays was killed on September 6, 1862; however, the *Official Records* has no action of any type taking place near Newtonia on that date. There was, however, a skirmish near there on September 13 between the rebels and elements of the Third Missouri Militia Cavalry, and the description fits what was said in the various Confederate accounts of the affair. Additionally, one veteran recorded that Hays was killed the day after he was elected colonel, on September 12, 1862.

36. Throughout his article, Jackman doesn't appear to brand Hays a coward; to the contrary he even notes that he was a "brave and experienced" officer, who "did his duty manfully." However there was a part of Jackman's account that could have left Hunter confused. According to Jackman, on the evening of August 15, 1862, "Coffee and Tracy had retreated upon a road south" of the main rebel force, "and that the enemy believing that they had fired on Hays and Quantrell [Quantrill], had now retired for the night." The force that "ran" before the Federals on the evening before the battle was not Hays's, but Coffee's command. Hays's command was located twelve miles northwest of Lone Jack on August 15 and did not arrive at the scene of the battle until just before dawn. Quantrill was not in the battle and even Jackman would later record that he took no part in the engagement. Banasik, *Embattled Arkansas*, 169; Eakin, *Lone Jack*, 8, 10; Norton, 5, 102, 108–109.

37. John C. Tracy was born in Kentucky about 1826, and lived in Columbus, Johnson County, Missouri, at the beginning of the war. He was elected lieutenant colonel of the Third Infantry Regiment, Eighth Division, MSG on June 19, 1861. Wounded at Wilson's Creek on August 10, 1861, Tracy recovered and during the winter of 1861–1862 was in the Lexington area recruiting for the rebel cause. In late spring 1862, Tracy was in Arkansas, having remained behind when the MSG moved to the east

# Battle of Lone Jack, Missouri
## (August 16, 1862)

CSA ASSEMBLY PT./ HOSPITAL/ AMMO

WEST FORK SINABAR CREEK

N

WOODS

CULTIVATED FIELDS

CORNFIELD

HAYS

FEDERAL RETREAT

TRACY

7TH MO CAV.

CORNFIELD

CORNFIELD

OVERGROWN HEMP FIELD

WOODS

JACKMAN

HOTEL

BLACK SMITH

UNION HORSES

HEDGE

2ND, 7TH & 8TH MSM CAV.

HUNTER

6TH MSM CAV.

CORNFIELD

CORNFIELD

PRAIRIE

ROADS

FENCE

PRAIRIE

PRAIRIE

COFFEE ARRIVES 11:00 a.m.

up near the sleeping enemy and then waited for an attack by Hays on the east. When we heard the Federals getting up[38] I went to Jackman and proposed to attack at once, but he would not consent, saying that the order would not permit. I told him that the circumstances were different from what Col. Cockrell expected, and in my judgment we should move at once. This he refused to do.[39] Had he and Tracy consented to charge at that time, the Federal host would have left the field dressed in white; but we must not take any advantage; consequently we waited until they had donned the blue, seized their guns, provided themselves with plenty of ammunition, formed

## Into Line

and counted off, as if on parade; and were thus ready and waiting for a foe to fight. Then it was that "I Did" gave the order to charge, when the entire line had been waiting all this time for the idea to get through his head that the proper time to charge had already come.[40]

When the charge was made, my command, being on the right, struck the south part of the town, my left near the hotel and my right out along the fence, when

---

side of the Mississippi River. On June 4, General T. C. Hindman authorized Tracy to return to Missouri to recruit for the Confederacy. On July 31, Tracy began recruiting a regiment and joined up with Cockrell, Hunter, Jackman, and Hays to fight and win the Battle of Lone Jack. There was no further record of Tracy found in the *Official Records* or the *Supplement to the Official Records*. According to a later comment in this article, D. C. Hunter wrote: Tracy "long ago sleeps under the sod." Banasik, *Cavaliers of the Brush*, 223; Banasik, *Embattled Arkansas*, 170; Bartels, *Forgotten Men*, 364; Hale, 324; Letter (June 4, 1862), Hindman to Tracy, Copy Letter Book (June 1–December 18, 1862), Hindman's Command, Peter W. Alexander Collection (hereafter cited as Copy Letter Book No. 1).

38. The Union force at Lone Jack was alerted to the rebel presence, by most accounts, when a single gunshot rang out in the early morning. Some sources say that an advancing rebel (Eakin and Edwards name him as William C. McFarland) stumbled and accidentally fired his gun. Yet another participant recorded: "Captain Thorp and I saw the Federal pickets and he remarked: 'Dick, there are the pickets, fire!' He and I fired simultaneously at the two pickets but neither of us hit them." Major Emory Foster, Union commander, noted that he was warned of the rebel approach by his pickets and makes no mention of a telltale shot. Banasik, *Embattled Arkansas*, 172; Eakin, *Lone Jack*, 12, 53, 61, 100; Edwards, *Shelby and His Men*, 74; Missouri Cavalryman, Collection No. 995, vol. 1, entry no. 6, State Historical Society of Missouri, 4.

39. Even the common soldier could see that action should have been taken instead of waiting. C. B. Lotspeich, of Jackman's command, recorded:

We had captured all the guards so far and had we charged them so soon as we got there, it would have been a bloodless victory, for we would have caught them all asleep. Orders must be obeyed and we waited until daylight and they discovered us and gave the alarm.

C. B. Lotspeich, Unpublished manuscript, "Personal Experiences of C. B. Lotspeich," Arkansas History Commission, 9.

40. According to Jackman, Hays's mounted force was to begin the attack on the Federal right flank. With the Unionist attention turned toward Hays, the remainder of the line would attack from the west of Lone Jack and completely destroy the Federals. Prior to the attack beginning, Hays was on the north while Tracy, Jackman and Hunter were to the west of Lone Jack. Tracy was next to Hays, then came Jackman in the center and finally Hunter on the far right of the Confederate line. Norton, 91.

the Federals were formed[41] in the street. My line and their left, being south of the houses, neither side had any protection. The Federals opposing my line soon gave way and retired down the line further north, forming behind the house in front of Jackman and Tracy. It was not long after the fight began until both parties took advantage of the houses on each side of the street, and fight was reduced to sharp-shooting—shooting behind the houses, from windows and from behind any object that would shield a man's carcass from the bullets of the enemy. After the fight had continued for some length of time and the Federals had been driven behind the houses, it was reported to me that there was a body of cavalry threatening my right flank and moving, as if it would attack the boys keeping our horses and our ammunition wagon.[42] When I heard this I sent my adjutant, Lieut. Frost[43] of Henry County, to see. He came back and reported to me that there was quite a body of Federal cavalry out there, and unless immediate steps for protection were taken, they would capture our horses and ammunition, and also be enabled to charge me in the right rear. At this time Jackman, Tracy and the Federals were all

---

41. The Federal command at Lone Jack consisted of 740 men with two pieces of artillery:

       7th Missouri Cavalry 265
       2nd Battalion Missouri State Militia Cavalry 81
       6th Regiment Missouri State Militia Cavalry 149
       7th Regiment Missouri State Militia Cavalry 69
       8th Regiment Missouri State Militia Cavalry 140
       Section, 3rd Indiana Artillery (2 guns) 36
       Total 740

Banasik, *Embattled Arkansas*, 504.

42. The Sixth Missouri State Militia Cavalry Regiment, under Captain William Plumb, held the Union left. According to Captain Plumb, the Confederates on his front, under Hunter, were initially repulsed, followed by an hour of relative quiet on his front. During this lull, Hunter, perceiving a threat to his right flank, turned his attention to that quarter. Meanwhile, Captain Plumb moved his command to support the Federal center and recapture the cannons which had been taken by the rebels in that section. Within the first hour, with the surprise gone, the focus of the battle shifted to the Union artillery. The Federals quickly moved into the buildings of Lone Jack, and used their horses and a thick hedge for protection. The Confederates, for their part, found cover wherever they could. *O.R.S.*, pt. 1, vol. 3:45–47. Emory S. Foster, "The Battle of Lone Jack," *Missouri Republican*, August 1, 1885.

43. Wayne Schnetzer does not list a Frost as a casualty or his presence at the battle. Schnetzer does list a W. B. Gibson as Hunter's Adjutant, who was present at the battle. Additionally, the only officer in Hunter's command that Schnetzer lists as killed at Lone Jack was a Lieutenant O. M. Cross. Was Hunter's memory faulty? Did Cross serve as an Adjutant or aid-de-camp during the battle? Eakin, *Lone Jack*, 147–149, 152.

# Behind the Houses,

each on his own side, keeping up a regular sharp-shooting match, neither trying to dislodge the other, and neither doing much damage. I had, by this time, lost seven men killed and many wounded; and when I left Jackman everything was safe, so far as an advance was concerned, and the enemy could not have turned his right flank without first coming out from behind the houses. This I knew they would not do; besides if they had, I was close enough at hand to meet them and drive them back.

I marched my command a little west of south, about 150 yards. When we started in that direction the cavalry retired east, in behind the Federal lines. During this movement we were exposed to a raking fire from Federals in front of Jackman, and my adjutant, Lieut. Frost, was killed and several others wounded.

When the Federals, against whom we were moving, retired from the south, I ordered my line into column facing the east, intending to march across the road, south of the two lines, and charge the left wing of the Federals and drive them from behind the houses. When the column started east some of my officers told me that the men had no ammunition. We had but a few cartridges and the men carried their ammunition in their pockets. (Jackman stated that we had only six rounds to start with.) I halted the column and passed down the line. I found some had two cartridges, some had none, except the one in their guns. In this condition and still under the fire of the Federals from behind the houses, I thought it best to retire to the wagon and get ammunition, and I think I got there about one minute before irate "I Did."

# He Came Up Blustering

but I was busy, and paid but little attention to him. Probably the electricity vibrating on the bristly red hair of his head so shocked my shattered nerves that I was dumb. However, be that as it may, it made no impression on my mind, or I had forgotten it.[44]

On our return to the town to renew the fight I may have fallen down (for I have a big foot), but that also slipped my memory.[45] At all events I went ahead and I got up behind the houses. I got behind one, and Jackman behind another. I fired several shots and supposed that he was equally busy, but I noticed that he was as careful to shield his carcass as I was to save mine. (By the way, neither of us died for our country at Lone Jack.)

---

44. According to Jackman, he, like Hunter had pulled his command back for ammunition, but more so because he felt that Hunter "had deserted" his flank. Jackman then accused Hunter of throwing his ammunition away. After a short tiff the two returned to the battle. Norton, 95–96.

45. Jackman stated that Hunter tripped and sprained his ankle while returning to the battlefield through a cornfield. Leaving Hunter "in disgust," Jackman returned to the battle. Gathering himself up, Hunter returned to the engagement, a point that Jackman never mentioned in his article, clearly leaving the impression that Hunter was either a coward or a slacker. Hunter, for his part, took Jackman's comments to mean that he, Hunter, was a coward. Ibid., 97–98.

Finally the Federals decamped. It might appear that said Jackman showed his fiery red head from behind the house, and the Federals, thinking it is a heretofore undiscovered comet threatening them with sure destruction, fled. But the facts are these: That man, Col. John T. Coffee,[46] that Jackman said had run off, happened to return just in the nick of time, when victory was poised over the field, uncertain where to perch. Col. Coffee came up, formed his line across the road north of the town,[47] and moved down on the field in grand style (and that was one time I was glad to see the gallant colonel), and the Federals not liking the looks of Col. Coffee's sharp-shooters, fled precipitately down the road to Lexington.[48]

This is a plain, fair and candid statement of facts. I was one of the boys that fought at Lone Jack, and only ask my part of honors.

As to me being a coward, the men that were with me at Lone Jack

## Did Not Believe.

When we reached Arkansas my recruits numbered 1,700. By order of Gen. Hindman these recruits were reduced to ten companies of 125 men, making 1,250 men, two or three hundred of them having been in the Battle of Lone Jack, and every one of them, by popular vote, voted for D. C. Hunter to be colonel of the Eleventh Missouri Infantry.[49] These men did not believe me to be a coward; the men who were with me at Prairie Grove in front of Gen. [James G.] Blunt[50] do

---

46. John Trousdale Coffee, a lawyer by profession and a veteran of the Mexican War, was born in Smith County, Tennessee. Prior to the Civil War, Coffee lived in Greenfield, Missouri, owned a local newspaper, and was elected to the Missouri Senate in 1854. At the beginning of the war Coffee raised a regiment of MSG cavalry. Later he organized a regular Confederate unit in the summer of 1862, and another one in 1864. He was at Lone Jack on Shelby's 1863 Missouri Raid, and Price's 1864 Missouri Raid. Following the war he relocated to Texas where he died on May 23, 1890, at Brownsville. See Appendix B for a complete biography. John K. Hulston and James W. Goodrich, "John Trousdale Coffee: Lawyer, Politician, Confederate," *Missouri Historical Review* 85 (October 1990), 272–273, 275–277, 283, 290, 292, 294; Peterson, 263.
47. According to Captain Milton Brawner, Coffee appeared on the Union left or southern flank, not the right or northern flank. *O.R.*, 13:237.
48. About 10:00 a.m., Major Foster, with 60 men, led the final Union assault to recapture the artillery. After fierce hand-to-hand combat, the guns were retaken, but at the loss of 48 men "disabled"—either wounded or killed. Foster was then wounded with a ball in his side and Captain Milton H. Brawner, of the Seventh Missouri Cavalry, assumed command of the Federal force. About 10:30, Colonel Coffee's command reappeared on the Federal left flank and prepared to enter the engagement, prompting Captain Brawner to order a retreat. *Ibid.*, 13:237, 239; Banasik, *Embattled Arkansas*, 173–174; Foster, "Battle of Lone Jack."
49. Hunter's command retreated to Arkansas, where it arrived near Bentonville on August 22. On August 31, Hunter's Battalion of seven companies was organized and the same day it was dismounted. On September 15, 1862, near the Pea Ridge Battlefield, at Camp Hindman, the Eleventh Missouri Infantry was organized with 1,248 men and elected Hunter its colonel. *O.R.S.*, pt. 2, vol. 38:609, 613, 617, 619; National Archives, Record Group 109, Confederate Muster Rolls, Eleventh Missouri Infantry; Quesenberry Diary, September 11.
50. James G. Blunt was born on July 21, 1826, in Trenton, Maine, obtained a medical degree in Ohio, and moved to Greely, Kansas, in 1856. An abolitionist and supporter of John Brown, Blunt led a militia company during the Kansas-Missouri border wars. At the beginning of the Civil War Blunt

not believe it; the Confederates from Missouri do not believe it, and now, Sidney, "honest injun," laying all jealousy and pride aside, you don't believe it yourself! Now own up and admit you just wanted to brag a little.

The boy that helped fire the hotel belonged to Capt. [William M.] Lowe's company.[51] His name was Lafayette Logan. He was killed before the fight was over and now sleeps under the Lone Jack tree.[52]

Col. Jackman makes a thrust at Col. Tracy. As to the facts I cannot say, but as Col. Tracy long ago sleeps under the sod, and cannot reply, I think it was a very small piece of business to use his vulgar slang to dishonor the dead, that he might boost of himself.[53] As to Capt. [H. B.] Brewster and Lieut. [Jesse P.] Herrill [Herrell],[54] both of whom he boasts about, I can say nothing as I do not know them.

---

enlisted as a private, was soon appointed the lieutenant colonel of the Third Kansas Infantry, and on April 8, 1862, was catapulted to the rank of brigadier general. Leading the Kansas Division in the fall of 1862, and later the Army of the Frontier, Blunt won the Battles of Old Fort Wayne, Indian Territory (October 22), and in Arkansas, Cane Hill (November 28), Prairie Grove (December 7) and Van Buren (December 28). Blunt spent his entire Civil War career in the Trans-Mississippi, participating in his last engagements during Price's 1864 Missouri Raid. A popular general with the soldiers, Blunt was promoted to major general on March 3, 1863, a grade he held until the end of the war. After the war Blunt returned to medicine in Leavenworth, Kansas, then moved to Washington, DC, where he died in a government hospital for the insane on July 27, 1881. See Banasik, *Reluctant Cannoneer*, 273–277, for a complete biography.

51. William M. Lowe, a resident of Schell City, Vernon County, Missouri, joined the Confederate Army on August 13, 1862, at Pleasant Gap, Missouri, just three days before the Battle of Lone Jack. His Company E, Eleventh Missouri Infantry, was organized on August 31, electing Lowe as its captain. Lowe resigned from the army on January 7, 1863, citing "chronic sore eyes." His resignation was accepted, but Lowe remained in the army and was paroled out of the service on June 15, 1865. At the Battle of Lone Jack, Lowe's company lost three killed and two wounded. *O.R.S.*, pt. 2, vol. 38:610, 613, 617; National Archives, Record Group M322 (roll no. 159), Confederate Compiled Service Records, Eleventh Missouri Infantry; Norton, 98; Wayne H. Schnetzer, *Men of the Eleventh: A Roster of the Eleventh Missouri Infantry Confederate States of America* (Independence, MO, n.d.), 53.

52. According to Sidney Jackman, Lieutenant James C. Martin, of Company I, Jackman's Regiment, came to him and suggested that they burn the Federals out of the hotel at Lone Jack. Lafayette Logan, of Lowe's Company, went with Martin and accomplished the deed. Eakin, *Lone Jack*, 157; Norton, 99.

53. After securing ammunition for his command, Jackman returned to the scene of the action, meeting Colonel Tracy en route to the rear. According to Jackman, Tracy told him that he was "shot all to pieces," but upon examination of his wound, a disgusted Jackman, returned to the battlefield "with a feeling of supreme contempt" for Tracy. Jackman "was thoroughly convinced" that Tracy was "mistaken, as to what it was running down his legs." Tracy, like Hunter and Hays, all seemed to be branded as cowards by Jackman. Norton, 97.

54. H. B. Brewster lived in Carroll County, Missouri at the beginning of the Civil War. He was elected captain of Company C, First Cavalry Regiment, Fourth Division, MSG on July 7, 1861. He was furloughed on October 8, but never returned to his command. He later joined the Confederate Army and served for a time as the Adjutant for Shelby's Cavalry Brigade. At the Battle of Prairie Grove, Shelby recorded that Brewster "was ever with me, brave and daring, carrying orders and forming regiments as if on dress parade." In addition to Lone Jack and Prairie Grove, Brewster also took part in the engagements at Carthage, Dug Springs, Wilson's Creek and the Siege of Lexington. *O.R.*, vol. 22, pt. 1:153; Eakin, *Confederate Records*, 1:146; Peterson, 139.

Jesse P. Herrell or Herrill was born about 1837 in Missouri, and lived in Butler County at the beginning of the Civil War. He joined the MSG in May 1861 and enlisted in Cockrell's Cavalry on July 18, 1862. Wounded at Lone Jack, Herrell recovered and went on to command an independent company

It is curious, with the reputation the Confederates have heretofore maintained, that the immortalized Jackman should have been thrown among so many cowards. I am sorry that any body of Confederate troops should have been commanded by a set of cowardly officers. And I might ask the "general" some questions about why

## He Left the Army

in Arkansas, depriving it of his valuable services at a most inopportune moment.[55] The army west of the Mississippi thus suffered about the same loss that the Army of Virginia did in the death of Stonewall Jackson; the difference is that one went to the grave, the other back into the brush. Had Jackman remained with the army and helped Gens. [Edmund Kirby] Smith and [Theophilus H.] Holmes,[56] the results of the war would have been far different.

Col. Jackman said nothing about the cannon.[57] I am surprised that he did not claim that he had captured them. After the fight was over there was a boy belonging to my command, who lived two miles east of Holcombe's Springs in Arkansas,[58] I have forgotten his name, who came and told me the cannon were down in the field. I, with others went back with him. We found that there were two pieces, and they were bravely defended, but we made a gallant charge and the

---

of cavalry, which became Company C, Sixteenth Missouri Infantry (Confederate), on September 1, 1862. Herrell was promoted to major of his regiment on March 24, 1863 (*O.R.S.* has the date as May 24). *O.R.S.*, pt. 2, vol. 38:637–638; Eakin, *Lone Jack*, 151; National Archives, Record Group 109, Confederate Muster Rolls, Sixteenth Missouri Infantry; National Archives, Record Group M322, (roll no. 168), Confederate Compiled Service Records, Sixteenth Missouri Infantry; Schnetzer, *More Forgotten Men*, 111.

55. Jackman resigned from the army on October 23, 1862, and his resignation was accepted by General Hindman two days later. In his letter of resignation, Jackman cited his desire to return to Missouri and recruit a mounted unit, which he felt he was better suited to command. Letter (October 23, 1862), Jackman to Hindman, Miscellaneous Correspondence, Peter W. Alexander Collection, Columbia University, hereafter cited as Miscellaneous Correspondence; Special Orders No. 22 (October 25, 1862), Special Order Book No. 1.

56. The Confederate War Department assigned Edmund Kirby Smith to command the Southwestern Army, embracing Louisiana and Texas, on January 14, 1863. Later the command was expanded on February 9 to include all troops west of the Mississippi River. Smith assumed his new post on March 7, 1863, and eleven days later was appointed the commander of the Trans-Mississippi Department. For a biography and photo see Banasik, *Missouri Brothers in Gray*, 152–153. *O.R.*, vol. 22, pt. 1:3; Harrell, *Arkansas, Confederate Military History*, 173.

Major General Theophilus H. Holmes was the commander of the Trans-Mississippi Department from July 16, 1862. He was promoted to lieutenant general to rank from October 10, 1862. On March 7, 1863 Holmes was relieved of the department command and placed in control of the District of Arkansas. Following the debacle at Helena, Arkansas, on July 4, 1863, Holmes was relegated to a minor role in the Trans-Mississippi and finally resigned in 1864. For biography and photo see Banasik, *Missouri Brothers in Gray*, 141–143; Boatner, 406; Sifakis, *Who Was Who in the Confederacy*, 133, 261.

57. Two pieces of artillery were captured at the Battle of Lone Jack—two 12-pound James rifles. They belonged to the Third Indiana Artillery Company. Banasik, *Embattled Arkansas*, 504.

58. Holcombe's Springs was located on the main road between Fayetteville and Springfield, Missouri. It was about nine miles north of Fayetteville. Letter (October 20, 1862), Hindman to Holmes, Copy Letter Book No. 1.

enemy surrendered. An old dun horse defended one piece and a boy and a sorrel the other. They made a gallant defense, but they could not resist our charge and so surrendered to Hunter and the Arkansas boy. Others may claim the honor of capturing the artillery but it rightly belongs to the boy from Arkansas. He wore yellow jean pants, a checkered shirt of homemade cotton cloth and a white wool hat.

## The Losses

As to the number of killed, after the dead had been carried up and laid in rows for burial, I went along the row and looked at the dead men. I asked the officer in charge how many there were. He said he had counted them and there were 119 Federal and 37 Confederates.[59] I did not count them, but from appearances, I thought he was correct. Nine of these belonged to Hunter's command. I never could ascertain as to the number of wounded. Several of my own men were left in the hospital, and several, who were slightly wounded, went out with me. Some also returned to their homes and there was no report made of the battle to my knowledge.

I do not know that it is necessary, at this late day, to answer the charges more fully than I have, that was never made, to my knowledge, until nearly a quarter of a century after the battle, when the majority of the participants on both sides are sleeping in the dust. And with all the social intercourse I have had with Col. Jackman, and with all the kind regards and personal friendships expressed through letters from him and from others, I had no idea there was any venom secreted in his heart against me, and I cannot now believe that it was anything else than his inordinate love of praise that prompted him to write as he did. It is likely the appointment of United States marshal from President Cleveland[60] may have also puffed him a little—but I am done for the present. Respectfully,

D. C. Hunter.

---

59. The Federal command lost 43 killed, 154 wounded with 75 missing. The Confederate losses varied depending on the source. The *San Antonio Weekly Herald* reported the loss of 34 killed and 70 wounded. G. W. Thompson reported that his command (probably just the troops from Independence—Hays's Regiment) lost 15 killed and 45 wounded. In searching individual Confederate records Wayne Schnetzer recorded 56 killed, 42 wounded and 4 missing. Banasik, *Cavaliers of the Brush*, 224; Eakin, *Lone Jack*, 149–152 (material provided by Wayne Schnetzer); "From Arkansas and Missouri," *San Antonio Weekly Herald* (San Antonio, TX), September 20, 1862.

60. Jackman was appointed the U.S. Marshall for the Western District of Texas in 1885. President Grover Cleveland was born in 1837, was elected President in 1884, defeated in 1888 and reelected in 1892. He died in 1908. Guralnik, 266; Norton, 9.

**Item:** David Shanks's Company, Upton Hays's Regiment, at the Battle of Lone Jack, by John S. Davis, Shanks's Cavalry Company.[61]
**Published:** September 12, 1885.

## A Voice From the Cavalry.

Lexington, Mo. Sept. 7

Editor, *Republican*

I am much pleased to see that the *Republican* is determined to bring out the facts about the Lone Jack battle, and hope you may find my short reminiscences worthy of publication.

With kindest feelings for both Gen. S. D. Jackman and Maj. E. S. Foster, allow me (an unfortunate eye-witness) to say that, certainly, Col. W. [U. or Upton] Hays's regiment of recruits (that portion having arms, except Co. G, commanded by Capt. David Shanks)[62] were engaged on Tracy's left, fighting dismounted.

Many of Hays's men and my neighbors were picked up dead or dying from that part of the field, after all was over; and that the "bloody" charge supposed to have been made by Quantrell [Quantrill] with 300 followers[63] was in reality

---

61. John S. Davis, a farmer by occupation, was a member of Company I, Hays's Regiment (Twelfth Missouri Cavalry). In 1901 he was living in the Van Buren Township, near Tarsney, in Jackson County, Missouri. Eakin, *Lone Jack*, 163; Hale, 81.

62. David Shanks was born in Kentucky about 1832, and moved to Jackson County, Missouri, where "he grew to manhood." At the age of seventeen he journeyed to California in search of gold and later returned to Missouri. He lived near Pleasant Hill, Cass County, at the beginning of the Civil War. He was elected captain of Company D, Third Infantry Regiment, Eighth Division, MSG on July 22, 1861. Listed as missing at Wilson's Creek, Shanks raised another company during the summer of 1862, which became Company C, Twelfth Missouri Cavalry. Shanks was promoted to major upon the death of Upton Hays on September 13, 1862, and colonel, with the resignation of Beal F. Jeans on May 11, 1863. Wounded during Price's 1864 Missouri Raid, Shanks was captured on October 8, 1864 at Jefferson City, Missouri, where he was recovering, and sent to the Myrtle Street Prison in St. Louis. On December 6, was forwarded to the Alton (Illinois) Prison, and from there to Gratiot Street Prison in St. Louis on July 1, 1865, where he was subsequently paroled. He died in Denver, Colorado in 1870. *O.R.*, 13:5; *O.R.S.*, pt. 2, vol. 34:742; pt. 2, vol. 38:260; Bartels, *Forgotten Men*, 324; Eakin & Hale, 389; Eakin, *Confederate Records*, 7:14; Eakin, *Missouri Prisoners of War*, "Shanks, David," two entries; Edwards, *Shelby and His Men*, 86; Hale, 289–290; National Archives, Record Group 109, Confederate Muster Rolls, Twelfth Missouri Cavalry Regiment; National Archives, Record Group M322 (roll no. 61), Confederate Compiled Service Records, Twelfth Missouri Cavalry Regiment.

63. William C. Quantrill was born in Ohio in 1837 and moved to Kansas in 1857. During the Civil War he became one of most notable guerrillas on the frontier border. For additional information on Quantrill's band see Banasik, *Cavaliers of the Brush*. See also *Serving With Honor*, pages 391–392 for a complete biography of Quantrill. Major Foster was the one who wrote that Quantrill was at Lone Jack with 300 men. Jackman, for his part, recorded that only Lieutenant Haller, with twenty-five men of Quantrill's command was present, but never fired a shot at the Battle of Lone Jack. Jackman wrote: When I came to the hospital I found Lieut. Haller and a few of his men at the door and inquired what part he had taken in the battle, and greatly to my surprise, he answered that they had not fired a shot. I then asked him if it was possible that twenty-five men, armed as they were, could witness a fight of that character and not participate in it. He replied that his captain (Quantrell) was not there and they would not go into battle without him.

made by Capt. Shanks and that portion of his company having arms, with one exception, and that was a man Dupee, who kept his place in ranks with only a rock in one hand to fight with. Capt. Shanks charged from east of the hedge, which readily accounts for Gen. Jackman's wrong conclusion as to the action of Hays' regiment.[64]

John S. Davis
A member of Capt. Shanks's Company

\* \* \* \* \* \*

---

Foster, "Battle of Lone Jack"; S. D. Jackman, "The Battle of Lone Jack," *Missouri Republican*, August 29, 1885.

64. In his comments on the Battle of Lone Jack, Jackman implies that Hays's entire command was east of the hedge, when in fact only Shanks's Company of forty men were in that position. Eakin, *Lone Jack*, 28; Norton, 98.

**Item:** The Battle of Lone Jack—the night preceding the battle and the action of Tracy's Regiment at the battle, by Henry C. Luttrell, Company G, Tenth Missouri Cavalry (C.S.A.), previously a member of Allison's Company, Tracy's command.[65]

**Published:** October 3, 1885.

## One More From Lone Jack.

Editor, *Republican*

I am very much pleased to see that you are inclined to bring out all the facts about the affair at Lone Jack. Perhaps there has been enough said already about it, quite likely too much, as a good portion of the statements exist only in imagination. For instance, Maj. Foster's imagination was busy when he told how he surprised Col. Coffee on the evening of the 15th. Now, I was a member of Capt. [Ephriam] Allison's company,[66] Tracy's regiment, and a soldier only six days old on the morning of the battle. When Foster arrived at Lone Jack on the evening in question he sounded his halt by a bugle blast. An 80-acre cornfield lay between our camp and the village. We marched out of camp on what I took to be the Warrensburg road at Augusta. It was the first road running east and west south of town and intersected by the Pleasant Hill road about a quarter of a mile south of the village. When the head of the column struck the Pleasant Hill road it turned south and halted just as Allison's company was at the angle of the two roads. Here a small number of men, ten or twenty, a flank guard, or, perhaps,

---

65. Henry C. Luttrell was enlisted by Colonel John C. Tracy in what became Company G, Tenth Missouri Cavalry (Confederate) on August 10, 1862. He survived the war and was paroled at Shreveport, Louisiana, on June 8, 1865. After the war Luttrell lived in Baldwin, Missouri, and wrote a series of articles on his wartime experiences, which appeared periodically in the *Missouri Republican* (These articles will appear later in this series). National Archives, Record Group M322 (roll no. 57), Confederate Compiled Service Records, Tenth Missouri Cavalry; War Echoes, *Missouri Republican*, October 29, 1885.

66. Ephriam Allison was born on November 27, 1835, in Copper County, Missouri. At the beginning of the Civil War Allison was a resident and promising businessman of Clinton, in Henry County. During the summer of 1862, according to Sidney Jackman, Allison was one of his commanders who accompanied him to Missouri to recruit a company (Schnetzer has Allison as part of Cockrell's command). However, according to the National Archives, Allison was enlisted by John C. Tracy on August 11, 1862, in St. Clair County, Missouri. Allison recruited his company primarily in Bates, Cedar, and St. Clair Counties, organized his unit on August 1, 1862, as a cavalry unit, and led it at Lone Jack. Wounded there, Allison recovered and upon organization of the Sixteenth Missouri Infantry on September 1, 1862, was elected captain of Company I, which was also known as "Allison's Company." Allison resigned his position on January 30, 1863, because of a foot disability. His resignation was approved on February 19, but he didn't leave his position until April 17, 1863. Remaining in the army, Allison served as a private in the cavalry, unit unknown, until the end of the war. Back in Clinton, Allison opened a grocery store and later became a judge. *O.R.S.*, pt. 2, vol. 38:640; Eakin, *Lone Jack*, 150; Eakin & Hale, 5; National Archives, Record Group 109, Confederate Muster Rolls, Sixteenth Missouri Infantry; National Archives, Record Group M322 (roll no. 166), Confederate Compiled Service Records, Sixteen Missouri Infantry; National Archives, Record Group M861 (roll no. 36), Record of Confederate Movements and Activities, Sixteenth Missouri Infantry; Norton, 74, 86, 97.

a rear guard, filed off north toward town. In ten or fifteen minutes a fusillade of small arms rang out, followed by a crash of artillery. The first cannon shot passed just above the tops of the fence-stakes to our right (west), the rest further to the right, inside the field. After the small arms fire had died out and only an occasional cannon shot came from the enemy we moved south of the Pleasant Hill road a short distance, then swerved to the right, west, and an all-night march followed.[67] We joined Col. Cockrell's command about 3 o'clock the next morning on the Independence road, not far from Lone Jack. And so this was all there was to the events of evening of the 15th.[68] I also think Col. Jackman's imagination was hard at work when he accused Col. Tracy of cowardice. He is the first man I ever heard speak to the detriment of Col. Tracy's courage. Tracy certainly did not show any signs of cowardice while leading his regiment to the charge that fated morning; he faced "the music" like a little man to my certain knowledge up to the time of his wound. What he did afterwards, I, of course, don't know, but I don't believe he acted the pusillanimous cur that Jackman described. If Col. Tracy was a coward, how did it come that he got his wound close up the enemy's guns? How, also, did it happen that his men didn't happen to hang up on the first "rail fence" they came too, as Jackman says his did, and "there fight it out?" But instead they captured the enemy's artillery and drove him into the cornfield to the east, then pushed him back south upon his center and held him there until about the time the roof of the hotel caved in at 9 o'clock. It was here—almost east of the hotel—that the writer was wounded, just on the inside of the hedge fence (east), and here that Tracy's men suffered from the fire of their friends on the west side of the street, and it was not Hays's men, whom Jackman supposed. The writer while being carried from

---

67. In describing the events on the evening of August 15, Major Foster recorded: "We surprised the camp about 9 o'clock that evening and completely routed the enemy." Captain Milton Brawner, who succeeded Foster in command after Foster was wounded, provided even more detail of the "rout." Brawner wrote in his official report:

Their cavalry charged down the lane upon us, but were received with a volley of musketry, which scattered them in all directions. Their camp was at the same time shelled by the battery with good effect. The enemy having fled, and no further demonstrations on their part being anticipated, the command returned to Lone Jack, arriving at 11 o'clock, and encamped for the night.

*O.R.*, 13:237, 239.

68. During the night, Coffee and Tracy's commands separated, with Tracy's finding the main rebel force at the George Kreeger farm, about three and one half miles west of Lone Jack. Coffee, for some unexplained reason, did not arrive until the battle was over. Eakin, *Lone Jack*, 7.

the field to a temporary hospital at the mill, met Hays's command marching to the battlefield. He carried a small Confederate flag and the men cheered lustily as they passed by, but did not get there in time to support Tracy's men, whose ammunition had been exhausted sometime before, and prevent the enemy from recapturing their artillery. Allison's company lost in killed and wounded thirteen men out of about forty who had arms and went into battle, including the captain and first lieutenant, his brother, wounded. So let the honors fall on them who deserve them. But after the sad story is all and truly told it reveals the sorry spectacle of contention for the honor or superiority in command among the officers, where unity should have existed. Even at this late day we see that the venom has not all been exhausted. No wonder the Confederacy collapsed.

Henry C. Luttrell
Hindman Escort, Co. G, Tenth Missouri Cavalry, C.S.A.[69]

* * * * * *

---

69. On November 8, 1862, General Thomas C. Hindman assigned John C. Lee's Company of Missouri Cavalry as his escort. Lee resigned from the army on December 13 but remained in the service as a private, being paroled out of Company G, Tenth Missouri Cavalry on June 15, 1865. With the departure of General Hindman on January 30, the escort company was probably incorporated into MacDonald's command, now led by M. L. Young. The Tenth Missouri Cavalry was originally commanded by Emmett MacDonald and consisted of three companies with two more added forming the "regiment" on December 1, 1862. The unit at that time was known as MacDonald's Regiment, even though it only contained five companies. MacDonald's command eventually joined other cavalry units to form the Tenth Missouri Cavalry Regiment in December 1863. At the time the Tenth was formed, Company G was commanded by Captain William Sims. *O.R.*, vol. 22, pt. 1:156; vol. 22, pt. 2:781; *O.R.S.*, pt. 2, vol. 38:253–259; Crute, 203; National Archives, Record Group 109, Inspector General Report, in Confederate Muster Rolls, Tenth Missouri Cavalry; Letter (November 8, 1862), Hindman to Lee, Copy Letter Book No. 1; John B. Lockman, Report of Ordnance Stores (March 2, 1863), Miscellaneous Correspondence; National Archives, Record Group M322 (roll no. 57) Confederate Compiled Service Records, Tenth Missouri Cavalry; Special Order No. 63 (December 13, 1862), Special Order Book No. 1.

**Item:** Colonel John C. Tracy at the Battle of Lone Jack; another account, by Granville C. Bowen; late Company E, Seventh Cavalry Regiment, Second Brigade, Eighth Division, Missouri State Guard.[70]
**Published:** October 10, 1885.

## One More From the Left Wing.

Troy, Mo., Oct. 5
Editor, *Republican*

There have been several accounts of the memorable "Lone Jack" battle given in your columns, and all more or less incorrect. My object in writing this article is to vindicate Col. John C. Tracy. Col. Jackman in his account of the battle located Tracy in the line of battle—Jackman forming the center, Hunter on the right and Tracy on the left. This was the exact position of the different commands at the time of forming; but Col J. does not give Tracy's position after the charge had been made. While Jackman and his command had stopped at the fence on account of warm firing, Tracy scaled the fence with the bravery and daring of a true soldier in the face of a scorching fire from small arms and artillery. In making this charge we had great obstacles to contend with—the fence—as Col. Jackman states, was a strong one and difficult to clear. Then we had the gardens in the rear to pull through, and three fences to climb before reaching the objective point. The street that Maj. Foster refers too where the hand-to-hand fight took place, Col. Tracy received a slight wound and was

## Taken From the Field.

What he told Col. Jackman down in the woods I do not know, but one thing I do know, while he (Col. Jackman) was down in the field hunting ammunition Col. Tracy part of the time at least was facing the "music" like a man. I think Col. Jackman did Col. Tracy a great injustice when he made his remarks about meeting him (Tracy) in the woods when he knew he was wounded. Such remarks should

---

70. Granville C. Bowen was born in Kentucky in about 1829, and lived near Nevada, Missouri, at the beginning of the Civil War. On July 15, 1861, he was elected captain of Company E (Compiled Service Records has Bowen commanding Company C), Seventh Cavalry Regiment, Eighth Division, MSG, and resigned on December 14, 1861. While in the Guard, Bowen took part in the engagements at Carthage, Dug Springs, Wilson Creek and Dry Wood. Bowen reentered the Confederate Service in the summer of 1862, joining John Tracy's Regiment (Compiled Service Records has Bowen joining Company B, First Missouri Infantry). Captured on February 3, 1863, in McDonald County, Missouri, Bowen was sent to Gratiot Street Prison in St. Louis. He was transferred to Camp Chase, Ohio, on January 31, 1864, and to Fort Delaware on March 25, and later exchanged. In April 1865 he deserted the Confederate Army and took the Oath of Allegiance in Memphis, Tennessee. Bartels, *Forgotten Men*, 28; Eakin, *Missouri Prisoners of War*, "Bowen, Granville," entry; Hale, 28; National Archives, Record Group M322, (roll no. 92), Confederate Complied Service Records, First Infantry Regiment; National Archives, Record Group M322, (roll no. 179), Confederate Complied Service Records, Missouri State Guard; Peterson, 269.

have been beneath the dignity of a Confederate colonel.[71] There is not a man, officer or private, who was personally acquainted with Col. Tracy, that would give credence to such a statement. Tracy had his men nearer the enemy than Jackman and stayed there longer—taking the colonel's own statement for it. Col. Tracy did not leave the field until the fight was over. After we got into the street it did not take long to satisfy both Federals and Confederates that the houses were the safest places. About this time in the engagement we found that our ammunition was running low and we detailed a man to the ordnance wagon for a supply—and unlike Jackman's man,[72] he went and secured what he went after and returned promptly. I did not learn the name of the gentleman, but he was not afraid to come back. In order that the public may know who the writer is, I will say that I had the honor to command a company of as brave men as ever shouldered a shotgun. My company was made up of men from Henry County, Missouri, and we were a part of Col. Tracy's fighting force at Lone Jack. Col. Jackman states that when he withdrew his men to go after ammunition that

## The Federals Charged

on him, and that he turned and gave them a volley that sent them back at a rapid gait. Now, the force must have been very small, for we held the houses on the west side of the street and Maj. Foster the houses on the east, and we did not miss any

---

71. In recounting the story Jackman wrote—

"Colonel Tracy, I am sorry you are wounded. Are you much hurt?"

"Yes,'" he answered, "I am all shot to pieces."

This remark rather opened my eyes, for I could see no blood. We were now face to face and I asked him, "How are you hurt?"

"Oh," said he as if in great pain, "when the first bomb was fired, it struck me in the breast and exploded, completely enveloping me in fragments, some of which cut my top of the head and some cut my legs terribly in front and one piece struck me in the fundament, and now the blood is running down my legs."

I made him take off his hat and examined his head. There was not a mark or even a speck of blood to be seen and no rents in his clothing. I left him with a feeling of extreme contempt and was convinced that he was mistaken, as to what was running down his legs."

S. D. Jackman, "Battle of Lone Jack," *Missouri Republican*, August 29, 1885.

72. Jackman sent Captain H. B. Brewster, his adjutant, to retrieve the ammunition, but Brewster never returned. Jackman then retreated his line as his ammunition was nearly exhausted. Halting his command at the original starting point, Jackman returned to the ammunition wagon, where he found his wayward adjutant. Brewster, for his part, refused to return to the fight, citing that it was "too hot of a place for him." Jackman then retrieved the ammunition and returned to his command to continue the fight. Norton, 95–96.

of Foster's men—and they were in front of us all the time until their retreat—nor did we know that Cols. Jackman and Hunter had abandoned the field until after the fight. As to Col. Hunter showing the "white feather," I never heard of it except through Col. Jackman. I also had the honor of commanding a company under Col. Hunter in the Missouri State Guards, and was with him at the Battles of Carthage, Dug Springs, Wilson Creek, Dry Wood and other engagements of the summer of 1861, and never knew nor heard of him flinching at any of them, nor do I believe that he had any cowards in his composition.

G. C. Bowen

* * * * * *

Chapter 3

# Fall and Winter 1862:
## Palmyra Executions and the
## Battle of Prairie Grove, Arkansas
## (December 7, 1862)

**Item:** The executions at Palmyra, Missouri, as seen through the eyes of a Confederate prisoner, held at that time in Palmyra and not selected for execution, by Joseph A. Edwards.[1]
**Published:** October 17, 1885

## The Palmyra Executions.[2]

Lexington, Mo., Oct. 13
Editor, *Republican*

I ask room for a few words in regard to the Palmyra (Mo.) executions in the fall of 1862, and also a word as to the [Andrew] Allsman case.[3] I have just read

1. This was probably Joseph A. Edwards, a resident of Lexington, Missouri, at the beginning of the Civil War. He enlisted in Company G, Clark's Missouri Infantry Regiment (Confederate), at Maysville, Arkansas, for a period of one year on June 16, 1862. There was no other record on Edwards. National Archives, Record Group M322, (roll no. 172), Confederate Compiled Service Records, Clark's Missouri Infantry Regiment.

2. On September 12, 1862, Joseph C. Porter entered Palmyra, in northeast Missouri. With a band of 300–400 men, Porter bypassed the Federal pickets just after dawn and captured the town within 15 minutes. The Federal command, consisting of 90 men belonging to the Missouri State Militia, including 6 or 8 citizens, had taken refuge in the city jail (22 men), the courthouse (30 men) and Loothan's brick store (30 men with 6 to 8 citizens). A "few shots were fired, and six or seven wounded on each side," according to one rebel participant. A local newspaper at the time reported the Union losses as one killed and four wounded, while the rebels lost one dead and one wounded. Within the first hour, the jail and Provost Marshal's Office had been taken, while the remaining Union strong points remained untouched. In taking the jail and Provost Marshal's Office, Porter captured 19 prisoners (3 had fled), freed about 40 rebel prisoners, and destroyed all the important papers, including personal bonds and Oaths of Allegiances. Two hours after he entered Palmyra, Porter left, giving parole to all his prisoners. Joseph A. Mudd, *With Porter in North Missouri: A Chapter In the History of the War Between the States* (Washington, 1909), 292-294, 409-414, hereafter cited as Mudd, *With Porter*; "Porter In Palmyra," *The Morning Herald* (St. Joseph, MO), September 13, 1862.

33. When Porter took Palmyra, he also surrounded the house of Andrew Allsman, "a notorious informer." After Allsman surrendered, he was taken by Porter when he left Palmyra, and not paroled like the remainder of the prisoners. According to Confederate sources, Allsman was still alive on September 15, when Porter offered to set him free. Allsman asked for an escort to a "safe place" which he defined as the public highway or a loyal man's house. Porter then provided Allsman a six man escort, three selected by Allsman, and three selected by Porter. During the night of September 15–16, Allsman was escorted to a "safe place," and Porter's escort returned the next morning. Allsman was never seen

the article on these subjects to-day as published in your issue of October 3.[4] As to who or what Allsman[5] was prior to the war I know nothing at all, but what I shall say in this article regarding both Allsman and the massacre of my Confederates will be from my recollections as a fellow-prisoner. As to Allsman, I learned whilst a paroled prisoner in Gen. [John] McNeil's[6] hands in the city of Palmyra in the fall of 1862 that Allsman was a cabinet workman, and had done a great deal of work in country residences in putting in closets and cupboards, and that being thoroughly acquainted in the country adjoining Palmyra he acted as an informer and guide to the marauding parties of militia and Unionists generally, and that in the summer of 1862 learning that Capt. Robt. Dunn[7] of the Confederate Army whose home was

---

again. On October 8, Colonel John McNeil, commanding the Northeastern Division of Missouri, gave in to local pressure and issued a notice in the local newspapers (See Appendix D), calling for the return of Allsman in ten days, or ten rebel prisoners would be shot. On October 18, the executions were carried out. This became commonly known as the "Palmyra Massacre." *O.R.*, 13:417; Mudd, *With Porter*, 293, 296-298; "Terrible Executions," *The Clinton Herald* (Clinton, IA), November 8, 1862.

4. On October 3, 1885, the *Republican* published an extensive article on the incident at Palmyra, by R. I. Holcombe, author of a small book on the Battle of Wilson's Creek. In his research on the Allsman affair, Holcombe concluded that during the night of September 15–16, the escort party, sent by Porter, shot and killed Allsman in the southern part of Lewis County. Only three of the men participated in the deed, after which his body was covered with leaves and "left to rot and shrivel where it fell." R. I. Holcombe, "The Allsman Murder," *Missouri Republican*, October 3, 1885.

5. Andrew Allsman was born in Kentucky, about 1798, and came to Marion County, Missouri in 1832. At one time or another, Allsman was a deputy sheriff, a Whig politician and a justice of the peace. He joined Company A, Third Missouri Cavalry (Union) on October 25, 1861, and left the service, with a Surgeons Certificate of Disability, for age, on June 14, 1862. He was age 64 when he left the army. A long time resident of Palmyra, Allsman assisted the local Provost, according to the *Palmyra Courier*, by providing "information touching the loyalty" of the local citizens. Allsman also served as "a guide to scouting parties sent to arrest disloyal persons." His actions earned Allsman, according to the *Courier*, "the bitter hatred of all the rebels in the city and vicinity." Holcombe, "The Allsman Murder"; Mudd, *With Porter*, 294-295; National Archives, Record Group M405 (roll no. 66), Union Compiled Service Records, Third Missouri Cavalry Regiment; "Terrible Executions," *Clinton Herald*.

6. John McNeil was born on February 14, 1813, in Halifax, Nova Scotia, Canada, moved to Boston, and in 1840, made St. Louis his permanent home. On May 8, 1861, he was appointed colonel of the Third Missouri Infantry, U.S. Reserve Corps, and participated in the Camp Jackson Affair. Later, McNeil was appointed colonel (to date from December 7, 1861) of the Second Missouri State Militia Cavalry Regiment. On June 4, 1862, McNeil was assigned to command the Northeast Division of Missouri a position he held during the incident at Palmyra. Branded a "butcher" for his actions at Palmyra and for his earlier execution of rebel prisoners during the summer of 1862, McNeil spent his entire Civil War career in Missouri, except for a short stint, commanding in Louisiana. See Appendix B for a complete biography. *O.R.*, 13:417; C. M. Farthing, *Chronicles of the Civil War in Monroe County (Missouri)* (Independence, MO, 1997), 69, hereafter cited as Farthing; General Orders of Missouri (1862), General Orders No. 12 (April 9, 1862), Missouri Historical Society; Heitman, 1:679; Mudd, *With Porter*, 308-309; Sifakis, *Who Was Who In the Union*, 259-260; Warner, *Generals in Blue*, 306; Winter, 114.

7. Robert Emmett Dunn was a resident of Marion County, Missouri and a would-be politician, who ran for the Missouri State Legislature in 1860, but lost. In June 1861, Dunn organized Company C, Third Infantry Regiment, Second Division, MSG, which he led at the Battle of Wilson's Creek. After his six-month term of service, Dunn returned to north Missouri where he was captured in February 1862, in Savannah, Andrew County. Dunn was sent to Palmyra, where he was imprisoned, but escaped on March 14. Securing a skiff, Dunn, with several companions made it to the Mississippi River and finally reached Memphis. Dunn later moved to Arkansas, where he married. He did not survive the war,

in Marion County, had returned at the expiration of his term in the service to see his mother and father. He (Allsman) piloted a Union party to Capt. D.'s father's house, where a thorough search was made for Capt. Rob, as he was called, but they failed to find the captain, and left. However, they had not gone far until Allsman halted them and said, "We will return, I know where he is, I made a closet for fruits, etc., we did not look into."

## They Did Return,

and, as he predicted, found Capt. D. in this same closet. They secured him and took him a prisoner, and lodged him in the Palmyra jail, where he was kept confined for about three months. Occasionally he was permitted to have a walk outside the jail yard, and that upon one and the last such occasion Capt. D. by strategy got the guard's gun, with which he knocked him down, and made his escape. And it was Capt. D. who captured Allsman when [Joseph] Porter[8] captured Palmyra. My informant claimed that Capt. Dunn took Allsman South with him.[9] Certain it is at the time John McNeil issued his order to shoot ten of our men if Allsman was not returned in ten days to his family. That Allsman with his captors was far beyond the reach of this order, or any possible chance to know of said order; and the story of the skeleton or shooting, as given by your correspondents, I believe to be guess work by their informants or out and out cheats. Now, as to the order for the killing our ten men.[10] It is all a great error that the Unionists were about to murder ten of the leading citizens of Marion County or Palmyra. I had a chance to

---

dying in Sunflower County, Mississippi, in the middle of 1864. Eakin & Hale, 123; *History of Marion County, Missouri, Written and Compiled from the Most Authentic Official and Private Sources Including a History of Its Townships, Towns and Villages* (St. Louis, 1884), 343, 381, 924, 931; R. I. Holcombe, "Nothing Like Being Exact," *Missouri Republican*, October 24, 1885; Peterson, 98.

8. Joseph Chrisman Porter was born in Jasmine County, Kentucky, on September 12, 1819, and moved to Marion County, Missouri, at the age of nine. Educated at Marion College at Philadelphia (Missouri), Porter married in 1844, moved to Knox County and in 1857, relocated to Lewis County, about five miles from Newark. He was a farmer and cattle trader and in 1849, went to California, with his brother, but soon returned. At the beginning of the Civil War, Porter raised Company K, First Cavalry Regiment, Second Division, MSG and was subsequently elected lieutenant colonel of the regiment in July 1861. Porter was promoted to colonel of his regiment on December 9, 1861, and later led the division. While in the Guard, Porter fought at Athens (August 5, 1861), Shelbina (September 4, 1861), the Siege of Lexington (where he was wounded), and the Battle of Pea Ridge. Following Pea Ridge, at the request of Price, Porter returned to Missouri, in April 1862, to recruit a new command. Operating in north Missouri, Porter fought numerous engagements with the Federal troops, and lost the disastrous Battle of Kirksville on August 6. In the early fall of 1862, Porter returned to Arkansas, where he commanded a brigade under John S. Marmaduke. At the Battle of Hartville, Missouri, on January 11, 1863, Porter received a mortal wound. He died at Batesville, Arkansas, on February 18, 1863. Eakin & Hale, 353; Hale, 256; Mudd, *With Porter*, 24–26, 327–328, 330, 332; Peterson, 81, 83, 85; Schnetzer, *More Forgotten Men*, 185.

9. Not true—see following article by R. I. Holcombe. The story of Allsman leading Federal troops to Dunn's house is not true. Per the previous note Dunn was captured in Savannah, Missouri, while organizing a secret Southern organization called "Imminent" or "Emminent." Hale, 123; Holcombe, "Nothing Like Being Exact."

10. See Appendix D for a list of the executed men.

know, as I had the freedom of the city, as a paroled prisoner, and had free access to papers and talked freely to and with many of the leading men of the city and county. I often met Rev. N. Lowthar, one of the wealthiest men of the county. He came frequently to the house where I was boarded and when it was known that

## Ten Of Our Men

were to be shot, I proposed to Mr. L. and others to raise $2,000 as a ransom for each man, making 20,000.[11] But the people were so utterly subdued and overawed by McNeil's and Dick Straghn's [Strachan][12] reign that they whispered to each other that it would never do to mention it upon the streets and forbad me from repeating it to anyone. I believe now, as I did then, that this amount would have saved those brave fellows. Now, as to why Capt. Thomas A. Snyder [Sidener][13]

---

11. According to C. M. Farthing, Jack Ragsdale, a prominent citizen of Monroe County and friend of Captain Sidener, made a personal plea to Provost Marshall Strachan, offering $1,000.00 to spare the captain's life. "For once," Strachan's "cupidity could not be tempted," according to Farthing, even after Ragsdale offered "any additional amount that might be named." Farthing, 100.

12. William R. Strachan was a Democratic member of the Missouri Legislature from Shelby County and at the beginning of the war was serving as a U.S. Deputy Marshal. He later joined Company I, Second Missouri Infantry (Union), Extra Battalion and in February, 1862, was appointed Provost Marshall of Palmyra by Governor Hamilton Gamble. With the arrival of John McNeil as commander of the Northeast Missouri Division, Strachan was made the Provost Marshall of the Division. Strachan, known as the "'beast,' and for his 'appetite' for women," had removed Thomas Humphry from the list of prisoners to be executed. To secure the favor, Humphry's distraught wife, agreed to pay $500.00 and offered herself as a sexual favor. Caught in the act, Strachan was later relieved of his position on October 20, 1862, two days after the executions. Strachan was later charged with embezzling $20,000.00 and "other offenses against morality of the most scandalous nature." John McNeil defended his ex–Provost, stating that all public funds had been "properly accounted" for prior to his assuming command of the Division. However, an instructor of cavalry in the local area seemed to imply in a letter to John M. Schofield that Strachan was a disreputable Provost, and that prisoners were being released by Strachan, when they should have been "hung." As to the incident surrounding Humphry, McNeil's defense was that he had already ordered the release of Humphry, and Strachan objected, remarking that Humphry was the "worst man of the lot." According to Griffin Frost, Strachan was a "fiend from hell in a human shape," who simply took advantage of the situation. Despite the controversy, Strachan remained in the army for a short time, serving as a volunteer aid to McNeil. Following the war, he fled to Mexico, was for a time in Paris (France), and returned to New Orleans, where he caught some disease and died. *O.R.*, 13:475; *O.R.*, vol. 22, pt. 1:260; *O.R.*, Series 2, vol. 1:207; Farthing, 69, 72–73, 85; Frost, 284; *History of Marion County*, 286, 431, 526; John McNeil, Letter in, "A Libel Suit Looming Up," *Quincy Whig and Republican*, November 21, 1863; Mudd, *With Porter*, 294–295, 305, 308.

13. Thomas A. Sidener lived near Shelbina, Missouri, at the beginning of the Civil War, when he joined what became Company C, First Cavalry Regiment, Second Division, MSG. Elected first lieutenant of his command, Sidener fought at Wilson's Creek and did not return to the north side of the Missouri River until the summer of 1862. Sidener, now a captain, accompanied Joseph Porter during his recruitment efforts and took part in the Battle of Kirksville on August 6, 1862. Following the disastrous battle, Sidener hid out in north Missouri and intended to flee to Illinois. Caught near Shelbyville in October 1862, Sidener was sent to Palmyra, where he was selected for execution. On October 18, he was shot and killed by the first volley, one of only two who died on the initial firing. The remaining eight men were subsequently killed by a second group of soldiers using small arms to complete the execution. Sidener was described as having a physique of a "Greek God," a man "born to war," and one, who was "fierce in combat." When he was buried, "hundreds" attended his funeral. Farthing,

was shot—I knew him personally. We served as lieutenants in the same company under Capt. Joe Thompson[14] of Monroe County. We met Col. Joe Porter on the north side of the Missouri River and followed him through his memorable raid which resulted so disastrously to so many of our command.[15] The killing of prisoners began at Kirksville[16] in Adair County, when McNeil had Col. Frisby McCullock [McCullough],[17] Dr. Davis, Lieut. [Lewis] Rollins and fourteen privates

---

*Monroe County*, 48, 92–96; Frost, 287; Eakin & Hale, 395; Peterson, 111.

14. Joseph Thompson, a resident of Monroe County, commanded a company under Joseph C. Porter in the summer of 1862. He was credited with the capture of Paris, Missouri, on July 30, 1862. Eakin & Hale, 427; Mudd, *With Porter*, 242.

15. After Porter returned to northeast Missouri in April 1862, he began organizing and recruiting what became the First Northeast Missouri Cavalry Regiment (Confederate). His camp was located in Marion County on the North Fabius River. On June 17, Porter struck his first blow near New Market, in Marion County, and began active operations. More than a "raid," Porter's activities had no set pattern or path to them, he simply tried to avoid contact with the Federal troops and selected attacks where and, normally, when he pleased—more like guerrilla operations. These would continue on and off until he finally departed the area in late October, crossed the Missouri River and moved to Arkansas. Highly successful, Porter eventually funneled about 5,000 men to the Confederate Army, mostly in Arkansas. Banasik, *Embattled Arkansas*, 116, 122, 141.

16. The Battle of Kirksville, Missouri, occurred on August 6, 1862, and marked the last major engagement that Porter fought in north Missouri. As senior officer of the multi–unit rebel command, Porter elected to deploy his troops in the town of Kirksville and await the arrival of the pursuing Federal troops. At 10:00 a.m. the Unionists began arriving but no action occurred until about noon, when the remainder of the Federal command arrived. The fight lasted about three hours and was largely conducted at long range—the bluecoated army had several cannon, while the Confederates had none. After battering the town for a length of time with artillery fire, Colonel Louis Merrill ordered in his command. The badly shaken rebels had already began to withdraw in an orderly fashion, but that quickly changed to a rout. Fortunately for Porter, the Federals were exhausted from the last ten days of constant pursuit and gave up the chase after only a few miles. By 3:00 p.m. the battle had ended. The Unionists lost 5 killed and 32 wounded; Confederates loses are sketchy at best, with one Federal source recording 58 dead, 84 wounded with 250 prisoners; while another put the rebel losses at 30 dead, 8 mortally wounded, 36 prisoners, with another 60 rebels buried five days after the battle. Banasik, *Embattled Arkansas*, 136–140; "Battle of Kirksville," *The Canton Weekly Press* (Canton, MO), August 14, 1862; Mudd, *With Porter*, 249, 255.

17. Frisby (not Frisbie) Henderson McCullough was born on March 8, 1828, in New Castle County, Delaware. At the age of twelve he moved to Marion County, Missouri, where he farmed with his parents. In 1849 he went to California with two of his brothers in search for gold, remained five years, returned to Round Grove Township, Marion County in 1854, and married in 1856. On July 26, 1861, he was elected captain of what became Company B, First Cavalry Regiment, Second Division MSG. He was with his command at the Siege of Lexington and was elected lieutenant colonel of his regiment on December 3 (Bartels has December 8), 1861. In April 1862, he accompanied Porter back to north Missouri and began recruitment for the Confederacy. He fought at Kirksville on August 6, but being ill left the command for home to recover. Caught on August 7, while asleep, he was returned to Kirksville, supposedly tried at a Court Martial as a guerrilla and executed on August 8. In giving the commands for his own execution, McCullough said, "'What I have done, I have done as a principle of right, Aim at the heart, Fire!'" The command caught the executioners by surprise, one soldier fired hitting McCullough in the breast, causing him to fall. The other soldiers fired, missing the falling McCullough. Reloading, the firing squad again fired at the kneeling McCullough, finally ending his life. Bartels, *Trans-Mississippi Men*, 41; "Col. Frisbie H. McCullough," *Canton Weekly Press*, August 21, 1862; Eakin & Hale, 294; Hale, 209; Mudd, *With Porter*, 274–275; Peterson, 84–85.

shot without an hour's warning.[18] But I have gotten out of line. Capt. Snyder after our defeat at Kirksville got separated from the main force and finally got home to his mother's (I think), who lived in Monroe County, near Granville or Kipper's Mill. He disguised himself in lady's attire, and in his mother's family carriage, closely veiled, had gotten nearly out of danger, but unfortunately unveiled his face too soon and was seen by a renegade Southerner, who hastened to Shelbyville and reported the fact. A squad of mounted men were sent after and captured Capt. S.[19] This I know to be his only offense. Now, as to the charge against the nine privates as oath-breakers, there was nothing in that all. Gov. [Hamilton R.] Gamble[20] had issued his order for every man to take sides, as there was no middle ground, and as Southern men, they had conscientiously done so.

Frisby H. McCullough

Joe A. Edwards

---

18. On August 7, the day after the Battle of Kirksville, Colonel McNeil charged fifteen captured prisoners with violating their "solomon oath and parole of honor not to take up arms against their country under penalty of death." Continuing, McNeil recorded, "I enforced the penalty." Lieutenant Lewis Rollins could have been Private Louis H. Rollins, a member of Company A, Rawling's Battalion, Second Division, Missouri State Guard. Following a six-month stint in the Guard in 1861, Rollins could have returned home and, with the advent of General Orders No. 19, reentered the service. As to Dr. John Davis, he was a resident of Lewis County, Missouri, and a physician who came into town with Colonel Porter and met a similar fate as the fourteen. According to E. M. Violette, Dr. Davis "had come into town with Porter" and "was attempting to give some assistance to the Confederate wounded who were in the southwest part of town when Federal soldiers came up and ordered him to go with them to McNeil's headquarters. It is told that after he started to go with them he was made to run and was then shot down for running." See Appendix D for the list of the executed prisoners following the Battle of Kirksville. *O.R.*, 13:215; Bartels, *Forgotten Men*, 314; *History of Adair, Sullivan, Putnam and Schuyler Counties, Missouri. From the Earliest Time to the Present; Together With Sundry Personal, Business and Professional Sketches and Numerous Family Records, etc.* (Chicago, 1888), 308; Peterson, 98; E. M. Violette, "The Battle of Kirksville. August 6, 1862," *Missouri Historical Review* 5, no. 2 (1911): 108.

19. Not true. According to both Farthing and Holcombe, Sidener was discovered when attempting to enter a carriage, with a Mrs. W. T. Ragsdale and two other ladies (Holcombe says Sidener was riding with his brother, a sister and another lady). Dressed in female clothing, Sidener lifted his skirt to enter the carriage, and revealed to some on looking Federal troops, his cavalry boots. Quickly unmasked, Sidener was captured and sent on to Palmyra, where he was executed on October 18. Farthing, *Monroe County*, 99; Holcombe, "Nothing like Being Exact."

20. Hamilton R. Gamble was born in Virginia in 1798, moved to Tennessee and then Missouri. He was a lawyer by profession and opened a law office in St. Louis. In 1858, he moved to Pennsylvania, but returned to Missouri during the secession crisis of 1861. Elected Provisional Governor of Missouri on July 31, 1861, Gamble did not survive the war, dying on January 31, 1864. Sifakis, *Who Was Who in the Union*, 147; Moore, *Rebellion Record*, 2:Diary-50.

**Item:** Rebuttal to Joe Edwards account of Allsman captured by Captain Dunn as told by a period historian, R. I. Holcombe, who wrote an account of the Battle of Wilson's Creek. Also comments on who constituted an "oath-breaker," by R. I. Holcombe.
**Published:** October 24, 1885.

## Nothing Like Being Exact.

Kingston, Mo., Oct. 19

I beg space to correct a few errors in the communication of Capt. Joe Edwards in the *Republican* of last Saturday [October 17] regarding the Palmyra executions. It is not true that Andrew Allsman was taken south by Capt. Robert Dunn, or that Capt. Dunn was taken prisoner at his father's house in Marion county, in a cupboard made by Allsman, as stated by Capt. Edwards in his communication.

Capt. R. E. Dunn took out the first company from Marion County for service in Gov. Jackson's Missouri State Guard. This was early in June, 1861, and the company was mounted, uniformed, armed with muskets and bayonets and well equipped. Six months later, his term in the State Guard having expired, Capt. Dunn came up north of the Missouri River and in February, 1862, he and one N. C. Kouns were arrested by the Federal military authorities at Savannah, Andrew County, accused of being engaged in organizing throughout Northern Missouri "camps" of secret Confederate organization called the "Emmanant." I may have heard it stated that well-known Missouri author, Maj. N. C. Kouns, was Capt. Dunn's companion, but I do not know this to be a fact.

Capt. Dunn was taken to Palmyra and placed in the county jail, then in use as a military prison. About 9 o'clock on the night of March 14, 1862, he called upon one of the guards to accompany him to the public spring to obtain some water for a sick man. When near the spring, Dunn suddenly drew a knife, sprang at the guard, threatened him with death if he moved a muscle without orders and then

## Disarmed Him

of his Sharp's carbine[21] and revolver and made him accompany him out of town. Three miles west of Palmyra, Dunn took the soldier's cartridge-box from him and sent him back with his compliments to the Federal officers at Palmyra.

About four weeks later, Capt. Dunn, Chas. McCutchen and David Dean (the

---

21. The Sharp's Carbine was patented in 1848 by Christian Sharp and was "one of the first successful breech-loading systems." A total of five models were produced for the Federal service, while the Confederates developed their own model using the Sharp's as their guide. The carbine was intended for cavalry use with .52 caliber bore as normal. A total of 80,512 were produced during the war for the Federal Government. To load the weapon the user cocked it, opening the breech, into which was inserted a paper cartridge. When closed the paper cartridge was cut allowing ignition of the powder and the firing of the weapon. A competent soldier could fire off 10 rounds a minute using this weapon, with accuracy up to six hundred yards. Boatner, *Civil War Dictionary*, 735–736.

latter, the present county surveyor of Marion County and a resident of Hannibal);[22] started from a point on the Salt River, in Ralls County, on a voyage in a skiff for Dixie's land and after a series of romantic and surprising adventures actually accomplished the trip and reached the Confederate lines at Memphis in safety. Capt. Dunn was never thereafter north of the Missouri River. He married a wealthy Southern lady and died in Sunflower County, Mississippi in the summer or fall of 1864. Of course he did not take Allsman prisoner September 12, 1862, for he was not in Missouri at that time. He has a number of relatives and acquaintances in Marion County, who will read these lines and know whether or not they are true.

As to Capt. Tom Sidener (not Snyder), he was on his way to Illinois when captured. He was in woman's clothing, and was riding in an open carriage with his brother, a sister and a lady cousin. He was not recognized because he removed his veil. A German militiaman named Fred Blessing, not a "renegade Southerner," recognized the ladies and the captain's brother, as the party drove through Shelbyville, and informed Col. John F. Benjamin[23] that "all those Sideners" had passed through town, and he believed they were going to where Tom Sidener was to give him some clothing and provisions. A small squad followed the party and brought it back, and Capt. Sidener was first discovered

By His Boots,

which were plainly visible as he alighted from the carriage. I believe Col. Benjamin removed the veil.

It is not "a great error" that ten prominent citizens of Marion county were about to be murdered in retaliation for the killing of Allsman. I am willing to refer

---

22. Charles H. McCutchen (or McCutcheon or McCuthen) was born about 1832, in Scotland, a sailor by profession and a resident of Hannibal at the beginning of the Civil War. After escaping from northern Missouri, McCutchen joined Company G, Sixth Missouri Infantry (Confederate). He was captured at the Battle of Champion's Hill in May 1863, later exchanged at City Point, Virginia, after which he disappeared from the Sixth Missouri rolls—McCutchen may have joined the Sixth Alabama Cavalry following his exchange. Following the war he became a Confederate pensioner, living in Campbell, Dunklin County, Missouri.

David Dean, was born on April 5, 1823, in Brown County, Ohio. Educated at Georgetown, Ohio, Dean moved to Hannibal in 1848, married in 1851, was a civil engineer by profession and owned a marble business until 1862. Dean joined the First Missouri Infantry (Confederate) and was detailed to the Confederate topographical corps after he reached Memphis. He survived the war and returned to Hannibal, where he latter became the County Surveyor for Marion County. Bartels, *Trans-Mississippi Men*, 213; Eakin & Hale, 110; *History of Marion County*, 920; National Archives, Record Group M322 (roll no. 136), Confederate Compiled Service Records, Sixth Missouri Infantry.

23. John F. Benjamin commanded Company A, Eleventh Missouri State Militia Cavalry Regiment at the beginning of the Civil War and was promoted to major of the regiment on May 6, 1862. He led the Eleventh at Kirksville, Missouri, on August 6, 1862, where Colonel McNeil cited him for "distinguished gallantry." He later transferred to the Second Missouri State Militia Cavalry Regiment, as the unit's lieutenant colonel and commanded them during Marmaduke's Second Missouri Raid (April 17–May 2, 1863). Following the raid, Benjamin was assigned to duty as a Provost Marshal, on June 2, 1863, a position he held until his resignation on May 11, 1864. Following the war, he was elected to the U.S. Congress and served until 1871. *O.R.*, 13:215, 218–219; *O.R.*, vol. 22, pt. 1:270–271; *O.R.*, Series 3, 5:908; General Orders 18 (May 8, 1862), General Orders of Missouri (1862); *History of Audrain County*, 41.

for the truth of this to Hon. Edward McCabe[24] of Palmyra and Hon. R. E. Anderson of Hannibal, and half a dozen other prominent citizens of Marion County, who resided there in the fall of 1862.

As to the "oath-breaker," Capt. Edwards states that there was "nothing" in the charge against them; that "Gov. Gamble had issued his order for every man to take sides, as there was no middle ground." Gov. Gamble never issued such an order.[25] The military order that caused so many men to break their paroles was known as "General Order No. 19," issued by Gen. Schofield at St. Louis, July 25, 1862.[26] This order called for "an immediate organization of all the militia in Missouri for the purpose of exterminating the guerrillas that infest the state," and required " every able-bodied man capable of bearing arms and subject to military duty," to report at once to the nearest Federal military post for service. Furthermore this order was based on one issued by Gov. Gamble at St. Louis, July 22, and denominated "Special Order No. 101," authorizing Gen. Schofield to organize the entire militia of the state." But neither Gamble nor Schofield's order allowed men of Missouri to "take sides," or said anything about "middle ground." Every able-bodied men, except ministers of the gospel, county officials and some others, was [were] ordered into the militia service noleus volens, to fight under the Federal flag against Confederates, and rather than do this many who had sworn not to fight at all joined the Confederate forces, and the Federals called them "oath-breakers."

R. I. Holcombe

* * * * * * *

---

24. Edward McCabe was born on August 6, 1827, in New Castle County, Delaware. He moved to New Orleans in 1849, St. Louis in 1850, and settled in Hannibal later the same year. He was a lawyer by profession. He supported John C. Breckinridge for President in 1860 and was a Union supporter during the war. In 1875 he was a member of the Missouri Constitutional Convention. *History of Marion County*, 343, 591–593.

25. Not entirely true. After consulting Governor H. R. Gamble, General John Schofield issued General Orders No. 19, on July 22, 1862, which called out the Missouri State Militia. The stated purpose of the order was to exterminate the "guerrillas" that infested the state. The men had six days to report. Over the course of the next two weeks Schofield attempted to clarify the order by issuing General Orders Numbers 20–24; however, the damage was already done. General Orders No. 24, would finally address the issue of "disloyal men and those who have at any time sympathized with the rebellion," but by then Missourians had already chosen sides. In the clarification, the Southern supporters would not be organized, but would have to report and then remain at home "and in no way give aid or comfort to the enemy." For many would-be Confederates, the clarification came too late, and many saw it as a death wish, which marked them as openly supporting the rebels. The would-be enrollees believed that they had only two choices, join the Union militia or the Confederate forces. Even John Schofield, commanding Missouri at the time, acknowledged the impact of his call to arms. Schofield recorded— "The first effect...was to cause every rebel in the State who could possess himself of a weapon of any kind to spring to arms." See Appendix C for a copy of General Orders No. 19 and 24. *O.R.*, 13:10, 506, 508–509, 516, 518, 534, 536; Banasik, *Embattled Arkansas*, 118, 121.

26. The order was issued July 22, 1862. *O.R.*, 13:506.

**Item:** The Twenty-seventh Arkansas Infantry at Van Buren, Arkansas, and the Prairie Grove Campaign as seen by a non-participant, by Silas C. Turnbo, Company A, Twenty-seventh Arkansas Infantry.
**Published:** April 3, 1886.

## Twenty-Seventh Arkansas Regiment.[27]

Pro Tem, Taney Co., Mo.
Editor, *Republican*

When our regiment, the Twenty-seventh Arkansas, on the 7th of November, 1862, arrived at the mouth of the Mulberry River and became attached to the main army, the total forces there assembled were said to number 14,000 effectives, excluding the cavalry.[28] At least eleven infantry regiments were there before our arrival, and it was no motley crowd, but a well-drilled force of Arkansans and Missourians. Rations were somewhat short, and there was a scarcity of tents and clothing, but we had enough to keep us good and lean so as be fit for dodging bullets. The army was under command of Maj.-Gen. T. C. Hindman, and was known as Hindman's Division.[29] Hindman was subordinate to Gen. Theophilus H. Holmes, irreverently known in the Trans-Mississippi as "Old Granny" Holmes. What his superior qualities were I don't know, but I remembered him as an unpopular officer.[30] Gen. Hindman had been criticized for his conduct in the cam-

27. This is an abbreviated version of a similar piece that appeared in an undated typescript manuscript that Turnbo wrote following the war. Turnbo, 145–156.

28. The Twenty-seventh Arkansas Infantry was part of Robert G. Shaver's Brigade. On October 11, 1862, Shaver's Brigade departed Pocahontas, in north Arkansas, and headed westward to Yellville, which they reached on October 22. Joining Mosby M. Parsons' command, Shaver's Brigade was supposed to proceed on an operation against Forsyth, Missouri, but the operation was abruptly canceled on October 26, by General Thomas C. Hindman. On October 29, Parsons's command headed southward, to the Mulberry River, near the Arkansas River, where Hindman was concentrating his army for a strike into Missouri. Parsons's command, with the Twenty–seventh Arkansas, arrived at the banks of the Mulberry at 1:00 p.m. on November 7. Banasik, *Embattled Arkansas*, 252–254; Turnbo, 143.

29. Thomas C. Hindman was born in Tennessee in 1828, fought in the Mexican War, and moved to Helena, Arkansas in 1856. At the beginning of the Civil War, he commanded an Arkansas Infantry Regiment and was promoted to general officer in November 1861. After the Battle of Shiloh, Hindman was again promoted and returned to Arkansas to command the Trans-Mississippi District. He went on the command the army at Fort Smith, fought and lost the battle of Prairie Grove, after which he departed the Trans-Mississippi for the east side of the river. On November 9, 1862, Hindman organized the First Corps, Trans-Mississippi Army, not Hindman's Division. The division was organized on January 24, 1863, and consisted of five brigades: Frost's, McRae's, Fagan's, Parsons's, and Shaver's. For a biography and photograph of T. C. Hindman see Banasik, *Missouri Brothers in Gray,* 139–141; *O.R.*, vol. 22, pt. 2:781; Letter (January 23, 1863), Hindman to Anderson and Circular (January 24, 1863), Hindman's Division, Copy Letter Book No. 2, 64–68.

30. As to Holmes's selection Michael Dougan provides this assessment:
Holmes was a North Carolinian and a close personal friend of Jefferson Davis. According to William Preston Johnston, an aide to the President, Holmes had given satisfaction in North Carolina and Davis trusted him not to be taken in by General Sterling Price. Some political maneuvering surrounded his appointment, as General Magruder, who it will be recalled had been appointed to his command [in Texas] at an earlier date, told Davis that Holmes did not want to go but that the Missouri delegation

paign, which resulted in the Battle of Prairie Grove and subsequent retreat to Little Rock, but from my personal observation I believe he was a true, zealous and active officer.[31]

## Reorganization

On Sunday, November 9, 1862, our regiment was inspected by Gen. M. M. Parsons,[32] an able general, of whom the Missourians were justifiably proud. Here Col. [James D.] White's regiment[33] was brigaded with the Missouri troops, and

---

had expressed a desire for Magruder. "Yes," answered the President, "because you assured them you would not interfere with Price, but would give him his own way. They care nothing for you general, it is Price they wish for." Holmes got the appointment.

Michael B. Dougan, *Confederate Arkansas: The People and Politics of a Frontier State in Wartime* (University, AL, 1976), 92–93.

31. On November 29, 1862, Hindman began crossing the Arkansas River at Van Buren, where he concentrated his corps. Following a meeting on the thirtieth, Hindman set the advance for December 3. On December 6, the Confederates engaged the advance Union elements at Reed's Mountain, near Cane Hill. During the night of December 6–7, Hindman skirted around James Blunt's Union command and attacked the Federal reinforcements that were coming from Springfield, Missouri. Following an indecisive battle on December 7, at Prairie Grove, Hindman withdrew his command back to Fort Smith and Van Buren. Tactically the battle was a draw but strategically, the Confederates suffered a significant defeat, giving up their last best chance to contest the control of Missouri. Following the battle, the press and Hindman's commanders blamed him for the loss. The Little Rock *True Democrat* labeled the campaign a "disastrous one." Colonel Alexander Hawthorn recorded: "We ought to have thrown our whole force upon one part [of the Federal army] and destroyed it;... instead of which we halted, fronted to all points of the compass, in the form of a hollow square, and waited for the enemy to attack us." Conversely, the common soldier believed, like at Pea Ridge, that they had won the engagement. One soldier in Parsons's Missouri Brigade wrote: "that we were whipped is false; that we got the worse of the fight is equally untrue; if there is anything to justify a retreat, it is want of ammunition." In assessing his overall performance and that of his command General Hindman recorded on December 12: "I am very proud of my troops, not satisfied with myself. I did not press the enemy as vigorously as I ought. The tremendous responsibility made me timid." Banasik, *Embattled Arkansas*, 292–294, 305–308, 310–311, 455, 457–458; Editorial comment, *The Arkansas True Democrat* (Little Rock, AR), January 7, 1863; A. T. Hawthorn, "The Battle of Prairie Grove," *Mobile Advertiser and Register* (Mobile, AL), January 31, 1863; Hindman to Holmes, Telegraphic Conversation (December 12, 1862), Telegrams, Hindman's Command, Peter W. Alexander Collection, University of Columbia, New York, hereafter cited as Telegrams.

32. Mosby M. Parsons, a resident of Jefferson City, Missouri, was born in Virginia in 1822, moved to Missouri at age thirteen, and was a veteran of the Mexican War. At the beginning of the Civil War, Governor C. F. Jackson appointed Parsons a brigadier general and commander of the Sixth Division, MSG on May 17, 1861. When General Price entered the Confederate Army, Parsons became the commander of the Guard. On November 5, 1862, he was commissioned a Confederate brigadier general, and led a brigade at the Battle of Prairie Grove on December 7. Parsons would later command a division in the Trans-Mississippi during the Red River and Camden Expeditions. Parsons spent all his Civil War years, save for three months, in the Trans-Mississippi Department. At war's end he went to Mexico, where he was killed on August 17, 1865. See *Missouri Brothers in Gray,* 146–148, for biography and photo; Peterson, 172.

33. James D. White was born in South Carolina about 1834, and lived in Fredericktown, Madison County, Missouri, at the beginning of the Civil War. He was elected captain of Company A, Third Cavalry Regiment, First Division, MSG on May 5, 1861, and lieutenant colonel of his regiment on October 5, 1861. White was mustered out of the Guard on December 27, 1861. General Hindman

Col. Grinstead's South Arkansas Thirty-third[34] was brigaded with the Twenty-seventh, which was ours, and the twenty-second, Col. Shaver's[35]—thus giving our brigade three Arkansas regiments, all under command of that excellent officer, Col. R. G. Shaver.[36] We were hardly rested from the march from Yellville

appointed White commander of a Missouri regiment on August 29, 1862. White's Regiment, which became known as the Twelfth Missouri Infantry (Confederate) was organized on October 22, 1862, at Yellville, Arkansas. White led the regiment at the Battle of Prairie Grove, after which he resigned from the service on February 19, 1863, but his resignation was never accepted. He departed his regiment on August 28, 1863, and went on to become the Provost Marshal of the Second Arkansas District, which encompassed the lower Arkansas River. After the war, White returned to Madison County, and eventually migrated to Texas where he was murdered—date unknown. *O.R.*, vol. 48, 249; Bartels, *Forgotten Men*, 387; Hale, 346; W. S. C. Lackey, "Sergeant Ancil Matthews in the Confederate Army," Miscellaneous Papers, Madison County Courthouse, Fredericktown, Missouri; National Archives, Record Group 109, Confederate Muster Rolls, Twelfth Missouri Infantry; Peterson, 53–54.

34. Colonel Hiram Lane Grinstead was born in Lexington, Kentucky, in 1829. He studied law, moved to Texas, and in 1854 was elected district judge. In 1859 he relocated to Camden, Arkansas, where in May 1862 he began organizing the Thirty-third Arkansas Infantry, which completed its organization on July 11, 1862, with Thomas C. Hindman appointing Grinstead colonel of the command. Grinstead led the regiment at Prairie Grove and during the Red River and Camden Expeditions commanded both a regiment and a brigade. On April 30, 1864, Colonel Grinstead died "with those who fell nearest the enemy," while leading a charge at the Battle of Jenkins Ferry. Special Order No. 28 (July 11, 1862), Special Order Letter Book No. 1; Lula Grinstead Smart, "H. L.Grinstead," Confederate Scrapbook, 548–550, Camden Public Library.

35. Robert Glen Shaver was born on April 18, 1831, near Bristol, Tennessee, in Sullivan County. Shaver was home-schooled after which he attended Emery and Henry College in Virginia (1846–1850) to become a lawyer. He moved to Batesville, Arkansas, with his family in 1850, married in 1856, and settled in Smithville, where Shaver was practicing law at the beginning of the Civil War. "Fighting Bob," as Shaver was known, raised the Seventh Arkansas Infantry, being elected colonel of the unit on June 16, 1861. He led the Seventh with distinction at the Battle of Shiloh in April 1862, returned to Arkansas in July, and began raising what would become the Thirty-eighth Arkansas Infantry, not the Twenty-second. The Twenty-second would become the Thirty-fifth Arkansas Infantry (part of Fagan's Arkansas Infantry Brigade), and it was commanded, in November 1862, by James P. King. Shaver was appointed colonel of the Thirty-eighth on September 24, 1862, and led the unit as either the regimental or brigade commander throughout most of the regiment's career. During the war Shaver fought at Prairie Grove, Pleasant Hill (April 9, 1864) and Jenkins Ferry (April 30, 1864). Following the surrender, Shaver returned to Arkansas, settling in Jacksonport. Shaver headed the Arkansas Ku-Klux-Klan and fled the state in 1868 for British Honduras to avoid murder charges. He remained in Central America until 1872, returned to Arkansas, had all charges against him dropped, and was appointed sheriff (1872) of the newly created Howard County. A resident of Center Point, Arkansas, until 1891, Shaver moved to Polk County. In 1896 he again relocated to Mena, Arkansas, then to Texarcana in 1914, and finally to Foreman by the end of the year, to live with one of his daughters. He died of a stroke on January 13, 1915. National Archives, Record Group 109, Confederate Muster Rolls, Thirty-fifth and Thirty-eighth Arkansas Infantries; "Old Comrades Called Him 'Fighting Bob'," *Mena Star* (Mena, AR), January 14, 1915; Wilson Powell, "'Fighting Bob' Shaver," *The Independence County Chronicle* 3 (October, 1961), 38–39, 42, 44; "Robert Glen Shaver," *Mena Star*, November 23, 1986; Special Orders No. 38 (November 9, 1862), Special Order Book No. 1.

36. When the First Corps, Trans-Mississippi Army was organized on November 9, 1862, Mosby M. Parsons was made the commander of the Third Division. The Division consisted of two Brigades organized as follows:

| 1st Bde.—Col. A. E. Steen | 2nd Bde.—Col. R. G. Shaver |
|---|---|
| Steen's Mo. Inf. Regt. | Shaver's Ark. Inf. Regt. |
| Hunter's Mo. Inf. Regt. | Shaler's Ark. Inf. Regt. |

when we were again under orders to march on the 12th. We started at dawn and camped at night on Frog Bayou. Next day we crossed the Arkansas River below Van Buren, the men being hauled across in the wagons of our regimental train. We camped that night on a hill, some distance from water, and the boys were sky-larking all night. On the 14th we moved a couple of miles to a better camp, marching in a heavy rain, which was bad for a number of men who had the mumps. The rain swelled the river and steamers began to come from Little Rock with supplies. On the 22d of November we were paid for the first time in Confederate money, the pay-roll being made out up to the 1st of June. Joe Trimble and I had enlisted only a few days before June 1, and only had $2 coming, which we gave for a half a pound of tobacco each. About the 25th

## Rumors Of War

began to float through camp. Gen. Blunt was pressing our cavalry, commanded by that steadfast soldier, Gen. [John S.] Marmaduke.[37] Hindman accordingly prepared to move forward. The sick were put into hospitals, and the barefoot men were left behind, if they would stay. The army broke camp with about 9,500 men, rank and file, and a large train of artillery.[38] Our regiment crossed at Van Buren on the 29th, but being badly armed, were left near that place, and did not take part in the Battle of Prairie Grove.[39] I can, therefore, tell nothing of that affair

---

| | |
|---|---|
| Caldwell's Mo. Inf. Regt. | Grinstead's Ark. Inf. Regt. |
| White's Mo. Inf. Regt. | C. W. Adams' Ark. Inf. Regt. |
| Tilden's Missouri Bat. | Robert's Missouri Battery |

Unattached
    Robert's Missouri Cavalry Company
Special Orders No. 38 (November 9, 1862), Special Order Book No. 1.

37. On November 28, 1862, General Blunt, with his Kansas Division, attacked Marmaduke's Confederate cavalry division at Cane Hill, in northwest Arkansas. The engagement began at 10:00 a.m. and lasted the entire day, being a running fight of about ten miles. In the end, the narrow passes of the Boston Mountains and the onset of night put an end to the engagement. John S. Marmaduke, the commander of the rebel forces, was born in 1833, graduated from West Point (Number 30 of 38) in 1857, and served on the frontier until the beginning of the Civil War. Resigning from the U.S. Army on April 17, 1861, he was appointed a colonel in the MSG, commanded the MSG troops at Boonville, and later entered the Confederate Service. On November 15, 1862, Marmaduke was promoted to brigadier general and major general on March 15, 1865. Following the war he was elected governor of Missouri in 1884, and died while in office in 1887. For complete biography see *Missouri Brothers in Gray, 143;* Banasik, *Embattled Arkansas,* 268–287; Boatner, *Civil War Dictionary,* 513.

38. For the up coming engagement the Confederate Army would have 9,040 infantry, 2,328 cavalry and 571 artillerymen, supporting 31 pieces of artillery. Banasik, *Embattled Arkansas,* 517, 528 (n. 12).

39. On November 30 Colonel Shaler "informed General Hindman that it would be counted no less than murder to carry his regiment into a fight without arms." At the time the Twenty-seventh was poorly armed with "old hunting rifles and shotguns," with only about 20 or 30 of the men having any type of acceptable arms. With Shaler's plea, the Twenty-seventh was sent back to Fort Smith, where Shaler was appointed Provost Marshal, while his regiment served as the Provost Guard. John B. Clark's Missouri Regiment took the place of Shaler's Regiment and was assigned to duty in Roane's Texas Brigade. Banasik, *Embattled Arkansas,* 291, 299; Daniel M. Frost Letters, November 30, 1862, Peter W. Alexander Collection; Turnbo, 152.

from observation, though we were within hearing of the guns on Sunday.[40] After a couple days of suspense we learned that our army was retreating. When the troops rejoined us we were told that the retreat began at midnight, the artillery wheels being wrapped with blankets to prevent noise on the stony ground. Our loss in killed and wounded was about 750, and the Federal loss was supposed to be about the same. The enemy captured about nine pieces of artillery and 350 prisoners. Our army captured seven guns and 265 prisoners, including a few officers.[41] This was the way our men figured it out at that time. The Federal prisoners passed our camp on the way to Fort Smith. They looked fat and hardy and were jolly enough. The retreat was said to have been conducted by our men in good order, though very exhausting, and the scarcity of rations was

## Fatal to the Hogs

along the road. Some of the boys who were hungry had just captured a razor-back and were in the act of dressing it when Gen. Hindman rode up. As depredations of that kind were against orders, the culprits were considerably abashed, and suspended operations, expecting to be punished. The general, however, looked at them a minute and asked, "is it fat?" and then rode away.

Sunday December 14, our regiment interred the remains of Cols. [Alexander E.] Stein [Steen] and [William C.] Chappel, who fell while gallantly leading their men in battle.[42]

On the 17th, another Arkansas regiment was consolidated with ours, its of-

---

40. The Battle of Prairie Grove was fought in northwest Arkansas on Sunday, December 7, 1862. The battle began just before dawn and lasted the entire day. Initially successful, the Confederates failed to hold the initiative for the battle, allowing the out-maneuvered Federal forces time to concentrate. By 3:15 p.m. the two wings of the Federal Army, commanded by James G. Blunt and Francis Herron, were united on the battlefield and managed to survive the day. During the night, General Hindman, believing he faced insurmountable odds and being short of ammunition, ordered his command to retreat, giving the field and the victory to Blunt. Banasik, *Embattled Arkansas*, 338–339, 428–429, 431, 458–459.

41. Confederate official losses were reported as 164 killed, 817 wounded with 336 missing; total 1,317, with the loss of no artillery. However this does not correspond with the losses listed by the various brigade or regimental commanders which reported 204 killed, 872 wounded and 407 missing; total 1,487. The Union command lost 175 killed, 813 wounded and 263 missing; total 1,251, with the loss of no artillery. Though no side lost any artillery during the battle, pieces on both sides were captured and recaptured. *O.R.*, vol. 22, pt. 1:86, 142; Banasik, *Embattled Arkansas*, 513, 515–517.

42. Lieutenant Colonel William C. Chappell was a private in the St. Louis Legion during the Mexican War. He joined the First Division, MSG in July 1861 and became a aide-de-camp to General M. Jeff Thompson. He was wounded at Fredericktown, Missouri, on October 21, 1861, but recovered sufficiently to assist in the capture of the river transport *Platte Valley* on November 18, 1861, at Price's Landing, Missouri. Thompson's command was at the Battle of Memphis (June 6, 1862) and there is every reason to believe that Chappell, as Thompson's aide, was also present. Chappell departed Thompson's staff in June 1862 while located at Grenada, Mississippi. He returned to Missouri during the summer of 1862 and helped organize Steen's Missouri Regiment (Tenth Missouri Infantry), in which he was second in command. *O.R.*, vol. 3, 367, 368; *O.R.*, Series 2, vol. 1, 137; Peterson, 43; Donal J. Stanton, Goodwin F. Berquist, and Paul C. Bowers, eds., *The Civil War Reminiscences of General M. Jeff Thompson* (Dayton, OH, 1988), 125, 126, 165.

Battle of Prairie Grove, Arkansas (December 7, 1862)

ficers being sent off "on recruiting service."[43] We were now supplied with good Enfield rifles,[44] and turned in our shot-guns and squirrel rifles to the Ordnance Department.

On the 20th, there was a grand review of the infantry and artillery an Mazzard Prairie, by Gen. Holmes.[45] The day was fine and the sight an inspiring one that will not soon be forgotten by those who witnessed it. Our brigade was first on the ground, then came Gen. Roan's [Roane's] brigade[46] on the left and the brigades of

---

43. The Twenty-seventh Arkansas was consolidated with Charles W. Adams's Arkansas Infantry Regiment following the latter's poor performance at the Battle of Prairie Grove. When ordered to charge the enemy, Adams's unit collapsed at the first fire of their foe; out of the 461 men engaged in the battle, only 100 could be rallied, while the rest disappeared. Adams's Regiment listed 167 men as missing following the battle, and on December 15, 511 men were listed as deserters. For his part Adams recommended that the enlisted men of his regiment be transferred to other units, while the officers of the command should be dismissed from the service. On December 16, 1862, Hindman issued Special Orders No. 66, ordering the termination of Adams's Regiment. The officers were ordered to report to headquarters for instructions, while the enlisted men were sent to the Twenty-seventh Arkansas. On December 18 Hindman ordered Major J. H. Williams of Adams's Regiment, with the other officers, to Clinton in Van Buren County. Williams was to open a camp of instruction and to find "the men of the regiment who have deserted or absented themselves without leave" and accept them back into the Confederate Service without penalty. They had until February 1, 1863, to complete their task. Adams's regiment was never reformed. *O.R.S.*, pt. 1 vol. 4:82; Banasik, *Embattled Arkansas*, 515; National Archives, Record Group 109, Confederate Muster Rolls, Adams's Arkansas Infantry Regiment; Special Orders No. 66 (December 16, 1862) and No. 68 (December 18, 1862), Special Order Book No. 1.

44. The Enfield Rifle was the standard issue for the British Army in 1855 and widely used by both sides during our Civil War. The military issue Enfield was manufactured at the Royal Small Arms Factory in Enfield, England, while the exported models were produced by private contractors throughout England. The weapon weighed 9 pounds, 3 ounces and was chambered in .577 caliber. It was very accurate to 800 yards and effective to 1,100 yards. About 400,000–500,000 were imported during the war. The Enfield was considered the most popular weapon in the Confederate Army, while the U.S. Springfield Rifle was the preferred weapon in the Union Army. Boatner, *Civil War Dictionary*, 266; Faust, *Historical Times Encyclopedia of the Civil War*, 243–244.

45. At the time of the review, Hindman's command consisted of four divisions. The First Division was commanded by John S. Roane and contained Douglas H. Cooper's Indian Brigade, which was located in the Indian Territory at the time, and William R. Bradfute's Texas Brigade. The only unit present at the review from the First Division was the Texas Brigade commanded by Roane. The Second Division, commanded by Francis A. Shoup contained James F. Fagan's and Dandridge McRae's Brigades. The Third Division was commanded by Daniel M. Frost, with brigades under Mosby M. Parsons and Robert G. Shaver. The Fourth or Cavalry Division, was commanded by John S. Marmaduke and was not present at the review, Marmaduke having departed the army on December 12, to regroup his division at Point Remove, near Clarksville, Arkansas. *O.R.*, vol. 22, pt 1:903–904; Special Orders No. 66 (December 16, 1862), Special Order Book No. 1; Telegraphic Conversation between Hindman and Holmes (December 12, 1862), Telegrams.

46. Brigadier General John S. Roane was born on January 8, 1817, in Tennessee, moved to Arkansas in 1837, and became a prominent political leader. He served in the Arkansas Legislature from 1842, until he joined the war effort against Mexico in 1846. After the war, Roane was elected Governor of Arkansas (1849–1852) and remained active in Arkansas politics until the Civil War began. Roane was appointed a general officer on March 20, 1862, and served in the Trans-Mississippi throughout his time in service. A lackluster officer, Roane participated in only one battle, Prairie Grove, after which he served in administrative positions until the end of the war. After the war Roane returned to Pine Bluff where he died in 1867. At the time of the review, Roane's Brigade consisted of the Twentieth, Twenty-second, Thirty-first, and Thirty-fourth Texas Cavalry Regiments (all dismounted). The other

Gens. McCrae [McRae],[47] Parsons and Frost on the right, and last, the handsome artillery train.[48]

On the 27th, we moved to new quarters, expecting to begin putting up cabins for winter quarters. Before Monday arrived, however, we were on our memorable retreat to Little Rock.

Silas C. Turnbo
Twenty-seventh Arkansas Infantry

\* \* \* \* \* \* \*

---

units, which were part of the brigade at the Battle of Prairie Grove, were sent to other stations or duties—Clark's Missouri Regiment returned to its duty as provost guard on December 14; Reid's Arkansas Battery was sent to outpost duty north of Van Buren at Log Town on December 14; and Shoup's Mountain Battery was reassigned to the Second Division. Anne Bailey, "John Selden Roane," *Confederate General*, 5:92, 93; Banasik, *Embattled Arkansas*, 498–481; Harrell, *Arkansas, Confederate Military History*, 10:412–414; Ross, 345; Special Orders No. 64 (December 14, 1862) and No. 68 (December 18, 1862), Special Order Book No. 1.

47. Dandridge McRae was born on October 10, 1829, in Alabama, graduated from the University of South Carolina in 1849, and moved to Arkansas to manage the family plantation. At the beginning of the Civil War, he was living in Searcy, where he practiced law. During the Civil War, McRae fought at Wilson's Creek, Pea Ridge, Prairie Grove, Helena (July 4, 1863) and participated in the Camden and Red River Expeditions. McRae was promoted to brigadier general on November 3, 1862. By the time of the review, McRae had become disgusted with the service and had offered his resignation, but it was refused. On the day of the review, General Holmes stopped at McRae's Brigade and remarked to McRae: "Colonel allow me to congratulate you upon your promotion! you have won it upon a bloody field and you are entitled to it. It affords me infinite pleasure to announce it in the presence of your command!" Shocked by the announcement, McRae learned that it had been approved for promotion two months earlier and for some reason the announcement had been delayed. At the review McRae's Brigade consisted of the Twenty-sixth, Twenty-eighth, Thirtieth, and Thirty-second Arkansas Infantries, with J. G. Marshall's Arkansas Battery (the battery was probably on the far left with the other artillery of the corps). McRae remained in the service until after the Camden Expedition, at which time he resigned. After the war, McRae returned to Searcy and resumed his law practice and in 1881 was elected the Arkansas Secretary of State. He died on April 23, 1899, at Searcy, where he was buried. *O.R.S.*, pt. 2, 14:563, 566, 567–570, 572–573, 575; Banasik, *Embattled Arkansas*, 513; Letters (November 3 and December 23, 1862), McRae to Wife, Samuel Spotts Wassell Collection, Arkansas History Commission; Warner, *Generals in Gray*, 206.

48. Parsons' and Fagan's Brigade, not Frost's were organized as follows for the review:

| Parsons' Brigade | Fagan's Brigade |
|---|---|
| 7th (16th) Mo. Inf. | 22nd (35th) Ark. Inf |
| 8th (11th) Mo. Inf. | 29th Ark. Inf. |
| 9th (12th) Mo. Inf | 34th Ark. Inf. |
| 10th Mo. Inf. | Hawthorn's Ark. Inf. |
| Mitchell's Mo. Inf. | |
| Pindall's Mo. Sharpshooter Bn. | |

Note: The regimental designation in "( )" represents the denomination that the unit eventually became known by.

*O.R.*, vol. 22, pt. 1:903–904; Banasik, *Embattled Arkansas*, 512–516; Banasik, *Serving With Honor*, 39–40

**Item:** Battle of Prairie Grove, Arkansas (December 7, 1862), by J. W. Cooper, Cavalryman under Marmaduke.
**Published:** February 6, 1886.

## Battle of Prairie Grove.

Beaumont, Kas., Jan. 6

Editor, *Republican*

Being one of Marmaduke's cavalry[49] at Prairie Grove I give you my account of the battle as I recollect it, and also from what I could learn from others and see from the topography of the ground by passing over the field and woods after the battle. Hindman marched up Cove Creek and struck the enemy on the mountain between its head and Cane Hill.[50] A collision took place between two regiments of cavalry under Col. [James C.] Monroe[51] and the enemy's advance, ending in

49. At the Battle of Prairie Grove, Marmaduke's Fourth Division, First Corps, Trans-Mississippi Army was organized as follows:

        Fourth Division or Cavalry Division (Brig. Gen. J. S. Marmaduke):

            First Brigade (Col. James C. Monroe)

                Ark. Regt. (L. L. Thomson)

                Ark. Regt. (A. N. Johnson)

            Second Brigade (Col. J. O. Shelby)

                Mo. Regt. (B. F. Gordon)

                Mo. Regt. (B. Jeans)

                Mo. Regt. (G. W. Thompson)

                Mo. Bn. (B. Elliot)

                Qunatrill's Guerrillas (W. Gregg)

                Mo. Art. (J. Bledsoe)

            Third Brigade (Col. Emmett MacDonald)

                Texas Regt. (R. P. Crump)

                Mo. Regt. (M. L. Young)

                Ark. Art. (H. C. West)

Banasik, *Embattled Arkansas*, 516–517.

50. On December 6, Marmaduke's Cavalry had a day-long battle for the control of Reed's Mountain, which barred the way to the Cane Hill Valley and the Union Army. Toward the end of the engagement on December 6, Parsons's Missouri Infantry Brigade, with artillery support, secured the mountain for the rebels. *Ibid.*, 305–308; *O.R.*, vol. 22, pt. 1:64.

51. James C. Monroe, a resident of Clark County, Arkansas, was elected the lieutenant colonel of the First Arkansas Infantry in May 1861. With the First Arkansas, Monroe journeyed to Virginia, where the regiment fought at the Battle of Bull Run in July 1861. Shortly thereafter, the First Arkansas was reorganized and Monroe departed the regiment, desiring to return home. From May to July 1862 Monroe helped organize a cavalry regiment with James F. Fagan, which became known as Fagan's or Monroe's Arkansas Cavalry Regiment. Monroe was appointed a colonel by General T. C. Hindman on December 6, 1862, to date from October 25. Monroe would lead his regiment or a brigade in the Battles of Cane Hill and Prairie Grove. Though given only lukewarm notice for his "daring and skill" during the Battle of Prairie Grove, Monroe made possible the Confederate night move that took the Union command completely by surprise. With only a small brigade of about 450 men, Monroe held Blunt's Federals in place at Cane Hill until the booming of cannon at Walnut Grove at 10:00 a.m. alerted the Unionists to Hindman's nighttime march. Monroe also fought in the Camden Expedition, after which he was noted for his "gallant" and "daring" conduct. Monroe also participated in Price's 1864 Missouri Raid. After the war Monroe moved to Mexico. *O.R.*, vol. 22, pt. 1:148; *O.R.*, vol. 41, pt.

driving them back to the positions A and B in the map. This was on the evening of 6th December, 1862. While the regiments[52] were taking position before the charge the enemy were sharp-shooting at us and occasional balls were passing through our ranks—one of the hardest things for soldiers to stand—and caused a constant dodging among the boys. Col. Monroe, who was a strict disciplinarian, would look at them and sternly order "stop that dodging." Soon a shell came along through the woods with its shrill sound and burst with a loud report almost above the colonel's head. This was more than flesh and blood could stand and the colonel went over his saddle with the rest. Regaining the perpendicular and seeing

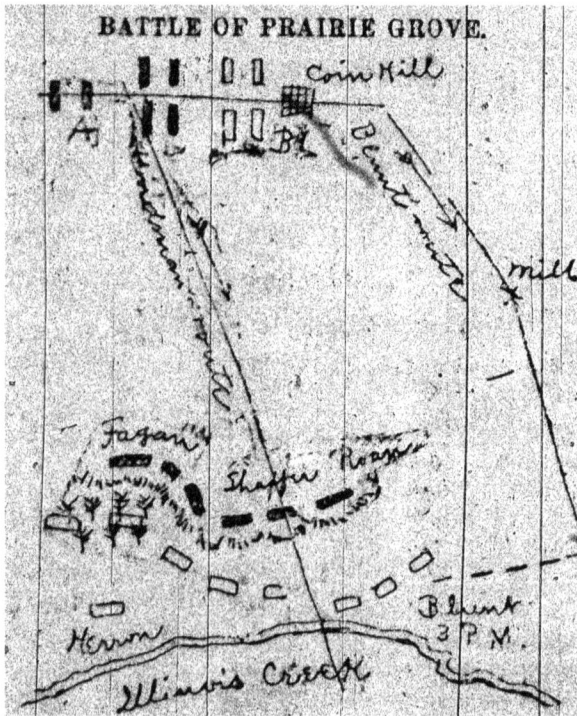

J. W. Cooper's map of the Battle of Prairie Grove

---

1:641; *O.R.*, vol. 41, pt. 4:1114, 1145; *O.R.S.*, pt.2, vol. 2:150, 271; Banasik, *Embattled Arkansas*, 516; Harrell, *Arkansas, Confederate Military History*, 281, 291, 324; Special Orders "no number" (December 6, 1862), Special Order Book No. 1; Letter (October 26, 1862), Newton to Parsons, Copy Letter Book No. 1.

52. At Prairie Grove, Monroe commanded a small brigade of two regiments with 450 men. Major L. L. Thomson and Major A. N. Johnson both commanded Arkansas cavalry regiments. Banasik, *Embattled Arkansas*, 516.

# The Boys Laughing

all around him he again sternly ordered "dodge the biggest."

Soon after night, leaving a detachment of cavalry[53] to watch Blunt, Hindman turned to the right on the Fayetteville road and on the morning of the 7th struck the advance of Gen. [Francis J.] Herron[54] marching from the direction of Fayetteville and drove it back to the prairie about three-fourths of a mile east of Prairie Grove Church where he met Herron. This prairie was from one-half to three-fourths of a mile wide. On the west side was a gentle rise of hills covered with a heavy growth of small stunted trees. The foot of these hills and the timber formed with the prairie a line convexed to the enemy.[55]

On the opposite side of the prairie ran Illinois Creek, or river; north of the road and west of the creek was a high precipitous bluff; south it had steep banks, the road passing across the creek through a narrow defile.

Hindman drew up his lines on the west side of the prairie. His right was posted on the northwest side of an orchard, making a reentrant angle, the salient towards the foe being protected from enfilade by a point of a hill. He had three brigades—one on the right commanded by [James F.] Fagan.[56] The center (I forget the com-

---

53. This detachment of cavalry was Monroe's Arkansas Cavalry Brigade. *O.R.*, vol. 22, pt. 1:148; Banasik, *Embattled Arkansas*, 334.

54. Francis Jay Herron was born in Pittsburgh, Pennsylvania, in 1837, and moved to Dubuque, Iowa, in 1855, where he entered into the banking business with his brothers. At the beginning of the Civil War he commanded the Governor's Greys, which later became Company I, First Iowa Infantry. Herron went on to become the youngest major general in the Union Army. See Banasik, *Reluctant Cannoneer,* 283–285, for a complete biography

55. Just before dawn on December 7, Confederate cavalry surprised elements of the First, Sixth, Seventh, and Eight Missouri Cavalries (Union) and First Arkansas Cavalry (Union), routing them near Prairie Grove church. The rebels pursued the Unionists, capturing about 250 prisoners, 21 wagons and three standards, including the Seventh Missouri's regimental flag. The rout did not stop until after the Unionists had passed through Herron's command at Walnut Grove church. After stabilizing the front, Herron advance his wing of the Army of the Frontier, crossed the Illinois River and fronted the Confederate position atop the Prairie Grove Ridge. About 12:30 p.m. the battle proper opened with an extended artillery duel, which served as a precursor of the upcoming infantry assault. Banasik, *Embattled Arkansas*, 338–346, 353, 364–371.

56. James F. Fagan was born on March 1, 1828, near Louisville, Kentucky, moved to Arkansas in 1839, where he became a plantation owner. At the beginning of the Civil War, Fagan organized the First Arkansas infantry and was elected colonel on May 6, 1861. He led the regiment to Virginia, where he participated in the Battle of First Bull Run, then transferred to the west, and fought at Shiloh in April 1862. Fagan resigned from his regiment on July 11, 1862, returned to Arkansas, and raised a regiment of cavalry. Appointed colonel of the First Arkansas Cavalry on August 5, 1862, Fagan was subsequently promoted to brigadier general on September 12. Fagan commanded a brigade at the Battles of Prairie Grove and Helena in Arkansas and led a division during the Camden Expedition. On May 13, 1864, Fagan was promoted to major general to rank from April 25, participated in Price's 1864 Missouri Raid and ended the war commanding the District of Arkansas. After the war, Fagan returned to his plantation, joined the Republican Party and obtained some minor government jobs. He died in Little Rock on September 1, 1893. For a complete biography see Banasik, *Serving With Honor*, 386–388; *O.R.S.*, pt. 2, vol. 2:271; Heidler, "Fagan, James Flemming," *Encyclopedia of the Civil War*, 673.

mander) lay across the road and Raon's [Roane] on the left.[57]

Herron drew up his lines on the west side of the creek and about 10 a.m. advanced to the attack of our right.[58] On entering the orchard he met a terrible crossfire from the angle and was repulsed with severe loss. This was repeated two or three times with the same results.[59] About 3 p.m. Blunt, who had marched to the sound of the guns about fifteen miles, came on the field, posted his divisions, his left regulating by Herron's right, and assaulted Hindman's left and

# Was Repulsed.[60]

Night closed the combat and during it Hindman retired from the field.[61]

---

57. As the Confederate infantry arrived at the battlefield, Hindman disposed his troops to deal with the advancing bluecoats. By 11:00 a.m., Joe Shelby's Cavalry Brigade held the rebel right, James F. Fagan's Arkansas Brigade held the center and MacDonald's Cavalry Brigade held the left. The remainder of the Confederate Army continued approaching the battlefield even as the artillery duel was progressing. Roane's Brigade would eventually join the far left of the rebel line, but that would not occur until the latter part of the battle at about 2:45 p.m.. Banasik, *Embattled Arkansas*, 364, 372, 377, 426–427.
58. Herron began his infantry assault on Prairie Grove Ridge at 2:00 p.m. At the time of the assault MacDonald's Cavalry Brigade held the far right of the Confederate line, next to Shelby's gray horsemen. Fagan's Arkansas Brigade was to the left of Shelby, while Dandridge McRae's Arkansas Brigade held the far left of the rebel line. Shaver's Arkansas Brigade was positioned behind McRae's and Fagan's command. The remainder of the Confederate forces were still farther behind and faced in the opposite direction of the main rebel line, fronting toward Cane Hill. *Ibid.*, 359–360, 377–378, 393.
59. Herron made two assaults on the Confederate lines. The first assault was made by the Twenty–Wisconsin and Nineteenth Iowa Infantries, which succeeded in capturing a Confederate Battery of four guns. However the ensuing Confederate counterattack overwhelmed the Union defenders, who retreated in disorder to their main line. This was followed by another assault by the Thirty–seventh Illinois and Twenty–sixth Indiana Infantries, that produced the same result. In less than an hour, Herron's wing of the Union Army was in a desperate condition, having been easily repulsed with a great loss of man–power. Indeed, according to one participant another Bull Run was at hand. However, just as Herron's troops began filtering back toward the rear, the booming of cannon on the Union right flank announced the late arrival of the other wing of the Army of the Frontier. *Ibid.*, 421–422, 427–428.
60. Blunt arrived on the battlefield at 2:45 p.m., having taken a detour to Rhea's Mills to ensure the protection of his trains. Prior to his arrival, Blunt's wing of the army had sat at Cane Hill, expecting the rebels to attack at any moment. Colonel James C. Monroe, commanding a Confederate cavalry brigade, had performed an outstanding job in deceiving Blunt as to the rebel intentions. Blunt fully believed that Hindman was about to attack him at Cane Hill and was startled into action at 10:00 a.m. when he heard cannon fire off to the northeast at Walnut Grove Church. Instead of taking a direct route to Prairie Grove, Blunt headed off to the north, and Rhea's Mill, where he was told that the rebels were about to attack his trains. Blunt would later claim that Dudley Wickersham, who led a cavalry brigade, had taken a wrong road, and that Blunt did not want to divide his command and so followed behind Wickersham. Had Blunt not taken the wrong road he would have arrived on the scene about the same time that Herron began his infantry assault. Ibid., 386–387, 427–428; *O.R.*, vol. 22, pt. 1:73–74.
61. After darkness set in, General Hindman evaluated his situation and determined that, like at Pea Ridge, his command was short of ammunition, and it was time to retreat. Muffling the wheels of his artillery to disguise their retrograde, the Confederate Army began moving back just before midnight. Even while Hindman was withdrawing Blunt had sent in a flag of truce to allow a cessation of hostilities until noon to tend to the wounded. Hindman agreed. Blunt would later claim that Hindman had requested the cease fire, but the record was clear—the request came to Hindman from Blunt via his chief surgeon for the cease fire. No matter the cause, the battle was at an end, and even though it was tactically a draw, the laurels of victory belonged to the Federal arms, as the Confederates had sur-

Hindman displayed good strategy the night before the battle by placing his army in the position he did, but seemed to lack that decision on the field of battle so much required in the make-up of a general.[62] Had he thrown forward the center brigade and pursued with his right on the first repulse of Herron, holding the left brigade in reserve, he would have undoubtedly forced him into the defile in his rear, captured his artillery and many prisoners, giving him a crushing defeat long before the arrival of. He held a position often used by good generals with complete success.

Napoleon made good use of a similar position at Castiglione, Rivoli and several other battles in the same campaign.

Stonewall Jackson gained his splendid battles around Port Republic[63] by this interior position, beating the enemy's separated divisions in detail. Hindman seemed to have the sense to gain his position but not the resolution to profit by it.

Truly yours.

J. W. Cooper

* * * * * *

---

rendered the field of battle. See Appendix C for Blunt's letter. Banasik, *Embattled Arkansas*, 457–460; Letter, Blunt to Commander Confederate Forces (December 7, 1862), Miscellaneous Correspondence.

62. General Hindman was indeed confused as to what actions to take at the Battle of Prairie Grove, though much of the fault lay with the intelligence he got while the battle was in its infancy. The head of the Confederate infantry column under General Francis Shoup arrived on the battlefield about 8:00 a.m. Shoup's orders were to strike the enemy "quickly and desperately." However, when Shoup conferred with Colonel Shelby, who had routed the Federal cavalry, Shelby informed the superior officer that the enemy coming from Fayetteville were "in no considerable force." Shoup interpreted this to mean that Herron's command had already passed in the night and that the bulk of the Federal Army was now at Cane Hill. Shoup halted and deployed his command upon Prairie Grove Ridge. Hindman would later approve Shoup's move, thus setting the stage for the battle. Hindman would later compound the inaction by sitting on the ridge and waiting for Herron to make a move, instead of attacking Herron before he could fully deploy his wing of the army. Hindman would latter telegraph to General Holmes, his superior officer, that he was at fault for the loss, being "timid" to engage Herron's wing. Banasik, *Embattled Arkansas*, 355–357; Francis A. Shoup, Manuscript report on Prairie Grove (December 11, 1862), Prairie Grove State Battlefield Park; Hindman to Holmes, Telegraphic Conversation (December 12, 1862), Telegrams.

63. Port Republic and Cross Keys, Virginia, were the final engagements of General Thomas "Stonewall" Jackson's 1862 Valley Campaign. The engagements were fought on June 8 and 9, 1862, with the main action occurring on the ninth. Jackson used part of his command to hold General John C. Frémont in check on June 8 and 9 at Cross Keys, while he used the remainder to successfully attack James Shield's Division at Port Republic, driving them from the field. The force blocking Frémont succeeded in retreating and burned the only bridge that he could have used to reinforce Shields. Federal losses at the two-day battle were 1,792, while Jackson lost about 1,088. Spencer C. Tucker, "Cross Keys, Battle of" and "Port Republic, Battle of," *Encyclopedia of the Civil War*, 527, 1549–1551.

Chapter 4

# Bits and Pieces, 1861–1862

**Item:** Missourians and Pilfering, by Richard Musser.
**Published:** September 4, 1886.

## The Few Pilfering.

Brunswick, Mo., Aug. 21
Editor, *Republican*

My attention has been called to a paper published in the Missouri *Republican* of the 14th inst. by Dr. John F. Snyder[1] of Virginia, Ill. The doctor served on the staff of Gen. Rains and well deserved distinction and ability. He had the best opportunities of witnessing the "few" instances of pillage committed by Confederate Missourians and the cases he relates are among the "few." Rains's soldiers in the first year of the war were raw and inexperienced, as is evidenced by the theft of the cross-cut saw. If they had been veterans, they would have known better how to steal and what.

Shortly after the Battle of Carthage, Clark's Division[2] encamped on Rains's plantation in Jasper County and very near to his mansion. The general was not at home, and his wife ventured to express the hope to one of Clark's soldiers, who did not know who she was, that the troops would not be permitted to burn the fences or deprecate on the property. The patriotic soldier assured her with perfect confidence that Gen. Clark's men were not permitted to steal, but ended the colloquy by informing the lady that, if it had been her misfortune to have Rains's[3]

---

1. Dr. John F. Snyder was born in St. Louis in 1830, lived in Bolivar, Polk County and edited the *Bolivar Courier* newspaper. He wore a variety of hats in the Eighth Division, MSG, including Inspector-General, Chief of Transportation, Chief of Ordnance, Division Chaplain, Provost Marshal-General and Assistant Division Surgeon. Dr. Snyder's article was published on August 14, 1886, and was republished in Part I of this volume. Peterson, 28, 211; Bartels, *Forgotten Men*; Walter Harrington Ryle, *Missouri Union or Secession* (Nashville, 1931), 151.
2. John B. Clark, Sr. commanded the Third Division, Missouri State Guard. Peterson, 107.
3. James S. Rains commanded the Second Division, MSG at Carthage, Missouri, in July 1861, even though he was listed as the commander of the Eighth Military District. Part of this confusion can be explained by how General Price arranged his army in July 1861. Price organized his command, on July 11, with five divisions, enumerated first through fifth, irrespective of the military district the general led. John B. Clark (Third Division), William Slack (Fourth Division) and Alexander Steen (Fifth Division), all led divisions corresponding to their military districts. Mosby M. Parsons (First Division) and James Rains (Second Division), commanding the Sixth and Eighth Military Districts respectively, were given division titles that did not correspond with their districts. By the Battle of Wilson's Creek in August 1861, Parsons's Division was labeled the Sixth Division while Rains's was still the Second Division. Finally, at the Battle of Pea Ridge, Rains's command was listed as the Eighth Division, MSG to correspond with his assigned District. *O.R.*, 3:20–22; *O.R.*, 8: 326; *O.R.*, 53:431, 710; Peterson, 81, 172, 209.

Division encamped on the place, there would not be a pig, chicken or a rail left on it, when they should march away. Very respectfully,

R. Musser

\* \* \* \* \* \* \*

**Item:** The Tallest Confederate, Henry Thruston, by Unknown.
**Published:** July 25, 1885.

## "Get Off That Stump."[4]

An old clipping from the Cairo *Democrat*,[5] of June, 1865, tells the following story:

Henry C. Thruston
at a Confederate reunion

Among the paroled rebel soldiers who came up on the steamer *Lady Gay* on Tuesday was a man a little over seven and a half feet in height. He started out with the Missouri troops at the commencement of the war and stuck to them until the "dog was dead" and never received a scratch.

Soon after he was mustered into the rebel service the regiment to which he belonged appeared before the colonel on dress parade, and the colonel, who prided himself on the fine appearance and good size of his men, cast his eyes along the line with a smile of self-satisfaction until they rested on the towering form of the tall Missourian, when he knit his brows and called out in fiercely thunder terms. "Get off that stump, you impertinent scoundrel, or I'll order you under arrest." The soldiers looked at each other, wondering what the colonel meant, but no one moved. Finding his authority tested with disrespect, he fairly boiled with rage, and advancing to the big soldier he exclaimed; "What in the devil are you

---

4. The incident related below is different from one in Eakin's & Hale's *Branded as Rebels*. "At Wilson's Creek," according to Eakin and Hale, Henry "earned his fame for his height. Thruston came up on his horse and the order was given to dismount. Thruston went marching on foot with the rest of his comrades. The infantry commander, who was then in command, saw Thruston's head so far above his comrades' he rode up, sword in hand, shaking his sword and said, 'Hey, you damn fool! Get down off that stump!' Thruston drawled in reply, "I ain't no fool an' I ain't on no stump." Eakin & Hale, 431.

5. The *Cairo Democrat* was both a weekly and daily newspaper, which was founded in 1863, and has since been merged or continued under various names, until the present, being titled the *Cairo Evening Citizen*. Library of Congress, *Newspaper in Microform United States 1948–1983, Volume A-O* (Washington, 1983), 1:210–211.

standing on?" The soldier respectfully replied: "On my feet colonel." The colonel was completely taken back as he surveyed this tall specimen of humanity from head to foot in blank amazement; he mumbled an apology for his rude remarks and hastened away, leaving his men convulsed with laughter. "Get off that stump" became the by-word with the Missouri rebels, and it will no doubt live as long as the long Missourian.

The hero of this incident was named Henry Thruston.[6] He enlisted in the Confederate army in Versailles, Morgan County, Mo., where his brother Dr. J. S. Thruston,[7] still resides. Henry is said, moved out to California, where he is still living comfortable, happy and tall as ever.

\* \* \* \* \* \*

---

6. Henry Thruston, or "Long Henry" Thruston as he was known, was born in West Morgan County, Missouri, on February 15, 1830. Also known as the "rebel giant," Thruston joined the First Cavalry Regiment, Sixth Division, MSG, under General Mosby M. Parsons in 1861. He later joined the Fourth Missouri Cavalry Regiment on October 27, 1862, and served throughout the war, being paroled out of the service at Shreveport, Louisiana, on June 8, 1865. He died in Mt. Vernon, Texas in 1909. Peterson, 172, 174, 176; Eakin & Hale, 431; Eakin, *Confederate Records*, 7:131; National Archives, Record Group M322 (roll no. 36), Confederate Compiled Service Records, Fourth Missouri Cavalry.

7. James S. Thruston was born on September 17, 1839, in Versailles, Missouri. His father was John B. Thruston, while his grandfather was Street Thruston. James was a lieutenant in the Morgan County Rangers, in Parsons's MSG Division at the same time as Henry. Surviving the war, James returned to Versailles, where he became a doctor. He died at home in Versailles on September 1, 1919. Eakin, *Confederate Records*, 7:132; Peterson, 176.

**Item:** Burial of Missouri Governor C. F. Jackson, by H. C. Miller.
**Published:** September 26, 1885.

## Gov. Jackson's Grave.

Arrow Rock, Saline Co., Mo., Sept. 15

Editor, *Republican*

In your Saturday morning's issue of September 12 I see a statement from Gen. [Justus] McKinstry[8] which should be corrected. The article refers to Gov. Clayborne [Claiborne] F. Jackson. He states that "Gov. Jackson died December 5, 1862, at a farmhouse in the state of Arkansas, and to this day no stone marks his resting place."[9] Again, he states, "amid war and its ravages, among stranger and unwept, he perished." I wish to state that the said clauses are not correctly stated. During Gov. Jackson's last sickness, and at the time of his death, he was kindly ministered to by his affectionate wife and daughter with many other near relatives and dear friends; that at the close of the war his remains were brought to Saline County and buried in the beautiful Sappington Cemetery four miles southwest of Arrow Rock, and a very handsome monument erected over his remains. Said monument was manufactured by Mr. Bedwell of Boonville costing over $700. "Honor to whom honor is due" should be Gen. McKinstry's motto in his forthcoming book and not wound the feelings of Jackson's many relatives in this state.[10]

H. C. Miller

\* \* \* \* \* \* \*

---

8. Justus McKinstry was born on July 6, 1814, in New York state, moved to Michigan, and received an appointment to West Point in 1834. He graduated in 1838 (number 40 of 45), fought in the Mexican War, where he was breveted a major for bravery. Following the war, McKinstry served in various Quartermaster positions and was serving in St. Louis as Quartermaster of the Department of the West, when the Civil War began. Under John C. Frémont, McKinstry served also as the Provost Marshall of St. Louis and on September 2, 1861, he was promoted to briagdier general. McKinstry commanded a division under Frémont, while still maintaining his position of Quartermaster for the department. Within days of Frémont's departure, General David Hunter arrested McKinstry on November 11, 1861, and in October of 1862, McKinstry was court–martialed for graft and corruption. Convicted, McKinstry was dismissed from the service on January 28, 1863, being the "only Union general officer cashiered for violation of his duty." Moving to New York, for a time McKinstry became a stock broker, but later returned to Rolla, Missouri, where he was a land agent. He died in St. Louis on December 11, 1897. See Banasik, *Missouri In 1861*, 358–359, for a complete biography and photograph of McKinstry.

9. Claiborne F. Jackson died at Little Rock, Arkansas, of stomach cancer, on December 7, 1862—the same day the Confederates lost the Battle of Prairie Grove. Ibid., 351–352.

10. The only book, noted in Dornbusch's *Bibliography of the Civil War*, that McKinstry ever authored was entitled *Vindication of Brig. Gen. J. McKinstry, Formerly Quartermaster Western Department*. The book was published in St. Louis in 1862. C. E. Dornbusch, *Military Bibliography of the Civil War* (1–3 vols., New York, 1961–62, 1967, 1972; vol. 4, Dayton, OH, 1987), 2:191.

**Item:** Biographies of famous Missourians; Congreve Jackson and Father Thomas B. Bannon, by R. H. Musser.
**Published:** November 14, 1885.

## Two Missouri War Characters.

In a recent address before the Southern Historical Society on the subject of the Battle of Pea Ridge, Col. R. H. Musser indulged in a slight digression, which may appropriately be given publication apart from the rest of the article, it was as follows:

It would be well for this society to follow the example of the French academy, and when a distinguished and honored member or citizen who had been a Confederate soldier dies, appoint one of its members to prepare and read a sketch of his life and character. When he has gone beyond the pale of personal malice and can no longer be affected by too partial or unseemly praise, and when death has silenced all cause for cavil and animosity, it would be well to write of their patriotism, their self-denial and their courage, embalming their virtue in charitable panegyric, so that what was excellent of them may be an example to posterity, and their faults, if any, be forgotten and untold. A proper object to be thus remembered and to be preserved in history was

## Congreve Jackson,

a native Missourian, born in Howard County early in this (nineteenth) century, and while the state was a territory, and even while the inhabitants were compelled to build forts to protect them against the Indians. Col. Jackson's was a locally historic family of pioneers. His father, James Jackson, had a brother who was stolen when an infant near Vincennes by the Shawnees and raised as an Indian. He became in time the well-known chief, "White Fish," of one of the tribes inhabiting the Upper North Grand River in Iowa and Missouri.

James Jackson fought with [Daniel] Boone in Kentucky when that beautiful land was new to civilization and culture. He had passed with the family through Indiana and Illinois when those now thriving prairie states were in, to him, unseemly nakedness, and to find in the rich soil and fine timber of Howard, lands like those in Kentucky where already the population had become too dense for him. Two miles from Glasgow [Missouri] on a section of land, which he subsequently purchased at the land sales, he settled. Here he remained in his old age till death removed him, and left it to his son as an inheritance. Amidst the scenes of simplicity and the hospitality his rural wealth afforded Congreve Jackson grew up. Those who would be truly great must live with nature and among scenes of sublimity and beauty, with no temptations to envy, and in all charity and good fellowship. With little scholastic learning Jackson became a man of wisdom, wisdom that is born of truthfulness and singleness of heart combined with experience. His reading of books was limited, yet his learning was great; his knowledge of details and facts comparatively small, yet his knowledge was instinctive of men and things and his judgment

# Without Error.

Born a slave-owner and a Democrat, he was the patriarch of his family, both white and black, and more of a father than a master to his household. He had been a captain in the Florida war under Col. Dick Gentry and commanded a battalion[11] in the Mexican War and was with Gen. Price in the campaign to Toas and Albuquerque. He returned with laurels to the modest occupation of a farmer and lived on his patrimonial acres. With his views of the relations of the states and the Union based upon the Virginia and Kentucky doctrine[12] of 1798-99, he naturally responded to the call of Gov. Jackson for 50,000 volunteers in 1861. He entered the State Guard as a private and was instantly elected colonel.[13] His age and infirmities soon after the Battle of Pea Ridge unfitted him for active service, and he modestly retired on the organization of the troops into Confederates instead of State Guard. He camped by the limpid waters of a mountain stream at the foot of the Mulberry range in Arkansas, and remained in exile the balance of the war. Returning in 1865 he found his paternal acres a desolation, with the exception that his mansion, with its bare walls and roof, was standing. Here he remained until his death, about two years ago, and died as he lived, an honest, fair-minded, brave man, unmarried, and on the spot where he was born.

# Father Bannon

Another of Col. Musser's happy personal sketches in the same address was the following:

I ought not to forget to mention the gallant and meritorious conduct of Father [Thomas B.] Bannon,[14] then secular priest, now of the Society of Jesus in Dublin,

---

11. Jackson was the lieutenant colonel in the First Mounted Missouri Volunteers. Heitman, 2:56.

12. On July 14, 1798, the Alien and Sedition Act was passed by the U.S. Congress, which prompted Thomas Jefferson and James Madison to craft what became known as the Kentucky and Virginia Resolutions. Jefferson and Madison believed that the Constitution did not give the Central Government the power to enact the legislation and as such that it was proper for the states to "nullify" it by legislation on their part. Jefferson wrote the Resolution for Kentucky, while Madison did the same for Virginia, hoping that other states would join by passing similar legislation. However, no other states joined in the protest and their actions produced no appreciable results. Ralph Ketcham, *James Madison A Biography* (New York, 1971), 394–403; Garry Wills, *James Madison* (New York, 2002), 48–49.

13. Jackson was elected colonel of the Second Infantry Regiment, Third Division, MSG on August 20, 1861. He went on to become commander of his division; date unknown. Peterson, 107, 118.

14. John Bannon was born in Ireland on December 29, 1829, educated at the Royal College of St. Patricks, and ordained a Catholic priest in May 1853. Immigrating to St. Louis shortly after he was ordained, Bannon was assigned to assorted parishes within the St. Louis Archdiocese. Prior to the Civil War, Bannon was the pastor of St. John's Church, chaplain of the St. Louis Militia, and participated in the Southwest Expedition in 1860. Bannon was captured at Camp Jackson and paroled on May 11, 1861. On December 15, he headed for Price's Army, joining it at Springfield in January 1862, and officially becoming a member of the Confederate Army on January 25, 1862. Bannon was at the

Ireland. He was attached to Gen. Little's personal staff, I believe, as chaplain, but had the general care of souls throughout the whole army. He was everywhere in the midst of the battle when the fire was the heaviest and the bullets thickest. He was armed with the viaticum, with tourniquet and with a bottle of whiskey. Whenever there was a wounded or dying man Father Bannon was at his side supporting his head; with the tourniquet he stanched his blood; with his spirits he sustained his strength till his confession could be told, or if necessary till he could baptize him from the waters of the nearest brook. Many a short shift was made that day; many lived to feel grateful to the good father for his gallant devotion to his profession and many more to admire his courage, and self-sacrifice by which he showed them the chaplain's peace was not back among the commissary wagons in time of battle, but among the wounded and dying in the strife. Father Bannon was an Irishman of splendid physique, full of grace and personal manliness, learned and eloquent, social and genial. He was formerly paster of the Immaculate Conception Church in St. Louis, over the site of which this society now holds its meetings.

\* \* \* \* \* \*

Battle of Pea Ridge as a member of Henry Little's staff, after which he headed for the east side of the Mississippi River. Bannon was captured at Vicksburg but was never paroled, and in September 1863 he was appointed a special agent of the Confederate Government. Traveling to Ireland and the Vatican, Bannon unsuccessfully lobbied the Pope to recognize the Confederacy, but did succeed in significantly reducing Union recruiting efforts in Ireland. Bannon never returned to the United States. He joined the Jesuit Order on August 26, 1864, in Ireland, and died in Dublin on July 14, 1913. Tucker, *Father Bannon*, 2–5, 7, 10, 17, 21, 23, 43–45, 155, 164, 175–178, 181, 184.

**Item:** Needed Aid for a Missouri Cemetery (CSA) in Fayetteville, Arkansas, by I. M. Baber.
**Published:** October 9, 1886.

## One Hundred and Fifty Missouri Dead.

The Richmond (Mo.) *Conservator*[15] publishes the following, which was addressed to G. W. Triggs, the editor:

Fayetteville, Ark., Sept. 26, 1866

Dear Sir: I have been requested by the president of the Southern Memorial Society (this society is composed of ladies) to write someone in Ray County and see what could be done in raising a fund to put a stone fence around the Southern Cemetery, asking no one to give over one dollar. The ladies have, since the war, raised the means and bought five acres on the side of the hill just east and facing the city, and fenced it and gathered the dead Confederates who were killed or died in this and Benton Counties, except those buried in the cemetery at Prairie Grove. But now the fence is decaying and they are trying to raise means to have a stone fence put around it and through me they ask if you will assist them in their worthy effort. There are buried here in the cemetery nearly 700 Confederates; of that number 153 are Missourians; of whom I send you a list of the names as far as could be obtained.

If a man will come here and go out southwest of town to the Federal Cemetery and see the marble and the ornaments and the fine residence, with an attendant paid $1,200 a year, with his blue suit and red stripes to guard and keep everything in trim, then pass through the city to the east and enter on the north side you will find lying near their homes, geographically, 150 Missourians, with nothing but a course sand rock to mark their graves. Then pass on to the center of the ground and you will find two dark sand rocks, barely discernable, above the ground. Nothing to distinguish whether it is the grave of a savage or a civilized man. When I walked up to it in July there was a lady kneeling at the side of it with a bunch of flowers in her hand, and the tears streaming down her face. I asked, "Who is that lady?" and the answer received was: "She is from North Missouri and is the cousin of Gen. Slack, and they were raised together, and she is here to visit his grave for the first time."

They have never called on anyone for outside help, but it is nothing but just as they have gathered together the lost and scattered dead of Missouri and buried them together at their expense, that we should contribute to protect their graves from spoilation.

I write to you because I thought your position would give you the advantage of seeing more parties than anyone else that I could think of. You can name this to

---

15. The *Richmond Conservator* began publishing in 1861, as a weekly newspaper, and went out of existence in 1945. Library of Congress, *Newspapers in Microform Volume A-O*, 560.

Capt. [John P.] Quesenberry,[16] Billie Ringo, Maj. [Robert J.] Williams and other old Confederates and if they feel interested in it see what they can do.[17] If anyone wishes to give anything you can send it to my address and I will see that it is appropriated to the purpose intended, or I will send you the address of the officers and you can send direct to them. Please answer and let me know what you think of it.

Below I give you the names of some of the Confederates buried here:

Lieut. Bliss, J. M. ———, H. A. Richardson, Rube Yates, Capt. Jack Cooper, Grundy Hawkins, M. Parsons, Thomas Pane, W. Allen, Lieut. Pane, ——— Mc-Gee, ——— Wilson, Wm. Butler, Albert Summers, Isaac Martin, N. O. Martin, J. Wiston, N. A. Hall, Sam Polk, J. W. Dunaway, P. H. Clark, James Roberts, H. J. Thorp, J. J. Stephens, ——— Bridges, R. F. Porter, R. J. Vaughn, T. H. Miller, Wm. Jobe, George B. Warinner, Allen Barnett, Charlie Clark, Willis Northcutt, James L. Owen, John H. Ball, W. S. Smith, J. W. Wells, Elijah Stenton, Bruce Ball, Frank A. Taylor, Dock Downing, R. Bibb, Henry Locket, A. Conroy, Doloss

---

16. John P. Quesenberry was born on September 13, 1818, in Glasglow, Virginia, and his family relocated to Richmond, Missouri, in 1840. Quesenberry opened a general store in 1848, and in June 1861 he joined Company A, First Cavalry Regiment, Fourth Division, MSG. During his six months in the Guard, Quesenberry fought at Carthage, Wilson's Creek and Lexington. He returned home briefly, then rejoined Price's army on December 19, 1861, and remained with the Guard serving as an Assistant Quartermaster. He entered the Confederate Service on June 23, 1862, and was elected a lieutenant of what became Company F, Thirty-fifth Arkansas Infantry. On August 27, the company was transferred to Hunter's Missouri Regiment and then became Company H, Eleventh Missouri Infantry. Quesenberry was promoted to captain in January 1863 following the death of his captain at the Battle of Prairie Grove. In addition to his duties commanding a company, Quesenberry appears to have served as an Assistant Quartermaster for his regiment. He was present at Little Rock in 1863 and fought at the Battle of Pleasant Hill in April 1864. Following the war, Quesenberry returned to Ray County and opened a hardware and implement business. He served for a brief time as a local sheriff and as the County Treasurer (1896–1902). He died a bachelor, on February 15, 1902. *O.R.S.*, pt. 2, vol. 2:779; Editorial note, *The Missourian* (Richmond, MO), August 24, 1933; Jewell Mayes, *"Ray County Chapters" Articles from the "Richmond Missourian,"* 7 vols. (Richmond, MO, 1930), 1:98, 3:61–63, hereafter cited as Mayes; Peterson, 137; Quesenberry Diary, notations in diary before entering regular Confederate Army.

17. William "Billie" Edward Ringo was born on March 30, 1841, in Richmond, Missouri. A druggist by profession, Ringo joined Company A, First Cavalry Regiment, Fourth Division, MSG in May 1861, during which time he was detailed to serve in General Price's band. On December 20, 1861, Ringo joined the Third Missouri Infantry (Confederate) and was mustered in for the war on January 25, 1862. Captured at Vicksburg, Ringo was exchanged and survived the war, being paroled on June 7, 1865, in Alexandria, Louisiana. Ringo returned home to Ray County, where he was still alive in 1923. Eakin, *Confederate Records*, 6: 172; Mayes, 3:63; National Archives, Record Group M322 (roll no. 119), Confederate Compiled Service Records, Third Missouri Infantry.

Robert J. Williams, was born about 1825, in Prince Edward County, Virginia, and lived in Richmond, Missouri at the beginning of the Civil War. A farmer and Mexican War veteran, Williams joined the Confederate Service on December 7, 1861, and was elected captain of company A, Third Missouri Infantry on December 28. He "was in every battle which his company was engaged in but one." Williams was wounded at Allatona, Georgia, survived the war and was paroled out of the service on May 13, 1865, in Meridian, Mississippi. Following the war he became the mayor of Richmond. Eakin, *Confederate Records*, 8:70; Mayes, 1:81; National Archives, Record Group M322 (roll no. 120), Confederate Complied Service Records, Third Missouri Infantry.

E. Payne, Wm. Barton, ——— Wilson, Joseph Snoddy, Andrew G. Smith, Bales Shumate, J. A. Noland, Jesse Brakefield, Wm. Balance, John A., Clark, Wm. Barrett, Lieut. Burgett, James Gash, Joseph Wells, Wm. Wells, H. C. Young, Silas C. Howard, Warren Moore, R. C. Beanlau, James Barnes, John Blackstone, Elijah James.

Yours Respectfully,
I. M. Baber
Box 225, Fayetteville, Ark

\* \* \* \* \* \* \*

**Item:** The importance of reunions, by C. S. Mitchell[18]
**Published:** October 10, 1885

## About Reunions.

The following letter is self-explanatory:
Dallas, Tex., Oct. 1, 1885
Capt. Celsus Price, President Missouri ex-Confederate Association, St. Louis, Mo.
Dear Sir:

In acknowledging the receipt of your kind letter of September 28, inviting my presence at the reunion of ex-Confederate Missourians to be held at Louisiana October 14 and 15, please accept my thanks and convey to our old army comrades my deep regret that I will not be able to join them.

I know from feelings realized at annual reunions of ex-Confederate Missourians in Texas what these gatherings mean, and that genuine brotherhood that is kept alive by coming together once a year; not to woe over the past in bitterness, but to count o'er the unwritten incidents of the battlefield, bivouac and camp-fires. There is a sad, sweet sentiment when each recurring year we count the new grey hairs and watch the mellow love borne towards each other as each mile-stone passes—awakening memories too dear to be forgotten—achievements that will be America's richest legacy—a heritage for posterity worthy of Achilles' grand-

---

18. Charles S. Mitchell was born in Franklin County, Virginia, on February 25, 1840, and moved to Saline County, Missouri, in 1840. Educated at private schools in St. Louis, Mitchell attended the Kemper Military Academy, in Boonville; Arcadia College, Arcadia; and Missouri and Central College of Fayette, Missouri. He joined the MSG on May 10, 1861, fought at Boonville (June 17, 1861), Lexington, and Pea Ridge. During the summer of 1862 he organized the Eighth Missouri infantry, of which he was elected colonel on August 8, 1862. He led the regiment at Prairie Grove, Pleasant Hill, and Jenkins Ferry. By war's end Mitchell had been recommended for general officer, but the war ended before it was approved. Mitchell returned to Missouri, but finding he was banned from the state, moved to Dallas, Texas, where he married and entered into the mercantile business. Mitchell was married twice and had six children. Date of death unknown. For a complete biography see Banasik, *Serving With Honor*, 390–391.

est heroism. All these belong to the Missouri Confederates, and why should they not meet periodically until the old guard shall have passed away? Such a history! Such soldiers! Worthy sons of Revolutionary heroes!

I thus refer to these reunions because I have been advised there are some of our old soldiers in Missouri who disapprove them—a misconception—Banquo's ghost[19] will not down, and let us make the most of it. Yours truly,

C. S. Mitchell

* * * * * * *

---

19. Banquo's ghost was a character in Shakespeare's play *Macbeth*. The ghost "appears to Macbeth, who had ordered his murder." Guralnik, *Webster's New World Dictionary*, 111.

# Appendix A
# Organization of Confederate Forces: Battle of Pea Ridge

Editor's Note: Most studies of Civil War battles contain a very basic Order of Battle, noting primarily the units and their commanders that were present at the battle or campaign. Occasionally you see information on losses, type of artillery used and, very rarely, the number of effective men engaged. The reader is oftentimes not given a clear picture as to the significance of a battalion, regiment, brigade, or division in a particular battle, since little is mentioned on the strengths of the opposing units. When a reader reads that a brigade withstood an attack by a division, is that significant—particularly when you have no idea how many men were involved in that particular action? Maybe the brigade outnumbered the division. The Battle of Pea Ridge has many of these inconsistencies, particularly on the Confederate side, when divisions were no bigger than companies or regiments, and brigades outnumbered any of the Union divisions that were present at the battle.

In presenting this Order of Battle, I am correcting many of the errors that Shea & Hess made in their book on Pea Ridge, including number and type of artillery present. I have also expanded the information on the losses sustained by the rebel command and added information on the effective strength that Van Dorn carried into the battle. The information on Price's command, with few exceptions, is fairly accurate, with assorted notes clarifying the numbers presented. McCulloch's command was more difficult to display due to lack of concrete unit information. However, I have made educated estimates of McCulloch's two brigades based upon available information, which is fully explained under the individual units.

I realize that the numbers presented in this Order of Battle probably have many inaccuracies, as many of them are estimates, but it will give the reader a better feel for the battle in terms of the number and losses of those units that were in the battle. It will also serve as a starting point for those who have other information concerning specific units that were at the battle and can adjust my logic accordingly to eventually obtain a full accounting of the Confederate Order of Battle at Pea Ridge.

Abbreviations:

| | |
|---|---|
| Bat. = Battery | Ltc. = Lieutenant Colonel |
| Bn. = Battalion | How.= howitzer |
| Capt. = Captain | M = Missing |
| Col. = Colonel | MSG = Missouri State Guard |
| Dmtd. = dismounted | Mtd. = mounted |
| EFF = Effectives | SB = smoothbore |
| (E) = Estimated | ukn. or ? = unknown |
| K = Killed | unorg. = unorganized |
| K/MW = Killed/ Mortally Wounded | W = Wounded |
| Lieut. = Lieutenant | [ ] = Losses |

## The Battle of Pea Ridge or Elkhorn Tavern (March 6–8, 1862)

Confederate Forces (Major Gen. Earl Van Dorn):[1]
  Body Guard:[2]
    Savery's MSG Cav. Co. (Capt. Phineas M. Savery)
    EFF = 34 [losses probably zero]
McCulloch's Division (Brig. Gen. Ben McCulloch):[3]
  Body Guard[4]
    Co. G, First Tx. Cav. Bn.( Capt. H. S. Bennett)
    EFF = 77 (E) [losses probably zero]

  First Brigade (Col. Louis Hébert):[5]

---

1. The composition of the Confederate command at the battle varies depending on whose account you read on the subject. The most extensive Order of Battle was presented by Shea & Hess, however, they provided no references on their data, making it impossible to either corroborate or refute their presentation. This order of battle represents a composite of all the information that I have located, making it more extensive and correct than previously presented by other authors. The references listed here are the general references. *O.R.*, 8:305; Anderson, *Memoirs*, 163; Bevier, 95–96; McElroy, 317–318; McGhee, *Letter and Order Book*, unnumbered page 75 (entry page 148); Moore, *Missouri, Confederate Military History*, 78; "Opposing Forces at Pea Ridge, Ark.," *Battles and Leaders of the Civil War*, 1:337; Shea & Hess, 334–339.

2. P. M. Savery's MSG Company was detailed as Provost Guard and Bodyguard, to the "commander of the corps," General Van Dorn, on March 3, 1862. Peterson noted that Savery's Company was part of Cearnal's 1st Cavalry Regiment, 5th Division, MSG, which served as Price's Body Guard at the battle. Price's Body Guard, according to Peterson, consisted of four companies, with an average strength of 31 effective men each (See note 29 for further details). *O.R.*, 8:784, 895; *O.R.S.*, pt. 2, vol. 38:154–15; McGhee, *Letter and Order Book*, unnumbered pages 29 and 78 (entry pages 55–56, 150); Peterson, 36–37, 156.

3. The strength of the individual units in McCulloch's Division was based upon their brigade's reported effective strength on March 2, 1862, just prior to the march. To obtain the effective strength for the individual regiments and battalion, I calculated the number using the regimental numbers from January 1, 1862, which reflected Total (meaning Aggregate Present) and Aggregate (meaning men present and absent). By January 1 the various units were fairly complete, with furloughs in the army being very limited or non-existent for enlisted men. The January 1 numbers should be a fairly good reflection of the men present when the advance began on March 4. To obtain the effectives on March 2, for the assorted units, I used the actual grand total values, as reported by McCulloch—4,637 for Hébert's Brigade and 3,747 for McIntosh's Brigade. These values were then adjusted to reflect the values of any known unit at the battle. The artillery and McCulloch's bodyguard were considered separately and not part of McCulloch's numbers for his infantry and cavalry. *O.R*, 8:718–719, 728, 763.

4. Also known as the "Lammar Cavalry." Effective strength based upon 97 percent of those present on January 1, 1862—the same percentage as used with the other cavalry units in McIntosh's Brigade. See McIntosh's Brigade for details. *O.R.*, 8: 719, 728; *O.R.S.*, pt. 2, vol. 68:267.

5. Hébert's Brigade had only one known value, the 16th Arkansas, which carried 664 officers and men into the battle. Removing the strength (Total column) of the 16th Arkansas from the January 1 values leaves 5,260 present in Hébert's Brigade. The effective strength on March 2 was reduced by 664, for the 16th Arkansas, leaving 3,973 effectives for the rest of the commands. The remaining 3,973 effectives were proportioned based upon a ratio of 75.5 percent of each individual command (3,973 divided by 5,260 present on January 1).
Neither Bearss or Tunnard account for Whitfield's Texas Battalion of dismounted cavalrymen. All the losses are from Shea & Hess unless otherwise noted. *O.R*, 8:718–719, 728, 763; Bearss, "Battle

4th Ark. Inf. (Col. Evander McNair)
EFF= 513 [16 K, 38 W, 6 M][6]
14th Ark. Inf. (Col. W. C. Mitchell)
EFF = 673 [losses ukn.]
16th Ark. Inf. (Col. J. F. Hill)
EFF = 664 [10 K/MW, 5 W, 12 M][7]
17th Ark. Inf. (Col. F. A. Rector)
EFF = 378 [losses probably zero to slight][8]
21st Ark. Inf. (Col. D. McRea)
EFF = 453 [losses ukn]
3rd Louis. Inf. (Major W. F. Tunnard)
EFF = 521 [16 K, 37 W, 38 M][9]
1st Ark. Mtd. Rifles (Dmtd.—Col. T. J. Churchill)
EFF = 604 [5 K, (?) W, (?) M][10]
2nd Ark. Mtd. Rifles (Dmtd.—Ltc. B. T. Embry)
EFF = 619 [6 K, 14 W, 23 M][11]
Texas Mtd. Rifles (Dmtd.—Maj. J. W. Whitfield)[12]
EFF = 212 [losses slight]

Brigade Total = 4,637 EFF
Losses (incomplete) = [53 K, 94 W, 79 M]

---

of Pea Ridge," 83; Mark Miller, *"If I Should Live" A History of the Sixteenth Arkansas Confederate Infantry 1861–1863* (Conway, AR, 2000), 32, 87–88, hereafter cited as Miller; Shea & Hess, 334–335; Tunnard, 129.

6. According to Colonel McNair, immediately after the battle the regiment had 40 missing of which "all except 5 or 6 have since returned to the regiment." Shea & Hess also noted that the regimental surgeon reported 5 Killed, 36 Wounded and 14 Missing, while the *True Democrat* reported the losses of 22 Killed, 23 Wounded, and 34 Missing. The difference in the numbers were probably the result of wounded dying or removed from a report as a minor wound and missing returned. I have used McNair's numbers in this case. *O.R.*, 8:296; H. G. Bunn, Letter (March 24, 1862), *The Arkansas True Democrat* (Little Rock, AR), April 3, 1862; Shea & Hess, 334.

7. Two of the wounded were captured and are listed under the wounded notation. Miller, 32, 87–88.

8. The 17th Arkansas, like many of the units in McCulloch's command, was never seriously engaged in the battle and probably suffered few if any losses. The unit was in reserve throughout most of the battle. Shea & Hess, 108–109, 123, 229.

9. The numbers presented here come from Tunnard, with the exception of the captured men, which comes from the *Official Records* and Bennett & Haigh. Shea & Hess have the losses as 10 killed, 15 wounded and 42 missing. *O.R.*, 8:231; Bennett & Haigh, 151; Shea & Hess, 334; Tunnard, 144.

10. "List of the Killed of Churchill's Regiment," *True Democrat*, April 10, 1862.

11. Shea & Hess listed the losses as 4 killed, 15 wounded, with 8 missing, but provided no source for their data. Leeper, for his part, provided a by-name list of the losses in the Second Arkansas Mounted Rifles, which I have used. Wesley Thurman Leeper, *Rebels Valiant: Second Arkansas Mounted Rifles (Dismounted)* (Little Rock, AR, 1964), 61–62; Shea & Hess, 335.

12. Of the four companies in the battalion, two reported total losses of 1 killed, 1 wounded and 1 captured. *O.R.S.*, pt. 2, vol. 68:211, 217; Sparks, 178.

Second Brigade (Brig. Gen. James M. McIntosh)[13]
1st Ark. Cav. Bn. (Maj. W. H. Brooks)[14]
EFF = 314 [6 K, 35 W, 0 M]
1st Texas Cav. Bn. (Maj. R. P. Crump)[15]
EFF = 245 (E) [minimal losses; probably zero]
3rd Texas Cav. (Col. E. Greer)
EFF = 931 (E) [2 K, 12 W, 0 M][16]
6th Texas Cav. (Col. B. W. Stone)
EFF = 854 (E) [3 K, 3 W, 13 M][17]
9th Texas Cav. (Col. William B. Sims)
EFF = 675 (E) [13 K, 24 W, 3 M][18]

---

13. The strength of the units in McIntosh's Brigade was calculated in a similar manner to Hébert's Brigade, with a few exceptions. There was no known value for Crump's Battalion prior to the Battle of Pea Ridge. From the *Supplement to the Official Records* we known that Crump's Battalion consisted of four companies, plus Bennett's Cavalry Company (Also known as the "Lammar Cavalry" or McCulloch's Escort). The only other cavalry battalion in McIntosh's Brigade was Brook's Arkansas Cavalry, which averaged 63.2 men per company on January 1, 1862. This would put Crump's Battalion, less Bennett's Company, at 253 men present on January 1. The six units comprising McIntosh's Brigade have a Total Present of 3,820 on January 1, The 9th Texas and Brook's Battalion have known values for March 2 of 989 men; this is subtracted from the 3,747-man Effective Strength of the brigade on March 2, leaving 2,758 men in the other four units. The known strength, on January 1, of the 9th Texas and Brook's Battalion was removed from the Total Strength, leaving 2,843 remaining in the other four units. The 2,758 Effectives on March 2 are divided by 2,843 Total Strength on January 1, giving a ratio of 97 percent, which is multiplied by the Total Strength of the remaining for units on January 1, yielding the estimated strength of the various units in McIntosh's Brigade at Pea Ridge. *O.R.*, 8:718–719, 728; *O.R.S.*, pt. 2, vol. 68:264, 275; George C. Robards, Letter (April 1, 1862), *True Democrat*, April 24, 1862; Gideon Smith, "Camp Near Van Buren, Arkansas," *The Standard* (Clarksville, TX), April 3, 1862.

14. Of the wounded, five were mortal. *O.R.*, 8:304; George C. Robards, Letter (April 1, 1862), *True Democrat*, April 24, 1862; Sparks, 174.

15. Indications are that Crump's Battalion, also known as the 1st Texas Cavalry Battalion, was only lightly engaged in the battle. Two of the four companies that were in the Battle of Pea Ridge, noted that they were not engaged or were "in a skirmish, not a general engagement." This skirmish would have coincided with the action that occurred on March 8, when the battalion was protecting Price's trains. *O.R.*, 8:304; *O.R.S.*, pt. 2 vol. 68:272, 277; P. R. Smith, Letter (March 13, 1862), *Washington Telegraph*, April 2, 1862.

16. One observer in Good's Texas Battery put the 3rd Texas Cavalry at 1,000 men. *O.R.*, 8:299; Douglas, *Douglas Battery*, 184; Hale, *Third Texas Cavalry*, 100.

17. Shea & Hess, 335.

18. On January 1, 1862 Sims's Regiment reported 713 men as the Aggregate Present, while Lieutenant George Griscom, the Adjutant of the regiment, reported that the command had "near 600" men available on February 17, 1862, with another detachment of 76 men joining the command on February 27, for a total of 676. Additionally, Griscom noted that more men joined the regiment as recruits and from furlough on March 3, the day before Sims's regiment marched—675 seems to be a fair estimate of the unit's strength for the Battle of Pea Ridge.

As to losses, three sources listed the losses of Sims Regiment at Pea Ridge. Crabb used the Confederate Service Records to compile the losses (the ones I used), while Gideon Smith, commanding Company B, listed the regiment's losses as 10 killed, 15 wounded and 3 missing (the missing all from Company B). Smith also noted that these losses were all as a result of the charge on the battery and makes no mention of any losses on March 6. Griscom listed the losses as 13 killed, 24 wounded (7

11th Texas Cav. (Lieut. Col. James J. Dimond)
   EFF = 728 (E) [losses were probably minimal][19]

   Brigade Total = 3,747
   Losses (incomplete) = [24 K, 74 W, 16 M]

Artillery Bn. (Capt. W. R. Bradfute):[20]
   Hart's Ark. Battery, four 6-lb guns
   EFF = 54 (E) [losses, minimal][21]
   Provence's Ark. Battery, two 6-lb. guns; two, 12-lb how.
   EFF = 53 (E) [losses probably zero][22]
   Gaines's Ark. Battery, two 12-lb rifles; two 12-lb. how.
   EFF = 53 (E) [losses probably zero][23]
   Good's Texas Battery (Capt. John J. Good),[24] four 6-lb SB guns; two,

---

mortally) with 3 missing—the same as Smith. *O.R.*, 8:728; Crabb, 76–77; Homer L. Kerr, ed., *Fighting With Ross' Texas Cavalry Brigade C.S.A.: The Diary of George L. Griscom, Adjutant 9th Texas Cavalry Regiment* (Hillsboro, TX, 1976), 12–15; Smith, "Camp Near Van Buren, Arkansas," *Standard*, April 3, 1862.

19. The losses which occurred in McIntosh's Brigade occurred either on March 6 or during the cavalry charge on 1st Missouri Flying Artillery (Union) on March 7. The 3rd Texas lost most of their men on March 6. Brook's Battalion, Sims's and Stone's Regiments suffered their losses when they charged the Federal Battery on March 7. In the charge on the Flying Battery, Shea & Hess have the entire brigade participating in the charge, with the exception of Greer's Third Texas. Gideon Smith, of the Ninth Texas, has the charge being made primarily by Sims' Ninth Texas, which took the battery head on, with part of Young's 11th and Stone's 6th Texas Cavalries. The Adjutant of Brook's Battalion also places his command in the charge of the battery where they lost most of their men for the battle. Robards, Letter (April 1, 1862), *True Democrat*, April 24, 1862; Smith, Letter (March 15, 1862), *Standard*, April 3, 1862.

20. Gun values all come from Shea & Hess, unless otherwise noted. James P. Douglas, of Good's Battery, has Bradfute as a major. Also, the manpower for the various batteries was based upon the strength present times 75.5 percent, the same percentage used to calculate the effectives in the infantry commands as seen under Hébert's Brigade. This percentage was similar to the percentage experienced by Douglass command when compared to March 21, 1864 figures of the number of men present verses the number of men listed as effective. *O.R.*, 8:719, 728; *O.R.*, vol. 32, pt. 3:699; Douglas, *Douglas Battery*, 163; Fitzhugh, 132; McElroy, 317; Shea & Hess, 335–336.

21. With the exception of the second day of combat Hart's command saw little action and from Shea & Hess' description of Hart's action on the second day they probably sustained few if any losses. Shea & Hess, 109, 233.

22. Provence's Battery was kept in reserve and never fired a shot according to a member of Douglas Battery. Douglas, *Douglas Battery*, 188; Fitzhugh, 164.

23. Shea & Hess make no meaningful mention of Gaines's Battery, having this battery in reserve throughout the battle. Members of Bradfute's Battalion, which included Gaines's Battery, make no mention of Gaines's Battery even being at the Battle of Pea Ridge. John P. Good, commander of a Texas Battery recorded that only his, Hart's and Provence's batteries were with McCulloch. Was Gaines's Battery with McCulloch's trains, similar to Kneisley's Missouri Battery being with Price's trains? or was it left behind and never marched with the army? Douglas, *Douglas Battery*, 188; Fitzhugh, 162, 164; Shea & Hess, 109, 144–145, 252

24. Shea & Hess have Good's Battery armed with four, 12-pound guns and two, 12-pound howitzers; this was not correct. A review of assorted sources clearly shows that the battery contained four,

12-lb how.
EFF = 76 (E) [1 K, 15 W, 0 M][25]

Battalion Total = EFF 236 (E)
Losses (incomplete) = 1 K, 15 W, 0 M
Unassigned:
19th Ark. Inf. Regt. (Lieut. Col. P. R. Smith)
EFF = 600 (E) [no losses—lightly engaged][26]
22nd Ark. Inf. Regt. (Col. G. W. King)[27]
EFF = 400 (E) [no losses—not engaged]

McCulloch's Division Total = 9,697 EFF
Losses (incomplete) = 78 K, 183 W, 95 M

**General Note on Sterling Price's Command:**
Price, in his official report on the Battle of Pea Ridge, places his strength at 6,818, with 8 batteries of artillery, as did the editors of *Battles and Leaders* (1:337). Shea & Hess have eleven batteries in Price's command at the battle, but

6-pound smoothbore guns and two, 12-pound howitzers. The guns were captured when the Confederate forces occupied San Antonio at the beginning of the war and were subsequently assigned to Captain Good by order of General Van Dorn. On May 10, 1862, the battery was reorganized, while at Corinth, Mississippi, being reduced to four guns—two sixes and two howitzers. They used these guns at Richmond, Kentucky in 1862, Chickamauga in 1863, and into March 1864. Between March 21 and April 2, 1864, the battery turned in their 6-pound guns, replacing them with two, 12-pound howitzers. On July 22, 1864, at the Battle of Atlanta, the battery took part in the capture of some Federal batteries, which allowed them to turn in their old guns for four 12-pound Napoleons. *O.R.*, vol. 30, pt. 2:159; *O.R.*, vol. 32, pt. 3:687, 698–699, 731; Douglas, *Douglas Battery*, 3, 116, 161, 188, 193, 197–198, 202; Fitzhugh, 14, 124; Shea & Hess, 336.

25. James P. Douglas, second in command of the battery, reported only 13 wounded and 1 killed, as did Sam Thompson of the battery. John J. Good reported the losses as stated in a letter to his wife as 1 killed 14 wounded and 2 missing; however, in a report issued in March 1864, Good noted that his losses at Pea Ridge were one killed and fifteen wounded, with none missing. This last figure would suggest that one of the two missing turned up wounded, while the other man returned to the battery with no injuries. *O.R.*, vol. 32, pt. 3:698; Douglas, 29, 186; Fitzhugh, 167.

26. The 19th Arkansas was with Price's trains and only lightly engaged on March 8, suffering no losses. I calculated their effective strength using their strength report from May 31, 1862. On that date they had an Aggregate Present of 397 men. However, at the time half the regiment was at home harvesting the wheat; or 451 men. This would suggest that if the entire regiment was present, its Aggregate Present would have been 794. I then treated the 794 the same as the other units in Hébert's Brigade on January 1, 1862, and multiplied it by 75.5 percent, yielding 600 Effectives for Pea Ridge. *O.R.*, 13:831, 935, 945; P. R. Smith, Letter (March 13, 1862), *Washington Telegraph*, April 2, 1862.

27. Shea & Hess have the regiment as the 20th Arkansas, while the *Official Records* have it as the 22nd Arkansas Infantry. According the *Supplement to the Official Records*, King's Regiment was known as the 22nd Arkansas Infantry from March 1862–February 1863, at which time it was known as the 20th Arkansas Infantry. At Pea Ridge, the 20th Arkansas guarded the trains and was not engaged. Maury placed the train guard at 1,000 men. Deducting the estimated men from the 19th Arkansas leaves the regiment 400 men at the Battle of Pea Ridge. *O.R.*, 8: 304, 317, 837; *O.R.S.*, pt. 2, vol. 2:634; Maury, 187; Shea & Hess, 336.

provided little documentation of that fact. As will be seen in the notes following, Price's command had ten batteries, not eight as Price stated, or eleven as Shea & Hess recorded. This in turn gives question to Price's reported strength of 6,818 men. The number of artillery pieces under Price's control varies depending on the account that one reads; Shea & Hess have 49 guns, Jay Monaghan has 42, John C. Moore places the number at 51, Frank Cunningham at 50 with R. S. Bevier and Franz Sigel correctly identify the number as 43 (Sigel for his part has Price with 38 guns, excluding Kneisley's five pieces that were with the trains, which resulted in 43 guns total) as shown below with an additional two unmanned guns; at 10 effective men per gun (allows for a typical nine man gun crew, three officers and one or two staff sergeants to a battery) would yield 430 artillerymen. With the artillerymen, Price's strength would be 7,248 effective men.

This compares favorably to the numbers provided by Bevier and E. Anderson, who put Price's strength at 7,450; though it was unclear as whether Bevier and Anderson included the artillerymen. In Bevier's statement of Price's strength, he does not include Parsons's command which I estimate at about 90 (see note 68); or an additional 185 men not included in the Third Brigade of Confederate Volunteers (see notes 55–57); or Cearnal's Missouri Cavalry Battalion of 94 men (Price's Escort—see notes 29 and 64); or McCulloch's Cavalry Battalion of 200 men (see note 30); or 120 cavalry men from the 7th Division MSG (see note 49). These additions, with artillerymen, would place Bevier's numbers at 8,569, which is reduced by six men to reflect General's Frost's adjustment in McBride's MSG division, leaving 8,563. Additionally, Bevier places the 5th Division, MSG at 600 men, while the *Official Records* places the command at 700 infantry; this additional 100 men would give Bevier's total of 8,663. However, Price may not have included those men with Green's 2nd Division, whom Bevier identifies as "details from other commands;" these men may not have been considered effective men by Price, because they were not seriously engaged or were possibly the stragglers of the command. Deducting these 1,350 men (See note 31) gives Bevier a total of 7,313 men of all types compared with Price's numbers of 7,248. Assuming Price's original figure was correct at 6,818, and with additions as noted above, the 65-man difference would suggest a "rounding" problem for Bevier's and Anderson's numbers and would be inconsequential in the remaining evaluation of Price's command.[28]

Price's Division (Maj. Gen. Sterling Price):
    Body Guard Bn.: 1st Cav. Regt., 5th Div., MSG (Ltc. J. T. Cearnal, wounded Mar. 7; Maj. D. Todd Samuels)[29]

28. *O.R.*, 8:325–326; Anderson, *Memoirs*, 163; Bevier, 96, 98–99; Coggins, 63; Cunningham, 54; Monaghan, 234; Moore, *Missouri, Confederate Military History*, 78; "Opposing forces At Pea Ridge," *Battles and Leaders of the Civil War*, 1:337; Shea & Hess, 336–339; Sigel, 1:334.
29. Cearnal's command was part of the 5th Division, MSG and per Colonel James P. Saunders, was detached from his command during the battle, and operated under the orders of Generals Price or Van

EFF = 94 [1K, 3 W, 5 M]
McCulloch's Cav. Bn. (Col. Robert McCulloch, Sr.):[30]
    Gause's Cav. Sqd., 4th Div., MSG (Maj. William R. Gause)
    Elements of 1st Cav. Regt., 6th Div. MSG, (Col. G. W. Riggins)
    Confederate Cav. Co. (1st Lt. G. W. Oglesby)
    Bn. EFF = 200 [ukn.]
Wagon Train (Brig. Gen. Martin Green):[31]
    2nd Div. MSG (Brig. Gen. Martin Green)
    EFF = 650 [probably zero][32]
    Elements of 3rd, 4th, 5th, 6th, 7th, 8th and 9th MSG
    EFF = 1,350 [not engaged—probably zero]
    Kneisley's MSG Bat. (Capt. James W. Kneisley),[33] 5 guns, 6-lb SB &
    12-lb How.

---

Dorn. When originally organized the unit was intended for the "immediate command of the Major General [Price] who may attach the same, or any part thereof, to any division whenever the exigencies of the service may require." The unit consisted of four companies, with an average strength of 31.25 (rounded to 31) effective men each at the battle. Since Savery's Company was detached as Van Dorn's Body Guard and Provost Guard, this would leave only three companies for Cearnal's control or 93.75 (rounded to 94) effective men. Losses are per Official Records, while Shea & Hess have the losses at 2 killed, 6 wounded with 12 missing. *O.R.*, 8:305, 321, 328–329; McGhee, *Letter and Order Book*, unnumbered pages 29 and 78 (entry pages 55–56, 150); Peterson, 36–37, 156; Shea & Hess, 337.

30. In his report on the Battle of Pea Ridge, Major D. H. Lindsay, commander of the 6th Division, MSG, implies that he also had cavalry present at the battle, but provides no information or details on them. A review of Colonel Thomas H. Rosser's and John T. Hughes official accounts of the battle identifies the command as Robert McCulloch's cavalry regiment or battalion. G. W. Riggins, commanding a battalion noted that his command was under the direct orders of both General Van Dorn and Price. Since Price commanded the left wing of the army, I have placed McCulloch's command under Price's control. Additionally, from Peterson's book, *Price's Lieutenants*, we find that McCulloch commanded the 1st Cavalry Regiment, 6th Division, MSG and that the command served at Pea Ridge. A review of the Supplement to the Official Records also supports the presence of four companies under McCulloch's command at the battle; Captains C. M. Sutherlin's and George B. Harper's Companies, First Cavalry Regiment, 6th Division, MSG; Major William R. Gause's Cavalry Squadron, Fourth Division, MSG; and McCulloch's recently organized company of Confederate cavalry under First Lieutenant G. W. Oglesby. The strength of McCulloch's command comes by comparing three sources—Moore's *Missouri, Confederate Military History* which places Slack's command at "700 Confederates" and Anderson's and Bevier's accounts which place Slack's Confederates at 500—The two hundred-man difference would be McCulloch's command. *O.R.*, 8:313, 315, 322; *O.R.S.*, pt. 2, vol. 38: 142, 146, 150, 160–161; Anderson, *Memoirs*, 163; Bevier, 96; Moore, *Missouri, Confederate Military History*, 78; Peterson, 142, 174–177.

31. Bevier has Green's command as 2000 men with elements from all the divisions in the MSG. Harding reported the strength of Green's Division as 650, leaving 1,350 for the remaining elements of the State Guard that traveled with Price's train. Bevier, 96; McGhee, *Service With the Guard*, 65.

32. According to Green's official report and a letter by Lieutenant Colonel P. R. Smith, commanding the 19th Arkansas Infantry, Price's trains were only lightly engaged. A Federal party came up on the trains, Green and Smith deployed their commands, and Kneisley's Missouri Battery (MSG) fired a few shots. The Federals replied with one shot, doing no damage and retreated. *O.R.*, 8:316–318; Smith, Letter (March 13, 1862), *Washington Telegraph*, April 2, 1862.

33. Also known as the Palmyra Light Artillery Battery or the "'Old Black Battery.'" *O.R.*, 8:317; Frost, 7; Peterson, 101.

EFF = 50 [probably zero]
Guibor's Mo. Bat. (cdr. ukn.),[34] 2 guns, 6-lb SB
    EFF = 0 [0 K, 0 W, 0 M]

Division/ Train Total = EFF: 2,050
Losses = No losses

Organized Confederate Troops (Maj. Gen. Sterling Price):
    First Brigade (Col. Henry Little)[35]
        1st Mo. Cav. (Col. Elijah Gates)
            EFF = 369 [ukn.]
        1st (2nd) Mo. Inf. (Col. John Q. Burbridge)
            EFF = 579 [173 K/W/M][36]
        2nd (3rd) Mo. Inf. (Col. Benjamin A. Rives)
            EFF = 579 [26 K, 45 W, 33 M][37]
        Clark's Mo. Art. (Capt. Samuel Chruchill Clark),[38] 2 guns, 6-lb SB; 2 guns, 12-lb How.
            EFF = 40 [ukn.]
        Wade's Mo. Art. (Capt. William Wade),[39] 4 guns, 6-lb SB; 2 guns 12-lb

---

34. Prior to the battle Guibor's command left two of their guns with the wagon train as they had insufficient men to man the pieces. Banasik, *Missouri Brothers in Gray*, 25.

35. In Bevier's account of the Battle of Pea Ridge, he has Little's Brigade with three regiments of infantry and one regiment of cavalry, with a total strength of 2,000 (Anderson has one less regiment, but maintains the same strength and fails to mention Green's 3rd Brigade). However in his official report of the battle, Little lists his command as containing only two regiments of infantry and one of cavalry—the missing infantry regiment would have been part of Colton Greene's 3rd Brigade, with a strength of 473 men (See note under Greene's Brigade). As such, 473 men are deducted from Little's 2,000 man strength to yield 1,527 effective cavalry and infantrymen. Bennett & Haigh place Gates's, Cearnal's and Shelby's cavalry strength at 500 men; Cearnal's strength was 94 (See note above for 1st Cavalry Regiment, 5th Division, Missouri State Guard), which leaves 406 for Gates's and Shelby's commands or 37 men per company; 369 for Gates's and 37 for Shelby. This further suggests that the two infantry regiments in the First Brigade contained 579 men each. Anderson in his account places these two regiments at about 600 men each, which compares favorably to the 579 calculation as seen above. The artillerymen are calculated at ten effective men per gun as seen in above note under "Price's Division," giving another 100 men, of all types, in the brigade, for a total strength of 1,627 *O.R.*, 8:305, 324–326; Anderson, *Memoirs*, 163, 180; Bennett & Haigh, 131; Bevier, 79, 95.

36. *O.R.S.*, pt. 2, vol. 38:411; Anderson, *Memoirs*, 180.

37. Shea & Hess, 336.

38. Clark's Battery, also known as the "Boy Battery" or the 2nd Missouri Artillery, initially contained two 6-pound guns, which they received at Lexington while assigned to Parsons's 8th Division, MSG. Following the capture of Lexington, Clark was given another two 6-pound guns, giving him a total of four. These final two guns were in turn exchanged before the end of 1861, for two 12-pound howitzers, which arrived in Springfield, Missouri, in November 1861. Anderson, *Memoirs*, 99; Bartels, *Trans-Mississippi Men*, 140; Peterson, 151–152, 286; Wilson, "Clark's Battery," *Missouri Republican*, November 28, 1885.

39. Wade's Missouri Battery was organized on December 28, 1861, at Springfield, Missouri. The unit contained six guns, four 6-lb smoothbores and two 12-lb howitzers. See note 127, of Chapter 1, for details on Wade's Battery. Wilson, "Clark's Battery," *Missouri Republican*, November 28, 1885.

How.
$$\text{EFF} = 60 \; [1 \text{ K, 8 W, 0 M}]^{40}$$
First Brigade Total = EFF: 1,627
Losses (incomplete) = 286 K/W/M

Second Brigade (Brig. Gen. William Y. Slack, mortally wounded March 7; Col. Thomas H. Rosser):
CSA Brigade (Brig. Gen. William Y. Slack, mortally[41] wounded March 7; Col. Thomas H. Rosser)
    Rosser's Mo. Inf. Bn. (unorg.—Col. T. H. Rosser, to brigade command)
        EFF = 125 (E) [losses ukn]
    Hughes' Mo. Inf. Bn. (unorg.—Col. John T. Hughes)
        EFF = 125 (E) [1 K, 3 W, 4 M]
    Bevier's Mo. Inf. Bn. (unorg.—Maj. R. S. Bevier)
        EFF = 250 [3 K, 8 W, 4 M]
    Jackson Mo. Art. (Capt. William Lucas).[42] 4 guns, 6-lb SB[43]

---

40. Tucker, *First Missouri Brigade*, 40.

41. In Bevier's account of the Battle of Pea Ridge, he has Eugene Erwin commanding an infantry battalion at the battle. However, Erwin was only a first lieutenant at the time, serving in Samuel F. Taylor's Company of Rosser's Battalion. Erwin would eventually be elected a lieutenant colonel commanding a Missouri battalion in April 1862, and he was appointed the colonel of the 6th Missouri Infantry on September 13, 1862. Additionally, Bevier has James McCown commanding a battalion at the battle, but there was no evidence that McCown was even at the battle. He could have possibly been with the train, but again, there was no evidence to that affect. Effective strength of the various units based upon Anderson's account which places Bevier's Battalion at 250 men, while the other two units equally divided the remaining 250 men. Losses per the *Official Records. O.R.*, 8:313, 316; *O.R.S.*, pt. 2, vol. 38:541, 544; Anderson, *Memoirs*, 168; Bevier, 78.

42. For artillery, Shea & Hess have two batteries assigned to the brigade for the Battle of Pea Ridge; the Jackson Artillery, commanded by Captain William Lucas and John C. Landis's Battery—This was not correct. Landis's Battery was not present at the battle as shown by the *Supplement to the Official Records* which stated:The battery "has been in service since March 1862 and has been engaged as follows. September 19—[Engaged] at Iuka. October 3–4—[Engaged] at Corinth, Mississippi;" no mention was made of Elkhorn Tavern. Additionally, on February 22, 1862, Landis and his men were at Jacksonport in eastern Arkansas to pick up their new battery, including 24-pound howitzers. On the morning of February 22, they were to march to Batesville, 25 miles distance, where they were to pick up horses for their new battery. From Batesville, the battery was directed overland to Clinton, Van Buren County, then to Dover in Pope County and finally to Clarksville in Johnson County near the Arkansas River. The path selected would encompass about 175 miles of overland travel, which would still place the command about 100 miles from the starting point of the Confederate forces that were march to Pea Ridge. At twenty miles a day, with no rest and over rough terrain, it would have taken Landis's command 14 days just to reach the Cove Creek Camp. Landis's Battery simply could not have been at the Battle of Pea Ridge. Also note, that when Van Dorn's Artillery Brigade marched to Des Arc, for transport to Memphis, it took nineteen days to march from the Van Buren area—which was a shorter distance than the march from Jacksonport to the Cove Creek Camp. *O.R.*, 8:313; *O.R.S.*, pt. 2, vol. 50:356; Douglas, *Douglas Battery*, 190; Peterson, 287–288; Shea & Hess, 337; Henry W. Williams Letter Book (December 1861–April 1862), Letters dated February 22 and 25, 1862, Mesker Papers, Missouri Historical Society.

43. The battery was organized on August 20, 1861, with one gun, received a second gun at Cassville, Missouri, in October 1861, and the final two guns at Springfield on January 1, 1862. *O.R.S.*, pt. 2, vol.

EFF = 40 [losses ukn.]

    CSA Brigade Total = EFF: 540
    Losses = 5 K, 34 W/ 3 MW, 0 M[44]

4th Div. MSG (Brig. Gen. William Y. Slack)[45]
    1st Cav. Regt. (Ltc. L. C. Bohanon)[46]
        EFF = 117 [losses ukn.]
    1st Inf. Regt. (Col. John T. Hughes)[47]
        EFF = 117 [losses ukn.]
    2nd Inf. Regt. (Col. T. J. Patton)[48]
        EFF = 116 [losses ukn.]

        4th Div. MSG Total = 350 EFF [losses ukn.]
        Second Brigade Total = 890 EFF
        Losses (incomplete) = 5 K, 34 W/ 3 MW, 8 M
        CSA Division Total = 2,517 EFF
        Losses (incomplete) = 336 K/W/M

Frost's Command (Brig. Gen. Daniel M. Frost):[49]

---

38:359.

44. In writing the official report on the battle Colonel Rosser only talks about the participation of the unorganized Confederate units and does not mention the 4th Division MSG, which was part of the command. The losses, as such, might only be those suffered by the regular Confederate units and not the MSG commands, though these losses could be all inclusive of that number. *O.R.*, 8:312–314.

45. Units per Peterson's book, *Sterling Price's Lieutenants*. Commanders as noted under the assorted units. Strength per Bevier or Anderson, estimated at one-third of 350 for each of the commands present at the battle. Anderson, *Memoirs*, 163; Bevier, 95–96; Peterson, 137, 141–143, 148, 150.

46. Eakin, *Confederate Records*, 1:107; Peterson, 137.

47. In Hughes's official report on the battle he stated that his command included two infantry companies from the Fourth Division, MSG, which I assumed came from his MSG regiment. Losses are probably embraced in Hughes's Battalion as seen above. *O.R.*, 8:314; Peterson, 143.

48. Hale, *Branded As Rebels Volume 2*, 247.

49. For the Battle of Pea Ridge, General Daniel M. Frost commanded the combined 7th and 9th Divisions, MSG and Colton Greene's 3rd Brigade, Missouri Volunteers. According to John C. Moore, Major James R. Shaler led the infantry units of Frost's MSG command, while Frost's overall command consisted of 500 infantry, with an additional 120 cavalry, and 7 pieces of artillery (artillery estimated at 70 men)—grand total 690. Of the cavalry, 20 were part of Rock Champion's command and served as General's Escort. In Frost's official report he stated that he commanded only MSG troops and further that he lost one-third of the "whole number" of his command prior to the battle. Assuming these losses were strictly in the infantry command would leave; 620/3 = 206 less infantry men or 294 infantry, 120 cavalry and 70 artillerymen—total 484 effective men of all types. Frost's command strength did not include Greene's command, which reported separate numbers to Frost following the battle.

Further, it was clear from Frost's official report that he commanded only MSG infantry, cavalry and artillery. Bevier and Anderson have MSG portion of the command at 300 men, and it appears that they have left out Frost's cavalry from the stated value to Price's command at the battle. From Greene's report we know that he commanded Confederate volunteer troops, with some MSG troops, no artillery and no mounted cavalry. *O.R.*, 8: 309, 323; Anderson, *Historical and Personal*, 163; Bevier, 96; Moore,

Body Guard, Mo. Cav. (Capt. John "Rock" Champion)
EFF = 20 [0 K, 2 W, 0 M][50]
7th & 9th Div. MSG (Maj. James R. Shaler)
5th Inf. Regt., 7th Div. MSG (Maj. James R. Shaler)[51]
EFF = 294 [ukn.]
Remnants 1st & 2nd Cav., 7th Div. MSG (probably Ltc. John H. Price)[52]
EFF = 100 [ukn.]
Artillery:
Guibor's 9th Div. MSG Bat. (Capt. Henry Guibor),[53] 2 guns, 6-lb SB; 2 guns, 12-lb How.
EFF = 40 [0 K, 1 W, 0 M]
MacDonald's 9th Div. MSG Bat. (Capt. Emmett MacDonald),[54] 3 gun, 6-lb SB, iron
EFF = 30 [ukn.]

7th & 9th Div. MSG Total = EFF: 464 [ukn.]

---

*Missouri, Confederate Military History*, 80.

50. *O.R.*, 8:324.

51. The 9th Division, MSG had no infantry units in the battle. Peterson has James R. Shaler commanding a battalion of infantry from the 9th Division, MSG, however, the unit that Shaler commanded was probably composed entirely of 7th Division units. Additionally, the 3rd and 6th Infantry Regiments, 7th Division, MSG were at Elkhorn, but served in Colton Greene's 3rd Brigade. The 4th Infantry Regiment, 7th Division, MSG was also in the battle but served with the 8th Division. It appears that only the 5th Infantry Regiment was under Shaler's command at the battle. *O.R.*, 8:325; Peterson, 204–206, 290.

52. Lieutenant Colonel John H. Price was captured on March 8, 1862, at Pea Ridge, though serving at what capacity was unknown. In Peterson's book he was listed as commanding the 2nd Cavalry Regiment, 7th Division MSG. From McGhee's book on the MSG, we know that Miscal Johnston or Johnson's 1st Cavalry Regiment, 7th Division, MSG was with the army in late January 1862, just before the battle. Also from Peterson's book we know that both the 1st Cavalry Regiment, 7th Division MSG was organized in September 1861, and was mustered out on March 17, 1862, following the battle. It was not known if Johnston was present at the battle. Eakin, *Missouri Prisoners of War*, "Price, John H." entry; McGhee, *Letter and Order Book*, unnumbered page 66 (entry page 130); Peterson, 197–198.

53. After Henry Guibor left the MSG in October 1861, he journeyed to Memphis, Tennessee, where he joined General Daniel M. Frost en route to join Price at Springfield, Missouri. Frost had in his possession six pieces of artillery which he assigned to Guibor. At Pea Ridge the battery had only enough men to man four of the guns—the other two guns were left with the wagon train. *O.R.S.*, pt. 3, vol. 1:618–619; Banasik, *Missouri Brothers in Gray*, 19, 25–26; Shea & Hess, 338.

54. Shea & Hess have the battery being armed with one 6-lb smoothbore and two 12-lb howitzers, which is not correct. Based on R. H. Musser's account of the Battle of Pea Ridge, he clearly stated that MacDonald's command contained "iron guns." The standard 12-lb howitzer was made of brass, and though the Confederates made a 12-lb iron howitzer, they did not do so until 1862. Additionally, the *Supplement to the Official Records* clearly stated that the battery contained "three 6-pounder smoothbores," which they used through the Battle of Elkhorn, after which they added a captured 6-pounder. *O.R.S.*, pt. 2, vol. 50:343; R. H. Musser, "The Battle of Pea Ridge," *Missouri Republican*, November 28, 1885; Peterson, 293; Ripley, *Artillery and Ammunition of the Civil War*, 46; Shea & Hess, 338.

Third Brigade Mo. Vol. (Col. Colton Greene)[55]
  Campbell's Cav. Co. (dmtd.—Capt. L. C. Campbell)
    [EFF: 80][56]
  7th Div. MSG—1st Cav. Regt. (remnants), 6th Inf. Regt, (remnants) & sqds. of CSA recruits (Maj. William Franklin)[57]
    [EFF: 105]
  3rd Inf. Regt. (parts of 2 Cos.), 7th Div., MSG & unorganized CSA Inf. (Maj. Waldo P. Johnson)[58]
    [EFF: 473]

  Third Brigade Total = EFF: 658: [6 K, 59 W, 0 M]
  Frost's Command Total = EFF 1,142
  Losses (incomplete) = 6 K, 62 W, 0 M

Missouri State Guard:[59]
  3rd Div. MSG (Col. John B. Clark, Jr.)[60]

---

55. In reviewing the *Official Records*, it appears that Frost's commanded, in addition to the 7th and 9th MSG units, Green's 3rd Brigade (See Greene's official report, which was addressed to General Frost). This can lead to confusion as to the strength of Frost's command at Pea Ridge, since Frost reported only 620 effective men on March 4, while Greene, supposedly a part of Frost's command, contained 658 men at the battle. A closer review of both Frost's and Greene's official reports leads one to believe that they were two separate units. When Frost wrote about the strength of men that he led at Pea Ridge, he was referring only to the 7th and 9th Divisions, MSG and not Greene's Brigade. Greene in his official report had no mounted cavalry for the battle, while Frost reported that he had 120 cavalry; Frost reported two batteries of artillery, Greene reported none; Frost reported his command as strictly MSG, while Greene's Brigade had regular Confederate troops as well as some MSG men. As such, Greene's Brigade should be listed under Frost's command as an attached brigade. Shea & Hess attach Greene to Frost's command in the body of their book, but not in their Order of Battle, which would have been a more accurate presentation. Anderson does not deal with Frost's command at Pea Ridge, with the exception of McBride's 300 men. *O.R.*, 8:325–326; Anderson, *Memoirs*, 163; Peterson, 197, 206; Shea & Hess, 176, 178, 337–338.
56. Commander and strength per Colton Greene. *O.R.*, 8:324, 326; Peterson, 207.
57. Strength per Colton Greene; commander per both Colton Greene and Daniel M. Frost. In his official report Greene highlights the service of two officers in his command; William Franklin and Waldo P. Johnson. From the *Supplement to the Official Records* we know that Johnson commanded the unorganized portion of the Confederate recruits, which leaves Franklin to command the MSG portion as detailed by Greene. *O.R.*, 8:324, 326; *O.R.S.*, pt. 2, vol. 38:479, 493; Peterson, 207; Schnetzer, *More Forgotten Men*, 84.
58. Commander per Colton Greene, Daniel M. Frost and *Supplement to the Official Records*; strength per Greene. *O.R.*, 8:324, 326; *O.R.S.*, pt. 2 vol. 38:479, 493; Peterson, 204–205.
59. Except as noted, the number of guns and caliber comes from Shea & Hess's book on Pea Ridge. Shea & Hess, 337–339.
60. For the effective strength of the individual regiments I estimated the strength of all the units, with the exception of the 4th Regiment which had a reported strength of 75. In estimating the regimental strength I removed the 75 from Clark's reported strength of 500, leaving 425 men. Each regiment was given equal weight except for the 5th Regiment which was rated at one-half the other commands, as it was consolidated with the 4th Regiment for the battle. In his official report Clark listed his losses in two places—his initial report has 14 killed and 104 wounded, while his "addenda" to the report has 11 killed, 101, wounded and 35 missing. Additionally, the Adjutant of the 4th Regiment, submitted his

1st Inf. Regt. (Maj. J. F. Rucker)
EFF = 94 (E) [1 K, 5 W, 5 M]

2nd Inf. Regt. (Col. Congreve Jackson)
EFF = 94 (E) [5 K, 27 W, 15 M]

3rd Inf. Ret. (Ltc. William Hyde, mortally wounded Mar. 7; Maj. J. C. Hutchinson)[61]
EFF = 95 (E) [1 K, 20 W, 6 M]

4th/5th Inf. Regt. (Col. John A. Poindexter)
4th Regt. EFF = 75 [1 K, 11 W, 6 M][62]
5th Regt. EFF = 47 (E) [1 K, 15 W, 0 M]

6th Inf. Regt. (Ltc. Quinton L. Preacher)
EFF = 95 (E) [2 K, 23 W, 8 M]]

Tull's MSG Bat. (Capt. Francis M. Tull),[63] 2 guns, 6-lb rifled; 2 guns, 6-lb SB
EFF = 40 [0 K, 0 W, 0 M]

3rd Div. MSG Total = 540 EFF
Losses Total = 11 K, 101 W, 40 M

5th Div. MSG (Col. James P. Saunders)[64]
1st Inf. Regt. (Ltc. J. H. R. Cundiff)
EFF = 234 (E) [ukn.]

---

losses as 1 killed , 11 wounded with 6 missing. These numbers were then used to calculate the losses in the 5th Regiment, which presented a consolidated loss report of both the 4th and 5th Regiments as 2 killed, 26 wounded with 1 missing. In the case of the missing I took the missing from the Adjutant of the 4th Regiment, which adjusts the overall missing in Clark's command by an additional 5 men. *O.R.*, 8: 319–320; Anderson, *Historical and Personal*, 163; Bevier, 96.

61. In his official report on the battle, Clark stated that Hutchinson commanded the regiment at the battle; however, Richard H. Musser, in his account of the battle has William Hyde being mortally wounded at the battle. It would have been strange if Hyde was not in command of the regiment; as such I placed Hyde in command with Hutchinson taking over after Hyde's wounding. Unknown as to why Clark does not mention the circumstances surrounding Hyde at the battle. *O.R.*, 8:319; Musser, "The Battle of Pea Ridge," *Missouri Republican*, December 28, 1885.

62. *O.R.*, 8:320–321; Bartels, *Forgotten Men*, 290.

63. This battery is often confused with Teel's Texas Battery in the *Official Records*. Anderson, *Memoirs*, 165; Peterson, 133.

64. Sanders in his official report gives the total strength of his command and number of guns present at the battle; the men in Kelly's Battery are estimated at 10 per gun or 50 men. However, Sanders does not list the units of his command that participated in the battle, except for Kelly's Battery. A review of Peterson's book *Price's Lieutenants* leaves little doubt as to what units of the 5th Division were in the battle. Of the three infantry units at the battle, only the 1st Battalion has a known commander at the battle, John R. Boyd, who was killed. The 1st Infantry Regiment has listed the most senior officer in the command, though the exact commander was not known. The cavalry, under Lieutenant Colonel James T. Cearnal, was detached at the beginning of the campaign and served as General Price's bodyguard and is not included under the 5th Division, but listed directly under Price's control. The effective strength of the various regiments are estimated based on an even division of the 700 men, with some rounding—or 233 men per. *O.R.*, 8:321; Peterson, 154–171.

2nd Inf. Regt. (Col. John. H. Winston)[65]
 EFF = 233 (E) [ukn.]
1st Inf. Bn. (Ltc. John R. Boyd, killed)
 EFF = 233 (E) [ukn.]

   Infantry = 700 EFF [ukn.]

Kelly's MSG Bat. (Capt. Ephriam V. Kelly),[66] 5 guns, 6-lb SB, iron
 EFF = 50 [ukn.]

   5th Div. MSG Total = 750 EFF
   Losses Total = 9 K, 32 W, 0 M[67]

6th Div. MSG (Maj. D. Herndon Lindsay)[68]
 Remnants 1st & 2nd Inf. Regts. (Maj. D. Herndon Lindsay)
  EFF = 90 [ukn.]
 Gorham's MSG Bat. (Capt. James C. Gorham),[69] 4 guns, 6-lb SB, iron
  [EFF= 40]

   6th Div. MSG Total = 130 EFF
   Losses Total = 0 K, 13 W, 34 M[70]

---

65. *History of Clay and Platte Counties, Missouri, Written and Compiled from the Most Authentic Official and Private Sources Including a History of Its Townships, Towns and Villages* (St. Louis, 1885), 671.

66. Shea & Hess have this battery commanded by Captain Joseph Kelly (the son of Colonel Joseph Kelly), but this was not correct. Kelly's Battery, 5th Division, MSG was commanded by E. V. Kelly, who tendered his resignation to General Price prior to the Battle of Pea Ridge. Kelly, in his own words, stated that he served at the Battle of Pea Ridge, commanding his battery. After the battle, Kelly left the army and was captured by Federal scouts on April 15, 1862. Prior to the Battle of Pea Ridge, the battery contained four, 6-lb guns that were captured at the Liberty Arsenal at the beginning of the war; a fifth gun was added sometime thereafter. *O.R.*, 8:788; Bartels, *Forgotten Men*, 195; Peterson, 169; Shea & Hess, 338.

67. Anderson, Bevier and Moore place Saunder's strength at 600 infantrymen. Anderson, *Memoirs*, 163; Bevier, 96; Moore, *Missouri, Confederate Military History*, 78.

68. Lindsay's command was a weak unit, being described by Bevier as "very small" in strength—no more than a battalion-sized unit. Lindsay in his official report stated that he had only 90 infantrymen to support his battery. Allowing ten men per gun at the battle, would give Lindsay's command 40 artillerymen and 90 infantry—total 130. The 1st Cavalry Regiment, 6th Division, MSG was also present, though it was detached and operated under direct orders of Generals Price and Van Dorn. *O.R.*, 8:308, 313; Bevier, 96; Peterson, 174–176, 184, 186.

69. Gorham's Battery was formed following the capture of Lexington, Missouri, in September 1861. Contrary to what Peterson presents in *Price's Lieutenants*, the battery obtained their guns from Guibor's Battery which disbanded in October 1861—this would have corresponded with the end of their six-month term of service in the MSG. The guns came from the Liberty Arsenal, not from those captured at Lexington. *O.R.*, 8:322; Patrick, 49–50, 59; Peterson, 192.

70. The missing probably occurred during the retreat; men who simply left and went home. *O.R.*, 8:322.

8th Div. MSG (Brig. Gen. James Rains)[71]
   Shelby's Cav. Co. (Capt. Joe O. Shelby)
      EFF = 37 [ukn.][72]
   6th Inf. Regt. (Ltc. J. P. Bowman)
      EFF = 291 (E) [ukn.]
   10th Cav. Regt (dmtd—Col. William H. Erwin)
      EFF = 291 (E) [ukn.]
   11th Cav. Regt. (dmtd.—A. J. Pearcy)
      EFF = 291 (E) [ukn.]
   13th Cav. Regt. (dmtd—Ltc. John M. Stemmons)
      EFF = 290 (E) [ukn.]

      Infantry EFF = 1,163

Bledsoe's MSG Bat. (Capt. Hiram Bledsoe).[73] 2 guns, 6-lb Model 1841, iron, 1 gun, 6-lb SB, brass, 1 gun 12-lb SB ("Old Sacramento")
      EFF = 40 [ukn.]

      8th Div. MSG Total = 1,240 EFF
      Losses Total = 2 K, 26 W, 0 M

      MSG Total = 2,660 EFF [22 K, 172, 74 M]
      Price's Command Total = 8,663 EFF
      Losses Total (incomplete) = 61 K, 324 W, 124 M, plus also =

71. The composition of Rains's Division differs from what was presented by Shea & Hess, who listed four infantry regiments (enumerated 1st through 4th Infantries) in the division. However, by reviewing the *Official Records* and Peterson's book, *Price's Lieutenants*, one can obtain the units of the 8th Division which were present at the battle; this was done by cross referencing known commanders, as listed by Rains, with Peterson's book. Peterson also listed several other infantry regiments which were in the battle, though not acknowledged by General Rains as present in the fighting. These additional regiments were the 2nd, 3rd, 4th and 5th Infantries and could have been units that were with the trains, as indicated by Bevier, or were left back in the pre-march camps. Peterson also listed the 4th Infantry Regiment, 7th Division, MSG as serving under Rains during the Elkhorn Campaign, but gives no indication as to what capacity. Effective strength of the individual regiments was estimated based on an even division of effective men present, after removing Sheby's command. *O.R.*, 8:327–328; Bevier, 96; Peterson, 206, 212, 227, 231, 239–242, 273–282.

72. See Note No. 35, of this Appendix, for the calculated strength of Shelby's company.

73. Shea & Hess have the battery armed with three, 12-pound Napoleons and "Old Sacramento"; however this is not correct. The initial battery consisted of one brass 6-pound smoothbore and "Old Sacramento," a bored out 12-pound gun. The battery added one 6-pound, Model 1841 iron gun from the Liberty Arsenal and added another Model 1841 gun following the Battle of Wilson's Creek. On December 23, 1861, the battery reported having four guns, with 42 men and 3 officers. At Pea Ridge the battery abandoned one gun, type unknown, but received a new gun upon their return to the Van Buren area. After the Battle of Pea Ridge, the battery moved to the east side of the Mississippi River where they were refitted with four new guns; "Old Sacramento" was sent to Selma, Alabama, where it was melted down and recast. *O.R.*, 8:788; *O.R.*, vol. 32, pt. 3:694; *O.R.S.*, pt. 2, vol. 38:372; Bartels, *Trans-Mississippi Men*, 136; McGhee, *Service With the Guard*, 6; Peterson, 287; Webb, 121.

173 K, W, M
Pike's Indian Brigade (Brig. Gen. Albert Pike):[74]
    Drew's Cherokee Cav. Regt. (Col. John Drew)
        EFF = 500 [? K, ? W, 4M][75]
    Watie's Cherokee Cav. Regt. (Col. Stand Watie)
        EFF = 417 (E) [? K, ? W, 11 M][76]
    Welch's Sqd. Tx. Cav. (Capt. O. G. Welch)[77]
        Co. I, 1st Choctaw & Chickasaw Regt. (Capt. O. G. Welch)
        Co. K, 1st Choctaw & Chickasaw Regt. (Capt. Robert A. Young)
        EFF = 83 (E) [ukn.][78]
    1st Choctaw & Chickasaw Regt. (Col. Douglas H. Cooper)
        EFF = 300 (not engaged) [0 K, 0 W, 0 M][79]

---

74. Pike, in his official report places the strength of his engaged forces at Pea Ridge at 1,000 men. Drew's command has a stated strength of 500 men while Welch's squadron, according to most sources had a strength of 200 men; however this would suggest that the two companies were at close to full effective strength. Further, these assorted sources provide no source for the strength of Welch's Squadron. I suspect that the various writers simply used Duncan's numbers, without any documentation. Overall, the 200-man strength does not seem possible since the unit was raised in June 1861. A closer reading of Volume 13 of the *Official Records* has the strength of Pike's Brigade at Pea Ridge as "a small body of Indians, 900 men" and says nothing about Welch's Squadron. Coupled with Pike's previous statements, as to his strength at Pea Ridge, would give Watie's command 400 men, leaving 100 men for Welch's Squadron (See also Note No. 77 of this Appendix). Pike, for his part, during the battle, also noted that he "gave permission" for Welch "to join any Texas Regiment he chose" until the end of the battle, thus leaving Pike with 900 Indians under his command. *O.R.*, 8:288, 289; *O.R.*, 13:820, 1062; *O.R.S.*, pt. 1, vol. 1:569–570; *O.R.S.*, pt. 2, vol. 73:542–543, 549–550; Bearss, "Battle of Pea Ridge," 94; Duncan, 207; Edwards, *Prairie Was On Fire*, 15; Gaines, 77–78; Josephy, *Civil War In the American West*, 337, 340; Josephy, *War On the Frontier*, 141.

75. *O.R.*, 8: 289; Gaines, 88.

76. Monaghan has eleven Indians taken prisoner and marched northward to Rolla, Missouri. Cunningham also states that eleven were taken, but says that they were half-breeds—this would make them part of Watie's command, not Drew's, which were pure bloods. Ingenthron also supports the eleven captures stating that they came from Watie's command. None of the eleven arrived at Rolla, all were shot while trying to escape. Gaines has four Indians from Drew's Regiment as captured and sent to prisoner of war camps, and all were exchanged at later dates. As such, the eleven Indians who were shot as escaping prisoners must have come from Watie's Regiment. Cunningham, 63; Ingenthron, 163; Monaghan, 249.

77. Welch's Squadron consisted of two companies from 1st Choctaw and Chickasaw Regiment—Companies I, and K. *O.R.S.*, pt. 2, vol. 73:542–543, 549–550; Special Order No. 1 (March 15, 1862), *Dallas Herald* (Dallas, TX), April 18, 1862.

78. Several sources list the strength of this squadron as 200 men, which was highly unlikely. This would suggest that the companies were at close to full effective strength. This does not seem possible since the unit was raised in June 1861. Watie's ten companies and two from Welch's Squadron, would suggest 41.7 men per company, for the remaining 500 men, or 417 men for Watie's Regiment and 83 men for Welch's Squadron. This compares favorably with the previous note on Pike's command. *O.R.S.*, pt. 1, vol. 1:569–570; *O.R.S.*, pt. 2, vol. 73:542–543, 549–550; Bearss, "Battle of Pea Ridge," 94; Duncan, 207; Edwards, *Prairie Was On Fire*, 15; Gaines, 78; Josephy, *Civil War In the American West*, 337, 340; Josephy, *War On the Frontier*, 141.

79. The strength of Cooper's command was calculated based upon the overall strength of Pike's Brigade as presented in *Kepis & Turkey Calls*, which placed the strength at 1,500 men. Since all the other commands have a known strength, Cooper's command would contain the remaining 300 men. Ray

1st Creek Regt. (Col. D. N. McIntosh)
EFF = 200 (not engaged) [0 K, 0 W, 0 M][80]

Brigade Total = EFF (engaged): 1,000
Brigade Grand Total = 1,500 EFF
Losses (incomplete) = [? K, ? W, 15 M]

Confederate Effectives Available (E) = 19,394
Engaged (E) = 17,144
Heavily Engaged (E) = 12,050

Confederate Losses = 185 Killed, 525 Wounded, 300 Missing
Total Losses = 1,010[81]

* * * * * * *

A. Clifford, "The Indian Regiments in the Battle of Pea Ridge," *Kepis & Turkey Calls: An Anthology of the War Between the States in Indian Territory* (M. L. Cantrell and Mac Harris, gen. eds.; Oklahoma City, OK, 1982), 63.

80. *O.R.*, 8:292; Gaines, 86.

81. Figures are those reported by Van Dorn's Surgeon General. Also note, that Bevier reported that the Confederates lost 169 killed, 431 wounded and 200 missing; total 800 (This could have been in just Price's command). As shown above in the assorted units the total losses (incomplete) were 139 Killed, 507 wounded with 226 missing. Additionally another 173 men are identified as killed, wounded or missing—Grand Total 1,045. Of all the units that have no reported losses only three would have been seriously engaged in the battle—the 14th Arkansas, 21st Arkansas and 1st Missouri Cavalry. The other units with no losses reported were either not engaged or probably suffered few if any losses. Using a "conservative estimate," Shea & Hess put the Confederates losses at 2,000, however; it would appear that a more appropriate number would be between 1,200–1,500 men of all types lost. In making their estimate, Shea & Hess cited the number of prisoners forwarded by Curtis following the battle, but they make no note that the captures included prisoners who were captured before the battle, plus private citizens or those Missourians who had left the army just prior to the battle and were on their way home (see Note No. 105, Chapter 1). Bevier, 106; Gaines, 87.

# Appendix B
## Selected Biographies

### Elias C. Boudinot

Elias Cornelius Boudinot was born on August 1, 1835, in the Cherokee Nation, near modern-day Rome, Georgia. His father was a full-blooded Cherokee and brother to Stand Watie, while his mother was a Caucasian from New England. After the assassination of his father on June 22, 1839, Boudinot was taken by his mother to Vermont where he was raised and educated.

A civil engineer by profession, Boudinot moved to Fayetteville, Arkansas, in about 1853. He became a lawyer in 1856, edited the Fayetteville *Arkanansian*, and in June 1860, became the senior editor for the Little Rock *True Democrat*. During the Arkansas secession crisis Boudinot was elected Secretary of the Secessionist Convention.

With the beginning of the Civil War, Boudinot aligned himself with his uncle, Stand Watie, joined Watie's Cherokee Regiment and became a leader in the Cherokee Treaty Party. Boudinot was appointed a major in Watie's command in the latter part of 1861, fought at the Battle of Pea Ridge, and briefly became the regiment's lieutenant colonel following the death of Lieutenant Colonel Thomas F. Taylor on July 27, 1862.

Boudinot left the regiment in the middle of 1862 to attend the Confederate Congress as a representative of the Cherokee Nation. When Boudinot took his seat in the Confederate Congress on October 9, he was described as "an intelligent, shrewd-looking man, youthful in appearance, with features denoting his Indian lineage." He returned to Arkansas in late 1862 and served as a volunteer aid to General Hindman at the Battle of Prairie Grove, after which he returned to Richmond, Virginia. Boudinot served in the Confederate Congress throughout the remainder of the war and came home to Arkansas in May 1865.

Following the war Boudinot spent most of his time in Washington, DC, first as a member of the treaty negotiations in 1866, and then as a representative the Cherokee Nation. He opened a tobacco factory in the Indian Territory in 1868 with the help of Stand Watie, but the factory failed. Accused of being a traitor to his people, Boudinot felt unsafe in his home land and spent the remaining days in Washington. He was a

Elias C. Boudinot

Mason "of the thirty-second degree" and the first Indian to be a member of the Supreme Court bar of the United States. Boudinot died in 1890.[1]

\* \* \* \* \* \* \*

Meriwether L. Clark

## Meriwether L. Clark

Meriwether Lewis Clark was born on January 10, 1809, in St. Louis. His father was William Clark, of the Lewis and Clark Expedition. Meriwether Clark graduated from West Point in 1830, (number 23 of 42) as a lieutenant in the Sixth U.S. Infantry and served in the Black Hawk War in 1832, fighting the Sac Indians. Clark resigned his commission in 1833 and began a career as an architect and engineer in St. Louis, at same time joining the St. Louis Militia. When the Mexican War began, Clark rejoined the U.S. Military to command a battery of artillery under Colonel Richard Weightman. Clark served from July 1846 to June 1847, after which he again left the service at the rank of major. (Note: Most sources have Clark leaving the Mexican War as a major of artillery, while Peterson has Clark as a major of mounted troops.) Returning to St. Louis, Clark continued on with his previous career and in 1854 commanded a force that quelled riots in St. Louis. Prior to the Civil War Clark was appointed the United States Surveyor-General for Missouri.

Shortly after the Civil War began, Clark was appointed a brigadier general commanding the Ninth Military District, vice Daniel M. Frost, who was captured at Camp Jackson. On November 11, 1861, Clark was appointed a major in the Confederate Service, but still retained his State Guard rank, commanding General Price's artillery. When Clark was transferred to the east side of the Mississippi River with Price's command, he gave up his rank in the Missouri State Guard, and on April 16, 1862, received an appointment as a Confederate colonel. Clark competed his military service on the east side of the Mississippi River and was captured at Sayler's Creek, Virginia on April 6, 1865.

After the war, Clark moved to Kentucky where he was the architect for the

---

1. *O.R.S.*, pt. 2, vol. 73: 521; Abel, *Slave Holding Indians*, 119, 153; Anderson, *Life of Stand Watie*, 54; Dale & Litton, xviii, 4, 84, 110–111, 222, 230, 259–260, 289; William Furry, *The Preacher's Tale* (Fayetteville, AR, 2001), 33, 156; Ross, 343; *Southern Historical Society Papers*, 18:93; *Southern Historical Society Papers*, 47: 69, 87, 89; Wright, 2:433–435, 438, 440.

"State Building" and also served as Commandant of Cadets and a mathematics teacher at the Kentucky Military Institute. He died in Frankfurt, Kentucky on October 28, 1881, and was buried in St. Louis.[2]

\* \* \* \* \* \* \*

### William F. Cloud

William F. Cloud was born 1825 in Ohio, received a common education, and was an apprentice tailor at the age of fifteen. When the Mexican War began, he enlisted in Company K, Second Ohio Infantry and served under General Zachary Taylor on the Rio Grande until the end of the war. At the beginning of the Civil War, Cloud was a resident of Emporia, Kansas. He organized Company H, Second Kansas Infantry and was made the unit's major on June 11, 1861. He was noted for his bravery at the Battle of Wilson's Creek and remained in the army after his unit went out of service following the battle. On April 3, 1862, Cloud became the colonel of the Tenth Kansas Infantry, and on June 1 he was given command of the Second Kansas Cavalry. During the course

William F. Cloud

of the war Cloud often served as a brigade commander, such as during the 1862 Indian Expedition and the Prairie Grove Campaign. One period writer called Cloud "one of the bravest of the Kansas soldiers" while another recorded—

> He is an accomplished gentleman, of fine personal appearance and affable manners, joined to great decision of character and a mind that comes rapidly to its conclusions, and adheres to them with unswerving tenacity. He has displayed more dash and enterprise than almost any officer of equal rank in the command. Day or night, rain and shine, he seems to feel the saddle to be his home, and he is restless unless in action.

As the war was winding down, newly elected Kansas Governor Samuel J. Crawford, appointed Cloud a major general and commander of the Kansas Militia. Following the election of a new governor in 1867, Cloud resigned from his Kansas Militia post, moved to Carthage, Missouri, and entered into private busi-

---

2. *O.R.*, 8:792; Allardice, 61–61; Boatner, 156–157; Hale, 58–59; Heitman, 1:305; Moore, *Missouri, Confederate Military History, Extended*, 258–259; Peterson, 16, 23, 290; Snead, 184; Winter, 114–115.

ness. At the turn of the century, Cloud was still alive and an accomplished writer, having written *Church and state, or Mexican politics from Cortez to Diaz, Under X rays*.[3]

\* \* \* \* \* \* \*

### John T. Coffee

John T. Coffee

John Trousdale Coffee was born on December 14, 1816, in Smith County, Tennessee. He studied law, by himself, and passed the Tennessee bar in the late 1830's, while at the same time joining the Masons. Coffee married in 1841 and settled in Cleveland, Tennessee. With the death of his first wife and his father in 1842, Coffee moved to Greene County, Missouri, where he again obtained a license to practice law. He remarried in April 1844, but unfortunately his second wife died two weeks after giving birth to their first child. Coffee married for the third time in 1845, and relocated to Greenfield, Dade County, Missouri, the home of his sixteen year-old bride.

With the coming of the Mexican War, Coffee raised a company of volunteers, but the war ended before they saw any action. Coffee entered politics and was elected Dade County's Circuit Attorney in 1849. In 1854 he was elected to the Missouri Senate, but resigned in 1855 to accept a commission in the United States Army. Illness caused Coffee to resign from the army on December 20, 1855, after only ten months of service. Returning to Greenfield, he bought the Greenfield *American Standard* newspaper and in 1858 changed its name to the Greenfield *Southwest*. Using the newspaper to his political advantage, Coffee was elected to the Missouri House, becoming its Speaker on January 1, 1859.

At the beginning of the Civil War, Coffee was living on his "800-acre farm," near Greenfield. He joined the Confederate cause and raised the Sixth Cavalry Regiment, Eighth Division, MSG, of which he was elected colonel on July 4, 1861. Coffee's command served at Wilson's Creek, though he was not present. After his regiment mustered out of the MSG, Coffee remained in the Guard and began recruiting anew. During the spring and summer of 1862, Coffee's irregular command was engaged in numerous small actions in both the Indian Territory and

Missouri, culminating in the Battle of Lone Jack on August 16, 1862. Withdrawing his command to Newtonia, Coffee went on to organize the Sixth Missouri Cavalry (Confederate), of which he was elected colonel in September.

On October 23, 1862, Coffee was arrested and charged with "conduct prejudicial to good order and military discipline"—being drunk and absent from his command during the Confederate retreat from northwest Arkansas. The charges were later dropped in favor of dismissing Coffee from the service on November 8, as he had not been properly elected to colonel of his regiment.

Coffee remained in the Missouri State Guard, returned to Missouri, and in 1863 raised an irregular force to confront the Union occupation. During Shelby's 1863 Missouri Raid, Coffee joined his 400-man command with Shelby's. Unfortunately, 1863 was not a good year for Coffee, as he lost his third wife, and he was passed over for promotion to general. He left his command, but in 1864 raised yet another regiment for the rebel cause, to participate in Sterling Price's 1864 Missouri Raid.

Coffee had mixed evaluations as a leader. General Holmes and Hindman considered him "worthless." Colonel Jo Shelby, following his 1863 Missouri Raid, noted that Coffee handled his command "with great skill; wherever the fire was the hottest and heaviest," he was present. His biographers, Hulston and Goodrich, probably summed up his life best: Coffee was a "hard-drinking and oft-married man noted for his 'positive convictions' on many subjects. But the most vivid recollections of the people would pertain to Coffee's military exploits as a successful recruiter for the Confederate cause."

Following the war, Coffee relocated to Waco, then to Georgetown, Texas, where he married a fourth and last time and owned a goat farm. He died on May 23, 1890, at Brownsville, Texas.[4]

\* \* \* \* \* \* \*

## Emory S. Foster

Major Emory Stallsworth Foster was born on November 5, 1839, in Greene County, near Springfield, Missouri, and moved to Warrensburg, Johnson County, Missouri in 1860. Locally schooled, Foster learned the printer's trade, and became the co-owner of the *Missourian*, a local newspaper, with his brother Marshall. In March 1861 Foster organized a local pro-Union militia unit nicknamed the "Red Shirt Company," which later became the Johnson County Home Guards and still later Company C, Twenty-seventh Missouri Infantry (Mounted).

---

4. *O.R.*, 8:75; *O.R.*, vol. 22, pt. 1:671, 677; "Charges and Specifications Preferred against Col. John T. Coffee," Miscellaneous Correspondence; Edwards, *Shelby and His Men*, 201; Heitman, 1:314; National Archives, Record Group 109, Confederate Muster Rolls, Sixth Missouri Cavalry (Confederate); Telegraphic Conversation, Hindman to Holmes (December 1, 1862), Telegrams; Hulston & Goodrich, "John Trousdale Coffee," 272–295; Peterson, 263; J. P. Wilson Letter (October 23, 1862), Miscellaneous Correspondence.

Elected major of the Twenty-seventh, Foster left the unit August 1861, at the request of U. S. Grant, and formed the "Frémont Scouts," with some men of the Twenty-seventh. Foster and the Scouts served on the western border of Missouri and returned to St. Louis in the latter part of December. They were mustered out of the service with the rest of the Twenty-seventh Regiment on January 27, 1862.

Foster returned to Warrensburg and recruited a three company squadron of Missouri Militia. He was wounded on March 26, 1862, at Post Oak Creek near his home town during an engagement with guerrillas. On May 1, 1862, Governor Gamble appointed Foster a major of the Seventh Missouri State Militia Cavalry. On August 16, 1862, Foster led the 740-man Federal force that lost the Battle of Lone Jack. He was wounded at that battle and never fully recovered, though he later rejoined his regiment. During Shelby's 1863 Missouri Raid, Foster served as the Adjutant for General E. B. Brown, after which he left the army on June 2, 1864, due to his wounds. Returning to the army in September 1864 at the request of General Brown, Foster raised a battalion which fought at the Battle of Westport in 1864.

Emory S. Foster

Foster survived the war and was elected the Missouri Public Printer (1865–1869), during which time he lived in Jefferson City. In 1869 he moved to Jefferson County, ran a fruit farm for two years, then relocated to St. Louis in 1871. As managing editor of the *St. Louis Journal*, Foster fought a duel with John N. Edwards over a derogatory article that Foster wrote on ex-President Jefferson Davis. Both duelists missed, after which they became close personal friends.

Foster's biographer George S. Grover wrote: "As a soldier, Major Foster was the peer of anyone who ever served in any war. Of rare judgment, dauntless courage and skill in the military science he had few equals, and no superiors. As a citizen his public spirit and impartiality in public service, rare zeal, and uniting ability and perseverance for public good, render him always a natural leader among men."

Foster continued living in St. Louis, when his health began to fail in 1901. In the fall of 1902 Foster journeyed to California to recover his health, but died on December 23, at Oakland, where he was buried. Foster and his wife, Sharon, had one child who died shortly after her father and was buried beside him.[5]

---

5. *O.R.*, 8:350, 354; Eakin, *Battle of Lone Jack*, 54; General Order No. 15 (May 1, 1862), Headquarters,

## Colton Greene

Colton Greene was born in South Carolina in July 1838 and moved to St. Louis in the late 1850s, where was a merchant in the wholesale grocery business. Prior to the Civil War, Greene was captain of Company E, Second Regiment, First Brigade, St. Louis Missouri Volunteer Militia. He figured prominently in the events surrounding Camp Jackson, being the officer who consigned the shipment of "marble"—siege guns, for the supposed reduction of the St. Louis Arsenal. His company was captured at Camp Jackson on May 10, 1861, though he was absent from the command.

Later, Greene served as aide to Governor Claiborne F. Jackson until appointed the Chief of Ordnance of the Seventh Division, MSG, on August 8, 1861. On October 28, 1861, he was appointed a lieutenant colonel and Adjutant General of his Guard division. He became the commander of the Seventh

Colton Greene

Division for a short time in February 1862, prior to the assignment of D. M. Frost to command the division on February 23.

Shortly thereafter, Greene joined the Confederate Army and commanded a Confederate brigade at Pea Ridge (March 6–8, 1862). In April 1862, he followed Sterling Price to Mississippi, but later returned and organized the Third Missouri Cavalry Regiment (Confederate) in October 1862, and was appointed colonel on November 4, 1862. With his command, Greene participated in John S. Marmaduke's First and Second Missouri Raids in 1863.

Greene commanded brigades in Arkansas at the Battle of Helena, Little Rock Campaign of 1863 (August 1–September 14, 1863), Pine Bluff (October 25, 1863) and during the Camden Expedition of 1864. Greene was also present during Price's 1864 Missouri Raid. Listed as a general officer in Heitman's *Historical Register*, there was no Confederate record of Greene having been promoted to that grade.

Following the war Greene returned to St. Louis, but found that his business partner had seized his property, leaving Greene broke. Greene moved to Mem-

State of Missouri, General Orders of Missouri (1862); George S. Grover, "Civil War In Missouri," *Missouri Historical Review* 8 (October 1913), 19–20, 25; George S. Grover, "Major Emory S. Foster," *Missouri Historical Review* 14 (April–July 1920), 425–432; National Archives, Record Group M405 (roll no. 179), Union Compiled Service Records, Seventh Missouri State Militia Cavalry; Bruce Nichols, *Johnson County Missouri in the Civil War* (Independence, MO, 1974), 26–28; Norton, 104, 106.

phis, where he became a successful banker and "civic leader." Never married, Greene helped found the Memphis Public Library and lived out his remaining days in Memphis. He died on September 23, 1900.

"No braver or better officer drew a sword," wrote John N. Edwards of Greene, while John McElroy recorded that Greene was a man of "great courage and constancy of purpose." Thomas L. Snead provides the most complete description of Colton Greene's personality. Snead wrote: "With a rather delicate physical disposition, he possessed fine sensibilities, a cultivated intellect, which was both sharp and strong, courage and determination. He was, with all, painstaking, laborious and earnest, upright and honorable."[6]

\* \* \* \* \* \* \*

### Sidney D. Jackman

Sidney Drake Jackman was born in Jessamine County, Kentucky, on March 7, 1826, and moved to Howard County, Missouri, in 1830, where he was educated. He married in 1849, then relocated his family to near Pappinville, Bates County, in 1855. Caught up in the border wars of the late 1850's, Jackman raised a company of defense forces to counter the raids from Kansas. At the beginning of the Civil War Jackman reluctantly joined the Confederate cause as the years of border warfare had taken its toll on his support of the Union.

Jackman raised a company in Bates County and was elected captain of the unit, which became part of the Ninth Cavalry Regiment, Eighth Division, MSG. Jackman and his company took part in the engagement at Drywood, after which he left the army to secure his family on the north side of the Missouri River with his mother in Howard County. His company disbanded a short time later, awaiting his return to Bates County. During the winter of 1861–1862, Jackman remained in Missouri while General Price led the Missouri Army southward. Recruiting a new command of partisans on the border, Jack-

Sidney D. Jackman

6. *O.R.*, 3:386, 387; *O.R.*, 8:325; *O.R.*, vol. 34, pt. 1:526, 730–731; Allardice, 104–105; Banasik, *Missouri Brothers in Gray*, 161, 162; Crute, 198; Edwards, *Shelby and His Men*, 251; Heitman, 2:177; McElroy, 38; McGhee, *Letter and Order Book*, unnumbered page 70–71 (entry page 139); Moore, *Missouri, Confederate Military History, Extended*, 302–303; Peterson, 35, 195, 196; Snead, 109.

man was again active, operating behind "enemy lines." By the summer of 1862, he had a substantial force and took part in the Battle of Lone Jack on August 16, 1862. Retreating into Arkansas, Jackman's Regiment was reorganized as the Sixteenth Missouri Infantry (Confederate) on September 1, 1862, at Camp Hindman, near Elkhorn Tavern. On October 23, 1862, Jackman submitted his resignation from his regiment, stating that his experience in "military affairs" had "been with mounted men" and his desire to return to Missouri to recruit a mounted unit. Two days later General Thomas C. Hindman approved his request, allowing Jackman to return to Missouri to recruit yet another command.

During 1863–1864 Jackman functioned basically as a guerrilla leader, operating in Missouri and the border region with Kansas. In the summer of 1864, he united his command with the regular Confederate Army and participated in Price's 1864 Missouri Raid.

After the war he moved to Kyle, Texas, where his wife, Martha died in 1870. As a respected member of the community, Jackman was elected to the Texas Legislature in 1874 and 1875. He again married in 1875 and had four children with his new wife Cass. In 1885 President Grover Cleveland appointed Jackman the U.S. Marshall of the Western District of Texas. Unfortunately he did not serve long, dying on June 2, 1886.[7] An obituary in the Austin *Daily Statesman*, probably sums up Jackman's life best:

> He was equal to every station in which he was placed and true to every trust reposed. Truth, honor and duty constituted his life creed....He was profoundly loyal to friends, family and country.[8]

* * * * * * *

## Henry Little

Lewis Henry Little was born on March 19, 1817, in Baltimore, Maryland, briefly attended St. Mary's College in Baltimore, and received a direct commission into the Fifth U.S. Infantry on July 1, 1839. In the course of time Little dropped the use of his first name "Lewis" and was commonly known as Henry Little.

During the Mexican War, Little was breveted to captain "for gallant and meritorious conduct in the Battle of Monterey, Mexico." After the war, he served on the frontier participating in Johnston's Mormon Expedition in 1858.

Little married in 1855 and had two daughters, one whom died in 1860 at the

---

7. Allardice, 133–135; Crute, 201, 208; Eakin, *Confederate Records*, 4:119; Letter, Jackman to Hindman (October 23, 1862), Miscellaneous Correspondence; Mullins, 93–96; National Archives, Record Group 109, Confederate Muster Rolls, Sixteenth Missouri Infantry; National Archives, Record Group M861 (roll no. 36), Records of Confederate Movements and Activities, Sixteenth Missouri Infantry; Norton, v, 3–9, 19, 25; Peterson, 242; Special Orders No. 22 (October 25, 1862), Special Order Book No. 1.

8. Norton, 9.

age of four. At the beginning of the Civil War Little was stationed at Jefferson Barracks in St. Louis, where he resigned his commission on May 7, 1861, moved his family to Boonville, and joined the Missouri State Guard on May 18, 1861, as a colonel and Assistant Adjutant General. Little was latter commissioned a major in the regular Confederate Army, but continued his duty as General Price's Adjutant General.

Henry Little

On January 23, 1862, Little was given the command of the First Missouri Brigade, which he led with distinction at Pea Ridge. With his command he was transferred to the east side of the Mississippi River in April 1862 and was commissioned a Confederate brigadier general on April 16, 1862. Little did not survive the war, being killed at the Battle of Iuka, Mississippi, on September 19, 1862. A soldier in his command noted that Little was "a fine tactician, an accomplished soldier" who "won for himself the love and esteem of the men he commanded."

Ephraim Anderson recorded this physical description of Henry Little: "He was of ordinary height and slightly built, quick and active in his speech and movements, with a look and manner somewhat French; his forehead was rather broad, eyes black and piercing, nose small and Grecian, and lips thin; when speaking, under his black mustache, a very white and regular set of teeth was displayed; the chin was rather massive; his hair black and straight, worn long, and surmounted by a small military cap."[9]

\* \* \* \* \* \* \*

## John McNeil

John McNeil was born on February 14, 1813 (Mudd has the date as February 4), in Halifax, Nova Scotia. At a young age he moved to Boston where he became a hatter and in 1840 made St. Louis his permanent home. Prior to the Civil War he served in the Missouri Legislature (1844–1845) and was president of the Pacific Insurance Company (1855–1861).

On May 8, 1861, he was named colonel of the Third Missouri Infantry, U.S. Reserve Corps, and participated in the Camp Jackson Affair. McNeil was mus-

---

9. *O.R.*, 8:285, 739; Castel, "The Diary of General Henry Little, C.S.A.," 4, 10; Anderson, *Memoirs*, 114; Davis, "Lewis Henry Little," *Confederate General*, 6:78–79; Peterson, 34.

tered out of the service at the expiration of his three month enlistment. On April 9, 1862, Governor H. R. Gamble, appointed McNeil a colonel (to date from December 7, 1861), and assigned him to command the Second Missouri State Militia Cavalry Regiment. General John M. Schofield, commanding the District of Missouri, appointed McNeil commander of the Northeast Division of Missouri on June 4, 1862, a position he held during the incident at Palmyra. Southern opinion branded McNeil a "butcher" and "murderer" for his actions at Palmyra and for his earlier execution of rebel prisoners during the summer of 1862 (see Appendix D).

McNeil spent his entire Civil War career in Missouri, except for a short stint commanding in Louisiana. He was promoted to brigadier general on November 29, 1862, and breveted a major general on April 12, 1865, "for gallant and meritorious service during the war."

According to one period commentator McNeil "was of medium stature, thick of body and lowering in aspects. There was courage of an indomitable kind marked in the huge neck and ferocity suggested in every line of the big body as it slouched in an easy relaxation on the seat" of his carriage. "There was whiskey on his breath and fire burning in the veins beating beneath the red skin. Here was a man of stormy passions, determined and restless. One dread to pity and disdainful of justice."

Much of McNeil's military service was fighting irregular forces in Missouri. However, during Price's 1864 Missouri Raid, he commanded a cavalry brigade under General Alfred Pleasanton. On November 19, 1864, following Price's Raid, McNeil was given command of the Central District of Missouri, which he held until he resigned on April 12, 1865.

John McNeil

After the war McNeil held several minor government jobs, including St. Louis Clerk of the Criminal Courts (1865–1867 and 1875–1876), county sheriff (1866–1870) and Inspector of Indian Service (1878 and 1880). McNeil died on June 8, 1891, at his desk, while serving as superintendent of a branch of the St. Louis post office.[10]

\* \* \* \* \* \* \*

10. *O.R.*, 13:417; *O.R.*, vol. 41, pt. 1:371; Farthing, 69, 71; General Orders No. 12 (April 9, 1862), General Orders of Missouri (1862); Heitman, 1:679; Mudd, *With Porter*, 308–309; Sifakis, *Who Was Who In the Union*, 259–260; *Union Army*, 8:170–171; Warner, *Generals in Blue*, 306; Winter, 114.

### Edwin W. Price

Edwin William Price, the eldest son of Sterling Price, was born on June 10, 1834, in Randolph County, Missouri. Educated locally, Price received a degree from University of Missouri at Columbia, after which he bought a farm in Chariton County, near Keytesville, which he named "Farm Place." Price married in 1855 and continued farming until the beginning of the Civil War.

Edwin W. Price

Elected captain of the Central Missouri Guards, of Chariton County, in early May 1861, Price was at the Planters' House, in St. Louis, when Camp Jackson was captured on May 10, 1861. Rising quickly in grade, Price was appointed lieutenant colonel of the First Infantry Regiment, Third Division, MSG, on June 23, 1861, then elected colonel of the Third Regiment on September 20, and finally elected brigadier general of the Third Division on December 2, 1861. He "gallantly" fought at the Missouri battles of Carthage, Drywood Creek, Wilson's Creek and Lexington.

In the latter part of 1861 Price went on recruiting service in north Missouri. Returning with 500 recruits, Price was captured at the home of Judge Foster Wright near Warsaw on the Osage River, on February 18, 1862. Sent to Alton Prison, Price was paroled on February 26 to Chariton County, and exchanged in October 1862 for General Benjamin Prentiss. Joining his father in Mississippi, Price resigned his commission in the Guard, which was never accepted, and returned to Missouri, where he took the Oath of Allegiance to the United States on October 22, 1862.

President Lincoln pardoned Price in November 1862, after which he was considered by many to be a traitor to the Confederacy. Others, including Edwin's father, weaved a tale that Edwin was undercover recruiting for the Confederacy. However, the most likely scenario was that Edwin Price had simply tired of the war, feeling that the Confederacy had no chance to win. In 1863, after being restored to the good graces of the Federal Government, Edwin purchased his father's lands at a sheriff's auction to prevent their loss because of his father's wartime actions.

After the war Edwin reconciled with his father and cared for his mother in St. Louis until 1871, after the elder Price had died. Edwin returned to his farm in

Chariton County in 1871 and lived out his remaining days raising wheat and running a tobacco factory. He died on in St. Louis on January 7, 1908.[11]

\* \* \* \* \* \* \*

### Albert Rust

Albert Rust was born in Virginia in 1818 and moved to Arkansas in 1837, settling near El Dorado on a plantation dubbed "Champagnolle," in Union County. Rust studied law for five years, became a lawyer, and entered politics in 1842 after winning election to the Arkansas Legislature. While still in the State Legislature Rust ran in a special election for a seat in the U.S. Congress in the latter part of 1848; he lost by less than 100 votes. Elected to the U.S. Congress in 1854, defeated in 1856, and elected again in 1858, Rust served until March 3, 1861, when he resigned and joined the Confederate cause.

Rust was elected to the Confederate Provisional Congress on May 10, 1861, and organized the Third Arkansas Infantry, of which he was elected colonel on July 5, 1861. Assigned to duty under Robert E. Lee and Thomas "Stonewall" Jackson in Virginia, Rust served with mixed results. Rust was promoted to brigadier general on March 6, 1862, to rank from March 4, and assigned to duty in the Army of the West under Earl Van Dorn.

On May 27, 1862, Van Dorn sent Rust to Arkansas, where he served under Thomas C. Hindman as his second in command for a short time, commanding either a brigade or a provisional division. Known by one Texan as a "clever gentleman and good officer," Rust was not well received by most of his Trans-Mississippi command, as another Texan recorded: "Great dissatisfaction prevails throughout the Brigade." Rust fought

Albert Rust

and lost the Battle of Cache River or Hill Plantation, Arkansas on July 7, 1862, for which he received poor reviews for his performance. One soldier noted that Rust went to the rear to get reinforcements, but never returned. Another simply recalled that it was a "badly managed affair."

On August 2, 1862, Rust was assigned to command the Camp of Instruction at

11. *O.R.*, 3:31; *O.R.*, Series 2, 4:642–643, 742; Allardice, 187–188; Bartels, *Forgotten Men*, 296; Eakin, *Missouri Prisoners of War*, "Price, Edwin W." entry; Hale, 258–259; Miles, 166; Peterson, 16, 107, 113, 116, 120; Shalhope, 36, 131, 281; Winter, 121.

Crystal Hill, Arkansas. Three days later, Hindman relieved Rust of command and sent him back to Van Dorn in Mississippi, with a letter to Generals Van Dorn and Johnston which said in part:

> I am laboring under very great and almost insurmountable difficulties to organize an army. For the accomplishment of that purpose I have announced a policy whose outlines, at least, have already been clearly defined in my orders. I believe that policy to be the only one that can be made successful, under the circumstances. In order to succeed, even with it, I must have the intelligent, active, and thorough cooperation of the officers serving under me, especially of my second-in-command.
>
> Between Brig. Gen. Rust and myself such cooperation appears to be impossible. Our ideas as to discipline, administration, and, in fact, everything of importance are at variance. The interests of the service therefore, in my opinion, demand that he shall serve elsewhere.
>
> I have no charges to prefer against him. He was sent to me without any application on my part and I return him in the same way.

Rust later led a brigade at the Battle of Corinth, but performed poorly and was again returned to the Trans-Mississippi on April 15, 1863. Rust never again played a major role in the Civil War, bouncing back and forth between the east and west side of the Mississippi River. Finally, Rust was removed from duty, according to one source, "for Union sentiments and his criticism of the rebel government." Following the war Rust returned to farming on a new plantation near Little Rock. He then joined the Republican Party and was elected to the U.S. Congress in 1869. He died on April 4, 1870.[12]

* * * * * * *

## Index to Previous Biographies

Found in *Missouri Brothers in Gray* (vol. 1), *Serving With Honor* (vol. 2), *Reluctant Cannoneer* (vol. 3), *Missouri in 1861* (vol. 4), *Cavaliers of the Brush* (vol. 5), *Duty, Honor and Country* (vol. 6), and *Confederate Tales of the War in the Trans-Missisippi, Part One* (vol. 7).

---

12. *O.R.*, 13: 829; Anne J. Bailey, *Between the Enemy and Texas: Parsons's Texas Cavalry in the Civil War* (Fort Worth, TX, 1989), 59, 70–71; Banasik, *Embattled Arkansas*, 56; Boatner, 714; Faust, *Historical Times Illustrated Encyclopedia of the Civil War*, 649; Harrell, *Arkansas, Confederate Military History*, 296, 415; Ross, 210, 232, 308, 333, 357–358; Sifakis, *Who Was Who in the Confederacy*, 249; Special Orders No. 23 (July 4, 1862) and No. 54 (August 2, 1862), Hindman's Command (June 11–August 19, 1862), Peter W. Alexander Collection, Columbia University; Warner, *Generals in Gray*, 266–267.

| | |
|---|---|
| Blair, Francis P. | vol. 7, pt. 1:183 |
| Blunt, James G. | vol. 2, 273 |
| Bowen, John S. | vol. 1, 135 |
| Brown, Egbert Benson | vol. 6, 442 |
| Burbridge, John Q. | vol. 3, 378 |
| Canby, Edward Richard Sprigg | vol. 6, 444 |
| Clark, John B., Jr. | vol. 3, 380 |
| Clark, John B., Sr. | vol. 3, 382 |
| Clarkson, James J. | vol. 7, pt. 1:184 |
| Clayton, Powell | vol. 2, 278 |
| Coleman, William O. | vol. 3, 383 |
| Curtis, Samuel R. | vol. 2, 279 |
| Dana, Napoleon J. T. | vol. 6, 446 |
| Davidson, John W. | vol. 2, 281 |
| Drayton, Thomas Fenwick | vol. 3, 385 |
| Ewing, Thomas | vol. 5, 175 |
| Fagan, James Flemming | vol. 3, 386 |
| Fremont, John C. | vol. 1, 135 |
| Frost, Daniel M. | vol. 1, 138 |
| Green, Martin E. | vol. 4, 347 |
| Gregg, William | vol. 5, 176 |
| Halleck, Henry Wager | vol. 4, 348 |
| Harney, William S. | vol. 7, pt. 1:185 |
| Harris, Thomas Alexander | vol. 4, 349 |
| Hays, Upton | vol. 5, 178 |
| Hébert, Louis | vol. 7, pt. 1:187 |
| Herron, Francis J. | vol. 2, 283 |
| Hindman, Thomas C. | vol. 1, 139 |
| Holmes, Theophilus H. | vol. 1, 141 |
| Jackson, Claiborne F. | vol. 4, 350 |
| Lane, James H. | vol. 2, 286 |
| Lane, Walter P. | vol. 7, pt. 1:188 |
| Lyon, Nathaniel | vol. 4, 353 |
| MacDonald, Emmett | vol. 1, 143 |
| Marmaduke, John Sappington | vol. 1, 143 |
| McBride, James H. | vol. 3, 388 |
| McCulloch, Ben | vol. 4, 356 |
| McIntosh, James McQueen | vol. 6, 447 |
| McKinstry, Justus | vol. 4, 358 |
| Mitchell, Charles S. | vol. 3, 390 |
| Parsons, Mosby M. | vol. 1, 146 |
| Pope, John | vol. 6, 449 |
| Price, Sterling | vol. 1, 148 |

\* \* \* \* \* \*

# Appendix C
## Assorted Correspondence and Orders for 1862

**Item:** General Pike's General Orders on the scalping that occurred at Pea Ridge on March 7, 1862.[1]

> Headquarters,
> Department Indian Territory,
> Dwight Mission, Cherokee Nation,
> March 15, 1862

Special Orders,
   NO.___.

1. The commanding General, with great regret, makes known to the troops of the department that in the action of Friday, March 7 he saw with horror a person unknown to him and who immediately passed beyond his sight, shoot a wounded enemy, prostrate on the ground and begging for mercy.

No degree of bravery can atone for such an atrocious act of barbarous and wanton cruelty. Exclaimed against by all who witnessed it, its odium ought not to attach to the troops under his command, but only to the perpetrator.

Often as such acts of inhumanity have been done by the enemy, the Indian troops are implored in no case hereafter to follow their cruel example since the braves should be always the most ready to spare fallen foe.

2. The commanding General has also learned with the utmost pain and regret that one, at least, of the enemy's dead was found scalped upon the field. The practice excites horror, leads to cruel retaliation, and could expose the Confederate States to the just reprehension of all civilized nations.

If the Indian allies of the Northern states continue it, let retaliation in kind be used as to them alone and those who with them may invade the Indian country and sanction it against forces that do not practice it, it is peremptorily forbidden during the present war.

3. Commanders of regiments, battalions and companies of Indian troops in the Confederate service will cause the foregoing order to be read and interpreted to their respective commands and will use all possible means to prevent the perpetration of the acts censored hereby.

> By order of,
> Albert Pike
> *Brigadier-general*
> Fayette Hewitt
> *Captain and Second Assistant Adjutant-General.*

\* \* \* \* \* \* \*

---

1. *O.R.S.*, pt. 3, vol. 3: 187-188.

**Item:** Letter to Joseph C. Porter, calling for the release of Andrew Allsman.[2]

Palmyra, Mo., October 8, 1862.

Joseph C. Porter

SIR: Andrew Allsman, an aged citizen of Palmyra and a non-combatant, having been carried from his home by a band of persons unlawfully arrayed against the peace and good order of the State of Missouri and which band was under your control, this is to notify you that unless said Andrew Allsman is returned unharmed to his family within ten days from date ten men, who have belonged to your band and unlawfully sworn by you to carry arms against the Government of the United States and who are now in custody, will be shot, as a meet reward for their crimes, among which is the illegal restraining of said Allsman of his liberty, and, if not returned, presumptively aiding in his murder.

Your prompt attention to this will save much suffering.

Yours, &c.,

W. R. Strachan

*Provost-Marshal-General District Northeast Missouri*

Per order of brigadier-general commanding McNeil's column.

\* \* \* \* \* \* \*

**Item:** General Orders calling out the Missouri State Militia.[3]

General Orders No. 19

Hdqrs. Missouri State Militia,

*Saint Louis, Mo., July 22, 1862.*

An immediate organization of all the militia of Missouri is hereby ordered, for the purpose of exterminating the guerrillas that infest our State.

Every able-bodied man capable of bearing arms and subject to military duty is hereby ordered to repair without delay to the nearest military post and report for duty to the commanding officer. Every man will bring with him whatever arms he may have or can procure and a good horse if he has one.

All arms and ammunition of whatever kind and wherever found, not in the hands of the loyal militia, will be taken possession of by the latter and used for public defense. Those who have no arms and cannot procure them in the above manner will be supplied as quickly as possible by the ordnance department.

The militia-men who shall assemble at any post will be immediately enrolled and organized into companies, elect their officers, and be sworn into service, in

---

2. *O.R.*, 13:719.
3. Ibid., 506.

accordance with the militia laws of the State, under the immediate superintendence of the commanding officer of the post.

The militia thus organized will be governed by the Articles of War and Army Regulations, and will be subject to do duty under the orders of the commanding officers of the post where they are enrolled, or such other officers of the United States troops or Missouri Militia, regularly mustered into service, as may be assigned to their command.

Commanding officers will report from day to day, by telegraph, when practicable, the progress of enrollment at their posts and the number of arms required.

Six days after the date of this order are allowed for every man fit for military duty to report to the commanding officer of the nearest military post and be enrolled. All persons so enrolled will be regarded as belonging to the active militia of the State until further orders.

The commanding officer of a post, or any higher commander, is authorized to give furloughs to such men of this militia force as cannot be absent from their ordinary business without serious detriment or such as are not needed for present service. Such leaves of absence will in no case be for longer period than ten days, and may be revoked at any time or renewed at their expiration, at the discretion of the officer granting them.

The same strict discipline and obedience to orders will be enforced among the militia in service under this order as among other troops and commanding officers will be held strictly responsible for all unauthorized acts of the men.

The enrollment and organization of the militia of Saint Louis will be under the general direction of Col. Lewis Merrill, commanding Saint Louis Division, who will establish rendezvous, appoint enrolling officers and make such regulations as he shall deem necessary.

By order of Brigadier-General Schofield:

C. W. Marsh,
*Assistant Adjutant-General.*

* * * * * * *

**Item:** General Orders clarifying the enrollment of Southern sympathizers in Missouri State Militia.[4]

General Orders No. 24

Hdqrs. Missouri State Militia,
*Saint Louis, Mo., August 4, 1862.*

General Orders, No. 23, from these headquarters, dated July 28, 1862 is hereby revoked. [deals with paying for exemptions to enrolling]

All loyal men of Missouri subject to military duty will be organized into com-

---

4. Ibid., 534–535.

panies, regiments, and brigades, as ordered in General Orders No. 19, from these headquarters, dated July 22, 1862.

All disloyal men and those who have at any time sympathized with the rebellion are required to report at the nearest military post or other enrolling station, be enrolled, surrender their arms, and return to their homes or ordinary places of business, where they will be permitted to remain so long as they shall continue quietly attending to their ordinary and legitimate business and in no way give aid or comfort to the enemy. Disloyal persons or sympathizers with the rebellion will not be organized into companies nor required nor permitted to do duty in the Missouri Militia.

Commanding officers of divisions will appoint enrolling officers and establish rendezvous at such places, in addition to the various military posts, as they may deem expedient.

On the 11th day of August instant each enrolling officer will proceed to ascertain and enroll the names of all men in his enrolling district who shall have failed to come forward and be enrolled as required, and report the same to the district commander.

By order of Brigadier-General Schofield:

C. W. Marsh,
*Assistant Adjutant-General.*

\* \* \* \* \* \*

**Item:** Blunt's letter requesting a cease fire at Prairie Grove.[5]

Head Quarters Federal forces
In the field
Dec. 7th 1862

To
Commanding Officer of Confederate forces

Gen'l:

The bearer Dr. Parker visits your lines with flag of truce for the purpose of caring for my wounded.

Jas. G. Blunt
Brig. Gen'l
Comd'g

\* \* \* \* \* \*

---

5. Letter, Blunt to Commander Confederate Forces (December 7, 1862), Miscellaneous Correspondence.

# Appendix D
## Executions of Colonel John McNeil

**Item:** The Kirksville Executions for violations of their paroles or for being a bushwhacker.[1]

From Adair County, Missouri; Executed on August 7, 1862.
    Kent, John
From Marion County, Missouri; Executed on August 7, 1862.
    Brannon, Hamilton
    Sallee, William
From Marion county, Missouri; Executed on August 8, 1862.
    McCullough, Ltc. Frisby H.
From Monroe County, Missouri; Executed on August 7, 1862.
    Bates, William
    Galbreath, R. M.
    Green, Reuben
    Harris, Columbus
    Rollins, Lewis
    Thomas or Thompson, Reuben
    Weld, Thomas
    Wilson, William
From Shelby County, Missouri; Executed on August 7, 1862.
    Christian, James
    Hayden, Bennett
    Wood, James
    Wood, Jesse

\* \* \* \* \* \* \*

**Item:** Palmyra Executions in retaliation for not returning Andrew Allsman to his family in Palmyra, Missouri.[2]

From Knox County, Missouri; Executed on October 18, 1862.
    Smith, Hiram
From Lewis County, Missouri; Executed on October 18, 1862.
    Baker, Lewis
    Bixler, Morgan
    Humston, Thomas
    McPheeters, John Y.

---

1. "Col. Frisbie H. McCollough," *Canton Weekly Press*, August 21, 1862; Mudd, *With Porter*, 342.
2. "Military Execution," *Weekly California News* (California, MO), November 1, 1862.

From Monroe County, Missouri; Executed on October 18, 1862.
    Sidener, Capt. Thomas A.
From Ralls County, Missouri; Executed on October 18, 1862.
    Hudson, Herbert
    Lair, Marion
    Wade, John M.
From Scotland County, Missouri; Executed on October 18, 1862.
    Lake, Eleazor

# Appendix E
## Confederate Pieces Not Used, 1862

Editor's Note: This Appendix includes pieces from both the east and west of the Mississippi River. In the case of those items in the Trans-Mississippi, they have been previously published and are noted when and where in each individual case.

**Item:** History of the Missouri State Guard from 1859–May 1862, by General James Harding, Quartermaster General, Missouri State Guard. Previously published in 2000 by Oak Hills Publishing, and titled *Service with the Missouri Guard: The Memoir of Brigadier General James Harding,* by James E. McGhee.
**Published:** July 18 and 25, 1885.

**Item:** The Delay at Shiloh, by P. J. E., late member of the Eighth Texas Cavalry. Events leading to the Battle of Shiloh and General Johnston's delay in advancing.
**Published:** April 30, 1887.

**Item:** Death of Gen. Albert S. Johnston, by R. B. Hutchinson, Sixth Arkansas Infantry. The Battle of Shiloh and the death of A. S. Johnston.
**Published:** April 9, 1887.

**Item:** Maj. Wickham's Recollections, by Watkin L. Wickham, major and aid-de-camp to General Johnston at the Battle of Shiloh. The Battle of Shiloh and the death of A. S. Johnston.
**Published:** April 9, 1887.

**Item:** The Chances of Victory at Shiloh. A short piece on the Battle of Shiloh.
**Published:** April 9, 1887.

**Item:** Crack Colonels, by "Reserve." The Battle of Shiloh by an ex-Confederate, probably a member of the Reserve Corps, commanded by General Polk.
**Published:** April 9, 1887.

**Item:** Early's Charge at Williamsburg, by John T. Mabry, Company A, Twenty-fourth Virginia Infantry. The Battle of Williamsburg, Virginia, May 5, 1862 as told by one of Jubal Early's men.
**Published:** December 19, 1885.

**Item:** Jackson as a Corps Commander, by General D. H. Hill. General Thomas "Stonewall" Jackson during the Peninsular Campaign of 1862.
**Published:** July 4, 1885.

**Item:** Stonewall Jackson's Way, no author listed. Poem on Stonewall Jackson in 1862.
**Published:** August 8, 1885.

**Item:** The Battle of Lone Jack, by S. D. Jackman. Previously edited by Richard L. Norton and published by Oak Hills Publishing in 1997 under the title of *Behind Enemy Lines.*
**Published:** August 29, 1885.

**Item:** Confederate retreat from Lone Jack and the capture of a Union spy from Illinois, by S. D. Jackman. Previously edited by Richard L. Norton and published by Oak Hills Publishing in *Behind Enemy Lines.*
**Published:** November 14, 1885 and April 17, 1886.

**Item:** The Confederate retreat from Lone Jack and reorganization of the Southern Army by General Thomas C. Hindman in the fall of 1862, by Sidney D. Jackman. Previously edited by Richard L. Norton and published by Oak Hills Publishing in *Behind Enemy Lines.*
**Published:** November 14, 1885.

**Item:** A Square Cavalry Fight, by "H.," Second Missouri Cavalry (Confederate). Operations on the Mississippi Central Railroad, death of Captain Rock Champion, Missouri Captain, and Union Lieutenant Colonel Harvey Hogg, Second Illinois Cavalry at an engagement near Bolivar or Denmark, Tennessee (August 30, 1862).
**Published:** November 13, 1886.

**Item:** Fight at Denmark, Tenn., by "H.," Second Missouri Cavalry (Confederate).The cavalry fight at Denmark, Tennessee (September 1, 1862), also known as the "Action at Britton Lane."
**Published:** August 7, 1886.

**Item:** Northern and Southern Battle Names, by D. H. Hill The Battle of Boonsboro or South Mountain, Maryland (September 14, 1862). Extracts for a paper prepared for the *Century Magazine.*
**Published:** May 1, 1886.

**Item:** Gen. Lee's Plans, author not identified. Extracts of a reported con-

versation with General Lee surrounding the Antietam Campaign (September 1862). Originally published in the June 1886 issue of the *Century Magazine*.
**Published:** May 29, 1886.

**Item:** A Critical Movement at Antietam, by General James Longstreet. Battle of Antietam, Maryland (September 17, 1862); excerpts from a piece published in the *Century Magazine* for June 1886.
**Published:** June 19, 1886.

**Item:** Doesn't Agree With Longstreet, by S. J. McMillian, Company I, Seventh Louisiana Infantry. The Battle of Antietam; comments on an article prepared by General James Longstreet by a member of Hay's Louisiana Brigade.
**Published:** August 7, 1886.

**Item:** The Superintendent of Libby Prison Talks, by Captain Jack Warner, ex-superintendent of Libby Prison, Richmond, Virginia. Federal generals in Libby prison—General Benjamin Prentiss, General E. N. Bates.
**Published:** September 5, 1885.

**Item:** Van Dorn's Raid on Holly Springs, by "H." Confederate raid on Holly Springs, Mississippi, as recounted by a "high private" in one of the cavalry regiments.
**Published:** December 19, 1885.

**Item:** Guibor's Battery at Corinth, by Hunt P. Wilson. Guibor's Missouri Battery (Confederate) at Corinth, Mississippi (October 1–2, 1862).
**Published:** June 19, 1886.

**Item:** Van Dorn's Attack on Corinth, by Major John Tyler, aid-de-camp to General Sterling Price. The Battle of Corinth, an official report, not previously published. The original is located in the Missouri Historical Society (St. Louis), John Tyler, Jr. Collection.
**Published:** October 30, 1886.

**Item:** Col. Streight's Tight Squeeze, by Captain Jack Warner, ex-superintendent of Libby Prison,
Richmond, Virginia. Colonel Streight's Raid to Rome, Georgia, in late 1862.
**Published:** November 21, 1885.

**Item:** A Story of Fredericksburg, by Herbert W. Collingwood. A poem on the Battle of Fredericksburg, Virginia (December 13, 1862); originally

published in the *New York Sun*.
**Published:** July 17, 1886.

**Item:** The Fredericksburg Opportunity, by J. W. Cooper. The Battle of Fredericksburg—why didn't the Confederates follow up their victory.
**Published:** September 18, 1886.

**Item:** Gen. Lee's Demijohn, author not identified. An incident following the Battle of Fredericksburg—Whiskey or Buttermilk; original published in the *Atlanta Constitution*.
**Published:** February 5, 1887.

\* \* \* \* \* \*

# Appendix F
## Jackman's Account of Lone Jack

Editor's Note: This is the account that appeared in the *Missouri Republican* on August 29, 1885. It differs only slightly from the account that appeared in Richard Norton's *Behind Enemy Lines*. Norton's account was found at the University of Arkansas, while the copy that appeared in the *Republican* was clearly an edited version of that account. Since Norton's account has been out of print for some time, it was felt that it should be republished here, as it is referenced by several of the other pieces presented on the engagement at Lone Jack in Chapter 2. However, it is presented without comment.

## The Battle of Lone Jack

In the summer of 1862 Col. J. V. Cockrell of Johnson county, Missouri, and I, who was from Bates county, Missouri, were engaged in recruiting a regiment of Confederate soldiers. Col. D. C. Hunter of Vernon county, Missouri and Col. S. P. Burns of Jasper county, Missouri, were engaged in the same business, and had collected 300 men. Cockrell and I had gathered together 400, and all were under the immediate command of Gen. Jas. S. Rains, who was encamped on Frog Bayou, twelve miles east of Van Buren, Ark. It became evident that the regiments could not be filled up to regimental standards without an invasion of Missouri. That, therefore, was determined upon. Preparation for the campaign immediately began, which required the work of near a month. A few days before starting, Capt. Jo O. Shelby, whom everybody knows of as Gen. Shelby, reached our camp, with seventy splendid soldiers from east of the Mississippi river and bound for Missouri.

This we regarded as a great acquisition, and, he and his men were equally rejoiced at finding us almost ready for marching.

The first day of August had now arrived and marching orders given. Col. Cockrell was assigned the command of the whole, I assumed command of 450 of our men, leaving the remainder under Capt. S. F. Cook of St. Clair county, Missouri, for camp and picket duty. Col. Hunter took 150 of his men leaving the balance under Col. Burns. Capt. Shelby was in command of his own men and was assigned the advance. Before leaving I called on the general and inquired how far we were permitted to penetrate Missouri. He replied by saying: "You have been anxious for some time to rescue your men in the hands of Col. Warren, who commands the part of Butler, Bates county. Go that far, if you think it safe, when you enter the state, but don't sink this command."

We now moved north, but many of the men were badly mounted and badly equipped. Many bridles were simply ropes and stringers and the naked backs of the horses constituted the saddles of many men. In appearance it was really the most amusing and laughable body of cavalry imaginable to start out on a recruiting and killing expedition, when those who were to be killed were the best mounted and armed men in the world, and backed by the strongest government in the world. But every man felt that he was a hero within himself, and many had long since learned what a little daring and dash would accomplish.

## My Company Commanders,

who accompanied me were Capts. L. M. Lewis of Clay county, Missouri a prominent minister of the Methodist church, afterwards Gen. Lewis, and now of Dallas, Tex., John M. Stemmons, Newton county, Missouri, later lieutenant-colonel, and now an able jurist at Dallas, Tex.; P. W. H. Cummings, McDonald county, Missouri and now a prominent merchant in the state of Louisiana; A. Bryant of Bates county, Missouri; Eph. Allison of Henry county, Missouri, now county judge of that county; Moses, Perry and Bullard of Southwest Missouri, their initials and counties not remembered—eight in all. Our march was rapid, and nothing of note transpired until we reached Cane Hill, Washington county, Ark., a beautiful and rich country and filled with a most excellent people. It being Saturday evening, it was decided to remain at this camp until Monday morning to prepare a few day's rations.

Our camp near the village church, and on Sunday morning, when the people gathered for worship, it was learned that we had several preachers among us and were requested to furnish one for the occasion. It was agreed upon, and as Lewis was always ready, he was selected. He took the stand with all the dignity of a presiding elder and began a ready and fluent talk. I tried to give him my attention, but it was soon so fixed upon his garb that I found it impossible. His coat was a brown jean or butternut roundabout and his pants were of blue jeans with an immense great white leather patch coving the entire seat. In fact, it was almost as large as the full moon and looked something like it. When he talked to the ladies my side of the house had the

## Benefit of the Moon,

and when he would turn to us the moon would rise on the ladies, and hence it became so amusing that I lost all interest in his discourse. The people, however, seemed pleased and came out in the evening to hear another discourse, when we put up Cockrell, who was also a Methodist preacher and who gave them one of his sledge hammer talks, and he was able to do it for he weighed about 300 pounds.

On the next morning the march was resumed, and continued to Newtonia, Mo., where a force of the enemy, under Maj. Hubbard, was reported several hundred strong, and quartered in a stone barn with considerable stone fencing about it, and having artillery. A demonstration was made upon him just before sundown, with Capt. Shelby's force thrown forward as skirmishers. The enemy shelled us without effect, and no small arms were brought into use. Our position was retained until after dark, when we withdrew.

I had supposed that this demonstration was made to house the enemy and give us the benefit of a night's march into the state without interruption, but to my surprise the colonel commanding headed due south and continued the march to Elm Springs, eight miles filling me with

## Apprehensions of Retreat.

Pickets were sent out and the command went into camp, and it being late all were soon asleep.

At a late hour the next morning the order to saddle up was given when Capt. Shelby came hurriedly to me and remarked: "Jackman, Cockrell is going back top Frog Bayou."

Said I: "How do you know?"

"He has just told me," said Shelby.

"Let us see him,: I replied.

We walked rapidly to here he was, and when I said to him: "Col. Cockrell, Capt. Shelby informs me that you are going back to Frog Bayou. Is it so?"

He answered: "Yes," and remarked that the danger and responsibility were so great that he was afraid to risk the command in Missouri.

Then said I: "If you are afraid, turn the command over to me and go back yourself."

After a moments reflection, he said: "No, I will go on myself, but you all must stick close to me." Shelby was an eager listener to this conversation and rejoiced at its result.

Right here I always felt that the expedition was at an end, and, but for this timely notice [of] Shelby and this earnest protest of mine, there never would have ever been any "Lone Jack" expedition and consequently any "Lone Jack" battle. I as fully appreciated the danger and responsibility as Col. Cockrell but I also fully realized the impossibility of retaining recruits without going into Missouri, and hence my great anxiety.

The command, now mounted and formed, moved north in fine spirits, and in blissful ignorance, as it is to this day, that it had been mounted to go south. Capt. Bullard, however, was left in this section to gather up recruits while we were gone north.

On September 9, 1883, I wrote Gen. Shelby, reciting the circumstances in conversation above and inquired whether he remembered the facts as given. Below is an exact copy of his answer, punctuation, underscoring and all.

## Shelby's Letter.

My Dear General—I have read the inclosed. The conversation occurred *just as you have stated in this sheet.* I was satisfied at the time, Col. Cockrell, from reports coming in, was apprehensive that he would be assuming too much responsibility and too great a risk of losing his men, not that he had any consideration for himself personally, but he did not at that time desire to hazzard the lives of his devoted followers. Col. Cockrell is a brave and good man, and was loyal to the South as any man whoever fought for her. In conclusion, however, I must say had it not been for your determination in the morning, the battle of Lone Jack would not have occurred. Yours truly,

Jo O. Shelby

To Gen. S. D. Jackman

I always regarded this as an important fact in the complete narrative of the events of that campaign, and one never known by anyone except Col. Cockrell, Shelby and myself. Let it be distinctively understood that I fully indorse every word uttered by Gen. Shelby about Col. Cockrell and much more. I know that not only is he a good and brave man and true friend of the South, but was also an honest man and Christian gentleman, which is about as much as could be said for anyone, and makes him about as good as a man could wish to be in this life. And hence, as my friend, I could not desire to rob him of one single honor to which he is entitled, and, as the brave and good man I know him to be, he should not, and does not, want any honors to which he is not entitled. The truth, the whole truth, and nothing but the truth, regardless of the honors, must and shall be told. The line of march was by way of Neosho, Carthage, and on up the great thoroughfare to the great Northwest until we reached the Osage river. There we learned that Col. Warren had hurried to Butler, rendering a march to that place unnecessary.

## Moving Northwards.

The command now turned north via Pleasant Gap, Butler county, and when a few miles north of that place a messenger from Cols. John T. Coffee and John C. Tracy, requesting our return to their assistance; that they were being sorely pressed by a body of Federals under Gen. Montgomery (I suppose Bacon Montgomery), a counter-march was made at once to Pleasant Gap, where Coffee and Tracy were met, having escaped without loss from the eager Federals. Coffee and Tracy had preceded our command into the state a few days, and bearing further east than the line of our march had encountered trouble. Coffee was in command of about 250 or 300 Missouri State Guards, and Tracy about the same number of Confederate troops. The exact number of troops commanded by those officers is unknown. Coffee having command of the State Guards the Confederate officers had no authority over him; and while Tracy was in command of the Confederate troops, he claimed to have some sort of authority from Richmond, giving him exclusive jurisdiction over his command. Here was some ground for confusion. Nevertheless, after an hour in consultation, it was agreed to remain together, when the entire command moved out in a northerly direction, with Shelby in advance, as he had been all the way.

We encamped that night in Deepwater, Bates county. The next day's march, being August 13, brought us to Dayton, Cass county, where went into camp for the night. This place, like most all others, in Western Missouri, had been reduced to ashes by those in the uniform of the federal government, and fighting for a restored Union. Of course it had its effect. Recruiting had been very rapid indeed for twenty-four hours, in fact, the woods seemed to be alive with men and all fleeing the wrath of what was known as the "Gamble Order." H. R. Gamble, the governor at that time, had recently issued an order required all men subject to military duty in the state, to enter the militia service which caused a general stampede to the woods of Southern men who refused to join the ranks of the enemy. This made recruiting easy, and was convincing proof that we had penetrated the state at the right time. This brought us to the morning of the 14th of August. As usual the command moved early but I was directed by the colonel commanding to organize three companies of men and then bring up the rear to the next camp. One company was organized with Capt. F. H. Rernaugh of Boonville, Mo., as captain; one with John H. McCombs, of Butler, Mo. as captain; the other, was one of the old squad, now having been filled up, was organized.

The command was overtaken at Rose Hill, Johnston county, where the night was spent. Here Prof. J. J. Searcy of the Missouri university, reported to me and rendered me valuable assistance during the balance of the campaign,

During this night, Capt. Shelby with his command left us for Lafayette county, Missouri. Col. Cockrell wishing to see his family, placed Col. Hunter in command, and proceeded north with Capt. Shelby for that purpose, stating that he would be with us next day at Lone Jack or vicinity.

## A Divided Command.

On the morning of the 15th, Col. Hunter proceeded to Lone Jack, distance about fifteen miles, and finding supplies scarce, moved west about four miles and went into camp. Cols. Coffee and Tracy, not recognizing Hunter's authority camped in Lone Jack. The battle of Independence having happened a few days before, had now filled the country with Federals determined on capturing or driving from the country the Confederates engaged in that battle. Col. Cockrell on reaching the vicinity of Warrensburg, learned of a large body of Federals moving in the direction of Lone Jack, and fearing danger to his command, came hurriedly back, reaching it about 9 o'clock of the night of the 15th, when very soon the "boom" of artillery was heard back at the town, and, of course, all knew that Coffee and Tracy had been fired upon.

During the evening Col. Upton Hays had joined us with a few hundred men, including Cols. Gid Thompson and Bohanon, two brave and experienced officers; also twenty-five men of Quantrell's command, under Lieut. Haller, who was killed in September following. Col. Cockrell formed his command and prepared for battle, expecting Coffee and Tracy to fall back upon him, pursued by the enemy, who was to receive a warm welcome. In this we were disappointed, when

Capt. E. Allison and Capt. Osborne were sent to reconnoiter the enemy and learn what had become of Coffee and Tracy. In the meantime our command was resting on their arms and in line of battle Allison and Osborne promptly discharged this duty, reporting that Coffee and Tracy had retreated upon a road south of us, and that the enemy, believing that they had fired upon and routed Hays and Quantrell, had retired for the night and was ignorant as to our presence in the country. As we had but one wagon, in all our command, and that our ordnance wagon, Maj. Foster's memory does not serve him correctly, when he states that he captured all of Coffee's wagons. Col. Cockrell now asked my opinion as to whether we had better fight or retreat. I urged strongly the importance of battle, and making the attack at daybreak the next morning and gave as reasons, the fatigued condition of the men and horses, as compared to that of the enemy, who was fresh and vigorous. With such a force in our rear, and the strong probability of meeting fresh troops pursuing us from the south, retreat was impossible. Let us fight the enemy in detail; whip these at hand now, and others

## As Occasion Might Require.

He fully concurred in my suggestion, and went to consult Hays and others, and make known his determination. The danger and responsibility talked about away South, seemed no longer thought of by him, although plainly visible on every hand. He seemed every inch a soldier, and I admired him greatly. I now made a little midnight speech to my men, and informed them of the decision and showed them the necessity. I urged that they "remembered that that was our country, the home of our mothers and sisters, and wives and children, and everything dear to us on earth. We must whip the enemy and hold it, or be whipped and driven from it. Let us meet them like men. Keep cool, shoot low, give them gut shots, boys, and the work will be done."

Tracy was now approaching from the west. He knew nothing of Coffee, they had separated in the dark, and Coffee was lost. Cockrell now returned and informed me of the plan of attack, as agreed upon by him and Hays. It was this: The commands of Hunter, Tracy and myself were to be used as infantry with Hunter on the right, I in the center and Tracy on the left. Those of Hays and Haller were to be retained as cavalry. The infantry were to receive six rounds of ammunition and move up as near the enemy as possible, without attracting attention, and there quietly remain until Hays should fire on the flank of the enemy, and when his attention was drawn to Hays, we were to charge home.

## A Cool Plan.

I protested strongly against the plan, and gave the following reasons for it; Let Hays be used as infantry also, and let us make a combined assault on the enemy while in bed, and in his confusion we can exterminate him, and that, too with out the loss of a man. But less should a few escape, retain Lieut. Haller's men, mounted, who can then complete the work.

But, he said, Hays would not be dismounted. "Then let him remain mounted; but let the infantry make the attack as I have suggested."

"No," he replied. "Hays must bring on the engagement."

"Then six rounds of ammunition will not do,"

Yes, he thought the enemy would run after a shot or two. Said I; "Col. Cockrell, the enemy having artillery, and knowing nothing of our presence here, is evidence to me that they have come to remain. Let them not get into line, we will need all our ammunition and lose many valuable lives with very doubtful chances to our favor. He thought not, the enemy would run after a fire or two. I viewed him with amusement and felt that his judgment in this matter was greatly at fault. The result proved who was right. Being a subordinate it was my duty to obey. The command was now mounted, and moved up to within a short distance of the town, where it was dismounted and formed as above. Capt. Osborne, who was familiar with that section, led the infantry where it was to remain, until Hays should bring on the engagement. The line of march was up ravine or branch west of the town into a wheat or oat field that had grown up in iron weeds sufficiently tall to entirely conceal and hide us from the enemy. We now moved up quietly in line of battle to within fifty or seventy-five yards of the enemy, when a halt was made as per orders. It was now daybreak and here we waited, seemingly an eternity, for Hays to begin the work; when to my great surprise and perfect astonishment, he came riding slowly and quietly up the front of my line. I hurriedly approached him and exclaimed: "Col. Hays, In the name of God, what are you doing here? Here we have been waiting a long half-hour for you to bring on the attack, as agreed upon, and instead of doing it, when the enemy is rallying, you come riding up this line as though you were a major-general of the Confederate army."

He replied in a very sassy and quiet way: "I will soon."

He then rode up a short distance up Hunter's line, and without suggesting anything, or making known any business, turned about and rode as slowly and quietly back. He was a very cool, and, no doubt, brave man, but this, I regarded, a great breach of good faith, and trifling with the lives of my men.

## The Fight.

Some little time before this a guard of the enemy discovered the movement of Hays, and gave the alarm, and the enemy was rallying with all possible speed.

During all this waste of precious time my men were eager and crazy for the attack. "Why halt here?" "Why not attack now?" "This is all wrong." "It won't do to remain here." "Now is the time." —and all such questions and remarks were continually in my ear from the time the halt was made. The worst that could have been done had now been done; to wait longer for the attack by Hays was nonsense. I gave the word to charge, and with a yell the men dashed forward in fine style. But an unexpected obstacle was in the way. A staked and ridered fence, and running parallel with our line, lay before us, not more than forty yards from the enemy. At this fence, we met a terrible fire of grape and musketry, which brought us to a halt, and here protected somewhat by the fence, we fought the thing out.

The enemy was formed in the street and rear of their horses and houses, and of course, greatly protected by both. Word soon ran up the line that Col. Tracy had been killed. This, I regarded a heavy loss, and filled me with sorrow. The first man was shot was a handsome young fellow on the extreme left of Hunter's force, whose name I did not learn. The next man I saw shot, was Capt. L. M. Lewis. He was hit with a spent ball, square in the forehead, but high up, and with sufficient force for the ball to stick. He picked it out with his fingers and called my attention to it. I told him if the wound was painful he had better retire. He replied, "No, not for that." Very soon he received a shot in the hand; the two was enough for him, and he left. I afterwards told him that in our association, I had hoped to convert him to Cambellism, but since Yankee bullets could not penetrate his head, there was no use in trying the water treatment, and I should have to give it up and he a Methodist to this day. Capt. Watson, another Methodist preacher and Christian gentleman, who was acting ordnance officer for the command, had had some experience in battle. Knowing him to be brave, I had placed him on the left of my force to aid me in its management. He was shot dead while faithfully doing his duty. He, Lewis, and Cockrell constituted my mess.

## Went to the Rear.

Very soon after the battle had opened, Col. Hunter came hurriedly to me and told me that he could hear the enemy's cavalry in the corn upon our right and asked if I did not think he had better take his command and protect my flank while I fought the battle. "No,: said I, "remain where you are and help to fight this battle. It is impossible for the enemy's cavalry to be there, they have not had time." He left, but only to come rushing back in a moment exclaiming, "I assure you they are there, for I can hear their sabres in the corn and hear them talking." "Then," said I, "If you know them to be there, which I don't believe, take your force and guard my flank." He then withdrew, when the enemy felt encouragement, and with a yell, came rushing upon us, but one well directed volley settled the business; they turned and fled, but only for protection to the horses [houses,] their horses having been mostly killed by this time.

The command of Col. Tracy, under Lieut. Col. Dick Hancock, of Bates county, Mo., was behaving nobly. Early in the engagement, and realizing that we would need more ammunition, I directed Capt. H. B. Brewster, of Carrollton, Mo., acting adjutant of my command, to furnish me a man to go for it, when he requested to go himself, stating that he would do it quicker than anyone else. I told him to go and lose no time. He went, but he never returned. The artillery had now been silenced by the left of my force and that of Col. Hancock, and our six rounds of ammunition almost expended. I took a man from the line and sent him to notify Col. Hunter that I was forced to retire for ammunition. The man returned reporting Hunter gone. He had abandoned my flank. I then gave the order to retire. It was done in good order.

## Another Charge.

The enemy now feeling greatly encouraged again raised a yell and came charging after us. I ordered about face and poured my last round into a yelling and advancing foe. It did its work well, and the enemy now showed us his back the second time. On reaching the low ground where the command had been formed in the morning, there I found Hunter with his command. I asked him why he had deserted my flank. He replied that he had "had no ammunition." Said I: "What did you do with it. You had no enemy in front. Did you throw it away?" He was dumb. "Now if ammunition is what you want let us get it and return to the battlefield." We proceeded down the field to the ordnance wagon, which had been brought up near the mill at the north or northwest of the town, and here I found hundreds of men congregated about the wagon with Col. Cockrell urging them with all the power that was in him to return to the battle, but with little or no effect. I here found Capt. Brewster, who approached me, and when I enquired as to why he had not returned with the ammunition. He frankly replied that it was too hot a place for him, he could not go back. Ammunition was now issued to my and Hunter's commands. I ordered my men to fall into line when to my great surprise, very few obeyed the order, many asking the question "Why should a few of us go back and be killed, when the whole command is here and refuses to go!" Really it did look that way, but a few gallant spirits followed me.

Capt. Lewis had been twice wounded, as stated above; Capt. Stemmons, dangerously; Capt. Allison, seriously; Capt. Watson, Moses and McComb, killed; all first-class men, anywhere in the world.

## Heroes and Cravens.

Hunter was less successful, because he had less men and was less anxious. Having treated me badly by leaving the field and my flank exposed, I determined that he should go back with me. A few splendid soldiers followed him. I returned upon a direct line to the battlefield, and on the way met Col. Tracy, supported by a man, under each arm. I rejoiced at this, for I had supposed him dead. When near enough to speak to him, said I, "Col. Tracy, I am sorry you are wounded; are you much hurt?"

"Yes," replied he, "I am shot all to pieces."

This remark rather opened my eyes for I could see no blood. We were now face to face and I asked him, "How are you hurt?"

"Oh," said he, as if in great pain, "when the first bomb was fired it struck me in the breast and exploded, completely enveloping me in fragments, some of which cut me in the head and some cut my legs terribly in the front and one piece struck me in the rear, and now the blood is running down my legs."

I examined his head. There was not a mark or a speck of blood to be seen, and no rents in his clothing. I left him with a feeling of extreme contempt, and was thoroughly convinced that he was mistaken as to what it was running down his legs. I moved on, and when passing through a corn patch of a few acres then in roasting ears, Col. Hunter fell reporting that he had sprained his ankle. There I left him. Two of his captains, Capt. Lowe of Shell City, Vernon county, Missouri, and old Capt. Frazier of Green county, Missouri (there was a young Capt. Frazier), went on with me to renew the fight, and requested that I take command of them, as they had no leader. I did so, and now take pleasure in testifying that they were among the bravest of the brave on that ever memorable occasion.

As I now approached the field I saw Confederates beyond the Bois D'Arc hedge, and which I learned was the command of Col. Hays. The enemy was directly between us, and as we were in easy range it's very probable that that command, and ours on the west had suffered from each others fire. It is, however, impossible to know the facts.

The enemy had now almost entirely gone into the houses and were firing from the holes made for that purpose, which gave them great advantage over us. Our little forces now engaging them were forced to break into squads and seek protection the best we could. I, with four others, took position near the corner of an old log cabin, when very soon a shot from an upper window of the hotel brought down one of my squad, shot directly through the temple. I did not know his name. In a moment more a shot from the same place brought down First Sergt. Montgomery of Bryant's company, and shot through the temple. Montgomery fell by the side of the other man. Another shot from the same place hit Capt. Bryant in the temple and felled him. He fell on top of the other two. Here lay three men out of five, all dead and all shot in the same place, and evidently

## By the Same Man

and the same gun. Good and brave men; what a cross it was to give them up. I remarked to Lieut. Harrell, that those men had all been killed by the same man; let us move. Before the suggestion escaped my lips, Lieut. Harrell, while in the act of moving, was shot in the arm. He left the field and I moved up with all my men engaged in the rear of the hotel, a two story frame structure, in which most of the enemy had now sought refuge. It being an old fashioned, weather boarded house, with thin walls, I felt that I might drive them out by shooting through the walls, but failing in that, and occasionally losing a man, Lieut. Martin of Johnstown, Mo. (afterwards Capt. Martin), came to me and suggested that that house

## Ought to be Burned.

Said I, "Lieutenant, I know it, but am afraid to risk a few men for that purpose." He then replied that if I would protect him he would do it. I told him to go; that I would do it or sacrifice this command. He called a man whose name I have forgotten—and which I regret—to go with him and burn the house. They jumped the fence and ran into the chimney corner, snatching up a little trash as they went. I now brought my men solidly up to the fence, with instructions for my man to be ready in case an attempt would be made for Martin's capture. We had not long to wait. A strong squad came boldly each way around the corner of the house, but after receiving one well directed volley, they wheeled and ran. Martin soon had the fire well under way, and very soon the house completely enveloped in fire. The house now burned. Thank God! The battle was over and the victory won, but dearly won; and it will be observed that my prediction to the colonel commanding, before the battle, had proven literally true. I desire here to say that a great many have claimed the honor of that brave and daring act, the burning of the hotel. In the future let the tongue cleave to the mouth of any man doing so except Martin and the man who went with him.

Someone named Buel, has written a book in which he states that Cole Younger burned the hotel with turpentine balls. Also that I was there but was a little slow in coming up with my command. Now, I don't know who Buel is, whether a Federal or Confederate soldier, or a shirk and a player from '61 to '65, but I presume the latter, as no brave soldier, friend or enemy would rob another of the honors to which he is entitled. He, however, has manifested considerable desire to be an author, and I am inclined to think from the genius he displays in certain directions had he been educated, would have made an author. But I am giving him too much notoriety.

## My Loss was Great.

I went into the battle with ten captains, including Watson, the ordnance officer, and about five hundred men. Four captains were killed and three wounded. Their names are as above. Three, Cummings, Hernaugh and Perry came out whole. In men it was also great, but I never knew the exact loss, which is to be regretted. There were no muster rolls and no company reports, for want of time, until we reached Arkansas, when we were organized, and then dismounted and reorganized; thus keeping up one everlasting confusion until the whole matter was lost sight of. My men behaved gallantly. Had I gone into the battle with ammunition to fight it through, I hardly think a man would have left the field until the close. A braver and more determined body of men never went into battle. Prof. Searcy, afterwards Lieut. Col. Searcy, was everywhere, carrying orders and encouraging the men. Little John Fisher of Bates county, Mo., a mere boy of 17 , recklessly exposed himself by crawling upon the fence, under a deadly fire, shouting for Jeff Davis and cursing the Federals. Those boy soldiers—what brave fellows they were. I never saw anyone who had any fear; but I can't particularize. Col. Hays did good work after the battle began. Col. Thompson, who had been wounded at the Battle of Independence, on the 11th, was not able to take an active part in the engagement. Col. Bohanon was fearless in the discharge of his duties. Capt. R. P. Bradley, of Tracy's command, and from Bates county, was killed—a great loss to his friends and country.

When hostilities ceased I found Col. Coffee had returned, but I do not know whether in time to take part in the battle. Col. Cockrell fully sustained the high opinion I had formed on him as a cool and brave man. So many behaved badly that he went into the battle himself, firing seventeen shots, as he informed me. With a half million such preachers as Cockrell, Lewis, and Watson, reconstruction would have been on the other side. As to the relative strength of the two armies I presume there was not much difference. Perhaps the Federals were

# A Little the Strongest.

Taking the Confederates as a whole, they were greatly in excess, but at least one-third or perhaps one-half were unarmed recruits and at a time like that are a positive burden. I, as stated above, had 500 armed men; Col. Hunter, 150; Cols. Tracy, Hays, Thompson and Bohanon , I suppose had about 700 men combined. It would be safe to say 400 went into the fight, and which would give us 1,050 men. I feel very certain that we could not have been less than that number. And it will be observed that I have not referred to Col. Coffee's command at all, because I do not know that he fired a single shot during the engagement. There is no question, however, as to his courage, either personally or in battle. Now I learn from Col. Cockrell, who captured the dispatches of Maj. Foster, who commanded the Federals, that he had 1,100 men, and thus it will be seen that the fighting strength of the two armies were about equal when the battle began. But the great body of unarmed recruits which had huddled together had a very damaging effect on our soldiers engaged in the battle, and especially so when we retired for ammunition. Not one-fourth the original number returned to the battle. The Federals had two splendid rifled cannon and better protection, better small arms, and hence it will be seen that they had greatly the advantage.

The battle opened before sunrise and closed about noon. The Federals fought us with great obstinacy. In fact, no man, from Grant on down to Foster, could have made a more determined and desperate resistance. The Federal loss was very great, far greater than ours, but I have never known their exact loss. On the street on which they were formed seemed literally covered with dead and wounded men, and dead and dying horses. Maj. Foster was dangerously wounded and fell into our hands. Also his brother Capt. Foster, together with many men. A very sad event occurred during the battle in the killing of a most excellent Southern woman, which filled all our hearts with sorrow. How, or by which party I do not know.

The captured property consisted of two cannon and caissons; several hundred guns, pistols and cavalry equipments.

I now called upon Maj. Foster in the hospital, in company with old Capt. Billy Mitchell, as he was familiarity called, acting commissary for our command. I found him on a bed with the floor covered with his wounded men. I expressed gratification at meeting him, having known him from reputation for some time, but the introduction had been warmer and more animated than I cared to receive. On learning my name, he and a great many others excitedly enquired if we were Confederate soldiers. When answered in the affirmative he expressed much regret in not knowing it in time to prevent the loss of so much blood and destruction of so much property, but thought he was fighting Hays' and Quantrell's guerrillas , and it was simply a matter of life and death.

When I came out of the hospital I found Lieut. Haller, and a few of his men at the door and enquired what part he had taken in the battle, and, greatly, to my surprise, he answered that they had not fired a shot. I then asked him if it was possible that twenty-five men, armed as they were, could witness a fight of that character and not participate in it. He replied that their captain (Quantrell) was not there and they would not go into battle without him. And thus it will be seen that Maj. Foster is mistaken as to the gallant charge by Quantrell It is very evident, however, that had he been there it would have been known and no mistake.

## Buried Near the Black Jack Tree.

Our first work after the battle was to care for the wounded and inter the dead. Our dead and that of the enemy were buried near the black jack tree from which the town took its name. A sad and sorrowful burial to me. A hospital was established, and the wounded who could not go South were left to fall into the hands of the enemy. Among them Capt. Stemmons, whose life was despaired of, was taken to Gratiot street prison, where he remained a few months, then making his escape by strategy, returned to his command to the great joy of his friends.

Exciting reports of large bodies of Federals pursuing us from the South were reaching us every moment. Being almost out of ammunition and crippled and bleeding, we were not in a very good position to make a stand, and very little better to make a run, but retreat was inevitable. Col. Cockrell now came up to me and remarked that his wife had come up to within a few miles, hoping he would be able to remain some days, but that being impossible, he must gallop out, let her know the result and bid her farewell; and in the meantime for me to get up teams for the cannons and caisson preparatory to retreat. He left, and I hurriedly began selecting teams by dismounting the men who had horses suitable for the service.

Col. Hays rendered me valuable assistance in the matter. It required twenty picked horses, and never a soldier hesitated a minute when he understood the purpose for which the horse was wanted. This was a great exhibition of devotion to principle. There we were 300 miles in the enemy's country with an overpowering, fresh and vigorous foe upon us giving up their only horses when the whole distance was to be traveled by day and night as rapidly as flesh and blood could endure—it was patriotism almost incomprehensible. Having had the example of the enemy for a year and half, we knew very well how to get horses when there were any to be had, but on the line of retreat that was impossible. Capt. Osborne was given charge of the artillery and Col. Cockrell not having time to return, and the enemy expected every moment, a move at once seemed absolutely necessary. A consultation was held and Col. Hays suggested that he had eight boxes of ammunition, eight miles from where we were, in a west direction, and thought we ought to have it, as we had very little. This seemed reasonable and was agreed then that we would retreat down the Western border of Missouri and thus keep the pursuing enemy all the time in the rear. The order of march was also agreed upon; Hays, knowing the country, was to take the advance, Tracy, Hunter and Coffee were to follow in order; the artillery next and I the rear.

## The Command Moved Out.

Now, almost dark, and very soon dreadfully so, after moving a short distance, I was brought to dead halt by the command in front of me. Remaining in this suspense for some time I rode forward to learn the cause and found a great part of the command dismounted and asleep and Hays gone. We saw nothing more of Hays for two or three weeks, when he came South with Capt. Shelby, both of whom brought regiments. Finding it impossible to arouse the men, I returned to the rear, where I found Col. Cockrell, who had just arrived and who disapproved the plan of retreat as agreed upon Hays and myself. I urged the reason as before mentioned, but without effect.

Finding it impossible to move the men, he was forced to let them sleep. I spent this night walking and nodding, with my bridle rein on my arm, expecting an attack at every moment. No guard or pickets were out this night, but morning came without the enemy. It was now thought best to feed the command before marching, for once moving, and the enemy after us, it would be impossible.

Marching orders were late coming and when we did move it was directly back to Lone Jack, at which place our advance met a small advance of the enemy, capturing one, the balance escaping. Cockrell turned to the left, passing around the enemy, which were in full view for several miles.

A few of our men gave chase to a small party of the enemy. The enemy seemed greatly amazed, and while equal to us in numbers gave no evidence of a desire to meet us in battle. Such an opportunity for martial glory I have never witnessed. A little pluck and dash by a few hundred men, with Foster at their head, would have retaken their artillery and put to rout our entire force. There is not a doubt about this.

The officer in command was not known by us, but was either wanting in perception or courage, perhaps both. Cockrell was soon completely in his rear and moving as fast as his tired men could move. He had accomplished exactly what he said he would when I was protesting against this line of retreat. Said he, "If I meet a force I can't whip I will pass around him and then have him in my rear."

The retreat and results of the campaign are full of interest, but my letter is already too long.

S. D. Jackman.

# Bibliography

**Books/Pamphlets/Articles**

Abel, Annie Heloise. *The American Indian Under Reconstruction*. Cleveland, OH: Arthur H. Clarke Co., 1925.

———. *The Slave Holding Indians: An Omitted Chapter in the Diplomatic History of the Southern Confederacy*. Cleveland, OH: Arthur H. Clarke Co., 1915.

Adamson, Hans Christian. *Rebellion in Missouri, 1861: Nathaniel Lyon and His Army of the West*. Rahway, NJ: Quinn & Boden Company, 1961.

Allardice, Bruce S. *More Generals in Gray*. Baton Rouge, LA: Louisiana State University Press, 1995.

Anderson, Ephraim McD. *Memoirs: Historical and Personal; Including the Campaigns of the First Missouri Confederate Brigade*. St. Louis: Times Printing Co., 1868. Reprint. Dayton, OH: Morningside Bookshop, 2005.

Anderson, Mabel Washbourne. *Life of General Stand Watie*. Pryor, OK: Mayes County Republican, 1915. Reprint. Harrah, OK: Brandy Station Bookshelf, 1995.

Bailey, Anne J. *Between the Enemy and Texas: Parsons's Texas Cavalry in the Civil War*. Fort Worth, TX: Texas Christian University Press, 1989.

Banasik, Michael E. *Cavaliers of the Brush: Quantrill and His Men*. Unwritten Chapters of the Civil War West of the River Volume V. Iowa City, IA: Camp Pope Publishing, 2003.

———. *Confederate "Tales of the War" In the Trans-Mississippi, Part One: 1861*. Unwritten Chapters of the Civil War West of the River Volume VII. Iowa City, IA: Camp Pope Publishing, 2010.

———. *Duty, Honor and Country: The Civil War Experiences of Captain William P. Black, Thirty-seventh Illinois Infantry*. Unwritten Chapters of the Civil War West of the River Volume VI. Iowa City, IA: Camp Pope Publishing, 2006

———. *Embattled Arkansas: The Prairie Grove Campaign of 1862*. Wilmington, NC: Broadfoot Publishing Company, 1996.

————. *Missouri Brothers in Gray: The Reminiscences and Letters of William J. Bull and John P. Bull*. Unwritten Chapters of the Civil War West of the River Volume I. Iowa City, IA: Camp Pope Publishing, 1998.

————. *Missouri in 1861: The Civil War Letters of Franc B. Wilkie, Newspaper Correspondent*. Unwritten Chapters of the Civil War West of the River Volume IV. Iowa City, IA: Camp Pope Publishing, 2001.

————. *Reluctant Cannoneer: The Diary of Robert T. McMahan of the Twenty-fifth Independent Ohio Light Artillery*. Unwritten Chapters of the Civil War West of the River Volume III. Iowa City, IA: Camp Pope Publishing, 2000.

————. *Serving With Honor: The Diary of Captain Eathan Allen Pinnell of the Eighth Missouri Infantry (Confederate)*. Unwritten Chapters of the Civil War West of the River Volume II. Iowa City, IA: Camp Pope Publishing, 1999.

Bartels, Carolyn M. *The Forgotten Men: The Missouri State Guard*. Shawnee Mission, KS: Two Trails Publishing, 1995.

————. *Trans-Mississippi Men at War, Volume I: Missouri C.S.A.* Independence, MO: Two Trails Publishing, 1998.

Bearss, Edwin C. "The Battle of Pea Ridge." *Arkansas Historical Quarterly* 20 (Spring 1961): 74–94.

————. "The First Day At Pea Ridge, March 7, 1862." *Arkansas Historical Quarterly* 17 (Spring 1958): 132–154.

Bearss, Edwin C. and Gibson, Arrell M. *Fort Smith Little Gibraltar on the Arkansas*. Norman, OK: University of Oklahoma Press, 1969.

Bek, William G. Ed. "Civil War Diary of John T. Buegel, Union Soldier." *Missouri Historical Review* 40 (April 1946): 307–329.

Bennett, L. G. and Haigh, Wm. H. *History of the Thirty-sixth Regiment Illinois Volunteers During the War of the Rebellion*. Aurora, IL: Knickerbocker & Hodder, 1876. Reprint. Marengo, IL: Prairie State Press, Inc., 1999.

Bevier, R. S. *History of the First and Second Missouri Confederate Brigades*

*1861–1865. And From Wakarusa to Appomattox, A Military Anagraph.* St. Louis: Bryan, Brand & Company, 1879.

Block, William Neil. *Shades of Gray Confederate Soldiers and Veterans of Randolph County, Missouri.* Shawnee Mission, KS: Two Trails Genealogy Shop, 1996.

Boatner III, Mark Mayo. *The Civil War Dictionary.* New York: David McKay Company, Inc., 1959.

Britton, Wiley. *The Civil War on the Border A Narrative of Military Operations in Missouri, Kansas, Arkansas, and the Indian Territory, During the Years 1861–1862, Based Upon Official Reports of the Federal Commanders Lyon, Sigel, Sturgis, Fremont, Halleck, Curtis, Schofield, Blunt, Herron and Totten and of the Confederate Commanders McCulloch, Price, Van Dorn, Hindman, Marmaduke and Shelby.* 2 vols. New York: G. P. Putnam's Sons, 1899.

———. *The Civil War on the Border A Narrative of Military Operations in Missouri, Kansas, Arkansas, and the Indian Territory, During the Years 1863–1865, Based Upon Official Reports and Observations of the Author.* New York: G. P. Putnam's Sons, 1899.

———. *Memoirs of the Rebellion the Border 1863.* Chicago: Cushing, Thomas & Co., 1892. Reprint. Florissant, MO: Inland Printer Limited, 1986.

———. *The Union Indian Brigade in the Civil War.* Kansas City, MO: Franklin Hudson Publishing Co., 1922.

Brock, R. A., ed. *Southern Historical Society Papers.* 52 vols. Richmond, VA: Southern Historical Society, 1876–1959. Reprint. Wilmington, NC: Broadfoot Publishing Company, 1990–1992.

Brown, Walter Lee. "Pea Ridge: Gettysburg of the West." *The Arkansas Historical Quarterly* 15 (Spring, 1956): 3–16.

Burke, W. S. *Official Military History of Kansas Regiments During the War for the Suppression of the Great Rebellion.* Leavenworth, KS: W. S. Burke, 1870.

*Burns, William S. Recollections of the 4th Missouri Cavalry.* Dayton, OH: Morningside House, Inc., 1988.

Byers, S. H. M. *Iowa In War Times*. Des Moines, IA: W. D. Condit & Co., 1888.

Cabell, William L. "Reminiscences From the Trans-Mississippi." *Confederate Veteran* 12 (April, 1904): 173.

Cantrell, M. L. and Harris, Mac., eds. *Kepis & Turkey Calls: An Anthology of the War Between the States in Indian Territory*. Oklahoma City, OK: Western Heritage Books, Inc., 1982.

Castel, Albert E. "The Diary of General Henry Little, C.S.A." *Civil War Times Illustrated* 11 (October, 1972): 4–11, 41–47.

Coggins, Jack. *Arms and Equipment of the Civil War*. Wilmington, NC: Broadfoot Publishing Company, 1987.

Cozzens, Peter. *General John Pope: A Life for the Nation*. Chicago: University of Illinois Press, 2000.

Crabb, Martha L. *All Afire to Fight: The Untold Tale of the Civil War's Ninth Texas Cavalry*. New York: Avon Books, Inc., 2000.

Crabtree, John D. "Recollections of the Pea Ridge Campaign, and the Army of the Southwest, in 1862." *Military Essays and Recollections. Papers Read Before the Commandery of the State of Illinois, Military Order of the Loyal Legion of the United States*. Chicago: The Dial Press , 1899. Reprint. 70 vols. Wilmington, NC: Broadfoot Publishing Company, 1992. 12:211–226.

Crawford, Samuel J. *Kansas in the Sixties*. Chicago: A. C. McClurg & Co., 1911.

Crute, Joseph H. *Units of the Confederate States Army*. Midlothian, VA: Derwent Books, 1987.

Cunningham, Frank. *General Stand Watie's Confederate Indians*. San Antonio, TX: The Naylor Company, 1959.

Dale, Edward Everett and Litton, Gaston. *Cherokee Cavaliers: Forty Years of Cherokee History As Told in the Correspondence of the Ridge-Watie-Boudinot Family*. Norman, OK: University of Oklahoma Press, 1939.

Davis, William C. Ed. *The Confederate General.* 6 volumes. Harrisburg, PA: National Historical Society, 1991.

Dornbusch, C. E. *Military Bibliography of the Civil War.* Vols. 1–3 New York: New York Public Library, 1961–1972. Vol. 4 Dayton, OH: Morningside House, Inc., 1987.

Dougan, Michael B. *Confederate Arkansas: The People and Politics of a Frontier State in Wartime.* University, AL: University of Alabama Press, 1976.

Douglas, Lucia Rutherford, ed. *Douglas's Texas Battery, CSA.* Tyler, TX: Smith County Historical Society, 1966.

Duncan, Robert Lipscomb. *Reluctant General: The Life and Times of Albert Pike.* New York: E. P. Dunton & Co., Inc., 1961.

Dyer, F. H. *A Compendium of the War of the Rebellion.* Des Moines, IA: The Dyer Publishing Co., 1908. Reprint. Dayton, OH: The Press of Morningside Bookshop, 1978.

Eakin, Joanne C. and Hale, Donald R. *Branded as Rebels: A List of Bushwhackers, Guerrillas, Partisan Rangers, Confederates and Southern Sympathizers from Missouri During the War Years.* Independence, MO: Wee Print, 1993.

Eakin, Joanne C. *Battle of Lone Jack August 16, 1862.* Independence, MO: Two Trails Publishing, 2001.

———. *Confederate Records From the United Daughters of the Confederacy Files.* 8 vols. Independence, MO: Two Trails Publishing, 1995–2001.

———. *Diary of a Doctor Missouri State Guards, 1861.* Independence, M: Two Trails Publishing, 1999.

———. *Missouri Prisoners of War From Gratiot Prison & Myrtle Street Prison, St. Louis, Mo. and Alton Prison, Alton Illinois Including Citizens, Confederates, Bushwhackers and Guerrillas.* Independence, MO: Two Trails Publishing, 1995.

Edwards, John Newman. *Shelby and His Men or the War in the West.* Cincinnati, OH, 1867: Reprint. Waverly, MO: General Joseph Shelby Memorial Fund, 1993.

Edwards, Witt. *The Prairie Was On Fire: Eyewitness Accounts of the Civil War in the Indian Territory.* Oklahoma City, OK: Oklahoma Historical Society, 2001.

Evans, Clement A. Ed. *Confederate Military History.* 13 Vols. Atlanta, GA: Confederate Publishing Co., 1899. Reprint. Secaucus, NJ: Blue & Gray Press, 1974.

Evans, Clement A. and Bridgers, Robert S. Eds. *Confederate Military History Extended Edition.* 19 Vols. Wilmington, NC: Broadfoot Publishing Company, 1987.

Farthing, C. M. *Chronicles of the Civil War in Monroe County (Missouri).* Independence, MO: Two Trails Publishing, 1997.

Faust, Patricia L. Ed. *Historical Times Illustrated Encyclopedia of the Civil War.* New York: Harper Perennial, 1986.

Fitzhugh, Lester Newton, ed. *Cannon Smoke: The Letters of Captain John J. Good, Good-Douglas Texas Battery, CSA.* Hillsboro, TX: Hill Junior College Press, 1971.

Frazer, Robert W. *Forts of the West: Military Forts and Presidios and Posts Commonly Called Forts West of the Mississippi River to 1898.* Norman, OK: University of Oklahoma Press, 1963.

Frost, Griffin. *Camp and Prison Journal.* Quincy, IL: Quincy Herald Book and Job Shop, 1867. Reprint. Iowa City, IA: Camp Pope Publishing, 1994.

Fry, Alice L. *Kansas and Kansans in the Civil War: First Through Thirteenth Volunteer Regiments.* Kansas City, KS: Two Trails Pub. Co., 1996.

Furry, William. *The Preacher's Tale.* Fayetteville, AR: The University of Arkansas Press, 2001.

Gaines, W. Craig. *The Confederate Cherokees: John Drew's Regiment of Mounted Rifles.* Baton Rouge, LA: Louisiana State University Press, 1989.

Gibson, J. W. (Watt). *Recollections of a Pioneer.* St. Joseph, MO: Press of Nelson-Hanne Printing Co., n.d. Reprint. Independence, MO: Two Trails Publishing, 1999.

Grover, George S. "Civil War In Missouri." *Missouri Historical Review* 8 (October 1913): 1–28.

———. "Major Emory S. Foster." *Missouri Historical Review* 14 (April–July 1920): 425–432.

Guralnik, David B., ed. *Second College Edition Webster's New World Dictionary of the American Language*. New York: The World Publishing Company, 1972.

Hale, Donald R. *Branded as Rebels, Volume 2*. Independence, MO: Blue & Grey Book Shoppe, 2003.

Hale, Douglas. *The Third Texas Cavalry in the Civil War*. Norman, OK: University of Oklahoma Press, 1993.

Heidler, David S. and Heidler, Jeanne T., eds. *Encyclopedia of the American Civil War: A Political, Social, and Military History*. New York: W. W. Norton & Company, 2000.

Heitman, Francis B. *Historical Register and Dictionary of the United States Army From Its Organization, September 29, 1789, to March 2, 1903*. 2 vols. Washington: Government Printing Office, 1903. Reprinted Gaitherburg, MD: Old Soldiers Books Inc., 1988.

Hewett, Janet B., ed. *Supplement to the Official Records of the Union and Confederate Armies*. 100 vols. Wilmington, NC: Broadfoot Publishing Company, 1994–2001.

Hinze, David C. and Farnham, Karen. *The Battle of Carthage: Border War in Southwest Missouri, July 5, 1861*. Campbell, CA: Savas Pub. Co., 1997.

*History of Adair, Sullivan, Putnam and Schuyler Counties, Missouri. From the Earliest Time to the Present; Together With Sundry Personal, business and Professional Sketches and Numerous Family Records, etc.* Chicago: The Goodspeed Publishing Co., 1888.

*History of Audrain County, Missouri, Written and Compiled from the Most Authentic Official and Private Sources Including a History of Its Townships, Towns and Villages*. St. Louis: National Historical Company, 1884.

*History of Clay and Platte Counties, Missouri, Written and Compiled from the Most Authentic Official and Private Sources Including a History of Its Townships, Towns and Villages*. St. Louis: National Historical Company, 1885.

*History of Howard and Chariton Counties, Missouri, Written and Compiled from the Most Authentic Official and Private Sources Including a History of Its Townships, Towns and Villages*. St. Louis: National Historical Company, 1883.

*History of Marion County, Missouri, Written and Compiled from the Most Authentic Official and Private Sources Including a History of Its Townships, Towns and Villages*. St. Louis: E. F. Perkins, 1884

Hulston, John K. and Goodrich, James W. "John Trousdale Coffee: Lawyer, Politician, Confederate." *Missouri Historical Review* 85 (October 1990): 272–295.

Ingenthron, Elmo. *Borderland Rebellion: A History of the Civil War on the Missouri-Arkansas Border*. Branson, MO: Ozark Mountaineer, 1980.

Josephy, Jr., Alvin M. *The Civil War in the American West*. New York: Alfred A. Knopf, Inc., 1992.

———. *The Civil War: War On the Frontier*. Alexandria, VA: Time-Life Books, Inc., 1986.

Kerr, Homer L., ed. *Fighting With Ross' Texas Cavalry Brigade C.S.A.: The Diary of George L. Griscom, Adjutant, 9th Texas Cavalry Regiment*. Hillsboro, TX: Hill Jr. College Press, 1976.

Ketcham, Ralph. *James Madison: A Biography*. New York: The MacMillan Company, 1971.

Kleber, John E. *The Kentucky Encyclopedia*. Lexington, KY: The University Press of Kentucky, 1992.

Krister, John S. "Captured Guns At Lone Jack, Mo." *Confederate Veteran Magazine* 24 (April 1916): 184.

Laughlin, Sceva Bright. "Missouri Politics During the Civil War." *Missouri Historical Review* 23 (July 1929): 583–618.

Leeper, Wesley Thurman. *Rebels Valiant: Second Arkansas Mounted Rifles (Dismounted)*. Little Rock, AR: Pioneer Press, 1964.

Lehr, Suzanne Staker. *As the Mockingbird Sang: Civil War Diary of Pvt. Robert Caldwell Dunlap, C.S.A.* St. Joseph, MO: Platte Purchase Publishers, 2005.

———. *Fishing on Deep River: Civil War Memoir of Pvt. Samuel Baldwin Dunlap, C.S.A.* St. Joseph, MO: Platte Purchase Publishers, 2006.

Lowe, Richard, ed. *A Texas Cavalry Officer's Civil War: The Diary and Letters of James C. Bates*. Baton Rouge: Louisiana State University Press, 1999.

Mayes, Jewell. *Ray County Chapters: Articles from the "Richmond Missourian."* 7 Vols. Richmond, MO: Ray County, Missouri Genealogical Association, 1930.

McElroy, John. *The Struggle For Missouri*. Washington, DC: National Tribune Co., 1909.

McGhee, James E. *Letter and Order Book Missouri State Guard 1861–1862*. Independence, MO: Two Trails Publishing, 2001.

———. *Service With the Missouri State Guard: The Memoir of Brigadier General James Harding*. Springfield, MO: Oak Hills Publishing, 2000.

Miles, Kathleen White. *Bitter Ground: The Civil War in Missouri's Golden Valley, Benton, Henry, and St. Clair Counties*. Warsaw, MO: The Printery, 1971.

Miller, Mark. *"If I Should Live": A History of the Sixteenth Arkansas Confederate Infantry, 1861–1863*. Conway, AR: Arkansas Research, Inc., 2000.

Monaghan, Jay. *Civil War on the Western Border 1854–1865*. New York: Bonanza Books, 1955.

Moore, Frank. Ed. *The Rebellion Record: A Diary of American Events*. 12 vols. Vols. 1–6, New York: Putnam, 1861–1863. Vols. 7–12, New York: Van Nostrand, 1864–1868. Reprint ed. New York: Arno Press, 1977.

Mudd, Joseph A. "What I Saw At Wilson's Creek." *Missouri Historical Review* 7 (January 1913): 89–105.

————. *With Porter in North Missouri: A Chapter In the History of the War Between the States*. Washington: National Publishing Company, 1909.

Mullins, Mrs. Mary Jackman. "Sketch of Col. Sidney D. Jackman." *Reminiscences of the Women of Missouri During the Sixties*. Jefferson City, MO: Missouri Division, United Daughters of the Confederacy, 1911. 93–96.

Musser, Richard H. "The War in Missouri." In *Southern Bivouac*. 6 vols. Wilmington, NC: Broadfoot Publishing Company, 1993. 4:678–685.

Nichols, Bruce. *Johnson County Missouri in the Civil War*. Independence, MO: Two Trails Publishing Press, 1974.

Norton, Richard L. *Behind Enemy Lines: The Memoirs and Writings of Brigadier General Sidney Drake Jackman*. Springfield, MO: Oak Hills Publishing, 1997.

"Opposing forces At Pea Ridge." *Battles and Leaders of the Civil War*. 4 vols. New York: Century Company, 1887–1888. 1:337.

Patrick, Jeffery, ed. "Remembering the Missouri Campaign of 1861: The Memoirs of Lieutenant William P. Barlow, Guibor's Battery, Missouri State Guard." *Civil War Regiments: A Journal of the American Civil War* 5, no. 4 (1997): 20–66.

Peckham, James. *Gen Nathaniel Lyon, and Missouri in 1861: A Monograph of the Great Rebellion*. New York: American News Company, 1866.

Peterson, Richard C., McGhee, James E., Lindberg, Kip A., and Daleen, Keith I. *Sterling Price's Lieutenants: A Guide to the Officers and Organization of the Missouri State Guard*. Jefferson City, MO: Two Trails Publishing, 1995.

Phillips, Christopher. *Damned Yankee: The Life of General Nathaniel Lyon*. Columbia, MO: University of Missouri Press, 1990.

Powell, Wilson. "'Fighting Bob' Shaver." *The Independence County Chronicle* 3 (October, 1961): 38–44.

Primm, James Neal. *Lion of the Valley St. Louis, Missouri*. Boulder, CO: University of Colorado Press, 1981.

Rainwater, Mrs. C. C. "Reminiscences From 1861 to 1865." *Reminiscences of the Women of Missouri During the Sixties*. Jefferson City, MO: Missouri Division, United Daughters of the Confederacy, 1911. 17–26.

Rampp, Larry C. and Rampp, Donald L. *The Civil War in the Indian Territory*. Austin, TX: Presidial Press, 1975.

Ripley, Warren. *Artillery and Ammunition of the Civil War*. New York: Litton Educational Printing, Inc., 1970.

Robley, T. F. *History of Bourbon County, Kansas to the Close of 1863*. Fort Scott, KS: Press of the Monitor Book & Printing Co., 1894.

Rose, Victor M. *Ross' Texas Brigade: Being a Narrative of Events Connected With Its Service In the Late War Between the States*. Louisville, KY: The Courier-Journal Company, 1881.

Ross, Margaret. *Arkansas Gazette: The Early Years 1819–1866*. Little Rock, AR: Arkansas Gazette Foundation, 1969.

Ryle, Walter Harrington. *Missouri Union or Secession*. Nashville: The Journal Printing Company, 1931.

Schnetzer, Wayne H. *Men of the Eleventh: A Roster of the Eleventh Missouri Infantry Confederate States of America*. Independence, MO: Two Trails Publishing, 1999.

———. *More Forgotten Men: The Missouri State Guard*. Independence, MO: Two Trails Publishing, 2003.

Schrantz, Ward L. *Jasper County, Missouri in the Civil War*. Carthage, MO: The Carthage Press, 1923. Reprint. Carthage, MO: The Carthage, Missouri Kiwanis Club, 1992.

Scott, Ernest. "Peter Van Winkle." *Arkansas Historical Quarterly* 21 (Summer 1962): 170–172.

Shea, William L. & Hess, Earl J. *Pea Ridge: Civil War Campaign in the West*. Chapel Hill, NC: University of North Carolina Press, 1992.

Shalhope, Robert E. *Sterling Price: Portrait of a Southerner*. Columbia, MO: University of Missouri Press, 1971.

Sifakis, Stewart. *Who Was Who in the Confederacy: A Comprehensive, Illustrated Biographical Reference to More Than 1,000 of the Principal Confederacy Participants in the Civil War*. New York: Facts on File, 1988.

————. *Who Was Who in the Union: A Comprehensive, Illustrated Biographical Reference to More Than 1,500 of the Principal Union Participants in the Civil War*. New York: Facts on File, 1988.

Sigel, Franz. "The Pea Ridge Campaign." *Battles and Leaders of the Civil War*. 4 vols. New York: Century Company, 1887–1888. 1: 314–334.

Simpson, Harold B. *Texas in the War, 1861–1865*. Hillsboro, TX: The Hill Junior College Press, 1965.

Snead, Thomas L. *The Fight For Missouri: From the Election of Lincoln to the Death of Lyon*. New York: Charles Scribner's Sons, 1866.

Sparks, A. W. *The War Between the States, As I Saw It. Reminiscent, Historical and Personal*. Tyler, TX: Lee & Burnett, Printers, 1901.

Stanton, Donal J., Berquist, Goodwin F. and Bowers, Paul C., eds. *The Civil War Reminiscences of General M. Jeff Thompson*. Dayton, OH: Morningside Bookshop, 1988.

Stone, Norman and Kenyon, J. P. *The Wordsworth Dictionary of British History*. Hertfordshire, England: Wordsworth Editions Ltd., 1994.

Stuart, A. A. *Iowa Colonels and Regiments Being a History of Iowa Regiments in the War of the Rebellion; And Containing a Description of the Battles in Which they Have Fought*. Des Moines, IA: Mills & Co., 1865.

Truman, W. L. "Battle of Elkhorn—Correction." *Confederate Veteran Magazine* 12 (January 1904): 27–28.

Tucker, Phillip Thomas. *The South's Finest: The First Missouri Confederate Brigade from Pea Ridge to Vicksburg*. Shippensburg, PA: White Mane Publishing Company, Inc., 1993.

————. *The Confederacy's Fighting Chaplain Father John B. Bannon*. Tuscaloosa, AL: The University of Alabama Press, 1992.

Tunnard, W. H. *A Southern Record: The History of the Third Regiment Louisiana Infantry*. Baton Rouge, LA: W. H. Tunnard, 1866.

*The Union Army: A History of Military Affairs in the Loyal States 1861–1865—Records of the Regiments in the Union Army—Cyclopedia of Battles—Memoirs of Commanders and Soldiers*. 8 vols. Madison, WI: Federal Publishing Company, 1908. Reprint. Wilmington, NC: Broadfoot Pub. Co., 1998.

Violette, E. M. "The Battle of Kirksville. August 6, 1862." *Missouri Historical Review* 5, no. 2 (1911): 94–112.

Volo, James M. and Volo, Dorothy Denneen. *Encyclopedia of the Antebellum South*. Westport, CT: Greenwood Press, 2000.

Warner, Ezra J. *Generals in Blue: Lives of the Union Commanders*. Baton Rouge, LA: Louisiana State University Press, 1964.

————. *Generals in Gray: Lives of the Confederate Commanders*. Baton Rouge, LA: Louisiana State University Press, 1959.

Watson, William. *Life In the Confederate Army: Being the Observations and Experiences of an Alien in the South During the American Civil War*. London: Chapman and Hall, 1887. Reprint. Baton Rouge, LA: Louisiana State University Press, 1995.

Webb, W. L. *Battles and Biographies of Missourians, or the Civil War Period of Our State*. Kansas City, MO: Hudson-Kimberly Pub. Co., 1900.

Weddle, Robert S. *Plow-Horse Cavalry: The Caney Creek Boys of the Thirty-fourth Texas*. Austin, TX: Madrona Press, Inc., 1974.

Wills, Garry. *James Madison*. New York: Time Books, 2002.

Winter, William C. *The Civil War in St. Louis: A Guided Tour*. St. Louis: Missouri Historical Society Press, 1994.

Wright, Marcus J. "Colonel Elias C. Boudinot." In *Southern Bivouac*. 6 vols. Wilmington, NC: Broadfoot Publishing Company, 1993. 2:432–440.

**Government Sources**

Davis, George B. and Perry, Leslie J, and Kirkley, Joseph W. *Atlas to Accompany the Official Records of the Union and Confederate Armies*. Washington, DC: Government Printing Office, 1891–1895.

Gorgas, J. *The Ordnance Manual for The Use of The Officers of The Confederate States Army*. Charleston, SC: Evans & Cogswell, 1863. Reprint. Dayton, OH: Morningside Bookshop.

Howe, James C. *Official Roster of the Soldiers of the State of Ohio in the War of the Rebellion, 1861–1866*. Akron, OH: Werner Ptg. & Litho Co., 1893.

Library of Congress. *Newspapers in Microform, United States, 1848–1983, Vol. I, A–O*. Washington, DC: Government Printing Office, 1984.

National Archives. Record Group 109. Confederate Muster Rolls. Assorted rolls and units. Washington, DC.

————. Record Group M317. Confederate Compiled Service Records: Arkansas. Assorted rolls and units. Washington, DC.

————. Record Group M322. Confederate Compiled Service Records: Arkansas. Assorted rolls and units. Washington, DC.

————. Record Group M405. Union Compiled Service Records: Missouri. Assorted rolls and units. Washington, DC.

————. Record Group M861. Records of Confederate Movements and Activities. Assorted rolls and units. Washington, DC.

State of Missouri. *An Act to Provide For the Organization, Government, and Support of the Military Forces State of Missouri, Passed at the Called Session of the Twenty-first General Assembly*. Jefferson City, MO, 1861. Reprint. Independence, MO, n.d.

Naval History Division. Navy Department. *Civil War Naval Chronology, 1861–1865*. 6 vols. Washington, DC: Government Printing Office, 1971.

United States War Department. *The War of the Rebellion: A Compilation of the Official Records of the Union and Confederate Armies*. 70 vols. comprising 128 books. Washington, DC: U.S. Government Printing Office, 1880–1901. Reprint. Harrisburg, PA: National Historical Society, 1985.

———. *The War of the Rebellion: Official Record of the Union and Confederate Navies*. 31 volumes. Washington, DC: U.S. Government Printing Office, 1894–1922.

**Manuscripts/Special Collections**

Aledo Museum (Aledo, IL.):
Ketzle, Henry. Typescript manuscript. "Military History of the 37th Reg. Ill. Vol. Infantry."

Arkansas History Commission (Little Rock, AR):
Lotspeich, C. B. Unpublished manuscript. "Personal Experiences of C. B. Lotspeich."
Skaggs Collection:
William O. Coleman Letter.
W. M. Moore Letter.
Wassell, Samuel Spotts. Collection,

Camden Pubic Library (Camden, AR):
Smart, Lula Grinstead. "H. L.Grinstead." Confederate Scrapbook.

Columbia University (New York):
Peter W. Alexander Collection:
Copy Book of Telegrams, June 2–October 9, 1862. Hindman's Command.
Copy Letter Book, June 1–Dec. 18, 1862. Hindman's Command.
Copy Letter Book, June 11–Dec. 30, 1862. Hindman's Command.
Frost, Daniel M. Letters.
General Orders. Various officers.
Miscellaneous correspondence.
Special Order Book, June 1–Dec. 18, 1862. Hindman's Command.
Special Order Book, June 11–August 19, 1862. Hindman's Command.
Telegrams. Hindman's Command.

Madison County Courthouse (Fredericktown, MO):
    Miscellaneous Papers
        Lackey, W. S. C. "Sergeant Ancil Matthews in the Confederate Army."

Missouri Historical Society (St. Louis, MO):
    Babcock, W. R. Collection.
        Missouri Volunteer Militia Scrapbook.
    Civil War Papers.
        General Orders of Missouri (1862)
    Mesker Papers.
        Henry W. Williams Letter Book (December 1861–April 1862)
    Missouri Militia Papers.
        List of Members of the Old National Guard.
        Parsons, G. A. Report (January 18, 1861).
    Rives, Col. B. F. Papers.
    Staff Correspondence. Missouri State Guard.

Prairie Grove State Battlefield Park (Prairie Grove, Ar)
    Shoup, Francis A. Manuscript report on Prairie Grove.

State Historical Society of Missouri (Columbia, MO):
    Western Historical Manuscript Collection:
        Tyler, Jr. John. Collection.
        Quesenberry, John P. Manuscript Diary.
        Rainwater and Fowler Family Papers.
    Missouri Cavalryman. Collection No. 995. Vol. 1.

University of Arkansas (Little Rock, AR)
    Turnbo, S. C. "History of the Twenty-seventh Arkansas Confederate Infantry With Many Interesting Accounts of the Counties Through Which it Passed During the Civil War and Accurate Accounts of the Battles in which it Engaged."

**Newspapers**

Alabama:
    *Mobile Advertiser and Register* (Mobile)

Arkansas:
    *The Arkansas True Democrat* (Little Rock)
    *Mena Star* (Mena)
    *Washington Telegraph* (Washington)

Illinois:
    *Chicago Daily Tribune* (Chicago)
    *Quincy Whig and Republican* (Quincy)
    *Waukegon Weekly Gazette* (Waukegon)

Iowa:
    *The Clinton Herald* (Clinton)
    *The Daily Gate City* (Keokuk)
    *Muscatine Daily Journal* (Muscatine)

Kansas:
    *The Emporia News* (Emporia)

Missouri:
    *The Canton Weekly Press* (Canton)
    *The Missouri Republican* (St. Louis)
    *The Missourian* (Richmond)
    *The Morning Herald* (St. Joseph)
    *Weekly California News* (California)

Texas:
    *Dallas Herald* (Dallas)
    *San Antonio Weekly Herald* (San Antonio)
    *The Standard* (Clarksville)

# Credits

## Photographs and Illustrations

Carlisle, PA. U. S. Army Military History Institute: Sidney D. Jackman
*Confederate Veteran* 17 (December 1909), 613: Henry C. Thruston
Harrell, John A., *Arkansas, Confederate Military History*, 10:409: Albert Rust
*Missouri Historical Review* 14 (April–July 1920), 426: Emory S. Foster
Mudd, Joseph A. *With Porter in North Missouri,* after 274: Frisby H. Mc-
 Cullough
Nevada, MO. Vernon County Historical Society: DeWitt C. Hunter
Osceola, MO. Colonel John T. Coffee Camp #1934 , Sons of Confederate Veter-
 ans: John T. Coffee
St. Louis, MO. Missouri History Museum:
 Meriwether Lewis Clark (IM001-006975)
 Samuel Churchill Clark (P0084-01)
 Edwin W. Price (IM001-007373)
*St. Louis Missouri Republican*, April 17, 1886: "Exchanging Civilities" name-
 plate
Topeka, KS. Kansas State Historical Society: William F. Cloud
Washington, DC. Library of Congress, Prints & Photographs Division:
 Brady-Handy Collection. LC-DIG-cwpbh-004585: Col. E. C. Boudinot; LC-
 B812-9496: Colton Greene
 Civil War Glass Negatives and Related Prints. LC-DIG-cwpb-05429: Gen.
 John McNeil
 Civil War Collection. B812-3902: Lewis Henry Little

## Maps

Michael E. Banasik, Battle of Lone Jack, Missouri (August 16, 1862)
*Battles and Leaders of the Civil War*, 1:263: Area Battle Map, 1862, modified
 and enhanced by Michael E. Banasik
*Battles and Leaders of the Civil War*, 1:322: Battle of Pea Ridge or Elkhorn
 Tavern
*Battles and Leaders of the Civil War*, 3:449: Battle of Prairie Grove, Arkansas
*St. Louis Missouri Republican,* February 6, 1886: J. W. Cooper's map of the
 Battle of Prairie Grove

# Index

9 7 8 1 9 2 9 9 1 9 3 6 9